Joseph Perl's
Revealer of Secrets

Modern Hebrew Classics

David Patterson, Series Editor

This series presents formative works of lasting significance that appeared in Hebrew between 1819 and 1939, as well as more recent critical work. The series is designed to acquaint the English reader with the quality of modern Hebrew writing in its period of revival and renaissance and to reflect the cultural, religious, and social conditions and conflicts in Jewish life in the nineteenth and early twentieth centuries.

Joseph Perl's *Revealer of Secrets:* The First Hebrew Novel,
translated with an introduction and notes by Dov Taylor

Tradition and Trauma: Studies in the Fiction of S. J. Agnon,
edited by David Patterson and Glenda Abramson

The World of Israel Weissbrem, *translated by Alan D. Crown*

Out of the Depths, *Joseph Chaim Brenner,*
translated by David Patterson

A Dream Come True, *Eliezer Ben-Yehuda,*
translated by T. Muraoka, edited by George Mandel

Joseph Perl's *Revealer of Secrets*

The First Hebrew Novel

TRANSLATED WITH AN
INTRODUCTION AND NOTES BY

Dov Taylor

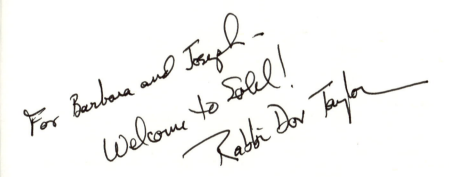

For Barbara and Joseph –
Welcome to Solel!
Rabbi Dov Taylor

WestviewPress
A Division of HarperCollins*Publishers*

Modern Hebrew Classics

Published in 1997 in the United States of America by Westview Press, 5500 Central Avenue, Boulder, Colorado 80301-2877, and in the United Kingdom by Westview Press, 12 Hid's Copse Road, Cumnor Hill, Oxford OX2 9JJ

A CIP catalog record for this book is available from the Library of Congress.
ISBN 0-8133-3212-5 (hc)—ISBN 0-8133-3213-3 (pbk.)

The paper used in this publication meets the requirements of the American National Standard for Permanence of Paper for Printed Library Materials Z39.48-1984.

10 9 8 7 6 5 4 3

For

Chanan Brichto
Rabbi, Teacher, Friend

שמע אמרי־אל אשר מחזה שדי יחזה נפל וגלוי עינים
במדבר כד:ד

Contents

Table of Transliteration

Yiddish		Ashkenazic Hebrew		Sephardic Hebrew	
א	a	א	--[1]	א	--[1]
אָ	o				
ב	b	בּ	b	בּ	b
בֿ	v	ב	v	ב	v
ג	g	ג	g	ג	g
ד	d	ד	d	ד	d
ה	h[2]	ה	h[2]	ה	h[2]
וו	v	ו	v	ו	v
ו	o/oo/oy	וֹ	o	וֹ	o
		וּ	oo	וּ	oo
ז	z	ז	z	ז	z
ח	kh[3]	ח	ḥ[3]	ח	ḥ[3]
ט	t	ט	t	ט	t
י	y[4]	י	y	י	y
י	i	יִ	i	יִ	i

(continues)

---

1. Between two vowels, sometimes represented by an apostrophe (').
2. Omitted at the end of a word in both Yiddish and Hebrew transliteration, except in words that have accepted English spellings, e.g., *Torah*.
3. Similar to *ch* in German *buch*.
4. When consonantal, *y* as in *you*. When vocalic, *i* as in *mir,* rhymes with *here*.

Yiddish		Ashkenazic Hebrew		Sephardic Hebrew	
ײֵ	ey[5]	ֵי	ei[5]	ֵי	ei[5]
ײַ	ay, ai[6]	ַי	ai[6]	ַי	ai[6]
כּ	k	כּ	k	כּ	k
כ	kh	כ	kh	כ	kh
ל	l	ל	l	ל	l
מ	m	מ	m	מ	m
נ	n	נ	n	נ	n
ס	s	ס	s	ס	s
ע	e[7]	ע	--[8]	ע	--[8]
פּ	p	פּ	p	פּ	p
פֿ	f	פ	f	פ	f
צ	ts	צ	ts	צ	ts
ק	k	ק	k	ק	k
ר	r	ר	r	ר	r
שׁ	sh	שׁ	sh	שׁ	sh
שׂ	s	שׂ	s	שׂ	s
תּ	t	תּ	t	תּ	t
ת	s	ת	s	ת	t

5. Rhymes with *day*.
6. Rhymes with *guy*.
7. As in *met*.
8. Between two vowels, sometimes represented by an apostrophe (').

Preface

אלולי דדלאי לך חספא לא משכחת מרגניתא תותא?
Had I not lifted up the shard for you
would you have found the pearl beneath it?[1]

This translation of Joseph Perl's *Megallé Temirin*, together with the sections preceding and following it, reflects the convergence of lifelong interests in Jewish thought, language and literature.

I am indebted to my teachers at the Hebrew Union College – Jewish Institute of Religion and Brandeis University, especially Abraham Aaroni, Chanan Brichto, Harry M. Orlinsky, Martin S. Rozenberg, Ezra Spicehandler and Chaim Brandwein, who filled me with love for the Hebrew language and its literature, and Joshua Rothenberg and Robert Szulkin, who made learning Yiddish a joy. Marc Saperstein, Goldstein Professor of Jewish History and Thought at Washington University, first made me aware of *Megallé Temirin* and its historical, literary and linguistic significance and suggested that I consider translating it. I have benefited from his friendly encouragement and profound erudition throughout this project. Chanan Brichto graciously read my manuscript and offered several incisive suggestions.

The translation and notes were essentially completed at The Oxford Centre for Postgraduate Hebrew Studies (now The Oxford Centre for Hebrew and Jewish Studies), where I was a Visiting Scholar during the first half of 1992. For this opportunity and so many others, I am grateful to David Patterson, founder and emeritus president of the Centre and renowned authority on modern Hebrew literature.

The scholarly researches of Shmuel Werses, Chone Shmeruk, Avraham Rubinstein, Zelig Kalmanovitch and David Patterson constitute by far the most extensive and significant critical literature on the works of Joseph Perl in general and *Revealer of Secrets* in particular. The influence of their work is present throughout this book.

My research was facilitated by the cooperation of the libraries at The Oxford Centre, The Bodleian, The British Museum, University College London, Hebrew Union College – Jewish Institute of Religion, The Jewish Theological Seminary, Spertus Institute of Jewish Studies, The YIVO Institute for Jewish Research, The New York Public Library, Hebrew Theological College, Lake Forest College, Congregation Solel and The City of Highland Park. In particular, I wish to acknowledge the generous assistance of Dan Sharon and Michael Terry, Reference Librarian and Director, respectively, of The Asher Library at Spertus.

---

1. Dov Ber ben Samuel, *Shivḥei ha-Besht* (Kopys, Lithuania: Israel Yafeh, 1814), 32:4, hereafter cited in notes as *SB;* and Dan Ben-Amos and Jerome R. Mintz, trans., *In Praise of the Baal Shem Tov* (Bloomington and London: Indiana University Press, 1970), 234, hereafter cited in notes as *Mintz*. The sentence is calqued on "אי לאו דדלאי לך חספא מי משכחת מרגניתא תותיה?" (Yev. 92b; B.M. 17b). Note that in Yiddish, "פערל" means both "pearl" and "Perl."

2. Baruch Kurzweil, "The Satire of Joseph Perl," in *In The Struggle Over Jewish Values* (Jerusalem and Tel Aviv: Schocken, 1969), 70.

The World of *Revealer of Secrets*

The map shows many of the places mentioned or alluded to in the text. The boundaries of Europe were redrawn at the Congress of Vienna in 1815. In East Central Europe, Russia, Prussia and Austria made the greatest gains.

Haskala: Jewish Self-Enlightenment

The emancipation of the Jews from the political and economic disabilities imposed upon them in medieval Europe began in the west with the French Revolution and moved east. One Jewish response to emancipation was Haskala. While its impetus came from the European Enlightenment movement, the unique circumstances of Jewish life gave Haskala its own character. It is, perhaps, best understood as the movement for Jewish *self*-enlightenment. David Patterson describes the phenomenon succinctly:

> When the Napoleonic armies swept across Europe and broke down the ghetto gates, the Jews emerged into a world that had changed beyond all recognition....They had become cultural laggards....If the glittering prizes of European culture were to be won, some radical adjustment was unavoidable....*Within the space of a few years a generation attempted to catapult itself through a process of intellectual and cultural development that Western Europe had undergone...in...two and a half centuries* [emphasis added]....
>
> Major change...was embodied in the Hebrew movement of enlightenment, known as *Haskalah.* The belief that a knowledge of...European culture was an essential step toward social acceptance led to a radical modification of the patterns of Jewish education....A demand arose to widen the syllabus, to introduce, side by side with religious instruction...secular studies....Instead of being able to speak only Yiddish, the Jewish child began to make his first acquaintance with the language of the country in which he lived! The aim of education was focused on enlightenment: the triumph of knowledge over ignorance, reason over superstition....
>
> The yearning for equality of opportunity, intellectual excitement, and social acceptance persuaded many Jews to believe that with the spread of enlightenment, prejudice would vanish....Once the peoples of Europe had been shown that hatred of the Jews was illogical...and contrary to the principles of brotherly love, they would welcome them...provided...that the Jews could prove their readiness to appreciate the benefits of European culture. The spread of enlightenment demanded a process of self-enlightenment, which in turn required changes in education.
>
> The growth of modern Hebrew literature...mirrors the broad aim of Jewish self-enlightenment, and was regarded as a major instrument for its fulfillment.[15]

The birth of Haskala is generally associated with the figure of Moses Mendelssohn in Berlin in the second half of the eighteenth century, though its characteristic call for secular education was heard as early as the 1740s. From Germany, its ideas spread eastward to Galicia, Lithuania and other provinces of the Russian Pale of Settlement, carried by itinerant scholars and abetted by the absolutist regimes of Germany, Austria and Russia which, in their attempt to assimilate the Jewish populace, deprived the traditional Jewish communal leadership of its coercive power, opening the way for the expression of dissenting tendencies.

Haskala thrived on the growth of commerce. Though Galicia remained feudal, agrarian and backward during the first half of the nineteenth century, significant trade developed along the Russian border, concentrated in Lemberg (Lvov), Tarnopol and Brody. These cities became marketplaces of ideas as well as goods and, consequently, the centers of Galician Haskala. The awareness of the interdependence of wholesale trade and Haskala was expressed by a leading *maskil:*

> Since God has taken pity on us and brought us under the rule of our lord, His Royal Highness the Emperor...trade with foreign lands has begun to flourish in our parts and instead of a life of poverty, a life of enjoyment has arrived...and since then the few brave ones have attempted to cast off the disgrace of ignorance and the shame of idleness and of poverty and they teach their children the vernacular and other languages and disciplines that men live by.[16]

The wealthy, enlightened merchant became the ideal of Haskala literature, though the movement included the bookkeepers and clerks of such merchants, *arendars* of various kinds, teachers, physicians, writers, bankers and other professional intelligentsia.

Among the fathers of Haskala in Podolia and Galicia was Joseph Perl's mentor and friend, Menaḥem Mendl Lefin, who was the first to propose that the war against Ḥasidism be waged through literary means, especially through ridicule. In 1792, he published a French pamphlet on the improvement of the situation of Polish Jewry -- *Essai d'un plan de reforme ayant pour l'objet d'eclairer la Nation Juive en Pologne et de redresser par la ses moeurs* -- in which he called for satirical works to be disseminated through journals founded expressly for this purpose. He believed that by exposing the superstition of Ḥasidism to reason and ridicule, the movement would wither away. Maskilic authors in Galicia responded, presenting an unflattering portrait of the ḥasidic way of life.[17]

That the war between Haskala and Ḥasidism was fought primarily with words is not surprising; faith in the power of the written word predates both movements. The Jewish tradition is primarily literary, beginning with the Bible and continuing with the two Talmuds and a variety of other works, which together constitute a literary corpus spanning almost three thousand years. Perl and his colleagues, as well as their intended readers -- *ḥasidim* no less than *maskilim* -- were heirs to this tradition of reverence for the written word.

This faith was reflected in all of Perl's activities. He tried to republish *Sefer ha-Vikkuaḥ,* Israel Loebl's anti-ḥasidic tract of 1797, which had been bought up and burned by the *ḥasidim.* The plot of *Revealer of Secrets* revolves around the protracted search for another book -- "the *bukh*" --

Perl's own German *Über das Wesen der Sekte Chassidim (On the Nature of the Ḥasidic Sect),*[18] which had been intended to expose the secret machinations of the *ḥasidim* to the Austrian authorities in the hope that they would suppress the new sect. The *ḥasidim* rightly fear the power of the *bukh.*[19]

Perl acknowledges the ascendance of Ḥasidism even in the literary realm: its misguided books, especially *Praises of the Balshemtov,* have become widespread, whereas no one wants books by the *maskilim:*

> We have seen plainly that all those publishers and authors of books by the *tsadikim* of our time have become...eminently wealthy....Conversely, we see that whoever publishes other books in language we call "beautiful" has lost a lot of money and been forced to forsake the publication....[20]

His high hopes eventually become more modest: "If only one in a thousand will be moved by our composition and will shrink from following the counsel of the deceivers and liars, then for the sake of the one it is our duty to do whatever we can."[21]

Solomon Judah Rapoport, Perl's colleague and friend, poignantly expresses the faith of a true *maskil* in words of reason in general and *Revealer of Secrets* in particular. Eulogizing Perl in 1839, Rapoport wrote:

> There isn't a *maskil* in our country, nor perhaps a Hebrew booklover in all of Ashkenaz,[22] who has not read it *[Revealer of Secrets]* and rejoiced....At the time it was published [1819] it worked wonders....Many of the *ḥasidim* hid in the gloom of utter cataclysm[23]....If one of them showed up at a gathering...he would quickly be recognized and named after the character who resembled him in *Revealer of Secrets,* e.g., "This is Reb Zaynvl Verkhievker," or "Reb Khayim Gavriel"....I said prematurely then that in a year or two the *ḥasidim* would be finished off....Alas, the ways of fate are hidden from man!....Instead of our eager anticipation that the *ḥasidim* would become fewer and fewer until they disappeared, from that time on they have multiplied prodigiously and swarmed like the frogs of Egypt....Perhaps you think that the book *Revealer of Secrets* made no impression at all? Not so! It did indeed, but in a different way than we had imagined.[24]

The dream of Haskala never materialized. By 1881, the Haskala had run its course, its hopes for emancipation dashed with the beginning of the mass pogroms in Russia, its faith in the good intentions of monarchs shown to be the product of wishful thinking. The Haskala *movement* came to an end, but it had given birth to modern Hebrew literature and had greatly influenced Zionism and virtually every other modern transmutation of Judaism.

The Life and Work of Joseph Perl

Joseph Perl (1773-1839) was a leading figure in the Galician Haskala. The son of a wealthy Tarnopol merchant family, he attended *ḥeyder,* was married at age fourteen and, unencumbered by the need to earn a living, devoted himself to the study of Talmud and other rabbinic literature and eventually to *kabbala,* which led him to the world of Ḥasidism. Perl

> was an ardent *ḥasid* in his youth. He prayed with exuberance and shouting, skipped like a ram,[25] believed in wonders, traveled to the *rebe* to listen in the dark to his obscure utterances, snatched some of the holy leftovers[26] consumed by the *ḥasidim* at dusk on *Shabbat* at the third meal.[27]

It was during these youthful years that Perl acquired the intimate knowledge of ḥasidic life and literature that would be reflected in his later writings.

Perl's father, Todrus Perl, was a *mitnagged.* Eager to distance his son from the company of *ḥasidim,* he sent him on regular business trips -- to Brody, the most important commercial center in Galicia at the time, and to Hungary and Germany -- that brought him into contact with the literature and luminaries of the emerging Haskala movement. From 1801-03, he studied with Dov Ginzburg, a *maskil* from Brody, whose influence on his student was decisive. Perl learned German language and literature, Hebrew literature, science, medieval Jewish philosophy, Bible and grammar. By 1803, the *khosed* had become a *maskil* -- an ardent proponent of western culture and a bitter opponent of Ḥasidism -- even as he continued to be a scrupulously observant Jew, to the consternation of some of the more radical Brody *maskilim.*

The motto of the Haskala was "education for Jews," and Perl became the quintessential educator. In 1813, while Tarnopol was still under Russian hegemony (1809-1815), he founded a modern school for Jewish children. In addition to Bible and Talmud, the curriculum included Polish and French, arithmetic and natural science, history, geography and Hebrew grammar, as well as practical trades. The language of instruction was German and there were also classes for girls. By 1819 the school had 118 students and its own building, and achieved legal status as a middle school, the *Deutsche-Israelitische Hauptschule,* of which Perl was made director for life. His school was to become the prototype for all the Hebrew schools in Galicia, Podolia, Volhynia, Poland, Russia and Bessarabia. Near it, Perl established a "Reform" synagogue -- not in the German style with choir and organ, but with decorum and with sermons in German by Perl himself.

His educational efforts also included a series of almanacs published in the years 1813-15, and a translation into Hebrew of Henry Fielding's novel, *Tom Jones,* probably from a German translation. Through his school, his writings and his personal contacts, he exerted a strong influence on the Haskala, both in Galicia and in Russia.

Perl's war against Ḥasidism began in earnest in 1816, when he submitted the manuscript of *On the Nature of the Ḥasidic Sect* to the provincial governor for approval, and continued with his successful publication in 1819 of *Megallé Temirin (Revealer of Secrets)*,[28] and his unsuccessful attempt in 1826 to republish Israel Loebl's *Sefer ha-Vikkuaḥ*. Though the *maskilim* held conflicting ideas as to the propriety of turning to the government for help in their struggle -- a means that had been employed frequently at the end of the eighteenth century by the *mitnaggedim*[29] -- Perl's hope for the modernization of Jewish life lay precisely in government intervention. He submitted a series of memoranda to the Austrian authorities, including several individual denunciations:

- on January 2, 1827, against the well-known ḥasidic *rebe,* Hirsh (Eichenstein) of Zhidotchuv, for harming the cause of enlightenment and of Perl's own school;[30]
- in 1829, seeking permission to publish *Katit la-Ma'or,* his Hebrew treatise attacking "the offensive custom" of the "Beshtians" of having collection boxes in their synagogues for the purchase of oil to keep lamps burning on the grave of Rabbi Meir Ba'al ha-Nes in Tiberias;[31]
- on March 6, 1838, against Rabbi Israel of Ruzhin, for illegally collecting funds in Galicia and transferring the money abroad, and for ordering the murder of two Jewish informers (the Ushitsa Affair);[32]
- on March 22, 1838, suggesting that the government censor Jewish libraries, close traditional Jewish schools ("a place of refuge for vagabonds, thieves, and similar types and...a nest of demoralization and of...nefarious, scandalous deeds"[33]) and prohibit meetings in Jewish ritual baths.

The struggle reached its climax in 1838, when Perl succeeded in having his scholarly and enlightened friend, Solomon Judah Rapoport, appointed as district rabbi of Tarnopol and, subsequently, of Tarnopol's old synagogue as well as of Perl's new one. The *mitnaggedim* and the *ḥasidim* were outraged. They rejected Rapoport and defiled the synagogue.

On July 6, Perl submitted his last and longest memorandum, accusing "this most dangerous sect of *ḥasidim*" not only of fanaticism and superstition, but of undermining the government's objective regarding "the rapprochement of the Jews with the rest of the population on the path of education and true morality," of being inspired only by self-interest, of trying to gain control over all of Galician Jewry, of caring only for power and worldly pleasures, and of stopping at nothing to attain these ends.[34]

He died a year later, probably of cancer, on Simḥat Torah, October 1, 1839. The gold medals that he had been awarded in 1816 by Czar Alexander I and in 1821 by Emperor Francis I for his achievements in education were pinned to his shroud, and his funeral was attended by the district chief, the mayor and a host of high-ranking officials and police officers. A report in a contemporary German newspaper, hotly denied by Rapoport, adds that "the men in civilian clothes who followed the coffin with bowed heads were armed police agents who were dispatched to guard the corpse against an attack by the Hasidim. On Perl's fresh grave the Hasidim let loose in a wild dance."[35]

Perl's Polemic Against Ḥasidism

The Books: Three Plus Two

Perl wrote three major works, which may be viewed as a trilogy. The first of these, *On the Nature of the Ḥasidic Sect,* was completed near the end of 1816. It was prompted by the publication in 1814-15 of two ḥasidic books -- *Praises of the Balshemtov,* a collection of legends about the patron saint of Ḥasidism, and *The Tales of Rabbi Naḥman* of Bratslav. Alluding to the former, which quickly became a bestseller, Perl states that "for some time now the members of the sect have been whispering about the miracles of the Besht by word of mouth until at last they have now, in the years 1814-1815, had the audacity to collect oral sources of this kind and present them to the public in print."[36]

Über das Wesen der Sekte Chassidim Aus ihren eigenen Schriften gezogen (On the Nature of the Ḥasidic Sect, Drawn from Their Own Writings) is a non-fiction critique of Ḥasidism, containing a synopsis of Lurianic *kabbala* and extensive quotations from *Praises of the Balshemtov* and and other ḥasidic works. Every citation is accurate, though the selection of texts is arbitrary and a few quotations are taken out of context so as to substantiate the author's views. The picture of Ḥasidism that emerges is uniformly negative.[37]

Perl composed this work in German because its intended audience was the Austrian authorities, whose power he sought to enlist against what he viewed as the growing menace of the ḥasidic sect. He published it anonymously, and for over a century scholars held conflicting views as to the authorship of his work. Dubnow was the first to suggest that Perl was the author of *On the Nature of the Ḥasidic Sect* and that it was this work that reappears as "the *bukh*" in *Revealer of Secrets.*[38] It was not until 1942, however, with Mahler's publication of documents from the Austrian archives in Lemberg -- including the cover letter that Perl had sent to the authorities along with the German manuscript, as well as an exchange of letters from 1816-17 among the authorities themselves -- that the identity of the author was finally confirmed.[39]

Why did Perl hide his identity? There is no objective evidence to support the theory that he was prompted to do so by fear of ḥasidic reprisals. In a different context, Perl vehemently denied that he chose anonymity out of fear:

> It should not enter your mind that the reason I did not reveal my name...is that I was afraid of the hot anger that certain of our kinfolk would pour out on me. Heaven forbid that I should think this way!....Even if they would issue a thousand indictments against me, I would fear "neither them nor their crowd nor their wealth."[40] The reason that induced me to hide my name I cannot reveal to you at present, but I hope to God that soon I shall be able to make known to you the reason for it.[41]

These words appeared in 1836. Perl died three years later without having revealed the reason.

Perl may have gotten the idea to publish anonymously from Lefin, whose French pamphlet had been written as a basis for debate in the Polish Sejm of 1788-92 about the status of the Jews in any program of political and social reform. Had the Polish legislators known that the author was a Jew, they might have regarded him as an interested party and rejected his arguments *a priori.* By remaining out of view, he had hoped that his case would be judged on its merit alone.[42]

Or the reason may have been less exalted. Perl was something of an exception among the leaders of the Haskala in his secret personal denunciations against individual ḥasidic leaders. Yet at the same time, he openly decried the state of morality among Jewish youth and urged a program that

> will strengthen in their hearts our faith and religion, and incline their hearts to virtue and right conduct, and purge them of bad and harmful traits that have recently been on the rise among our countrymen, such as money-lust, extravagance and wastefulness, envy of one another, enmity toward people, flattery, usury, cheating in weights and measures, insulting words, *denunciations and calumnies* [emphasis added].[43]

We will probably never know how he justified to himself his own denunciations, or whether his condemnation of denunciations was simply an attempt to cover his tracks, but we can at least hazard the guess that his anonymity in *On the Nature of the Ḥasidic Sect* may have followed from his wish *not* to be seen as informing against his own people.

In any case, in 1816, as required by law, Perl submitted the manuscript to the Supreme Imperial Police and Censorship Office in Vienna. He was denied permission to publish, however, as the government sought "to maintain the good will of all classes and sects of the population" and did not wish to place itself "in opposition to one sect even though it may run counter to the aims of the state through its fanatical principles."[44] Furthermore, it feared that the book would incite the enlightened gentiles against *all* the Jews.

Perl tried unsuccessfully to publish the book outside the country, and the manuscript remained in his library in Tarnopol until World War II, when it was brought to Jerusalem. In 1977, The Israel Academy of Sciences and Humanities published a scientific edition of the German text with the addition of a Hebrew Introduction and annotations by Avraham Rubinstein.[45]

But while *On the Nature of the Ḥasidic Sect* did not see the light of day during Perl's lifetime, it was reincarnated by its author as a work of *fiction* entitled *Megallé Temirin (Revealer of Secrets)*, and published in Vienna in 1819. The new incarnation contains virtually the same source citations and arguments as the old, but in a different guise. Unlike its predecessor, *Revealer of Secrets* was written in Hebrew, intended not for the Austrian authorities but for a Jewish readership. Despite his ideological opposition to Yiddish, Perl also translated it into Yiddish to make it available to the masses, and wrote a new and significantly different *Prologue* that anticipates the differences between a Yiddish and Hebrew readership. The Yiddish translation, however, was not published until 1937 by YIVO in Vilna, and the Yiddish *Prologue* the following year.[46]

In *Revealer of Secrets,* Perl again chose to hide, this time behind a fictional editor named Ovadye ben Psakhye. He may have wished to strengthen the credibility of his hoax that this was actually an authentic ḥasidic work; or his anonymity may be a literary device designed to heighten the air of mystery.

Perl wrote *Revealer of Secrets* as if *On the Nature of the Ḥasidic Sect* had been published, anticipating the reaction to it -- the consternation it would engender among the *ḥasidim* and the opposition to Ḥasidism that it would elicit among the Austrian authorities. In *Revealer of Secrets, On the Nature of the Ḥasidic Sect* reappears as "the *bukh,*" the pivot of the plot.

> On the pages of *Revealer of Secrets*...a bitter struggle is played out between the supporters of the *bukh* and those who wish to get rid of it once and for all. It is this struggle that creates the complicated plot of *Revealer of Secrets* and gives rise to many comic possibilities, which gave the author countless opportunities to make fun of the *ḥasidim* and to describe their downfall....[Perl] anticipated future events, and through the letters in *Revealer of Secrets* he described what he saw in his mind's eye as an event that had actually taken place, namely, that the *bukh* brings about the downfall of the sect.[47]

It is significant that the struggle depicted in *Revealer of Secrets* takes place not between *ḥasidim* and *maskilim* but between *ḥasidim* and the Austrian authorities. Indeed, there is only one *maskil* in the entire book and he, remarkably like Perl, appears cultured and generous and remains above the fray. This is consistent with the hope Perl harbored for his German work -- that the defeat of Ḥasidism would come about at the hands of the civil authorities, which is precisely what happens in *Revealer of Secrets.*

In this Hebrew work of fiction, as in its non-fiction German predecessor, the author's strategy is not to debate principles, but rather, through the selective use of ḥasidic sources, to denounce the ḥasidic way of life as asocial, unethical and anti-religious.

> Whoever has eyes to see and has not befouled his pure soul will know full well that it is nothing but [the plain] truth my mouth utters here. Yet I know that some of our contemporaries are confused about this and do not yet know the way of truth, so...I am fully prepared for the sake of truth and righteousness to support and substantiate these words with the holy books by the *tsadikim* of our time.[48]

One of his non-Jewish characters, a Polish prince, confirms that "the author of this *bukh* knows them [the *ḥasidim*] quite well. Everything he wrote in his *bukh* he reproduced from their books and he copied everything from their own words."[49]

In the *Prologue* to the Yiddish edition, Perl's first-person narrator says:

> Do you...think that the one who wrote *Revealer of Secrets* just wanted to write stories and entertain the public? It seems to me that when the author copied the letters, more than once there were tears in his eyes, and it was with a bitter heart he copied them because he saw our gloomy condition -- that one can't address people nowadays in a serious vein as one could in the past. Because of our many sins, we're deaf to serious talk and our eyes are closed. I compare us to a sick child. When you have to give him medicine, you need to mix it in sugar or in preserves for him because otherwise he won't take the medicine. He doesn't see that he must have the medicine, he doesn't know that he's sick. That's how it is with us. The author of the *Revealer of Secrets* knows his brothers. He didn't just want to write stories, he intended something different. He sees we're critically ill and we won't take any medicine, so he mixed the medicine with sugar for us. But what good is it? The public, I see, laps up the sugar, and the medicine they don't touch![50]

If this narrator speaks for his creator, and if we take him at his word, it would seem that Perl was writing a polemic on behalf of a people he loved deeply and in the service of a cause in which he believed passionately -- even as he realized its futility!

With the publication of *Revealer of Secrets,* Perl became the first *maskil* to attack Ḥasidism openly.[51] The book was widely read in Galicia, Podolia, Volhynia, Congress Poland, Lithuania and even Germany, and it inspired many imitations. Perl had escalated the war between Haskala and Ḥasidism to a new level and set a standard for Hebrew satire that has never been surpassed and for Hebrew prose fiction that, in the opinion of one modern critic, remained without equal until Mendele.[52] In the process, he managed to write the first Hebrew novel before modern Hebrew even existed!

The third book in his anti-ḥasidic trilogy, another Hebrew work aimed at a Jewish readership, is *Boḥen Tsaddik (The Test of The Righteous).* Written in 1825 and circulated in manuscript form for several years, it was finally published in 1838. *The Test of The Righteous* is a sequel to *Revealer of Secrets,* consisting of a discussion of readers' reactions to the earlier work, including criticism of the author's use of ḥasidic sources. Each of the criticisms is, of course, convincingly rebutted, as the entire work is crafted to lend authenticity to *Revealer of Secrets.* Ovadye reappears as the narrator in *The Test of The Righteous.* Its plot revolves around the search for a completely honest man, in the course of which, representatives of the various elements of Jewish society are reviewed and their defects exposed. The parade of failures here includes not only *ḥasidim* but also rabbis, traders, craftsmen and even *maskilim.* As the search concludes, the honest man turns out to be neither a *tsadek* nor even a *maskil,* but a pious farmer in a Jewish agricultural utopia somewhere in southern Russia. Perl's vision of utopia thus rejects not only Ḥasidism but also the idea of a return to Palestine, envisioning instead a life of productive labor in the Diaspora.

In the spirit of these three major works is a fourth composition that was never completed, *The Tale of The Loss of the Prince.* Intrigued by reports of Rabbi Naḥman of Bratslav's extended stay in Lvov without his faithful disciple and recording secretary, Rabbi Nathan, Perl seized upon the opportunity to create a fiction. He invented a correspondence between two imaginary Bratslav *ḥasidim,* one of whom was supposedly in Naḥman's entourage during this stay, and appended to this correspondence several stories from *The Tales of Rabbi Naḥman,* which had been published in 1815.[53] Having achieved credibility through the inclusion of some of Naḥman's actual tales, he then proceeded to append a continuation of Naḥman's story, *The Tale of the Loss of the Princess,* as well as an entirely new story supposedly told at Lvov, *The Tale of the Loss of the Prince,* a parody of *The Tale of the Loss of the Princess.* The clear intention of the work was to present itself as a previously unknown yet authentic Bratslaver holy book, when in fact it was the very antithesis of what it purported to be.[54]

The author probably worked on it during 1816 but gave it up in favor of *Revealer of Secrets,* which targets the *entire* ḥasidic movement but which retains several aspects of the earlier hoax. The outline of the work and some of its parts were recovered from the Perl archives and published by Shmeruk and Werses in 1969 -- together with an introduction, notes and extensive appendices -- under the title, *Yosef Perl: Ma'asiyyot ve-Iggarot (Joseph Perl: Ḥasidic Tales and Letters).*

To this list must be added *Katit la-Ma'or.* Originally envisioned as a brochure, it was finally published in the form of three letters in the journal, *Kerem Ḥemed,* volume 2, in 5596/1836. The subject is the alms boxes in which the *ḥasidim* collected money for the purpose of buying oil for the lamps on the grave of Rabbi Meir Ba'al ha-Nes in the Land of Israel. Perl states that this second-century rabbi, in whose name the funds are collected, "has no standing among the great and has just been elevated by the poor people who don't know their right hand from their left," and that "the custom of pledging for the soul of Rabbi Meir Ba'al ha-Nes is contrary to the holy Torah."[55] His goal is to put an end to this practice, which is not only rank superstition but also violates the law against sending money out of the country.[56]

To the best of my knowledge, the present translation of *Revealer of Secrets* is the first appearance in English of any of Perl's works.

The Critique

A consistent critique of Ḥasidism emerges from these compositions. In *The Test of The Righteous,* Perl describes the mission he had set for himself in writing *Revealer of Secrets:*

> Would anyone be angry at the sentry who sees an enemy approaching the city in the thick of night and sounds the alarm to rouse the city-dwellers to gird their loins and take up their weapons and join in battle against their enemies who beset them? Would anyone find the lookout guilty for having roused the people from their sweet sleep so that fear and trembling seized them? That is the situation with me. I saw how the enemies of my people and my faith wax mightier each day, seducing people and causing the people to stray from the straight path....I could not restrain myself from publicly proclaiming their reproach.[57]

As a faithful lookout, Perl is warning the inhabitants of the impending danger, in the hope that they will defend themselves by rejecting Ḥasidism and its leaders. Indeed, already in *On the Nature of the Ḥasidic Sect,* Perl had stated that he wrote

> because I am a human being, because I belong to a people that this sect has mortally wounded, and because the pain that I feel over the fact that my

> co-religionists, despite the efforts of the rulers to enlighten them, sink deeper and deeper in the mire of superstition and devote themselves more and more to hating and persecuting people who do not think as they do.[58]

It is only fitting, therefore, that he expose them for what they are, and he believes that what they are may be gathered from what they read as well as from what they do -- hence the proliferation of quotations from ḥasidic literature in Perl's works.

In typical maskilic fashion, Perl ignores the Zohar and the teachings of Isaac Luria, arguing that Ḥasidism lacks any Jewish authenticity and directing all his complaints about Jewish mysticism against Ḥasidism. With most *mitnaggedim* and *maskilim,* he maintains that it is an utterly new sect without past or present analogy and that its fundamental principles are qualitatively different from those of Judaism. Those principles are, first, blind faith in and loyalty to the *tsadek,* and second, communion with God. And the former is far more important than the latter, as spiritual awakening can be attained easily enough with the help of alcohol and the *tsadek.* In reality, says Perl, it is only blind faith in the *tsadek* that is essential among all *ḥasidim,* since communion with God is the prerogative of the *tsadikim.*

We discover that "faith in *khakhomim*" is the *sine qua non,*[59] that "the whole of Judaism depends on" the pilgrimage to the *tsadek.*[60] In classical Judaism, the *ḥakham* is the rabbinic sage, but for Ḥasidism, the *khokhem* is the *tsadek,* who is "the foundation of the universe."[61] He is omnipotent[62] and God-like[63] -- indeed, even greater than God,[64] teaching God how to act[65] and nullifying or tempering Divine judgments.[66] He can obtain abundance[67] -- children, life, food[68] -- for his followers and for all the world. He can heal the sick,[69] decree death for a person[70] or punish the celestial prince of a nation, thereby causing that nation to suffer.[71] It is he and not God to whom prayers should be directed.[72] All of the *tsadek*'s words,[73] thoughts,[74] movements[75] and acts[76] are filled with religious significance -- laying his head on the table,[77] smoking a pipe,[78] arguing with his wife,[79] shooting an arrow,[80] switching the hand in which he holds an object,[81] competing with rival *tsadikim* for followers or money.[82]

The *khosed* is obligated to believe in the *tsadek,* to bind himself to him and to obey him unquestioningly, repressing his own critical judgment.[83] He must love,[84] serve and support him,[85] make regular pilgrimages to him,[86] tell his praises,[87] guard his reputation at all costs[88] and help him extend his sphere of influence and increase his wealth[89] so that he may live in appropriate luxury.[90] The most vile sinners can make amends simply through their generous gifts to the *tsadek.*[91]

Perl charges Ḥasidism with using mystical exegesis to subvert the plain meaning of Scripture,[92] thereby permitting what is forbidden and vice versa.[93] According to Perl, Ḥasidism permits bloodshed,[94] vengeance,[95] lying,[96] stealing,[97] cheating,[98] bribery,[99] sexual immorality,[100] abortion,[101] intimidation[102] and character assassination.[103] It promotes idleness and panhandling[104] and their accompanying vices of alcohol[105] and tobacco.[106] It spreads superstition and ignorance,[107] and opposes science, culture and enlightenment.[108]

Despite their disclaimers to the contrary, *ḥasidim* are contemptuous of Christians,[109] whom they regard as no better than idolators[110] -- husks waiting to be emptied of whatever holy sparks might still be trapped inside them.[111] The *ḥasidim* are forever hatching schemes to subvert the rights of the individual[112] and the laws of the state.[113] Since the *tsadek* is likened to a king[114] and a prince, and since his followers are protected and provided for by *him* and not by the state, it is only *his* command that is obligatory on the *khosed,* who is thus freed from having to obey the law of the land. The *khosed* is not afraid of the punishment of the state.[115] If anything, it is the state that should be afraid of the *ḥasidim,* who shamelessly pervert justice -- bribing officials,[116] forging documents,[117] arranging for false testimony[118] smuggling persons[119] and contraband[120] across borders, and sending money out of the country in violation of the law.[121] All is permissible in the name of "faith in *khakhomim*" or of earning a living.

Perl sees Ḥasidism as an easy form of Judaism[122] that attracts the young and naïve[123] who reject discipline and obligation in favor of carousing and fun. He acknowledges the movement's ability to win followers and its phenomenal spread,[124] as well as the fear it strikes in the hearts of its opponents, who must often suppress their opposition and make a show of loyalty to some *rebe* in order to keep their jobs[125] and assure their physical safety. He is highly critical of the explicit sexual imagery that ḥasidic literature borrows from kabbala to describe activity within the divine realm and between the human and divine realms, disdaining the erotic metaphors as tantamount to pornography.[126]

Perl regards the dissemination of the ḥasidic story as one of the principal reasons for the spread of the sect. He abhors the fact that what began as an oral tradition has been canonized in writing, whereby the ḥasidic legends are rapidly becoming articles of faith among the faithful. *Praises of the Balshemtov* in particular is regarded as so holy that simply reading it serves magical purposes.[127] It earns his special contempt[128] and provides the impetus as well as the subtext for much of *Revealer of Secrets.*

In the *Prologue* to *Revealer of Secrets,* the "editor" articulates Ḥasidism's claim to divine authority for its holy books:

> There isn't the slightest reason to doubt that all those [ḥasidic] books...from the days of the Besht until now, must already have been known in the days of the Besht and his holy disciples. The reason they didn't publish them

> was that the generations were not yet worthy of them, and they also knew that the generation would not accept them....For this reason they didn't publish more than what each and every generation was capable of receiving and was worthy of, because in every single generation, by the help of G-d...faith in *khakhomim* is progressively revealed to us.[129]

This is the ḥasidic equivalent of and counterclaim to the rabbinic notion of Oral Torah, according to which all holy books composed in the generations since Sinai were already revealed to Moses at Sinai and passed down through the centuries by word of mouth. It is the Oral Torah that underwrites rabbinic authority. This alternative Oral Torah, by contrast, underwrites the authority of the ḥasidic teachers and casts the Besht in the role of Moses.[130] And it is this alternative Oral Torah that Perl attempts to invalidate in *Revealer of Secrets.*[131]

In his classic essay on "The Satire of Joseph Perl," Baruch Kurzweil perceptively argues that by using the *bukh* (i.e., Perl's German *Über das Wesen der Sekte Chassidim*) to demystify the book (i.e., the ḥasidic holy book) in order to defend The Book (i.e., The Book of Books), Perl willy-nilly calls into question the holiness of all sacred Scripture:

> What is the criterion -- asks Kurzweil -- for the true book...? The idea of absolute truth, for whose sake the satirist goes forth to battle against books for the sake of books, is problematic and utopian, because the historical-scientific examination of The Book and the books will never cease, the critical enterprise once having begun. And this issue...is not a scholarly issue alone, but in itself becomes an existential issue, because in the unique situation in which the Jewish people lives among the nations, it has no other existential justification as a nation except for the authority of The Book of Books and the books. And consequently...this subject is the soul of our modern literature, which is a war of books against books.[132]

This is the enduring challenge of modernity -- the problem of faith in the sanctity of *anything.*

Literary Considerations in *Revealer of Secrets*

Authorship

The author's name never appears explicitly in *Revealer of Secrets.*[133] Perl employs a fictional editor named Ovadye ben Pesakhye,[134] identified as an ardent *khosed* "who dwells among all the *tsadikim* and eminent men of our time."[135] The anonymity of the work, however, is merely a literary device, as there is ample evidence that the identity of its author was public knowledge even during Perl's lifetime. Meir Letteris, editor of the literary anthology, *Ha-Tsefira,* lists *Revealer of Secrets* in the New

Polish Woods, set in the nineteenth century, the young *khosed,* Shmuel, says:

> Do you remember when both of us studied *Revealer of Secrets,* which can be found in every little khsidic prayer-room? Every *khosed* knows that it's an old, holy text....What if I were to tell you that this *Revealer of Secrets* isn't even twenty years old? And that it was written not by an ancient scholar but by a Galician Jew! Ha, what would you say to that?!....You think I'm joking? Not at all! Your father-in-law...knows the author of *Revealer of Secrets.* He's a Jew from Tarnopol, a wealthy man, a follower of the Haskala. Can you imagine a bigger joke?![143]

It seems doubtful that such a deception could have prevailed for very long. Indeed, ḥasidic tradition maintains that the real nature, purpose and author of *Revealer of Secrets* were known from the start. There is a legend that in the 1820s the wealthy Warsaw matron, Tomorl, a supporter of the *ḥasidim,* announced a reward of two gold coins for every copy of *Revealer of Secrets* brought to her, which copies were promptly burned. As she is the object of ridicule in *Revealer of Secrets,* the story seems plausible.[144] The tradition that the *ḥasidim* were taken in by *Revealer of Secrets* remains unproven and may possibly have been a rumor planted by Perl himself, expressing his own wishful thinking. In any event, as indicated above, the author's identity was public knowledge by 1824 at the latest.

In Dispraise of the Balshemtov

Of the nineteen ḥasidic holy books listed in the *Bibliography of Ḥasidic Texts* at the end of *Revealer of Secrets,* the great majority of references within the novel are to the works of Rabbi Naḥman of Bratslav and to *Praises of the Balshemtov.* Perl mines the Bratslaver texts, always managing to emerge with a statement that, especially out of context, sounds outrageous. But the works of Rabbi Naḥman were by no means held in universal esteem even within the ḥasidic camp, and it is *Praises of the Balshemtov* that occupies pride of place in Perl's Rogues' Gallery.

Praises of the Balshemtov is a collection of legends about the life and works of Israel ben Eliezer, known as the Balshemtov. It was compiled by Dov Ber ben Samuel, the ritual slaughterer of Linits, who had served for eight years as his scribe. First published in December 1814 in Kopys (Kopust), Lithuania, it became an immediate best seller, going through several editions in the course of only a few years.[145] *Praises of the Balshemtov* was both the proximate cause of *Revealer of Secrets* and a factor in its plot, which may be viewed as a battle between two books symbolizing two worlds and two worldviews, i.e., *the bukh,* Perl's German composition, which epitomizes Haskala, and *Praises of the*

Balshemtov, which embodies ḥasidic faith and provides Perl with a ready-made target -- both substantive and symbolic -- for his parody.

To begin with, he casts doubt on the authenticity of the accounts in *Praises of the Balshemtov* and, by implication, on the authenticity of the Besht himself: "Who guarantees us that all the things found in *Shivkhey ha-Besht* are true? Does *he* know the ritual slaughterer of Linits, or is it signed by witnesses and a court? And why didn't they publish the book *Shivkhey ha-Besht* while the Besht and his generation were still alive? Why did they wait until the whole generation who knew and saw his deeds and acts had died?" asks the *mitnagged* judge.[147]

Using sources from *Praises of the Balshemtov,* Perl has his characters impugn the person and activities of the Balshemtov[148] so as to raise doubts about the movement from its very inception, based on its own sacred literature. Ovadye affirms that "he who looks at the holy book *Shivkhey ha-Besht* will see that in many places -- and almost everywhere at the time -- they didn't think anything of the Besht, and some reverent and faithful people made fun of him. Even in Mezhebush where he lived for some years they thought nothing of him."[149]

The ferocity with which Perl derides *Praises of the Balshemtov* testifies to its hold on the popular imagination and its importance in shaping early Ḥasidism. "And most of all, be sure to get the holy book *Shivkhey ha-Besht*...because there's nothing small or big, spiritual or material, either in the higher worlds or in the lower worlds, that does not have its root in the book *Shivkhey*...," advises one *rebe*'s personal secretary.[150]

The book impresses the young and unsophisticated, seducing them away from the study of Talmud. Mikhal Kahane, the judge, describes the scene with Eyliohu, the contractor's son:

> When I entered his room I saw a book in his hand. When he saw me he wanted to hide the book but it was too late to conceal it and I saw that it was the book *Shivkhey ha-Besht.* As I had never seen it, I had wanted to have a look at it ever since it was published. When I opened it I saw in it that the Besht was expecting to ascend in a tempest like Elijah of blessed memory but he didn't ascend because his wife died on him and he became half a man. When I read this, I was aghast and I said to my student, "Can you believe such heretical things?" He replied to me that he believes it with perfect faith....[151]

Simply reciting *Praises of the Balshemtov* with proper enthusiasm and concentration can change reality:

> Afterward he gave the order to notify all our Faithful they should meet after noon to recite the whole *Shivkhey ha-Besht* from start to finish....All our Faithful gathered and we began reciting *Shivkhey ha-Besht* with dread and fear of G-d. When we finished three folios, our *rebe* rapped on the book

The Ḥasidic Letter

Letters were a popular form of communication used by the ḥasidic leadership to clarify teachings and to discuss Jewish current affairs and social problems. There developed an epistolary genre known as *Iggerot ha-Kodesh,* "Sacred Letters," which constitutes a mine of historical, ideological and literary source material. *Iggerot ha-Tanya u-Venei Doro (Letters of [the Author of] the Tanya and His Contemporaries),* for example, is an important collection of the letters of Shneur Zalman, founder of *ḤaBa"D* Ḥasidism.

One of the richest collections of such letters is *Alim li-Terufa* (1896), by Nathan Sternharz of Nemirov. Rabbi Nathan was the personal secretary and amanuensis of Rabbi Naḥman of Bratslav, a contemporary of Perl. Naḥman and his works figure prominently in the footnotes to *Revealer of Secrets* and, as already noted, provided the impetus for a work that Perl ultimately left unfinished in favor of *Revealer of Secrets.*

R. Nathan's letters lend credence to the image painted by Perl. A prominent theme in *Revealer of Secrets* is the interception of letters and the accompanying fear that letters may fall into unfriendly hands.[163] In a letter written in 1825 to his son, R. Nathan writes: "Be very careful from now on to guard my letters well, for they are forbidden to strangers who turn words of truth into mockery...."[164] In another letter ten years later, he concludes with a caution: "You'll understand of your own accord to give the letter to our true friends to read and to hide it well from strangers, so that 'no alien may consume that which is sacred.'"[165] His words suggest that it is not uncommon for "sacred letters" to fall into the wrong hands and to be used against their authors.

In yet another letter he writes: "For now, you should know that I found out from Reb Shmuel...that the letter I sent you via Reb Khayim Nathan Tsese's of Nemerov fell into the hands of strangers because this Reb Khayim Nathan forgot to deliver the letter to you and he remembered [it] on his way to Tultchin and sent it to you by way of someone or other. The letter was already opened in Bartnik and I don't know where they[!] are....So make sure to write to that Reb Khayim Nathan and let me know what's happened with this, and ask that he write you who he delivered the letter to -- maybe you'll be able to go back to get the letter...."[166] He continues this theme the following week: "The letter I sent by way of Reb Khayim Nathan, I already wrote you that I had notification that it was opened in Bartnik. The notification came by way of Reb Yaakov Stromvasser who mentioned it to Reb Shmuel...so make sure to hurry up and meet with him [Reb Yaakov] -- maybe you'll be able to get him to tell you where the letter is, and if it's possible to go back and get them[!], try as hard as you can of course to get them[!] and let me know about it."[167]

A particularly significant incident involving letters is reported by Shmeruk. In 1818, there was a real publisher named Meyer Yaakov of Zaslav who was smuggling ḥasidic books into Galicia for illegal distribution. In a contemporary letter written by Reb Hirshele of Zhidotchev to Reb Joshua Heschel of Apt, this Reb Meyer Yaakov is mentioned in connection with the printing of a new edition of Vital's *Eits Ḥayyim* and *Peri Eits Ḥayyim.* Reb Hirshele writes: "Last week Meyer Yaakov of Zaslav, who deals in book-publishing, came and told me...."[168]

In Letter #55 of *Revealer of Secrets,* Meyer Yankev is introduced as the emissary whom the *ḥasidim* will send to Galicia:

> To cover expenses, we'll give him some of our holy books to sell there because right now it's very easy at the border to bring the books over there. Not only will we do something important by spreading the holy books in Galicia where it's forbidden to print them, but we'll also make a big profit, because I heard that in Galicia they sell our holy books at high prices.[169]

Subsequently, the connection between Reb Hirshele of Zhidotchev and Reb Meyer Yankev concerning the reprinting of Vital's book is mentioned explicitly: "I had a correspondence with the *rebe* of the holy community of Kalktsig [= Zhidotchev[170]] and with other people there to supply them the holy books *Toldes Yankev Yoysef, Eyts Khayim* and *Pri Eyts Khayim.*"[171] Commenting on the arrest of Meyer Yankev, Ovadye reports that "I was overjoyed when I saw from this letter that I had brought it about that they didn't find Reb Zelig's letters on Reb Meyer Yankev because I continually took them away from him when I was invisible, so even Reb Meyer Yankev didn't know where they were."[172]

When the historical Meyer Yaakov was arrested by the Galician authorities for smuggling Hebrew books into the country, his letters were taken from him and *brought to Joseph Perl to be translated!* Ovadye's claim that "I continually took them away from him when I was invisible" is based on this episode.[173]

The "editor" of *Revealer of Secrets* also refers several times to the destruction of holy books by opponents.[174] And in a letter from 1835, R. Nathan writes: "There is fear of mortal danger and sacrilege involved, because they go and tear up the holy books that...the holy Rabbi [Nakhmen]...composed, and they trample them underfoot and throw them in the trash and in the toilet. Has such a thing ever been heard or seen?! It doesn't even occur to them to look inside the book to see and consider whether such scorn is appropriate."[175]

The style, typographical form, ideas, subjects, language, syntax and even grammatical inconsistencies that characterize the letters of Rabbi Nathan all appear in *Revealer of Secrets.* Since Perl's work was published three quarters of a century before *Alim li-Terufa,* and in light of the striking similarities between the ḥasidic letters in both works, it is clear

accompany the text and constitute part of its satire, he has created an ironic and ambiguous aura of fictitious scholarship and feigned trustworthiness, while simultaneously providing himself with an additional vehicle for his parody.[185] As one of the discussants in *The Test of the Righteous* says of *Revealer of Secrets,* "In that book almost the main thing is the footnotes."[186] Indeed, because Perl made them part of the story, they imply that Ḥasidism in theory, as reflected in the passages from ḥasidic holy books presented in the footnotes, is as perverse as it is in practice, as reflected in the events described in the letters themselves! Furthermore, the voice of Ovadye the "editor," "the fervent *khosed*" whose personal reactions appear in the footnotes in conjunction with events in the story *and* citations in the footnotes, furnishes the author with additional room for satiric comment on the thought and behavior of his characters. Each new attempt "to substantiate the point that appears within the composition by means of some quotation that appears in the holy books" has the effect of further undermining that which it ostensibly substantiates![187] The real objective of the footnotes is to denigrate Ḥasidism by "praising" and "defending" it.

Werses has further demonstrated that many of the satirical devices used by Perl -- the multiplication of mock-serious introductory sections, the elaborate and scholarly footnote apparatus, the extensive use of quotations from the very writings of those who are the objects of the satire, the motif of the invisible observer/participant who can go wherever he wishes -- are already found in the works of Wieland and Jean Paul, which were well known to the *maskilim* of Galicia. He suggests that Perl's mentor and friend, Mendl Lefin (1749-1826), may have been his link with the European epistolary tradition, particularly as it is known that Lefin himself wrote an unpublished anti-ḥasidic satirical work, *Maḥkimat Peti (Making Wise the Simple),* which was inspired by that tradition and which, in turn, furnished Perl with some of his ideas and forms.[188]

Revealer of Secrets uses all of these elements of the European epistolary tradition, of the ḥasidic holy book and of the ḥasidic letter, weaving them into a broad tapestry. The "editor," Ovadye ben Psakhye, claims to be a loyal *khosed* who has been singled out for a sacred purpose -- to strengthen people's faith in *tsadikim.* Endowed with the magical ability to become invisible at will, he has used his special gift to collect the letters of the *tsadikim* and of their opponents so that the reading public can draw its own conclusions. Perl, however, goes well beyond simply allowing the epistles to speak for themselves. He provides footnotes, ostensibly "in order to substantiate the point that appears within the composition by means of some quotation that appears in the holy books" and so that "people will recognize the righteousness of the *tsadikim* from the passages...quoted."[189] In fact, the footnotes, structurally tied to the letters and to the supplementary sections that bracket them, give the story additional levels of meaning.[190] They include a multitude of quotations taken from ḥasidic texts, occasionally taken out of context and invariably chosen by the author for their likelihood to shock and to repel. They permit the "editor" to add his own perspective to the multiple perspectives of events already expressed in the letters. And they enable him to play a subtle but significant role as a protagonist -- perhaps the *main* protagonist -- in the story.

As Patterson observes,

> An examination of the influences of the European epistolary tradition upon Hebrew literature in the nineteenth century leads inevitably to the conclusion that...the satirical genre in the tradition of Montesquieu's *Persian Letters* eventually finds its way into Hebrew literature in the fully fledged guise of Perl's *The Revealer of Secrets* and *The Test of the Righteous,* which take advantage of a long literary chain.[191]

Plot

In his 1831 review of *Revealer of Secrets,* Rapoport was the first to point out that the letters all fit together and constitute a unity, that none is extraneous and each adds something new that is necessary to the whole.[192] While the plot of the novel is loosely woven, allowing its author plenty of room for sub-plots, intrigue, adventure, comic situations, social commentary and other discursive elements, the letters are virtually all interconnected and integral to the story, which unfolds clearly in the letters:

> When I began to read your letter...I saw in it the news you bring me of a *treyf* travesty that was recently published against our Faithful and against the real *tsadikim,* and that this *bukh* was sent from Galicia to the prince of your community to read!....It's full of wickedness, deceit and mockery aimed at the *tsadikim* and real *rebes*....We got to make sure to do something about the *bukh*....I'm informing you that...you should do whatever you can to get hold of this *bukh* so we can know what's written there and so we'll know the name of the *bukh,* so as to direct our Faithful to buy the *bukh* and burn it and wipe it out, and also to find out who the author is so as to take revenge against him. [Letter #1]

> I knew the infamous *bukh* is in the German language. [Letter #2]

> I heard the *bukh* is making an impression on all the noblemen who read it and they want to translate it into Polish. All the lords reading it roar with laughter at our people and at the *tsadikim.* [Letter #3]

> I don't know what's going on. Your prince didn't used to be so very wicked...and now I see from your letter he's an enemy and a foe of all our Faithful and of all the *tsadikim* and it seems this is all on account of the

Moshe Fishl's, the young talmudist, is pure, unsophisticated, even naïve, yet thoughtful and strong in his convictions. He is the object of unsuccessful attempts by the Dishpoler *ḥasidim* to win him over.

Eyliohu Bisinger, the innocent and naïve son of a wealthy contractor, is similar prey. Having begun as a student of the judge and talmudist Mikhal Kahane, he is temporarily won over by the wiles of the Dishpoler's men, but eventually returns to the fold. In his wavering, he represents the younger generation of Jews in Eastern Europe in the early nineteenth century, and in his rejection of Ḥasidism, Perl's hoped-for outcome. His name -- Eyliohu/Elijah -- identifies him with both the biblical prophet who confronts royal power in the name of divine justice and with the Gaon of Vilna, leader of the early opposition to Ḥasidism.

Meyer Yankev, who is sent by Zelig as an emissary to Galicia to try to uncover the whereabouts of a gentile maid who has fled there with her father after having been impregnated by one of the *ḥasidim,* functions in the additional role -- common in European epistolary literature -- of a picaresque, a traveler in a foreign land who sends back reports about the social situation there. He provides the author with an additional discursive vehicle through which to present his social commentary.

Mordekhai Gold, the lone *maskil* in the novel, is princely, honest and generous to a fault, helpful to everyone, loyal, learned, a successful entrepreneur and ahead of his time in his social attitudes. He is handsome, dresses smartly, reads and speaks German, is on good terms with the Polish prince -- and is, consequently, detested by the *ḥasidim.* He represents the ideal of Haskala thought and, in many ways, Perl himself.

Ovadye ben Psakhye, the fictional editor and sometime protagonist,[196] begins as a fervent *khosed* surrounded by a quasi-legendary aura in emulation of *Praises of the Balshemtov,* but becomes progressively less so as the story develops. His change of character is reflected in his language, which improves with the progress of events. He, too, is in some ways a reflection of Perl, who left a youthful flirtation with Ḥasidism and became an ardent *maskil.*

Symbolism

There are two primary symbols in the novel, and the various parties vie with one another for ownership of them.

"Unless a man knows of the darkness he would not know the delight of the light."[197] Light is the first symbol. The *ḥasidim* use it frequently with reference to their *rebes* and their beliefs, e.g., "our *rebe,* our Light,"[198] "The Light of Israel and its Holy One, the Besht,"[199] "The Holy Light...Rabbi Dov Baer,"[200] "The Most High and Worthy Light, The Hidden and Secret Light...Rabbi Nakhmen,"[201] "The Light of Israel...The

Lamp of Israel...Rabbi Menakhem Nokhem,"[202] "the reference therein is...not to the few Talmudists still found in our land...upon whom light has not yet dawned,"[203] "The Jews in Ashkenaz, who our group's divine light didn't yet shine on,"[204] "By recounting the tales of *tsadikim,* we draw the light of *meshiekh* [messiah] into the world."[205]

The *mitnaggedim,* too, use light as a symbol. They refer to the Gaon of Vilna, the greatest rabbi of his day and the leader of the first wave of opposition to Ḥasidism, as "The Great Light, Rabbi of All The Exiles, Our Teacher the *Rov,* Rabbi Eyliohu."[206]

And of course, light is the quintessential symbol of the Haskala, the Enlightenment, which seeks to kindle the light of reason and science and modern education in the darkness of Jewish existence.

Whose light is pure? Whose is brightest?

The other symbol at the heart of *Revealer of Secrets* is "the book" in its various incarnations, i.e.,

- The Book, i.e., The Book of Books, i.e., The Torah;
- the ḥasidic holy books;
- the *bukh,* i.e., the anti-ḥasidic German book, the search for which gives rise to the plot of the novel;
- *their* books, i.e., books on secular subjects by non-Jewish authors.

Which is the *real* holy book? For Perl's *ḥasidim,* it is the works of "the *tsadikim* of our time,"[207] i.e., the ḥasidic *rebes,* that are really holy. When Zaynvl pawns the silver Torah ornaments in order to raise cash to bribe the housekeeper to steal an incriminating letter, Ovadye "explains" the sacrilege as follows: "The L-rd loves those *tsadikim* more than all synagogues and study halls...[and] if the synagogues and study halls are not as important as the *tsadek,* the sacred vessels are even less so."[208] As for secular books by non-Jewish authors, even the insolent young *khosed* who reads German "doesn't go to *their* trash-sellers because he's afraid to buy from them *bikher* that can harm him."[209] And all the Zaliner *ḥasidim* are engrossed in the effort "to get hold of this *bukh* so we can know what's written there and so we'll know the name of the *bukh,* so as to direct our Faithful to buy the *bukh* and burn it up and wipe it out...."[210]

The Language of *Revealer of Secrets*

In addition to expressing the ideas of its author and characters, language is itself the *subject* of *Revealer of Secrets.* In more ways than one, *maskilim* and *ḥasidim* did not speak the same language. Yiddish was their common vernacular, but the linguistic ideal of Haskala was for Jews to know German and French as the vehicles of western culture and science,

Hebrew, is a literal rendering of the colloquial Yiddish, "לאז ער זעך פּיטטער אריין לאזען אין זיין כתב נשיאות, The Zaliner can put butter on his letter of presidency!", i.e., his letter of presidency is worthless![220]

In his discussion of the linguistic results of Jewish bilingualism, Max Weinreich points out that

> Those who wrote Loshn-koydesh [traditional Hebrew] had no puristic scruples; if one did not know how to say something in Loshn-koydesh, one unhesitatingly incorporated the appropriate Yiddish word....Calques in vocabulary are observable in both languages....Calques in Hebrew modeled on the Yiddish are abundant....
>
> The creators of the Ashkenazic types of words were well versed in both languages; in writing Loshn-koydesh they could coin written words without resorting to the unmediated language....Between Yiddish and Loshn-koydesh there is a zone with a joint dominion of both languages....
>
> The Yiddish speaker well versed in Loshn-koydesh was not necessarily a great grammarian or a puristic pedant....Loshn-koydesh was his writing language, therefore he could coin neologisms with much greater freedom than in an acquired foreign language....
>
> The writers in [maskilic] Hebrew, even those who also wrote in Yiddish, sharpened their sense for the specificity of Hebrew and sought "purity of language" to a much larger degree than the writers of Loshn-koydesh in previous periods. The most trenchant expression of contempt for the Yiddishizing of Hebrew style is found in Joseph Perl's satire *Megale temirin*.[221]

Robert Alter describes the challenge faced by Haskala writers: "Their mother tongue, *mama loshn,* was Yiddish; their immediate models of literary emulation were in a European language...and yet they composed their works in Hebrew, a language that nobody, themselves included, as yet spoke." The result was a clumsy Hebrew, linguistically "pure," yet "one senses the shadow presence of a second language on which Hebrew, with its different lexicon, syntax, grammar and associations, is imperfectly mapped."[222] In this connection, it is worth noting that the Hebrew the Haskala called "pure" was, in its own way, no less clumsy than is the "barbarous jargon" of Perl's characters.

Challenges of Translation

Corrupt Hebrew Into Corrupt English

The challenge for the translator was implied by Nathan Gordon in 1904:

> Megalleh Temirin is written intentionally in a barbarous jargon....*The possibilities of translating any passages are precluded altogether* [emphasis

> added], as their humor would necessarily become tame and insipid. There is an utter disregard of correct grammatical construction. Hebrew, Yiddish, and Polish words are mixed indiscriminately; sentence after sentence is a direct rendition of Yiddish phraseology.[223]

How might it be possible, without rendering its caustic comedy tame and insipid, to translate a text whose language has been intentionally corrupted by its author in emulation of his characters and in pursuit of his goal? It would be relatively easy to turn the language of *Revealer of Secrets* into elegant English. It would also be treason. Gordon's resigned conclusion that "the possibilities of translating any passages are precluded altogether" is thus our starting point.

Satire does not work unless the reader *recognizes* the characters, be they drawn larger, or smaller, than life. Perl places a barbarous jargon in the mouths of his ḥasidic characters, but Ovadye's disclaimer that he has reproduced "all the tales and the letters in the very same language as I have them from the writers of the letters" is trustworthy.

The mimicry of his characters' speech is a conscious part of the author's craft. The challenge is not how to translate some artificial, obscure and corrupt language that an author has created out of his imagination, but how to translate the real language of "real" people into a contemporary English idiom. There are English speakers in parts of the United States and the United Kingdom, for example, whose English is no less idiosyncratic than the language of some of Perl's characters. Their manner of speaking may be unconventional but their meaning is perfectly clear. *Their way of speaking can even be imitated* -- as Perl imitates the language of his characters -- so it must have its own coherence.

How might that coherence be conveyed in another language? Is there a model that approximates in English the way Perl's ḥasidic characters express themselves in Hebrew? The language of *Revealer of Secrets* is that of Hebrew-speakers whose native tongue is Yiddish and who have not mastered Hebrew. The equivalent in English would be that of English-speakers whose native tongue is Yiddish and who have not mastered English. To be sure, the mistakes our hypothetical English-speaker makes are not "translations" or accurate reflections of the mistakes Perl's ḥasidic Hebrew-speakers make. Rather, they are intended to give a flavor of the ungrammatical Hebrew of the original.

Fortunately, our link through time and space with the characters behind the characters in *Revealer of Secrets* is not completely severed. Though the entire world of Eastern European Jewry that provided both text and context for *Revealer of Secrets* was destroyed in the Holocaust a century after the death of Joseph Perl, still today one can hear in New York, London, Jerusalem and elsewhere, the English spoken by Jews whose mother-tongues are Yiddish and Polish. It is they who provide

- his place of domicile, e.g., Zelig Letitshiver[233] = Zelig of Letitshev, Zaynvl Verkhievker[234] = Zaynvl of Verkhievk, Shloyme Umner[235] = Shloyme of Uman, Mendl Barer[236] = Mendl of Bar; or
- his father's given name, e.g., Aharon Lozer's[237] = Aharon, Lozer's son; Moyshe Fishl's[238] = Moyshe, Fishl's son; or
- (in the case of a sick person requesting an intercessory prayer,) his mother's given name, e.g., Moyshe son of Rivke;[239] or
- (in the case of a married woman,) her husband's given name, e.g., Freyda Reb Isaac's[240] = Freyda, Reb Isaac's wife; or
- his family name,[241] e.g., Mordekhai Gold,[242] Mikhal Kahane.[243]

In polite discourse, the name of a married man might be preceded by the title *"Reb,"*[244] the equivalent of "Mr.," and the name of a woman by the denominative, "the lady, the woman,"[245] and/or by the title *"Moras,"* the equivalent of "Mrs." or "Mistress,"[246] or both.[247]

Format and Punctuation

True to traditional Hebrew typography, Perl uses only rudimentary punctuation. Ovadye's major *Prologue* is a single paragraph, four pages long in Hebrew. Several of the epistles, too, consist of only one paragraph and punctuation within paragraphs is minimal. Run-on sentences are endemic, interspersed with commas and the conjunction "and." There are no quotation marks and only occasional periods. This style is typical of the texts Perl parodies, but makes for great difficulties in comprehension. For the sake of the reader, I have chosen to break the text into paragraphs and insert appropriate punctuation throughout the text.

The Treatment of Quotations

Rabbinic and ḥasidic texts frequently cite earlier Jewish literature without citation or attribution, as their authors assume that the reader will recognize the sources. This is true for *Revealer of Secrets* as well, where the use of quotations and allusions becomes a prominent part of the parody. In addition to Ovadye's footnotes, where sources are meticulously identified,[248] Perl uses quotations significantly and *without attribution* in the body of the novel. In the *Notes,* I try to identify all of his sources and I occasionally explain the irony or satire in his (ab)use thereof, but the sheer number of such instances precludes the possibility of explaining them all. The reader is invited to examine the quoted sources in their original context to appreciate fully Perl's use of them.

In order to make the English reader aware of quotations without a profusion of quotation marks, such marks are used in the translation only to identify direct discourse. Biblical quotations appear in SMALL CAPITAL LETTERS and quotations from *Praises of the Balshemtov* appear in **bold-face print**. Passages appearing in **BOLD-FACE SMALL CAPITAL LETTERS** are biblical quotations that appear in *Praises of the Balshemtov.* The source of such quotations is *always* identified in a note.

When it is not my own, the translation of biblical passages is from The Jewish Publication Society's *TANAKH: A New Translation of The Holy Scriptures,* also known as the NJV (New Jewish Version).

Fonts and Other Conventions

Perl's novel is set in square Hebrew typography, except for the *Approbation* and footnotes, which are set in Rashi script, as is customary in the printing of Hebrew holy books to this day. His attention to this convention was part of the hoax. Since the use of multiple English fonts would not create an equivalent aura of holiness for the English reader, the translation of the entire novel is set in *Palatino.*

Italics are used for book and story titles, for non-English words and to express special emphasis. Such emphasis is occasionally expressed as well by i n c r e a s e d l e t t e r s p a c i n g , but only when this device is employed in the Hebrew. [Brackets] indicate that the word or phrase is not explicitly present in the original, but has been added in the translation for clarity.

An asterisk* may appear in the body of the text or in the footnotes, indicating a translator's note that identifies a quotation from a source other than the Bible or *Praises of the Balshemtov,* or explains something of a literary, linguistic, historical or religious nature. *Notes* to the novel begin on page 283. In these *Notes,* as well as in the *Notes* to the translator's *Preface, Introduction, Afterword* and *Excursuses, RS=Revealer of Secrets* and *SB=Shivḥei ha-Besht (Praises of the Balshemtov).*

The Hebrew *name* of God is never pronounced by pious Jews. And the Hebrew words corresponding to the titles "God" *("Elohim")* and "Lord" *("Adonai")* are pronounced only in prayer and written only in holy books. In other contexts, it is the custom among pious Jews intentionally to misspell *"Elohim"* as *"Elokim"* and to substitute *"Ha-Shem"* ("The Name") for *"Adonai."* The corresponding practice in English is to write the words "God" and "Lord" as "G-d" and "L-rd." Whenever "G-d" or "L-rd" appears in the translation, they reflect the use of equivalent euphemisms in the original.

Brody, alienated the early critics of Hebrew literature as well. Or perhaps his denunciations of individual *ḥasidim* to the Austrian authorities made him *persona non grata* even among literary critics.[264]

If *Revealer of Secrets* is not a novel, what then is it? Chanan Brichto's observations with regard to "genre" are apposite here. He calls genre

> a misleading tool for interpretation. To say that a piece of literature is a satire...is to offer an interpretation (which may or may not be correct); but the genre label is in itself no tool at all....Is the perception of a narrative's genre an assumption that will...shape or determine the interpretation of that narrative; or is the reverse the case, namely, that a given interpretation of a narrative will then determine the genre to which it is assigned?[265]

A literary genre comes to be defined through examples. When epistolary works came into vogue, the novel genre was broadened to include the subspecies of the epistolary novel. The primary difficulty with classifying *Revealer of Secrets* is its unusual form, or rather, combination of forms. Absent its preliminary and concluding sections, it would be quickly recognizable as an epistolary novel. But as we have seen,[266] such use of satirical prefatory and concluding sections is found in the works of Wieland and Jean Paul. Once we realize that these sections are an essential part of the satire, we should have no difficulty in concluding that we have before us a satirical epistolary novel, whose successful emulation of the colorful language of many of its characters represents artistry of a high order -- some thirty-four years before the appearance of Mapu's romance, whose biblical Hebrew style was created in the service of Haskala ideology and is itself artificial and highly unrealistic!

In any event, few critics would disagree that *Revealer of Secrets* represents the beginning of modern Hebrew fiction or that it had a profound influence on its subsequent development. In the realm of satire, Perl's work was often emulated, though never equaled. Yehuda Leyb Meises' *Kin'at ha-Emet,* published in 1828, was heavily influenced by Perl's satirical descriptions of the battle between the courts of the competing *rebes.*[267] His narrator further states that "I also knew for certain and saw with my own eyes that many people from the sect of the Beshtians read the important book *Revealer of Secrets,* even though the fact that the author intended to expose their shame and to tear away the mask from their faces was not hidden from them."[268] And *Megillat Yoḥasin,* an important satire composed in 1834 and ascribed to Rabbi Mendl Landsberg of Kremenitz, makes extensive use of ungrammatical Hebrew style as a means of parody. Friedlander observes that "there are grounds for the view that the author of *Megillat Yoḥasin* knew well Joseph Perl's satire *Revealer of Secrets* and his way with linguistic mistakes and their use in parodying the language of *ḥasidim.*"[269]

Many of the elements that would later characterize the style of Mendele, such as his use of Yiddish words and incorrect Hebrew idioms in his Hebrew works, and even comic elements in the stories of Agnon, have their source in Perl's works.[270] The theme of the undermining of the authority of the book, so prominent in *Revealer of Secrets* and *The Test of the Righteous,* reappears in the works of Y. L. Gordon, Berditchevsky, Lilienblum, Tchernichowsky, S. Ben-Tsion, Hazaz and especially Agnon, as well as in the poetry of Bialik.[271] Writers such as Erter and Smolenskin were indebted to Perl for his descriptions of ḥasidic life and the courts of the *rebes.* And Mapu's debt to Perl is discernible in his penchant for the melodramatic, in his use of epistles and dreams, and in the didactic element in his writing.[272]

Certain stock figures, which Perl borrowed from the European literary tradition and Judaized, became part of the repertory company of subsequent Hebrew authors. Thus, for example, the figure of Meyer Yankev, the itinerant bookseller and "Jewish picaresque," is reincarnated by S. Y. Abramovitz in his Mendele Moykher Sforim (Mendele the Bookseller) and Alter Yaknehaz.[273] The noble whore, originally celebrated in the Book of Esther, returns to Hebrew literature in Perl's *Revealer of Secrets* in the character of Freyda Reb Isaac's, and subsequently in Mapu's *The Hypocrite* as Tsaphenat the innkeeper, and in Mendele's *The Book of Beggars* as Beyle the hunchbacked girl.[274] And the figure of Mordekhai, the hero of the Book of Esther, who had become a comic character in pre-Haskala dramas at the end of the seventeenth century, was rehabilitated by Perl and thereafter enjoyed a successful career until the rise of modern Jewish nationalism made the "Court Jew" an object of derision.[275] Perl may thus be regarded as the father of both modern Hebrew fiction and of the Hebrew novel.

Revealer of Secrets is also important for the study of ḥasidic literature, as Perl's footnotes contain some three hundred quotations, mostly from rare first editions of ḥasidic texts. Subsequent editions of *The Tales of Rabbi Naḥman* may have been corrected on the basis of Perl's parody.[276]

From a linguistic point of view, *Revealer of Secrets* is an important source for the study of the development of modern Hebrew. Perl was a master of language, including biblical and rabbinic Hebrew, as well as the "mutilated" Hebrew written and spoken by the *ḥasidim* and the "pure" Hebrew used by the *maskilim* of his day. And Perl's Yiddish version of *Revealer of Secrets,* though it remained undiscovered and unpublished for over a century, is one of the primary sources for the study of the Yiddish language in the early nineteenth century.

Revealer of Secrets is historically significant as well. It is a rich contemporary source for the study of Jewish life in Galicia and the Pale. From it we learn, for example, that the ḥasidic holy book, *Keter Shem Tov,* was torn into pieces, dipped in sulphur and made into matches by the *mitnaggedim.*[277] Perl's book conveys the historical milieu, the workings of a small Jewish town and the tenacious influence of Ḥasidism on the lives of its adherents. Indeed, the end of Perl's novel finds the *ḥasidim* on the run, but -- with the possible exception of Ovadye -- it does not find them any less committed to the *tsadek* or any more "enlightened" than they were at the start. Dubnow claims that *Revealer of Secrets* "is a faithful portrait, despite its historical exaggerations, of the life of the *ḥasidim* and the *tsadikim* at the beginning of the nineteenth century."[278]

To the Reader

Revealer of Secrets is an intriguing book, one that speaks on many levels. It challenges the modern English reader -- far removed from its historical context and thought-world -- to keep track of its somewhat free-ranging plot and numerous sub-plots, as well as of its many characters. The basic plot is related in the *Prologue,* the *Letters* and the *Epilogue,* which constitute a coherent, if somewhat digressive, whole. Then there are the footnotes! And bracketing the whole are the prefatory and concluding sections.

Suggestion: *First* read the *Prologue, Letters* and *Epilogue* for your enjoyment. *Then* read the prefatory and concluding sections, which will not be confusing if you bear in mind that they are part of the satire and intended to be humorous. The translator's *Notes* may prove useful as navigational aids.

Clearly, *Revealer of Secrets* failed to accomplish its author's goal of destroying Ḥasidism, a failure that Perl himself acknowledged.[279] By the time it was first published, the movement it satirized had already triumphed in most centers of Jewish life in Eastern Europe. But the fact that the book continued to be popular for more than a century after its publication was a function neither of its political success or failure nor of the personal virtues or shortcomings of its author, but of its considerable literary merit. People would refer to corrupt Hebrew as "*Megale Tmirin* language" in the same way one might characterize a certain kind of English as "Brooklynese"; or they would speak of "a satire in the style of *Megale Tmirin*" as one might describe the style of a literary work as "Dickensian" or "Kafkaesque." *Revealer of Secrets* came to be viewed as the prototype as well as the pinnacle of the satirical novel genre in Hebrew literature. Although it is historical fiction and offers a highly antagonistic view of Ḥasidism, it is to be read, in the final analysis, neither as history nor as a religious polemic but as a novel.

1. A *treyf-posl* is a secular book -- forbidden reading for a pious Jew in pre-modern times. See note to Letter #1, *Line 22: treyfe travesty.* See also *Glossary.*

2. A *seyfer* is a Hebrew holy book. See *Glossary.*

3. David Roskies, *A Bridge of Longing* (Cambridge: Harvard, 1995), 59f..

4. Terms based on Hebrew or Yiddish usage are defined in the *Glossary.*

5. See, for example, Raphael Mahler, *Hasidism and the Jewish Enlightenment* (JPS: Philadelphia, 1985), 39f., 45f., 229-33. See also David Patterson, *A Phoenix in Fetters* (Savage, Maryland: Rowman & Littlefield, 1988), 5-8.

6. Lit., "Dispersion." The countries outside the Land of Israel in which Jews have lived since the end of Jewish sovereignty in 70 C.E..

7. See Mahler, *The Jewish Enlightenment,* 64-7; also Eisig Silberschlag, *From Renaissance to Renaissance: Hebrew Literature from 1492-1970* (New York: KTAV, 1973), 102.

8. In discussing Woody Allen's "Hasidic Tales, with a Guide to Their Interpretation by the Noted Scholar," William Novak and Moshe Waldoks point out that "whether or not he is aware of it, Woody Allen is contributing here to a venerable strain of Jewish humor: parodies against Hasidism. The first major work in this tradition was *Megalleh Temirin* (Revealer of Secrets), published in 1819; it was so skillfully rendered that it was accepted as genuine -- *even by Hasidim."* See Novak and Waldoks, *The Big Book of Jewish Humor* (New York: Harper & Row, 1981), 200. I am grateful to Daniel A. Richman for calling this reference to my attention.

9. See Letters #4, #23, #24, #62, #114, #115 and notes thereto.

10. Silberschlag, *Renaissance,* 130.

11. See Mahler, *The Jewish Enlightenment,* 5f.. See also Hillel Levine, *Economic Origins of Antisemitism* (New Haven and London: Yale, 1991), 9f., 140-5, 169-71, 188, 214.

12. Literally, *Praises of the Balshemtov.* Cited in notes as *SB.* Translated into English by Dan Ben-Amos and Jerome Mintz and published in 1970 by Indiana University Press under the title, *In Praise of the Baal Shem Tov.* See *Select Bibliography.*

13. Concerning the differing transliterations of the same Hebrew words, see below, "The Nightmare of Transliteration," pp. *lvi-lvii.*

14. See especially Letter #109, *Lines 43ff.: Seyfer ha-Vikuakh, Zemir Aritsim, Kivres ha-Taavo...Zikhron Yoysef...Merkeves Mishne.* See also M. Wilensky, *Ḥasidim and Mitnaggedim* (Jerusalem: Bialik Institute, 1970).

15. Patterson, *Phoenix,* 3-5.

16. Written by Samson Bloch Halevi in 1828 in the dedication of his book to Solomon Judah Rapoport. See Mahler, *The Jewish Enlightenment,* 32 and note 7 thereon.

17. See, for example, Shmuel Werses, "Joseph Perl's Methods of Satire" in *Story and Source* (Ramat Gan: Massada, 1971), 16-18. See also Silberschlag, *Renaissance,* 129 and Israel Zinberg, *A History of Jewish Literature* (New York: KTAV, 1977), Vol IX, 237. Roskies takes a dim view of the means employed by the Haskala: "To rally their benighted brethren, the first generation of east European Jewish innovators became wolves in shepherds' clothing....They learned to imitate the sacred tale, the sermon, the spoken anecdote, so as to laugh them off the stage of history, once and for all. They were predators feeding off the seemingly unusable past." *A Bridge of Longing,* 6. It is worth noting that Perl has the author of the *Approbation* denounce the *mitnaggedim* as "predatory preachers who prey upon the word of the L-rd...and strengthen the demonic forces...." See p. 3, lines 21ff..

69. See, for example, Letter #27, lines 26ff. and footnote 1 thereto; Letter #87, lines 14f. and footnote 1 thereto; Letter #88, lines 16f..

70. See, for example, Letter #1, lines 54ff.; Letter #15, lines 132f. and footnote 6 thereto; Letter #87, lines 14ff.; Letter #123, footnote 1.

71. See, for example, Letter #15, lines 129ff. and footnote 5 thereto.

72. See, for example, Letter #84, footnote 1.

73. See, for example, Letter #38, lines 13ff. and footnote 1 thereto; Letter #39, lines 6ff.; Letter #40, lines 16ff.; Letter #45, lines 15ff.; Letter #64, lines 28ff.; Letter #76, lines 39f. and footnote 3 thereto.

74. See, for example, Letter #15, line 245f.; Letter #16, line 15.

75. See, for example, Letter #17, lines 28ff. and footnote 2 thereto; Letter #45, lines 52ff.; Letter #47, lines 33ff.; Letter #103, lines 39ff..

76. See, for example, Letter #15, footnote 5.

77. See, for example, Letter #25, lines 11ff.; Letter #64, lines 28ff..

78. See, for example, Letter #16, lines 13ff.; Letter #17, lines 14ff.; Letter #19, lines 20ff..

79. See, for example, Letter #80, lines 17ff..

80. See, for example, Letter #45, lines 65ff..

81. See, for example, Letter #45, lines 53ff..

82. See, for example, Letter #113, lines 28ff.; Letter #114, lines 17ff.; Letter #127, lines 6ff. and footnote 2 thereto; Letter #128, lines 8ff.; Letter #133, lines 14ff.; Letter #139, footnote 3.

83. See, for example, Letter #4, lines 15f. and footnote 6 thereto; Letter #78, lines 48ff. and footnote 6; Letter #141, footnote 3.

84. See, for example, Letter #4, line 10 and footnote 5 thereto.

85. See, for example, Letter #2, lines 17f.; Letter #16, lines 25f., 32f.; Letter #46, lines 39ff. and footnotes 2, 3 and 4 there; Letter #50, lines 6ff. and footnote 1 thereto.

86. See, for example, *Prologue,* lines 157ff. and footnotes 14 and 15 thereto.

87. See, for example, *Prologue,* footnote 11; Letter #4, lines 7f. and footnote 2 thereto.

88. See, for example, Letter #48, lines 29ff. and footnote 1 thereto.

89. See, for example, Letter #15, lines 242f. and footnote 7 thereto; Letter #19, lines 55ff.; Letter #115, lines 30ff..

90. See, for example, Letter #141, lines 13ff. and footnote 2 thereto.

91. See, for example, Letter #2, lines 16ff.; Letter #102, footnote 1; Letter #104, lines 56ff. and footnote 1 thereto.

92. See, for example, *Approbation,* lines 25ff..

93. See, for example, Letter #23, lines 24ff.. In *On The Nature of The Ḥasidic Sect,* Perl specifically charges the movement with moral anarchy. See Rubinstein, *On The Nature,* 36-9, 92, 96, 103, 118, 131, 142-4, 146, 148.

94. See, for example, Letter #17, lines 39f.; Letter #39, lines 21ff.; Letter #76, lines 26ff..

95. See, for example, Letter #1, lines 54ff.; Letter #17, lines 52ff.; Letter #30, lines 47ff.; Letter #33, line 34; Letter #45, lines 72ff..

96. See, for example, *Prologue,* lines 129ff. and footnote 13 thereto; Letter #10, lines 25ff.; Letter #15, lines 140ff.; Letter #21, lines 20ff.; Letter #22, lines 5ff.; Letter #28,

lines 6ff.; Letter #41, lines 29ff.; Letter #70, lines 15ff.; Letter #130, lines 10ff.; Letter #142, lines 31ff..

97. See, for example, Letter #2, lines 21ff.; Letter #10, lines 10ff.; Letter #11, lines 17f.; Letter #48, lines 24ff.; Letter #90, lines 12ff..

98. See, for example, Letter #15, lines 89ff.; Letter #32, lines 10f..

99. See, for example, Letter #10, lines 10ff.; Letter #14, lines 34ff.; Letter #86, lines 14ff..

100. See, for example, Letter #35, lines 28ff..

101. See, for example, Letter #35, lines 34ff.; Letter #36, lines 29ff.; Letter #37, lines 11f.; Letter #61, lines 26ff..

102. See, for example, Letter #16, lines 85ff. and footnote 4 thereto; Letter #24, lines 11ff.; Letter #30, lines 22ff., 45ff.; Letter #49, lines 44ff.; Letter #86, lines 20ff..

103. See, for example, Letter #21, lines 20ff.; Letter #23, lines 6ff.; Letter #65, lines 10ff.; Letter #112, footnote 1.

104. See, for example, Letter #91, lines 24ff.; Letter #95, lines 19ff.; Letter #151, lines 14ff..

105. See, for example, Letter #1, lines 46f.; Letter #5, lines 9ff. and footnote 1 thereto; Letter #8, line 41; Letter #9, lines 34f.; Letter 15, lines 23f.; Letter #32, lines 9ff.; Letter #34, lines 35ff.; Letter #51, lines 20f.; Letter #60, lines 86ff.; Letter #122, lines 15ff..

106. See, for example, Letter #1, lines 12ff.; Letter #8, line 41; Letter #16, lines 13ff.; Letter #40, lines 50ff.; Letter #66, lines 8ff.; Letter #71, footnote 3.

107. See, for example, *Prologue,* lines 153ff.; Letter #2, lines 25ff.; Letter #4, lines 72ff.; Letter #22, lines 43ff. and footnote 1 thereto; Letter #45, footnote 1; Letter #51, footnote 1; Letter #56, footnote 1; Letter #65, footnote 2; Letter #70, footnote 1; Letter #104, lines 99ff.; Letter #109, footnote 2.

108. See, for example, Letter #54, lines 27ff.; Letter #60, lines 54ff.; Letter #104, lines 116ff..

109. See, for example, Letter #3, lines 18ff. and footnote 2 thereto; Letter #8, lines 40f..

110. See, for example, Letter #3, footnote 3; Letter #15, lines 99ff..

111. Letter #3, lines 19f. and footnote 2 thereto.

112. See, for example, Letter #33, lines 26ff.; Letter #36, lines 12ff..

113. See, for example, Letter #18, lines 17ff.; Letter #21, lines 39ff..

114. See, for example, Letter #114, footnote 1.

115. See, for example, Letter #121, lines 32f..

116. See, for example, Letter #3, footnote 2; Letter #8, lines 7ff.; Letter #18, lines 16ff.; Letter #20, lines 72f.; Letter #21, lines 39ff.; Letter #30, lines 11f., 25ff.; Letter #52, lines 9f.; Letter #55, lines 14ff..

117. See, for example, Letter #5, lines 23ff.; Letter #8, lines 17ff.; Letter #33, lines 27ff.; Letter #35, lines 49ff.; Letter #36, lines 17ff..

118. See, for example, Letter #21, lines 20ff.; Letter #120, lines 22ff..

119. See, for example, Letter #41, lines 27ff.; Letter #42, lines 10ff.; Letter #43, lines 13ff..

120. See, for example, Letter #54, lines 38ff.; Letter #55, lines 14f.; Letter #100, lines 14ff..

original in *SB* alluded to in footnote 1 there; the incident in the woods in Letter #20 with the original in *SB* related in footnote 1 there; the encounter between the Zaliner *Rebe* and Mordekhai Gold in Letter #8 with that between the Besht and a demon quoted in footnote 2 there.

162. See Werses, "Joseph Perl's Methods of Satire," 34-41.

163. Cf. Letter #6, lines 21ff.; Letter #8, lines 4ff.; Letter #9, lines 14ff.; Letter #33, lines 12f..

164. Nathan Sternharz to his son Isaac, Friday, *Vayigash* 5585 [1825], *Alim li-Terufa* (Jerusalem: Breslov Research Institute, 1968), 15, Letter #11.

165. Sternharz to his son, Sunday, *Kedoshim* 5595 [1835], *Alim li-Terufa,* penultimate letter in #172. The quotation at the very end is from Lev. 22:10.

166. Sternharz to his son, Wednesday, *Vayeitsei* 5596 [1836], *Alim li-Terufa,* 157, beginning of Letter #184.

167. Sternharz to his son Isaac, Tuesday, *Vayishlaḥ* 5596 [1836], *Alim li-Terufa,* 159, middle of Letter #186.

168. See Chone Shmeruk, "Authentic and Imaginative Elements in Joseph Perl's 'M'galeh T'mirin," *Tsion* 21 (1956): 95. See also "Meyer Yankev" in *Excursus 2: Deciphering the Names,* pp. 256-7.

169. Letter #54, lines 38ff..

170. See "Kalktsig" in *Excursus 2: Deciphering the Names,* p. 258.

171. Letter #121, lines 25ff..

172. Letter #121, footnote 1.

173. Shmeruk, "Imaginative Elements," 94-8. Cf. Letter #33: "Only when Mordekhai Gold will come to him [the landlord], then he'll give *him* the letter to translate it for him into Polish in order to know who were the men...."

174. Cf. *Prologue,* lines 32ff.; Letter #1, lines 64f.; Letter #60, lines 68f..

175. Toward the bottom of the first page of #181.

176 Israel Davidson, *Parody in Jewish Literature* (New York: Columbia University Press, 1907), 61.

177. Heinrich Graetz, *History of the Jews,* vol. V (Philadelphia: JPS, 1956), 612: "[Perl] made incisive attacks upon the Chassidim in a work...which was in no way inferior to *The Letters of Obscure Men* in the monkish Latin of Rubianus and Hutten...."

178. Werses, "Joseph Perl's Methods of Satire," 10f.. Cf. also Halkin, *Trends and Forms,* 170f.. Cf. also Patterson, *Phoenix,* 23.

179. A. D. McKillop, "Epistolary Techniques in Richardson's Novels," *Rice Institute Pamphlet* 38 (April 1951): 36. Quoted in Patterson, *Phoenix,* 24.

180. See above, p. *xli.*

181. Werses, "Joseph Perl's Methods of Satire," 11f.. This possibility was first suggested by J. L. Landau in his *Short Lectures on Modern Hebrew Literature* (London: E. Goldston, 1938), 213.

182. *Jüdische Briefe,* 1764-66 and 1770-73.

183. Introduction to vol. I of *Lettres juives.* Quoted by Werses, "Joseph Perl's Methods of Satire," 12.

184. *Prologue,* lines 197ff..

185. Werses, "Joseph Perl's Methods of Satire," 21f.. Cf. Kalmanovitch, "Linguistic Analysis," LXII, n. 2.

186. Perl, *The Test of the Righteous,* 23.

187. E.g., "And of course, it *had* to be so, as is known" (Letter #57, footnote 3); "And it stands to reason that...Rabbi Nakhmen *must have known better* than the 'experts' in Greater Tsidon" (Letter #109, footnote 2); "There is no doubt at all that he comprehended this matter, for had he not comprehended it how did he know by virtue of which trait we could understand this matter?" (*Prologue,* footnote 1); "Who is fool enough to believe the words of those who say that the printers of the holy community of Mezhebush, in a community that, since the time of the Besht, became a wonder to behold, are ignoramuses!" (*Prologue,* footnote 3).

188. Werses, "Joseph Perl's Methods of Satire," 12-18.

189. *Prologue,* lines 197ff..

190. Werses, "Joseph Perl's Methods of Satire," 21-4.

191. Patterson, *Phoenix,* 24.

192. Solomon J. Rapoport, review of *Revealer of Secrets,* by Joseph Perl, *Bikkurei ha-Ittim* (1831): 178. Cited in Werses, "Joseph Perl's Methods of Satire," 18.

193. Kurzweil, "The Satire of Joseph Perl," 71.

194. See also *Excursus 2: Deciphering the Names.*

195. Isaiah Rabinovich, *Major Trends in Modern Hebrew Fiction* (Chicago and London: University of Chicago Press, 1968), 6.

196. E.g., Letter #121, footnote 1; Letter #139, footnote 3; Letter #124, footnote 3; Letter #69, footnote 1.

197. *Prologue,* lines 225f..

198. Letter #13, line 10.

199. Letter #71.

200. *Acknowledgments,* lines 25ff..

201. *Acknowledgments,* lines 35ff..

202. *Acknowledgments,* lines 40ff..

203. *Important Notice,* lines 8ff..

204. Letter #16, lines 80f..

205. *Prologue,* footnote 11.

206. Letter #76, lines 11f..

207. Cf. *Title Page,* line 14.

208. Letter #10, lines 18ff. and footnote 1 thereto.

209. Letter #109, lines 14f..

210. Letter #1, lines 63ff..

211. *Prologue,* lines 143ff., 161ff., 173ff., 218ff..

212. Davidson points out that Perl was the originator of this technique, which was subsequently employed by others who acknowledged their debt to him. See Davidson, *Parody,* 62 and note 8 there.

213. Werses, "Joseph Perl's Methods of Satire," 33f.. Cf. Patterson, *Phoenix,* 31.

214. Kalmanovitch, "Linguistic Analysis," XCVIX-C: "It is without a doubt bad Hebrew...a parody of Hebrew. Perl didn't have to invent a thing....In hundreds of books and in countless letters and documents this very language was used....Perl could rightly say that he wrote 'in their language.'"

215. In Vaynlez, *The Yiddish Writings of Joseph Perl.*

216. Letter #104.

217. See Letter #8, lines 15f.; Letter # 15, lines 208f.; Letter # 29, lines 14f.; Letter #35, line 32; Letter #87, line 13. In Letter #106, lines 27f., we find "אינם שוים החיות," "they're not worthy of the living."

218. Letter #50, line 27.

219. Letter #130, line 38. Cf. Letter #97, lines 9f..

220. Letter #130, lines 34f.. Both of these examples are cited by Rapoport. See Rapoport, review of *Revealer of Secrets,* 178.

221. Max Weinreich, *History of the Yiddish Language* (Chicago and London: University of Chicago Press, 1980), 306-10.

222. Robert Alter, *Hebrew & Modernity* (Bloomington and Indianapolis: Indiana University Press, 1994), 6.

223. Nathan Gordon, "Joseph Perl's Megalleh Temirin," *Hebrew Union College Annual,* 1904, 241.

224. Leo Rosten's *The Education of Hyman Kaplan* is probably the best-known fictional treatment of this subject. See his *O Kaplan! My Kaplan!,* which includes the earlier work. The colloquial English I use to approximate the colloquial Hebrew is just that -- an approximation. The Hebrew style that Perl lampoons is intended to show the cultural backwardness of the *ḥasidim* at the beginning of the nineteenth century, while the "Yinglish" style I have employed in the translation resonates with the cultural world of the Borsht Belt more than a century later.

225. Letter #104, lines 93f..

226. Letter #77, line 101.

227. David Patterson, *Hebrew Literature: The Art of the Translator* (London: Jewish Book Council, 1958), 10.

228. Rosten, *Hyman Kaplan,* xvi.

229. The historical places mentioned in the text can be located in Gary Mokotoff and Sallyann Amdur Sack, *Where Once We Walked* (Teaneck, New Jersey: Avotaynu, 1991).

230. Letter #55, line 5.

231. Letter #64, line 2.

232. Letter #96, lines 37f..

233. Letter #1, line 2.

234. Letter #1, line 3.

235. Letter #2, lines 15f..

236. Letter #62, line 74.

237. Letter #5, line 9.

238. Letter #7, line 2.

239. Letter #26, line 51.

240. Letter #2, line 20.

241 For a discussion of the introduction of surnames into Jewish life, s.v. "Mordekhai Gold" in *Excursus 2: Deciphering the Names,* p. 255.

242. Letter #8, line 22.

243. Letter #64, line 22.

244. E.g., Reb Zelig Letitshiver, Letter #1, line 2.

245. E.g., the lady Khaye, Letter #64, line 12.

246. E.g., Mrs. Odel, Letter #71, line 41.

247. E.g., the lady Mrs. Freyda, Letter #91, line 4.

248. See above, pp. *xlv-xlvi.*

249. Alter, *Hebrew & Modernity,* 43.

250. Nahum Slouschz, *The Renascence of Hebrew Literature* (Phila.: JPS, 1909), 56.

251. *Jewish Encyclopedia,* s.v. "Perl, Joseph."

252. Cf. Silberschlag, *Renaissance,* 369, n. 71. Cf. also Kalmanovitch, "Linguistic Analysis," LXXIV, n. 5: "It is apparent that the learned author of the article did not even bother to glance at the book before scribbling...."

253. Kalmanovitch, "Linguistic Analysis," LXXV.

254. Kurzweil, "The Satire of Joseph Perl," 70ff..

255. Kurzweil, "The Satire of Joseph Perl," 71f..

256. Rapoport, review of *Revealer of Secrets,* 178.

257. Halkin, *Modern Hebrew Literature,* 152f., 164ff., 184f..

258. Davidson, *Parody,* 63.

259. Halkin, *Modern Hebrew Literature,* 166f.. See also above, note 46 and *Excursus 3: Perl's Yiddish Prologue.*

260. Silberschlag, *Renaissance,* 130.

261. Werses, "Joseph Perl's Methods of Satire," 19.

262. Patterson, *Phoenix,* 10f..

263. Diaspora Jews, lit., "Exile Jews." A term of disdain.

264. See above, p. *xxvi.*

265. Chanan Brichto, *Toward A Grammar of Biblical Poetics* (New York and Oxford: Oxford University Press, 1992), 4-5, 20.

266. See above, p. *xlvi.*

267. Yehuda Friedlander, *Hebrew Satire in Europe in the Eighteenth and Nineteenth Centuries,* vol. 3 (Ramat-Gan: Bar-Ilan University: 1984) 35 and 141, n. 43/1.

268. Friedlander, *Hebrew Satire in Europe,* vol. 3, 60f..

269. Friedlander, *Hebrew Satire in Europe,* vol. 2, 136, n. 119.

270. Cf. Kurzweil, "The Satire of Joseph Perl," 73. Cf. also Kalmanovitch, "Linguistic Analysis," LXXIX.

271. Cf. Agnon's story, "Until Now," quoted by Kurzweil: "It is true that Dr. Levy left her two rooms full of books, but in the meantime the rats will consume them. And even if the rats don't consume them and they remain as they are, the entire generation that would have needed those books has died." See Kurzweil, "The Satire of Joseph Perl," 83. Cf. also Agnon's "Forevermore," and Bialik's poems, "In Front of the Bookcase" and "On the Threshold of the House of Study."

272. See David Patterson, *Abraham Mapu: The Creator of the Modern Hebrew Novel* (London: Horovitz Publishing, 1964), 101f..

273. In his *The Book of Beggars.* See also Shmeruk, "Imaginative Elements," 99.

274. I am grateful to Ezra Spicehandler for this insight.

275. See Chone Shmeruk, "The Name Mordecai-Marcus -- Literary Metamorphosis of a Social Ideal," *Tarbiz* 29 (1959-60), 76-98. See also "Mordekhai Gold" in *Excursus 2: Deciphering the Names,* p. 255.

276. See Letter #109, footnote 2 and note thereto.

277. *Prologue,* lines 34f..

278. Dubnow, *History of Hasidism,* 397.

279. Perl, *The Test of the Righteous,* 112.

THE BOOK

REVEALER OF SECRETS*

IT IS JUST WHAT ITS NAME SAYS

For it reveals things that have hitherto been
secreted away AND HIDDEN FROM ALL HUMAN SIGHT
and whoever reads the PROLOGUE
will understand the reason for revealing these things
for therein this matter is explained at length.

And appended thereunto
at its end is a lexicon of the expressions
common amongst our kinfolk the Jews of Poland*
and used in this book and in other books by
the *tsadikim* of our time*
so that our kinfolk who are not amongst the Jews of Poland
will understand the holy books composed by
the *tsadikim* of our time
who reside in the land of Poland.
MAY IT PLEASE THE WISE.*

MEGALLÉ TEMIRIN

VIENNA*

Printed by ANTON STRAUSS, royal imperial licensed printer.*

1819

THE APPROBATION* OF

A saint, a man of G-d, brimful* of blessings from the L-rd,
Filled with ancient wine, a vessel new [and fine],*
The *Rov* most eminent, *khosed** and deferent,
The Lamp [exceeding] bright, with him resides the light* --
His Excellency, Our Teacher the *Rov,*
Rabbi Yehude, son of Our Teacher the *Rov,*
Rabbi Moyshe of Turbusme,* may his light shine.

Whereas the author of the book *Revealer of Secrets* has come before me and requested that I give him my Approbation for his book, which he proposes TO DISSEMINATE IN JACOB and to SCATTER OVER THE FACE OF THE WHOLE EARTH so that ALL DWELLERS ON EARTH AND ITS INHABITANTS will recognize and know* THAT THE NAME OF THE L-RD IS PROCLAIMED UPON us AND WILL FEAR us, and even ONE WHO IS UNCLEAN OR FAR AWAY, who has not yet SEEN THE DELIVERANCE OF THE L-RD, which He has brought about in order to FULFILL THE WISHES OF THOSE WHO FEAR HIM and WHO TREMBLE AT HIS WORDS, WILL RESOLVE NOT TO DEFILE HIMSELF WITH THE FOOD OF THE KING* -- the kings of the rabbis* of our day serving as teachers WHO ARE BENT ON MISCHIEF. For they are predatory preachers who prey upon* the word of the L-rd through *drosh* (דרָשׁ)* and thereby mutilate the sacred books and strengthen the demonic forces, G-d save us!, as is known to the Kabbalists.*

SUCH MUST NOT BE DONE, for the essence of Toyre study is through *pshot* (פְּשָׁט), *remez* (רמז) or *sod* (סוד)* -- the letters of *sephor seypher sipur* (סְפָר סֵפֶר סִפּוּר) of *Seyfer Yetsire** -- and not through *drosh* (דרָשׁ). Delete ***d*** (ד) from the word *drosh* (דרָשׁ) and there remains ***rosh*** (רָשׁ, poor man), as in, *VELOROSH EYN KOL* (THE POOR MAN HAD NOTHING). Remove ***r*** (ר) and there remains ***sheyd*** (שֵׁד, demon) -- this is a Jewish demon.* [The second word of] *LEMI SIYAKH* (למי שיח), WHO HAS COMPLAINTS?, is an acronym of ***Khokhem*** ***sheyd*** *yehudo'ey* (חכם שד יהודאי),

"A [Talmud] sage is a Jewish demon", as is explained in the book.* Strike ***sh*** (ש) and there remains ***reyd*** (רֵד, descend), as in *LEKH-REYD KI SHIKHEYS AMKHO* -- DESCEND, FOR YOUR PEOPLE HAVE ACTED BASELY. This is the truth.

Now the aforementioned author-rabbi has been stirred TO GIRD HIMSELF WITH STRENGTH and to HASTEN IN THE VANGUARD to wage a war of *mitsve,* an obligatory war,* FOR IT IS A LAW UNTO ISRAEL to gather the camps that ARE ENCAMPED AT THE COMMAND OF THE L-RD and go forth against the demon Samoel and his troupe,* namely, those who GROUND THE MANNA BETWEEN MILLSTONES OR POUNDED IT IN A MORTAR because they didn't know what it was.* Therefore have I promised that HE HAS MY UNFLAGGING SUPPORT to bring his idea to fruition, and so that none would come to APPROACH THE SACRED ALTAR to COMPOUND ITS LIKE* or slander the author.

Consequently, I hereby give him my blessing, THE BLESSINGS OF HEAVEN ABOVE, boundless blessings* ASCENDING AND DESCENDING from the Sanctuary on high to the Sanctuary below,* TO COUPLE THE TENT* so that the Tabernacle SHALL BE ONE AND ITS NAME ONE.* By virtue of this blessing from the highest cistern and the conduits that bring abundance,* may it be absolutely certain that NO HARM WILL BEFALL him. For the L-rd WILL POUR OUT His SPIRIT, A FAVORABLE SPIRIT, ON ALL FLESH* and then the HERALD* will come speedily. *Omeyn.*

These are the words of the undersigned writer for [the purpose of dating] the week* and year:*

ויאמר לו משה המקנא אתה לי
ומי יתן כל־עם ה׳ נביאים
כי־יתן ה׳ את־רוחו עליהם.

BUT MOSES SAID TO HIM: ARE YOU WROUGHT UP ON MY ACCOUNT?
WOULD THAT ALL THE L-RD'S PEOPLE WERE PROPHETS,
THAT THE L-RD PUT HIS SPIRIT UPON THEM!*

[(by the abbreviated count) *Beha'alotekha* 5579, June 1819]*

Yehude, son of Our Teacher the *Rov,*
Rabbi Moyshe of Turbusmi. BE STRONG.

[ACKNOWLEDGMENTS]*

THE BOOK

REVEALER OF SECRETS

IT IS JUST WHAT ITS NAME SAYS

For it reveals things that have hitherto been secreted away AND HIDDEN FROM ALL HUMAN SIGHT.

And it is incumbent upon us* to acknowledge and to praise The Source and Conduit of Divine Wisdom, The Crown Jewel of Israel, The Master, Our Teacher the *Rov*, Rabbi Israel Balshemtov* -- may his merit protect us and all Israel our brethren -- through whom the aforementioned things have been revealed to us, as is explained at length in the PROLOGUE.

Also, everyone will find in it *toyre* and moral instruction bequeathed to us by his holy and pure disciples who DWELT IN his SHADE,* namely:

- the eminent, great and brilliant rabbi, pious and modest, a man of G-d, renowned as a saint -- Our Teacher the *Rov*, Rabbi Yankev Yoysef the priest,* may his light shine brightly;
- the great rabbi, sharp-witted and erudite in that which is revealed, and in that which is concealed* -- The Pride of The Glory of Israel; godly, pious and abstinent, The Holy Light, Revealer of Profundities, whose good name is known far and wide -- His Reverence, Our Teacher

the *Rov,* Rabbi Dov Baer, remembered for eternal life,* who was Preacher of the holy community of Meziretch;

- the eminent, pious and prominent* rabbi, a man of G-d, renowned as a saint -- Our Teacher the *Rov,* Rabbi Elimelekh, remembered for eternal life, of Lizhensk;
- our revered master, Our Teacher and Our Rabbi, The Holy *Rov,* The Most High and Worthy Light, The Hidden and Secret Light* -- His Holiness, Our Teacher the *Rov,* Rabbi Nakhmen, THE SAINT and Holy Man OF BLESSED MEMORY, the great-grandson of the Besht;*
- The Light of Israel and its Holy One, **The Lamp of Israel, The Right-hand Pillar, The Strong Hammer,*** The Prodigy of the Generation* and its Splendor, THE HOLY DIADEM, the distinguished saint of the L-rd, THE PRIDE OF our STRENGTH and LIGHT OF OUR EYES, Teacher of his folk and Leader of his people -- His Holiness, Our Teacher the *Rov,* Rabbi Menakhem Nokhem, Preacher and Spiritual Guide of the holy community of Tchernobil;
- the eminent, pious rabbi, a man of G-d, renowned as a saint -- Our Teacher the *Rov,* Rabbi Moyshe, scribe for Toyre scrolls, *tfiln* and *mezuzes,* of the holy community of Prshevorsk;
- and others comparable to them in holiness and purity.

All these stories were recorded and truthfully reported by A HOLY ONE SPEAKING, the great sage, wonderful and distinguished in Toyre and fear of G-d,* the eminent *khosed,* Our Teacher, Rabbi Ovadye ben Psakhye,* who dwells among all the *tsadikim* and eminent men of our time.

The year

TURN TO ME AND BE ASTONISHED [JOB 21:5].* פנו־אלי והשמו [איוב כ״א: ה]

[579 (by the abbreviated count) = 1819]*

IMPORTANT NOTICE*

Let it be stated emphatically that everywhere this book indicates the designation "Rabbi *(Rov)*," "*Rebe*," "Real *Rebe*," "*Tsadek*," "*Tsadek* of the Generation," "Perfect *Tsadek*," "True *Tsadek*," "Worthy," "Worthy of the Generation," "Real Worthy," "Sage," "Sage of the Generation," "True Sage," "Real Sage," "Scholar," "Prince," "King," "G-d-fearer" and the like, the reference therein is only to those *tsadikim* who serve G-d with *dveykes* and *hislayves*, and not to the few "Talmudists"* still found in our land, because of our many sins, upon whom LIGHT HAS not yet DAWNED.

Even though the matter is common knowledge, all the same we have felt compelled to announce this because we know that some of those syphilitics* do not read the holy books by the *tsadikim* of our time and do not know that it is not to *them* [the "Talmudists"] that all those epithets are regularly ascribed. When they see the aforementioned epithets in this book, they might think that these designations are for *them* and might thereby assume a haughtiness that, thanks to the *tsadikim*, has been taken from them for some time now.*

Therefore we have presented this Notice at the beginning of the book for all to see, so that they may not attire themselves in a *tales* that is not theirs.[1]*

---

[1] Whoever has eyes to see and has not befouled his pure soul will know full well that it is nothing but [the plain] TRUTH MY MOUTH UTTERS here. Yet I know that some of our contemporaries are confused about this and do not yet know the way of truth,* so I give my promise: Whoever discloses his troubled mind and FEELS A CRAVING to be shown clear proofs of this, I am fully prepared* for the sake of truth and righteousness to support and substantiate these words with the holy books by the *tsadikim* of our time.

Only the expenses of publishing, which are considerable, have prevented me from getting them published at this time, especially since I know that currently, thank G-d, there are few people who will not know that all the titles mentioned in the *Notice* from the books by the *tsadikim* of our time are used only of real *tsadikim*, the essence of whose worship of the Creator is *dveykes* and *hislayves*.

Even the designation "scholar," which seems at first sight to signify Talmudists -- as the Talmudists think, because of our many sins -- it too refers only to the aforementioned *tsadikim*. For proof see the holy book *Yesamakh Leyv* 24:3[ff.] on the rabbinic statement, "Rabbi Elozor said in the name of Rabbi Khanine: 'The scholars increase peace in the world, as it is written, ALL YOUR CHILDREN SHALL BE TAUGHT OF THE LORD AND GREAT SHALL BE THE PEACE OF YOUR CHILDREN. Do not read, YOUR CHILDREN *(BAWNAIYIKH)*, but rather, 'your builders' *(bonaiyikh)*.'"* This is his unadorned language: "The scholars are called 'builders' by virtue of the fact that they once again uplift to the *Eyn Sof*, blessed be He, the sparks that are in everything, which fell in the Shattering....Because all this has to be done by the *tsadikim* of the generation. As we say elsewhere, 'There is a single pillar from heaven to earth and *Tsadek* is its name,'* because the *tsadek* unifies all things and connects them from earth to heaven, and raises the lower things, categorized as 'Female' *(Nukvo)*, up to the Source of Abundance, named 'Word' *(Dovor)** [because the category 'Female' is so named, as it is written, THIS IS THE TOYRE *(Zos ha-Toyre)*, because the Toyre that is hidden among the lower things...is called 'This' (f., *Zos)*, and the Celestial Root is called by the name 'This' (m., *Zeh)*, as it is written, THIS IS THE WORD *(Zeh ha-Dovor)*, namely, the Word of the Celestial Source of Abundance. Therefore it is necessary to raise the category of 'This' (f., *Zos)* up to 'This' (m., *Zeh)* by means of the *tsadikim*...]."

It is known that all worship and all actions, everything without exception, is [effective] only through *dveykes* and *hislayves*, and despite all this the Talmudists sorely mislead themselves and imagine that the designation "scholar" was coined just with reference to them. But there will yet be an occasion to show them their error with the rest of my compositions, which I hope to publish soon, G-d willing. There they will see that this title is not theirs, for they just GROPE in darkness LIKE BLIND MEN, and the name that is really fitting for them* you will see in the holy book *Toldes Yankev Yoysef, Parshes Shoftim*, fol. 45, and in the *Kitser Likutey MohoRa"N*, Book 2, par. 174.

PROLOGUE

PraISed* be the name of our RAbbi.[1] We have nonE Like unto him among prophets. His feats have long BEeN known to us, ever since thE LIght of his *toyre* was revEaled to our gaZE thRough[2] his disciples who succeeded him. The first was "the eminent, great and brilliant rabbi, pious and humble, a man of G-d, renowned as a saint, Our Teacher the *Rov,* Rabbi Yankev Yoysef the priest, may his light shine brightly, may his Rock and Redeemer protect him -- the light of whose *toyre* shone in the holy communities of Rashkov and Sharigrod and Nemerov, and whose SECURE POSITION at present is as Chief Judge of the Court, Head of the *Yeshive* and Spiritual Guide* [rabbi] in the holy community of Polnai, and Spiritual Guide* here in the holy community of Nemerov"[3] -- who gave us the privilege of revealing to us

---

[1] **VERILY, THE WORD OF G-D WAS in the agency of The Balshem. He was unique. None of the ancients were like him** NOR WILL THERE EVER BE ANY LIKE HIM ON EARTH. Introduction to the holy book *Shivkhey ha-Besht,* Kopust edition, first printing.* It is also known that Moyshe Rabeyne, may he rest in peace, was premier among the prophets, nevertheless he was unable to attain the measure of "a *tsadek* whom evil befalls," and our rabbi, the Hidden and Concealed Light, Our Teacher the *Rov,* Rabbi Nakhmen, the great-grandson of the Besht, THE SAINT and Holy Man OF BLESSED MEMORY, shows how to attain this measure in his book *Likutey MohoRa"N,* Book 2 [5:15], 16:1-2.* There is no doubt at all that he attained this measure, for had he not attained it how would he know that by virtue of this trait we could attain this measure? We also know from his holy book *Sipurey Mayses,* Part 2, that he used to comport himself with this trait, and so he certainly attained this measure. And if *he* attained it, how much the more so must the Besht, THE SAINT and Holy Man OF BLESSED MEMORY, have attained it! So he must have been greater than all the prophets and even than Moyshe Rabeyne, may he rest in peace.

[2] Israel, son of Eliezer* is the name of our founder, whose title is "The Balshemtov." See *Shivkhey ha-Besht* 25:2 [Mintz, 181].

[3] This is all copied from the title page of the holy book *Toldes Yankev Yoysef,* which was printed for the second time in the holy community of Mezhebush in the year 5576 [1815-1816]. And I have copied it directly because the scoffers of the generation deride it and say that the printers copied the title page from the title page of the first edition in the year 5540 [1780] when the *Rov* who composed it was still alive, and the printers in the holy community of Mezhebush were ignoramuses and did not know that in the year 5576, when the *Rov* who composed it had already died, we could not have said of him, "May his light shine brightly, whose secure position at present is as Chief Judge of the Court and Head of the *Yeshive* and Spiritual Guide of the holy community of Polnai, may his Rock and

an infinitesimal part* of the Besht's *toyre* in his holy books, *Toldes Yankev Yoysef,* Tsofnas Pa'aneyakh* and *Poyres Yoysef.*

His successors followed in his holy and pure footsteps and published the books *Likutey Amorim, Likutey Yekorim, No'am Elimelekh, Tsavo'as MohoRY"BaSH, Keser Shem Tov, Or ha-Meyer, Yesamakh Leyv, Me'or Eynayim, Mevaser Tsedek, Kedushas Levi, Or Peney Moyshe, Darkhey Tsedek, No'am Megodim, Orakh le-Khayim, Be'er Mayim, Or ha-Khokhme* and thousands and tens of thousands like these. Were all the oceans ink and all the reeds quills and all the grasses paper,* we would be unable to write the titles of all the holy books that have been published and disseminated among our kinfolk by the *tsadikim* and the great men of the generation from the time of the Besht until now.

There isn't the slightest reason to doubt that all those books -- that is to say, the *toyre** and moral instruction that we see in them -- from the days of the Besht until now, must already have been known in the days of the Besht* and his holy disciples. The reason they didn't publish them was that the generations were not yet worthy of them,* and they also knew that the generation would not accept them, as was the case with the holy book, *Toldes Yankev Yoysef,* mentioned above, which they burned in the holy community of Brod,[4] as well as with the holy book,

---

Redeemer protect him...." And a few of the scoffers say that the printers were afraid of the censor and printed the title page as it was, and the proof is that they printed the old date, 5540 [1780].

What a disgrace!* For anyone can see that they are lying and no one is FOOL ENOUGH TO BELIEVE the words of those who say that the printers of the holy community of Mezhebush, in a community that, since the time of the Besht, became a wonder to behold, are ignoramuses! It is also a lie that they were afraid of the censor, because they printed the *Approbation* of the *tsadek* of Apt -- where the year 5576 is explicitly stated -- right there on side 2 of the title page!

But the truth is that all the scoffers are the real ignoramuses and do not seek the truth, for in the holy book *No'am Elimelekh,* it says explicitly, "The vitality of the *tsadek* also becomes essentiality and eternality, for they cling together to the same essence (to G-d)", 90:3.

Also in *Shivkhey ha-Besht* 18:4 [Mintz, 136], the following terminology appears explicitly: **I heard from Rabbi Zusya of Anipoli when he left his brother Rabbi Elimelekh and traveled through Zolkva: "I stood at some spot in the** ***besmedresh*** **to pray and the prayer was almost as pure and clear as the prayers of the Besht. I didn't know what the reason was, and they said that this very spot was the** [praying] **place of the author of the book** ***Toldes*** ***Yankev Yoysef."*** So it was intentional that the printers wrote about the *Rov,* "Our Teacher the *Rov,* Yankev Yoysef, may his light shine brightly, whose secure position at present...." For he is even now still alive and to this day he serves as teacher in all the places mentioned above.

[4] *Shivkhey ha-Besht* 36:3 [Mintz, 260]. Even though it is not written there *where*

Keser Shem Tov, which they took and tore into pieces, dipped in sulphur and made into matches, G-d save us! For this reason they didn't publish more than what each and every generation was capable of receiving and was worthy of, because in every single generation, by the help of G-d, blessed be He, faith in *khakhomim* is progressively revealed to us, as is explained in the holy book, *No'am Elimelekh.*[5]

Therefore in the generation of our rabbi, The Hidden Light, Our Teacher the *Rov,* Rabbi Nakhmen, the great-grandson of the Besht, THE SAINT and Holy Man OF BLESSED MEMORY, he favored the generation -- he and his delightful disciple, the young gentleman, Our Teacher, Rabbi Noson, may his light shine -- by publishing wonderful and sweet compositions, like the three *Likutim* and the abridged *Likutim,* the *Mides* and *Sipurey Mayses,* in which he showed everyone the foundation on which rest the pillars and structure of our faction* and sacred fellowship.* So we see that in each and every generation the true *toyre* and faith in

---

they wanted to burn the aforementioned book, this too is well-known -- that in the holy community of Brod, because of our many sins, they burned the holy book *Toldes Yankev Yoysef* in front of the home of Our Teacher the *Rov,* Rabbi Mikhel of Zlotchuv, in compliance with the order of the court and the community there.

[5] "Thus said my master, my father, my teacher and my rabbi, may his light shine. He commented regarding the verse, GENERATION TO GENERATION WILL PRAISE YOUR DEEDS, that it says in the *Gemore,* 'Before the sun of Eli set, the sun of Samuel rose; before the sun of Rabbi [Yehude Hanosi] set...,'* because the generation is not lacking in *tsadikim,* who are in every generation, but they have no faith, except for the one who has a holy soul, who has not befouled it with sins. Although we bring them proof from the *tsadikim* and from the earlier generations, they speak in this manner: 'We believe in the early *khakhomim* who had attained the rung of the holy spirit [revelation], but now, in this generation, it is impossible for this to be.' And so they say in every generation, as we find with King Saul, may he rest in peace, as is known."

"My beloved brother, rest assured that even in the days of the saint, the AR"I* of blessed memory, there were also those who quarreled with him, and that is the meaning of the verse, GENERATION TO GENERATION WILL PRAISE YOUR DEEDS, that is to say, the current generation themselves acknowledge that the preceding generations had attained [high] rungs, which is the meaning of, WILL PRAISE YOUR DEEDS -- that they praise and acknowledge that the deeds of the L-rd that He performs for the *tsadikim* are great, but not in *this* generation. That is the meaning of the *Gemore,* 'The *tsadikim* are greater in death than in life,'* because while they were alive people would quarrel with them, but after their death everyone acknowledges and praises him that he had attained the aforementioned rungs." *Igeres ha-Koydesh* in *No'am Elimelekh* 111:2.

strengthen and to extend faith in *khakhomim,* and to make known the virtues and the fundamentals of the circle of the *Rabbon,* the Besht, in general, and of the *tsadikim* of the generation. There is nothing more important than this."[11] The moment he finished speaking, the old man vanished from my sight.

I was standing not on the mountain but in the ravine between the mountains, and since I knew that on this route there were many highwaymen,[12] I put the manuscript in my right pocket and I immediately became invisible, and when I got near my home I put the manuscript in my left pocket and I became visible as before.

I resolved to go to all the *tsadikim* in an invisible state, because when I was around them previously I saw that their Faithful publicize their holy deeds, but I saw that many things they don't reveal, and many things that the *tsadikim* do in secret they don't know. So I thought, "There is nothing more important than this -- to reveal to the public all the dealings of the *tsadikim,* those who serve them and their Faithful -- even the things that they do humbly and in secret. As a matter of fact, the things they do in secret are liable to be more important to us, because from them their greatness and their thought is most recognizable."

---

[11] "Whoever recounts the tales of what happened to the *tsadikim,* by virtue of this good thoughts are drawn to him." *Seyfer ha-Mides* of *MohoRa"N,* 20:4.

"Whoever recounts the tales of the *tsadikim,* The Holy One praised be He treats benevolently." *Ibid.,* 55:174.

"By recounting the tales of *tsadikim,* we draw the light of *meshiekh* [messiah] into the world and push much darkness and trouble out of the world and also merit nice clothes." *Ibid.,* 73:1.

"By virtue of recounting the tales of the great real *tsadek,* the arousal of the *Shkhine* comes about. Fortunate is he who is privileged to come to such a *tsadek* who can arouse him from his slumber so that he should not waste his days in slumber, G-d forbid!" *Kitser Likutey MohoRa"N* 56:564.

"By virtue of recounting the tales of a real *tsadek,* the childless are taken note of." *Ibid.,* 57:565.

"IN PROPORTION TO THE NUMBER OF PERSONS *(NEFOSHOS),* meaning that one should always tell of the great *tsadikim* and should always enumerate their upright qualities, and *'nefoshos'* is an allusion to the *tsadikim* and their qualities." *No'am Elimelekh* 36:4.

The Besht said, "Whoever recounts the praises of the *tsadikim* is as if he were occupied with [the study of] *Mayse Merkove.*" *Shivkhey ha-Besht* 28:1 [Mintz, 199].

He who looks into the holy books will see that they are filled with the praiseworthiness and the significance of the virtue of recounting the tales of the real *tsadikim.* If I tried to write them down, the paper would run out but they wouldn't run out.

[12] *Shivkhey ha-Besht* 3:2 [Mintz, 22].

Thus I went to all the *tsadikim* and I heard what they say in secret, and I also took the letters that they or those who serve them sent to one another and they didn't see, because by means of the cloud I went easily from one place to another when I put the manuscript in the corners of the *tsitsis.* I have reproduced some of their letters in this composition of mine in order to publicize them, so as to reveal to the public secret things that are of paramount concern. And I have named this composition ***Revealer of Secrets,**** because it really reveals secrets that hitherto were HIDDEN FROM EVERY HUMAN EYE.

I ask whoever reads this composition not to think that I made -- G-d forbid! -- any change of language in the letters I reproduced, or that I fabricated -- G-d forbid! -- any tale -- perish the thought! -- for I never attempted to utter any falsehood, even though we have already discovered through our rabbi, The Hidden Light, Our Teacher the *Rov,* Rabbi Nakhmen, the great-grandson of the Besht, that a lie is only with the mouth, not in a manuscript.[13]*

All the same I thought, who am I to permit this to myself? Surely our Master, Our Teacher the *Rov,* Rabbi Nakhmen, THE SAINT and Holy Man OF BLESSED MEMORY, intended this only concerning the real *tsadikim* and the great men of the generation, because they know which falsehood would accomplish good on our behalf and which, G-d forbid!, would be harmful.* But for people of little worth like me, surely such a deed as this would not be permissible without asking permission from the real *tsadikim,* since *we* can't make this distinction. But I couldn't ask permission of them, for I knew that because of their exceeding humility they would not agree to make public those things they do in secret.

Therefore I have reproduced all the tales and the letters in the very same language as I have them from the correspondents.* Only in this respect have I made a change -- in that several names of people and towns I have not transcribed as they are in my letters, for I thought, "Perhaps it is not the wish of these *tsadikim* to make themselves and their deeds public, because much publicity can, G-d forbid!, cause death, as happened in the time of our Master, Our Teacher the *Rov,* Rabbi Nakhmen."* So I disguised their name and the name of their town and wrote them in the secret language of *gimatrie* and such,* AND THE ONE WHO IS ENLIGHTENED WILL UNDERSTAND. But the rest I left as it is in my letters, even though I saw several times, because of our many sins, that the scoffers of the generation make a dreadful mockery of our Faithful and say they can't write properly in the holy tongue and always write full of errors and mistakes like common ignoramuses.*

---

[13] *Seyfer ha-Mides* 6:11.

to write in this language of ours, which makes one wealthy and healthy, particularly since we have seen plainly that all those publishers and authors of books by the *tsadikim* of our time have become, thank G-d, eminently wealthy, particularly the publisher of the holy community of Slavita,* may he live. And of course, if they were ill, G-d save us!, they were healed from illness by virtue of this language.

Conversely, we see that whoever publishes other books in language we call "beautiful,"* has lost a lot of money and been forced to forsake the publication, as we have seen with the press in the holy community of Greater Tsidon*, where many times they began publishing other books but didn't publish the holy books by the *tsadikim* of our time. What more proof do we need that the language of our Faithful must make one wealthy and healthy? In the merit of this may we too be favored with wealth and health. *Omeyn Selo* forever.

Since I knew that people who do not belong to our faction -- who haven't read or looked into the holy books by the real *tsadikim* -- would also read this composition of mine, therefore I have provided footnotes* in the necessary places in order to substantiate the point that appears within the composition by means of some quotation that appears in the holy books. And there will derive from this another great benefit in that those people will recognize the righteousness of the *tsadikim* from the passages I have quoted, and they will be privileged to read words of the *tsadikim* of the highest standing.*

But let it be known that I have taken all the passages and proofs only from the holy books by the *tsadikim* of our time. Even those sayings that are found in the *Gemore* or *Medroshim* and also in the books by the *tsadikim* of our time, I have taken as they appear in the books by the *tsadikim* of our time because the unbelievers would be able to explain the sayings from the *Gemore* and from the *Medroshim* based on the sages and *tsadikim* in a previous age, as is explained above in the name of the godly, eminent *tsadek,* The Hidden Light, Our Teacher the *Rov,* Rabbi Elimelekh of Lizhensk, in his holy book, *No'am Elimelekh.*[18] Therefore I have brought the quotations from the books by the *tsadikim* of our time -- which refer only to the real *tsadikim* in our generation and in recent generations -- in their actual language, in order to strike dumb THOSE WHO SPEAK WANTONLY and TO BOW LIKE A BULRUSH THE HEAD of the slanderers to acknowledge the truth, which is clear as the noonday sun.*

I beg of all our Faithful, may they live, not to blame me* for the fact that I copied the letters verbatim* from those of little faith* and from the disputants* -- just as they wrote their letters, in their very own words. I did this deliberately so that they should not have the privilege of wealth

---

[18] See above, footnote 5.

and health, for had I made changes in their letters, perhaps their language would have been elevated thereby. I did this also so as to show the whole world the distinction between the language of truth and THE LANGUAGE OF FALSEHOOD, for it is known that unless a man knows of the darkness, he would not know the delight of the light.

I also announce that I have, by the help of G-d, blessed be He, many more matters and tales and letters of the real *tsadikim* and of our Faithful, which I hope to publish soon, G-d willing, and to privilege our fellow-Jews with them. At present, however, I have not yet been able to publish them because I heard from an eminent man that the current generation is not yet worthy* of all the secret things. But through this composition I hope that G-d, blessed be He, will make them capable of receiving such precious words as these.

Then the L-rd will overturn CLEAR LANGUAGE* SO THAT together ALL WILL CALL UPON THE NAME OF THE L-RD and the hearts of the Israelites -- credulous children of credulous parents* -- will no longer be divided, and the Toyre will no longer be as two Toyres -- G-d forbid! -- because whoever has A HEART TO KNOW AND EARS TO HEAR, whoever has not STOPPED UP HIS EARS and has not MADE his HEART INSENSITIVE, will see plainly the naked truth, and from that which is concealed may judge that which is revealed.

Today is Tuesday, the 17th of Kislev, a lucky day,* in the year*

נסגו אחור יבשו בשת הבטחים בפסל
האומרים למסכה אתם אלהינו
החרשים שמעו העורים הביטו לראות

ישעיה קאפיטעל מ׳ב פסוק י׳ז

THWARTED, HUMILIATED SHALL BE THOSE WHO TRUST IN AN IMAGE,
WHO SAY TO IDOLS, 'YOU ARE OUR GODS!'
HEARKEN, DEAF ONES! BLIND ONES, LOOK AND SEE!

Isaiah, Chapter 42, Verse 17[-18]

[5579 (by the full count) =1819]

These are the words of the compiler and publisher, Ovadye ben Psakhye, who dwells among all the *tsadikim* and great men of the generation and thirstily drinks in their words.*

[LETTERS]

#1

From Reb Zelig Letitchiver in Zalin
To Reb Zaynvl Verkhievker in Kripen

Yesterday after evening prayers I stayed by our holy *rebe,* The Lamp of Our Generation, and listened to his words, which are SWEETER THAN HONEY OR THE HONEYCOMB. It was such a great pleasure for me because after the prayers, our holy *rebe,* his light should shine, was in total bliss and everything he said was with intense *dveykes,* as usual. During this time I learned from his talking and from his storytelling, thank G-d, more than what A HUMAN BEING can learn from the *toyre* of other *rebes.* I could go for days without eating or drinking to hear his holy speech.

But our holy *rebe* wanted to smoke his pipe* and go to the outhouse. I gave him the pipe but I wasn't privileged to light it for him because while I was giving our *rebe* the pipe, another of our Faithful* scrambled to light it. When I saw it wasn't our *rebe*'s wish to be accompanied to the outhouse,* I went home overjoyed that I am worthy to be among our *rebe*'s people and that G-d gave me the privilege of hearing great things from our *rebe* that day.

When I got home, my wife gave me a letter brought by a visitor from your community, and my pleasure was doubled when I recognized your handwriting. But when I began to read your letter, IT SHOOK ME UP because I saw in it the news you bring me of a *treyf* travesty* that was recently published against our Faithful and against the real *tsadikim,* and that this *bukh** was sent from Galicia to the prince of your community to read! According to your letter, it's full of wickedness, deceit and mockery aimed at the *tsadikim* and real *rebes!*

I wouldn't have believed it if anyone else had told me such a thing, because in my opinion it just isn't possible that in these times -- when the generation is very near to the coming of the *meshiekh;*[1] and when everyone sees plainly and openly the signs and the wonders that the *tsadikim* perform continuously -- clearly, no secret is hidden from them,* and who am *I* to tell of their praise? -- for them PRAISE IS SILENCE*; and the times -- and there were many -- are past when there were still those among our

[1] See in the *Prologue* to this composition, footnote 7.

kinfolk who opposed us,* but now, with G-d's help, THE WHOLE PEOPLE, SMALL AND GREAT, OLD AND YOUNG, MAN AND WOMAN, MALE AND FEMALE SLAVE, believe and know very well the power of the real *tsadikim* and all the opposition have already suffered an overwhelming public defeat and now all of them alike answer and speak respectfully,* so that there is no one on earth but our Faithful; and when the *tsadikim* can do whatever their heart desires and compel G-d to do whatever they want; and when they perform the most extraordinary wonders, even just by their holy speech[2] -- if *this* is so, how could it be that someone could rise against them now of all times by composing a *bukh* and publishing it? The author himself must know that if our holy *rebe* wishes, he can do to him whatever his heart desires.[3] Believe me, I would've fallen into deep melancholy because of your letter, but the pleasure I had before and the vodka* I drank after I read your letter helped me push away melancholy with both hands,* and with G-d's help, now I'm not the least bit melancholy.

But all the same, we got to see about doing something with regards to the *bukh.* For the time being, I'm afraid to inform our holy *rebe* of this news for two reasons. Because for the blink of an eye he'll be aggravated, G-d forbid! Even though our *rebe* must've already seen this in the higher worlds, all the same he might be aggravated, G-d forbid!, when he hears this in the lower world. And I'm also afraid maybe he'll instantly take some revenge against the writer of this here *bukh,* burning him by means of the Prince of the Toyre[4] or some such thing, and we won't have the privilege of seeing this sinner and of getting sweet revenge -- of hitting him, denouncing him, burning everything he owns and so forth. So I want to get your advice what to do, whether to tell our holy *rebe* and ask him not to take revenge against the author on his own but just through us, or not to tell him anything and do our part.

For right now, I'm informing you that first of all you should do whatever you can to get hold of this *bukh* so we can know what's written there and so we'll know the name of the *bukh,* so as to direct our Faithful to buy the *bukh* and burn it up and wipe it out,* and also to find out who the author is so as to take revenge against him. In case the author's name isn't written in the *bukh,* maybe it contains the author's picture, the way

---

[2] "For behold, the *tsadek* performs the greatest, most extraordinary wonders. Through his holy speech all the judgments against Israel are tempered." *No'am Elimelekh* 94:1.

"There are *tsadikim* who can do anything through their holy speech and do not need to cry out and pray so much because their speech has an impact and it can stop the judgments so that they will not come to pass at all." *Ibid., ibid..*

[3] "As the Holy One, praised be He, grants dominion over the earth, meaning, to the *tsadikim,* so that the *tsadek* is like a king." *No'am Elimelekh* 41:2.

[4] See *Shivkhey ha-Besht* 2:3 [Mintz, 17 and note 5 thereon].

the sinners print their picture at the beginning of their trashy books.* Then, even if he's from another country, our *rebe* will look at his picture and punish him by looking.* So don't be lazy about this! Be quick to get hold of the *bukh* and send it to me. A word to the wise....*

From me,

....

The main thing I forgot. Last *Shabes* there was here by our *rebe* a visitor from Galicia from the Lubliner's people* and he brought our *rebe* greetings from the *tsadek* of Lublin with some *nigunim.** Our *rebe* added a few sections to them and made them whole. When you'll be by us, G-d willing, you'll have great satisfaction because you'll see from this that our holy *rebe* is the king among the *tsadikim.*[5]

[5] "Know that the king has the whole *nign,* all of it in perfection, but the ministers have only some part of the *nign."* *Likutey MohoRa"N,* Book 2, 43:2.

#2

From Reb Zaynvl Verkhievker
To Reb Zelig Letitchiver

I got your letter [#1] and I had from it otherworldly* pleasure when I heard how our holy *rebe* is and how you are. I want you should always let me know how you're doing and about your good works.

As for the *bukh,* since you wrote me I should send you mine advice whether to tell our holy *rebe,* mine opinion leans toward still keeping the thing secret 'til we see a strong need to reveal it to our *rebe,* 'cause maybe they *didn't* inform our *rebe* of this in the upper worlds.[1] Also, I'm afraid our holy *rebe* would instantly pluck up the author by the root and we wouldn't have even the privilege of doing toward his defeat a small thing, so better you shouldn't tell our *rebe.*

With regards to the *bukh,* I tried a few schemes but I couldn't get hold of it yet. I spoke with Shloyme, who's called in our community Shloyme

[1] Look in *Shivkhey ha-Besht* 22:4 [Mintz, 163] and elsewhere in that holy book and you will see that on a number of occasions there were matters that they did not wish to show the Besht in the upper worlds and he did not hear of them at all in the court.

Umner. Even though he's an awful hedonist and don't have the least fear of Heaven, all the same he's a good man and very attached to our *rebe* and gives him lots of money. I brang him regards in the name of our holy *rebe* and talked with him about the business of the *bukh* and he promised me to discuss this with his relation, Freyda Reb Isaac's -- she's a wonderful clever creature and respected by our prince -- she should steal the *bukh* when she's by the prince. He kept his word, 'cause two days later I was at this Freyda's and she gave me the *bukh* she stole the night before when she was by the prince.

I took the *bukh* and showed it to mine son-in-law, he should live, who's from Galicia and studied there in the German schools.* Even though he forgot, thank G-d, what he learned, at least he knows still the German letters and can recognize the difference between German and other scripts. When mine son-in-law, he should live, seen the title page of this *bukh,* he told me the *bukh* isn't German, 'cause on the title page he seen something that by them is the letter *khes,*[2] and by them -- I mean, by the German Jews -- the sound of *khes* don't come at the beginning of a word 'cause they always make the sound of *hey* instead of *khes.* For instance, *"Khayim"* they pronounce *"Hayim," "Khaye"* they pronounce *"Haye," "Yekhezkl"* they pronounce *"Hezkl"* and so forth.

He also said he knows for certain all the large lettering on the title page isn't German, but maybe Latin.* Since I knew the infamous *bukh* is in the German language, I thought, "This *bukh* definitely isn't the one." I gave the *bukh* back to Freyda so she could return it to the prince before he finds out he's missing a *bukh* and locks up all the *bikher* so she can't steal the infamous *bukh* no more -- whereas if she returned it first, then of course she might be able to steal the infamous *bukh* some other time.

When I seen she didn't visit the prince for several days, I talked with the *arendar* from the village of Slabudshik. His prince is a relation of our prince and I know his prince always needs cash. So I told the *arendar* to promise his prince to find money for him, and while discussing this he should mention to him the *bukh* that's by our prince, and that he heard we recommend it highly. He'll make sure to make him want to borrow the *bukh,* and when he borrows the *bukh* then we can rely on the *arendar,* who'll steal the *bukh,* of course, and bring it to us. I sure hope everything will be alright. Be well.

These are the words of

....

---

[2] The letter[s] he saw [for the sound] *Kh* was from the word *"Chassidim."**

#3

From Reb Zelig Letitchiver To Reb Zaynvl Verkhievker

I'm amazed you *still* didn't get hold of the *bukh!* I already wrote you the matter is very urgent and still you didn't do nothing. Maybe, G-d forbid!, you're being lazy about this matter, so I'm telling you this is no trifle. I heard the *bukh* is making an impression on all the noblemen who read it and they want to translate it into Polish. All the lords reading it are roaring with laughter at our people and at the *tsadikim.*

Today I bumped into Councilman Glakhav's agent and he told me yesterday there were several officials by his gentile for tea. Among them were many who read the *bukh* and they were discussing this *bukh* the whole time. Some of them made a mockery and laughingstock* of the agent and said *he's* a *khosed* too.

One asked him if he knew the reason why the Jews sway during the *Tfile* prayer,* and the agent said, "I don't know." The nobleman said to him, "I'll tell you the reason -- because the *Tfile* is like intercourse. That's what's written in the book *Likutey Yekorim.*"[1] And another asked him if it's true that the justice of gentiles is husks* and that your *rebe* goes to gentile justice* so as to extract holy justice from among the husks.[2]* And the third asked him if he too speaks with them only so as to extract the holy sparks* from them so that they should be left empty,[3] and so on.

They asked him so many questions he forgot the one because of the

---

[1] 1:2.

[2] "Now in exile, since we do not have the power ourselves to punish the sinners at all, even TO PUT THE FEAR OF YOU IN THEIR HEART,* we have to bring them to justice and exact vengeance from them through gentile justice because sometimes there is a reason from G-d that wickedness surrounds the *tsadek,* and we ourselves do not have the power to push it away except through gentile justice, through which holy justice emerges from among the husks. It follows that when we endure suffering from sinners who deny holiness we have to subdue them precisely through the aforementioned gentile justice. We also have to bribe them [the gentiles] with money in order to subdue the sinners, but it is forbidden to reveal this matter to the masses so that they should not seek justice for their needs through gentile justice and say that their intention is for the sake of Heaven." *Kitser Likutey MohoRa"N* 15:130.

[3] "When (the *tsadek*) speaks with an idolator, then the *tsadek* extracts the good from him and he [the idolator] remains an empty nothing." *Likutey MohoRa"N,* Book 2, 58:1.

other, but all the questions they were asking him, they were all [full] TO HIGH HEAVEN with *apikorses* and he couldn't bear them. The agent swore to me that when he got home he couldn't sleep all night. When I saw him he still wasn't feeling well on account of the aggravation.

So for God's sake, don't be lazy about this because we're terrified the thing will become public and our *rebe* will find out. So I'm urging him* again and again he shouldn't be lazy at all, G-d forbid!, and he should do everything in great haste as befits our Faithful. A word to the wise....

From me,

....

#4

From Reb Zaynvl Verkhievker
To Reb Zelig Letitchiver

In your letter [#3] I seen you're very melancholy -- it should never be worse! -- about the *bukh.* I'm surprised on you! *I'm* the one who don't got the good fortune to be by our holy *rebe* every day, to see him and his face, shining like a mirror.[1] But still, just 'cause I sing his praises, melancholy can't rule over me.[2] But *you* see him[3] and you hear when he sings[4] and still you become melancholy sometimes, G-d save us! This must be 'cause you're lovesick for our *rebe* more then for women,[5] and you're concerned he shouldn't have aggravation, G-d forbid!, over the *bukh.*

But in mine opinion, since it's been a long time they been talking

---

[1] "Through the reflection of the light that the heart receives from the heart of G-d, as mentioned above, his face sparkles with this light, in the sense of, A HAPPY HEART MAKES A LOVELY FACE. When his face shines with this transparency, then the other can see his face in this face." *Likutey MohoRa"N* 35:2.

[2] "Whoever spreads the *tsadek*'s fame merits happiness." *Mides* 59:16.

[3] "By virtue of seeing the face of the *tsadek,* the bad traits are abolished...that is, melancholy and laziness and their consequences." *Kitser Likutey MohoRa"N* 3:6.

"Whoever is melancholy should look at the *tsadek* and joy will enter his heart." *Mides* 44:6.

[4] "As a remedy for removing melancholy, let him listen to a distinguished *tsadek* singing." *Ibid.,* 45:27.

[5] "The essence of attachment is love -- that he loves the *tsadek* with perfect love so that his soul is bound up with the other's, to the point that through his love of the *tsadek,* his love of women is abolished [in the sense of, YOUR LOVE IS MORE WONDERFUL TO ME THAN WOMEN'S LOVE.]" *Kitser Likutey MohoRa"N* 32:302.

about this *bukh* in your community, our *rebe* too must've heard of this on high and knows all about the *bukh* but didn't want to do nothing yet in this affair. He must have a reason for this and we don't got to create problems, 'cause just as problems are hard for G-d....[6] So don't be melancholy about this 'cause everything is sure to be alright, but all the same it's really up to us to do our part. Of course I'm exhausting mineself every which way to get hold of the *bukh,* but from Heaven they hindered me so our *rebe* must not wish yet to get hold of it. And in case our *rebe,* he should live, wills,* then for sure we'll get hold of it.

The *arendar* I wrote you about done what I told him. He took from his prince a letter to our prince to lend him the *bukh* by way of the *arendar.* But our prince sent to the Slabudshik prince an answer in a letter, and when the *arendar* asked him if he'd give him a certain *bukh* for his prince, he answered, "I wrote him in the letter an answer about the *bukh."* Since you wrote me that some noblemen who were by Councilman Glakhav read the *bukh,* I thought maybe he didn't send him the *bukh* since he didn't have this *bukh* in his house 'cause he gave it to them noblemen, and when he gets the *bukh* from them he'll send it to him.

I went straight to our Freyda Reb Isaac's she should return the *bukh* she stole 'cause I was getting scared. If he finds out he's missing a *bukh,* he'll think he lost it on account of borrowing and he'll get angry and won't want no more to lend nobody no *bukh,* and even the Slabudshik prince he won't lend the infamous *bukh.* I really pleaded with Freyda she should go right away since maybe he'll find out about it today yet. She wouldn't go 'cause he didn't send for her for several days* and she was angry at the prince. I says to her, "You know, Queen Esther wasn't called to the king neither, but still, in time of trouble, she went on her own," and she went at once.

When she got back from the prince I went straight to her and asked her about the *bukh.* She told me she returned the *bukh* so cleverly he didn't suspect nothing, 'cause he opened the bookcase and took some *bukh* and went to the candle to have a look at it, and in the meantime she went to the bookcase and hid the *bukh* she stole in the bookcase. Then he came back from the candle and closed the bookcase.

---

[6] "Let not your imagination confuse you when some problems about the real *tsadikim* are incomprehensible to you, because the *tsadikim* are like their Creator. Just as problems are hard for G-d, so too problems are hard for the real *tsadek*...and of necessity there should be problems for him for thus it is fitting and proper." *Likutey* and *Kitser Likutey MohoRa"N,* Book 2, 40:3 and 140.

"For indeed, there are people who come to the great *tsadikim* and it is incomprehensible to them that the *tsadek* has difficulties...and all this is because of his [the visitor's] lack of perfection." *No'am Elimelekh* 58:2.

She's really such a wonderful clever creature and smart as they come! She told me she was wheedling him into talking about the infamous *bukh.* He told her for several days he didn't saw the *bukh.* Also his relation, the Slabudshik prince, asked him to lend him this *bukh,* and he told him he didn't know where it was, but he said in any case he still wouldn't lend it to him 'cause he's a scatterbrain, and especially *this bukh* he's not lending nobody to read outside his house 'cause it's not for sale in our country. He also told her a few days ago there were by him some provincial lords and they begged him to lend them the *bukh* to take home and he wouldn't, but in his house they read from it a few pages. Some of them who didn't know German asked the others to tell them in Polish or Russian what's written in the *bukh* and they all thought the *bukh* was very good. She started sweet-talking him again and asked him if the *bukh* was so thick they didn't read the whole thing and he said, "Wait, I'll look for it. Maybe I'll find it among the *bikher* and I'll show it to you." He opened the bookcase and looked and found it. He showed it to her and she seen it was the very *bukh* she had stole from him.

The prince opened the *bukh* and looked at it. He says to her, "Did you know that G-d has a wife, not to mention a concubine?"[7] She started laughing and says, "What is my lord saying?" He answered her, "That's what Rabbi Wolf of Zutomir wrote in his book."* Then he says, "This *bukh* is very valuable to me, and since I haven't seen it for several days I'm going to lock it in the small bookcase inside the large bookcase."

When Freyda told me all this, I BEGAN TO TREMBLE and I also got very angry at mine son-in-law, on account of who I returned the *bukh.* But I calmed mineself down. Why should I be angry at mine son-in-law that he can't read German? On the contrary, for this he deserves to be *more* admired in mine eyes, that he studied by royal edict in school* and *still* he don't understand the language of wickedness!* I came home and kissed him 'cause I had from this episode clear proof he don't understand German at all, so of course, G-d willing, he'll be a great vessel.*

In any case, RELIEF AND DELIVERANCE are sure to ARISE for us FROM SOMEWHERE ELSE. Why should I want this should come about through mine son-in-law, if only he understood German? Better the deliverance should come about some other way.

These are the words of

....

---

7 "REUBEN WENT AND LAY WITH BILHOH HIS FATHER'S CONCUBINE, and it can cause...that is, lying with the concubine of our Father in Heaven." *Or ha-Meyer* 18:4.

#5

From Reb Zelig Letitchiver To Reb Zaynvl Verkhievker

Truly, I saw from your letter [#4] you're not being lazy about this matter and you made many attempts to get hold of the *bukh,* so it must not have been yet our holy *rebe*'s wish to get hold of it. But all the same, the blaspheming of the real *tsadikim* and of all our people gets worse every single day among the *goyim.*

Today Reb Aharon Lozer's, our wineseller, told me last night some provincial lords rented rooms by him and made a mockery and a laughingstock of our *rebe* and all the *tsadikim* and all our Faithful. One asked him if a *khosed* can enter a state of *hislayves* through wine too just like through mead,[1] and another one said he was sitting and drinking wine like the king's son and cleaving to his father the king.[2] At one point his [Reb Aharon's] daughter gave a flask of wine to one of them lords and the nobleman asked her if she knew that in studying Toyre one has to take off her clothes because the Toyre is a bride[3] -- and dirty talk like that, which he couldn't stand nohow.

I couldn't bear the aggravation neither and I went to Reb Yosl Fradel's. He's a wonderfully clever creature and his handwriting is as wonderful as wonderful can be. You must know him since he's one of our holy *rebe*'s people too. I told him everything and he actually started crying. He gave me a sealed letter written in Polish, from the lieutenant governor* -- with his seal -- to your prince, to please lend him the infamous *bukh* for a few days. This Reb Yosl assured me whoever knows the handwriting of the lieutenant governor would testify that the letter is his [the lieutenant governor's] very own handwriting.

So for G-d's sake, see to it you deliver the letter enclosed here to your prince by someone your prince don't know and you're sure to get the *bukh* because he certainly won't refuse the lieutenant governor, especially since last *Shabes Koydesh** we heard from our holy *rebe* over the

---

[1] "It is known that it is the custom of most of the masses to drink mead on the holy *Shabes* eve after the bath. The reason is, as mentioned previously, so that extra love will come to them in the afternoon and evening prayers, because the prayers of the holy *Shabes* eve require more *hislayves* and greater *kavone* than all the weekday prayers." *Likutey Yekorim* 31:4.

[2] *Likutey Amorim* 11:3.

[3] See in the *Prologue* to this composition, footnote 6.

*shaleshudes,** who said about Reb Yosl Fradel's that he's a wonderfully clever creature. So I decided our holy *rebe* must agree and wants us to get hold of the *bukh* through him, because of course I believe and know for certain that whatever our *rebe* speaks and does* is altogether miraculous.[4] Live and be well.

From me,

....

[4] "PLACE IT ON AN ENSIGN(*NES*), meaning, that you should place the *tsadek* as an eternal ensign *(nes olam)* so that everyone will understand that all his actions and doings are altogether miraculous."* *No'am Elimelekh* 54:1.

#6

From Reb Zaynvl Verkhievker To Reb Zelig Letitchiver

Since the matter is very urgent I'm sending you a special messenger. When I got your letter [#5], I went to the marketplace to find someone we could depend on and who our prince don't know. I seen the *melamed* from the village of Verbitch. He's one of our holy *rebe*'s people. Since he's teaching for many years in the villages he knows how to speak Polish, and he's also a little bit of a clown.* I handed over to him in great secrecy the letter, and he went off very happily to the prince and gave him the letter. But the prince answered him that [since] in any case in two days the mail goes from here to your community, he'll send an answer to the lieutenant governor by mail. The *melamed* asked him in a different vein if he had anything to send to the lieutenant governor and the prince said he didn't have nothing to send. The *melamed* pretended to be simple-minded and asked him if he'll give him back the letter he brang since it didn't accomplish what he [the lieutenant governor] had wrote there. The prince started laughing and says to him, "Fool! The letter stays here. I'll answer his letter by mail."

So I'm sending you a special messenger to let you know this, so you'll do there all you can to get hold of the letter from the mail so it won't reach the lieutenant governor, 'cause if he gets the letter he'll order a thorough investigation,* and maybe he knows Reb Yosl Fradel's who wrote the letter and it'll be, G-d forbid!, bad for us and for him.

These are the words of

....

#7

From Moyshe Fishl's in Nigrad To Reb Gedalyohu Balter in Aklev

I hereby inform you that, with G-d's help, from the day I arrived at the home of my father-in-law the dignitary, may The Merciful One protect and bless him, I became more beloved to my father-in-law and the members of his household every day. Thank G-d, my father-in-law supports me in every way possible [to enable me] to engage in Toroh. And I, too, when I saw this, turned my heart away completely from all the material things of this world. I just DWELT IN THE HOUSE OF THE L-RD -- would that it could be so all the days of my life!

Never did I try to follow in the footsteps of my contemporaries, to gad about or sit at games or listen to their idle conversations, for my whole purpose is to engage in His Toroh, praised be He, and to spend therein all the days of my life, that I might be privileged to attain as much as is incumbent upon me. And, thank G-d, it is now more than ten years that I have toiled in the house of my father-in-law AND ON MY WATCH I SHALL REMAIN. I have not frittered away a single day, G-d forbid!

But in this am I smitten -- when I consider that I shall have to take leave of my father-in-law's house according to the law* of our holy Toroh, for I have not yet merited children. I do not know from whom the lack stems, whether from me or from my spouse,* may she live. My spouse has already tried several remedies and cures from old women and midwives and wonder-workers and she has even paid for *pidyoynes* to a few *tsadikim* of our time but it has not helped. Even though I knew that there is nothing of substance in these things, I was compelled to fulfill the wish of my spouse, may she live, for she pestered me. Even now she is still chasing after such things, like all women.

Now she's heard that in your community too there's some *rebe* and she's begun to badger me to travel with her to your community. But in this I put her off for awhile until I could ask your opinion, whether or not there is anything of substance in it, for I'm confident that in the old friendship between us, you will surely guide us in the way of truth.* Please, oh please, my beloved friend, let me know the truth about this, for if there is no substance in it, I shan't have to neglect my studies and squander money fruitlessly. WE AWAIT the grace of a letter by your own hand.

Sholom from me,

....

#8

From Reb Zelig Letitchiver
To Reb Zaynvl Verkhievker

In G-d's great mercy and kindness, praised be He -- and by the merit of our holy *rebe,* which stood us in good stead -- a great miracle* happened for us and a credit to our *rebe,* by whose merit we got the letter from the post office! The same day the mail arrived here we sent the postmaster's agent and he gave the postmaster a handsome gift, and he [the postmaster] handed over to him the letter that arrived from your prince for the lieutenant governor. I ran straight to Reb Yosl Fradel's and brang him the good news of the great miracle that happened for us. He fell on my neck and kissed me a thousand times. He told me this was an important thing for him because there's right now a big lawsuit against him and only the lieutenant governor can help him, and if the lieutenant governor had found out about this, he surely would've taken away his livelihood, G-d forbid!

Since you gave us the news of this letter, he told me to send you his regards and he promised me that if you'll need more receipts* for installments of the *arende* for your brother, he'll write for you for nothing.

I'm also informing you that a few weeks ago, Wolf Dubner, a wine merchant in our community, made a wedding for his daughter with a widower from Galicia whose name is Mordekhai Gold.* He's a big adversary of our *rebe* and of all the *tsadikim,* so he must be a big fornicator.[1] He's worse than his father-in-law, because his father-in-law wouldn't be so openly opposed, but *he* is really an *apikoyres* and a heretic. He studies the forbidden books* and speaks evil of the L-rd and His *meshiekh,* that is, our *rebe,* The Light of Israel. And he incites his father-in-law to attack our *rebe* openly. Even though his father-in-law can't be so defiant toward our holy *rebe* openly, all the same he does his wickedness in secret and informs on our *rebe.*

Since this Mordekhai sometimes travels to buy merchandise and may come to your community too, so know how to act with him. So you'll recognize him, let me write you features* by which you'll recognize him. He's **good-looking, his hair is curly** (but when our *rebe* passed his hand in front of my face I **saw that he's a brand plucked from fire**),[2] and he

---

[1] "Fornicators are generally opponents of the *tsadikim.*" *Mides* 55:163.

[2] **Once the Besht went with the rabbi, Our Teacher the *Rov,* Rabbi Dovid Purkes, to the bathhouse. On their way a good-looking man with curly hair and nice clothes came toward them. When the man approached them the**

has long hair on his head.* He goes about **nicely dressed** and with a cravat around his neck. His speech is measured* and he knows arithmetic.[3]* He has book learning but he's never read any holy book by the *tsadikim* of the generation. And he's a little crazy because, first of all, he can't stand a stain on his clothes,[4]* when he sees a poor *goy* he gives him charity,* and he doesn't drink vodka or smoke a pipe.* Since throughout our province there's no one, thank G-d, like him -- I doubt very much if in our whole country there are men like him nowadays* -- therefore you're sure to recognize him by the [distinguishing] features and you'll know what to do with him, because he's a ruthless sinner and a major adversary.

From me,

....

Besht jumped very far to the side and when he had passed by them the Besht returned. He passed his hands over his eyes and said, "Look what has passed before us!" And he [Rabbi Dovid Purkes] **saw that it** [the good-looking man] **was a brand plucked from fire. Fire had singed all the locks of his hair.** *Shivkhey ha-Besht* 30:4 [Mintz, 220]. I wrote this so that those of little faith will not dispute what Reb Zelig wrote.

[3] "Most arithmeticians are full of lustful desires." *Mides* 87:18.

[4] This is against the Toyre because we are obliged to roll ourselves in mud and mire as is explained in *Likutey MohoRa"N*, Book 2, in these words: "He must roll himself in all kinds of mud and mire in order to do His will and please G-d. Then, when his love for G-d is so strong that he discards all his wisdom and casts himself into mud and mire for the sake of worshiping and pleasing Him, praised be He, then it is good for the intellect because then he is privileged to grasp even that which is higher than the intellect, that which even Moyshe in his lifetime did not comprehend." *Likutey MohoRa"N*, Book 2, 16:1.

#9

From Reb Zelig Letitchiver
To Reb Zaynvl Verkhievker

This very minute the postmaster's agent, who's also the lieutenant governor's agent, came to me and told me that today your prince was by the lieutenant governor and gave him the *bukh* and apologized he didn't send him the *bukh* by way of the messenger. The lieutenant governor was surprised and said, "I didn't write and I haven't heard about any *bukh."* He urged your prince to send back the letter the emissary delivered to his [the prince's] home in his [the lieutenant governor's] name. The prince said as soon as he gets home he'll send him the letter. He meant to take the letter with him but forgot it on the table by his bed, and when he returns home he'll send it to him by special messenger.

So hurry, quick, get going* for cryin' out loud!!! Make sure to get hold of the letter before your prince gets home, because not only did the lieutenant governor take the *bukh* and will he read it, and our *rebe* and our whole group will have such an enemy as your landlord, but also he'll order an inquiry -- Who wrote the letter? Who delivered it to your prince? -- and there'll be, G-d forbid!, big trouble for us and for the writer who in any case has a big lawsuit in the province right now. So be sure to get hold of the letter the moment you see this note!

The letter must be lying on the table by the bed. So you don't take a different letter and ruin the thing like you did with the *bukh* that Freyda Reb Isaac's took, I'm giving you unmistakable signs. On the envelope of the letter there's a drop of ink and on the back where the seal is there's one drop of *treyf* wax that Reb Yosl Fradel's, the letter writer, sealed. For G-d's sake, don't let this matter slide! Step lively! Whatever money you need for this take from the *Ertsisroel** or Rabbi Meyer Balanes funds,* because there's no greater *mitsve* than to save many Jewish lives, especially in a matter that relates to the members of our fellowship* and our holy *rebe,* he should live.

Believe me, we had yesterday a pleasure greater than all the pleasures of this world and the world-to-come. Last night the moon was so very clear and we went with our holy *rebe* in the lead -- we were all mellow after the *shaleshudes* -- and we sanctified the [new] moon.* Then we went to our holy *rebe*'s home and sang. Our holy *rebe* was smoking a pipe with a long stem and [had] a very good Turkish shawl on his shoulders. He walked back and forth in his house and occasionally said something to us that PUT FAT ON all OUR BONES. This went on 'til after midnight. Believe me, if they offered me the whole [reward in this] world and the whole [portion in the] world-to-come of all the rabbis and Talmudists in the world, I wouldn't trade for it the pleasure I had. A word to the wise....

From me,

....

#10

From Reb Zaynvl Verkhievker
To Reb Zelig Letitchiver

How great is the merit of our holy *rebe,* he should live! -- 'cause with G-d's help I got hold of the right letter before the prince got home, and now I'm sending it to you tucked in here! So you'll know the miracle what happened for us in this affair, let me tell you.

Now you know, of course, Reb Yankl Rivke's, the grocer in our community. He's one of our holy *rebe*'s people and he has an "in" with our prince's housekeeper. Reb Yankl went to the housekeeper and really begged her and gave her a gift of half a dozen ducats. She sneaked with him into the room where the prince sleeps and he took from the table by the bed the letter with the signs what you wrote me.

Since there wasn't *Ertsisroel* or Rabbi Meyer Balanes money more then two czerwone zlotys* 'cause a few days ago I sent our holy *rebe* all the cash around here by way of the emissaries from your community that were here, and the housekeeper wouldn't have it no other way but to pay her all the cash at once, I took the pointer and the breastplate from the *Seyfer Toyre*[1] and pawned them by the local forester. I borrowed

---

[1] When I was in Kripen I heard that one old householder who no longer sided with our faction complained bitterly against Reb Zaynvl that he had pawned the pointer and the breastplate, but that was because he does not read the holy books and did not know what the *tsadek,* Rabbi Nokhem of Tchernobil, said about the verse, THE L-RD LOVES THE GATES OF ZION MORE THAN ALL THE DWELLINGS OF JACOB. This is his unadorned language: "The *tsadikim* are called 'gates' who are distinguished in *halokhe* (going) because they are the gate through which enter blessing and much goodness for all the worlds...because their speaking has an impact above. That is why the L-rd loves those *tsadikim* more than all synagogues and study halls, even though they too are busy with Toyre and prayer. In any event, since they are not on this rung to have their word have an impact above...like the *tsadikim....* Therefore 'their *toyre*' is called 'their profession *(umanus)*',* which makes firm *(omenes)* [because their *toyre* and their speech is their faith], through which an eternal edifice is built to perfection as in the beginning of the Creation." *Yesamakh Leyv* 20:4 and 21:1.

I abbreviated his language because it's too long for me to copy it as it appears there in context. But he who browses there will find contentment. And it follows that if the synagogues and study halls are not as important as the *tsadek,* the sacred vessels are even less so.

against them four czerwone zlotys for three groschen a week interest for each czerwone zloty.

It was very lucky I done this quickly 'cause two hours later the prince came home and looked for the letter. When he didn't find it he got very angry at his household staff and would've hit them 'cause a letter was missing from the room where he slept. But our Freyda, who went to greet him, and the housekeeper too, acted shrewdly and begged him not to get so angry. They said he must've put the letter in his pocket before his trip and it got lost on the way. He calmed down but he ordered his servant who was in his room when the *melamed* delivered the letter to him to search for the messenger who handed him the letter and if he should recognize him, to bring him [the messenger] to him, and he would give his servant a handsome gift for this.

Since the *melamed* is in the village and not here, he didn't find him. I'll get word in the meantime to the *melamed* he shouldn't come to our community until the thing is all forgotten.

These are the words of
....

#11

From Reb Zelig Letitchiver
To Reb Zaynvl Verkhievker

I got your letter [#10] with the right letter enclosed in your letter and I delivered the letter at once to Reb Yosl Fradel's. He said this was the very letter he wrote. It was clear to him all this was brought about by the *pidyen* he gave our *rebe* as soon as we had the news of the letter through the agent, because our holy *rebe,* he should live, said a number of times there were many judgments pending against him* [Yosl Fradel's] but by means of the *pidyen* he tempered them. In my opinion we got nothing to worry about in this matter.

But because of our many sins, the wickedness of the lieutenant governor against our people has got worse ever since he read the infamous *bukh.* We can't bear the aggravation this *bukh* makes for us. We did what we could around here but we couldn't get hold of it. When we found out from the agent that your prince had got back the *bukh* from the lieutenant governor, we sent our people to the house where your prince was staying and they stole all the forbidden books* he had there in his room. I went with them to Reb Yosl Fradel's but he told me they're all other *bikher* and that this infamous *bukh* isn't among them. I asked the householder your prince is staying with and he told us he always carries a certain *bukh* the size of a *Reshkhoydesh* prayer booklet[1] in his pocket.

We returned all the *bikher* to his room and agreed to send [someone] to his room at night to take the *bukh* from his pocket, or maybe at night he'll lay it on the table -- but the prince left for home before night and I couldn't get hold of it. So for G-d's sake, be sure to do there everything possible to get hold of the *bukh*.

From me,

....

---

[1] The householder was an old man who had come from Galicia to Zalin because, thank G-d, in our land they do not know what a *Reshkhoydesh* prayer booklet is at all because they all pray the Sephardic rite.* Neither is it at all important to us, so Reb Zelig did not record the distinction, or maybe he forgot to do so.

#12

From Reb Zaynvl Verkhievker
To Reb Zelig Letitchiver

I hereby inform you that today our Freyda told me she was by the prince and he ordered his servant that was in his room when the *melamed* delivered to him the letter to go to the fair there in Pulshtin to buy for him horses. He told him to keep an eye out at the fair maybe the messenger who brang him the letter from the lieutenant governor might be there, and to have him arrested there. And he gave him a letter to the Pulshtin prince to give him help with this. So make sure to send at once one courier after another to the holy community of Pulshtin to notify our Faithful there they should be on guard to save the *melamed* in case he's at the fair and the servant recognizes him.

I wanted to send to the *melamed* to inform him of the whole business, but when I gave him the news earlier that the prince ordered his servant to search for him in our community, he was frightened and he left the village of Verbitch and I don't know where he went. So I got to inquire around here where he went and you be sure to do your part 'cause this is no trifle, on account of the prince is furious and he said if he gets hold of the messenger then he'll give every cent he has to send him to Siberia if he won't reveal the forger and the others who were in on the plan.

These are the words of
....

#13

From Reb Gedalye Balter in Aklev To Moyshe Fishl's in Nigrad

Now this man Moyshe I don't know what's become of him. It has been a long time since I have seen him or heard from him, and he is almost like a dead man, unremembered in my heart. Now you have made me very happy with your lovely letter [#7]. Moreover, I am inclined to fulfill your fondest wish in every way possible, especially in such a matter. With G-d's help, I am able to fulfill your request in the best way possible, because it is in *me* that our *rebe,* our Light, trusts in all his affairs, whether in regard to a trip through the country, or regarding the innumerable* activities and affairs that he undertakes. Never has our *rebe* done anything, small or big, without me, so our *rebe* must have found some spark in my soul that **belongs to his soul-root*** And I am certain that in your case he will surely do everything for my sake, particularly as it concerns children. This is a trifle for him. Our holy *rebe* already has experience in this thousands upon thousands of times and he is more famous in this than all the *rebes* of our generation.

Probably even you have heard of the magnitude of the renowned miracle that was performed by our holy *rebe* a few days ago for Reb Shloyme of the holy community of Ramishl. Whoever hears about it, his heart burns with passion to be privileged to draw close to our *rebe,* our Light, may he live, for surely, so great a miracle as this has not been performed or reported* of the *tsadikim* who have existed since the days of the Besht, remembered for eternal life, until now, and how much the less so by the *rebes* in our generations, who are surely all **like the skin of a garlic clove*** compared to our holy *rebe.* Since this miracle is the most renowned, and probably heard of even by you -- because at the time, Reb Itsik Kalker from your community was by us -- you'll understand that your matter is a mere trifle and our *rebe* will fulfill your requests and mine the moment you get here.

But **what can I do for you** at present, since our *rebe* left last Sunday for the holy community of Belzitse, because next week, may it come to us for good, there's a gathering there of the *arendars* with regard to the *arendes* of all the localities around there and he'll have to give each and every person a form for written petitions* and to be busy with *pidyens* and other vital matters. Since our holy *rebe* knows that he has no one in his household to depend on in his affairs, he has left me in his home for the time being to receive letters that are written to him from far and wide. Right now there are in my safekeeping about ten letters, and I have to respond to each and every one as it requires.

This very moment I received from our *rebe,* too, a letter with two hundred rubles in banknotes that he has sent home, and he has directed me to take some forms that he forgot to take with him and to come with them to the holy community of Belzitse, because in any case, I, too, must be there to instruct the recipients of the notepapers for written petitions the way they should proceed and how they should conduct themselves with our *rebe*'s scribe.

So for the present, the time is not ripe to save you, until our holy *rebe,* may he live, comes home. But because of the love between us let me advise you, first of all, that you should be sure to acquire the books by the *tsadikim* of our time and study them, for I see from your letter that you have not yet read any of those holy books. And most of all, be sure to get the holy book *Shivkhey ha-Besht* and the books of Our Teacher the *Rov,* Rabbi Nakhmen, THE SAINT and Holy Man OF BLESSED MEMORY, especially his *Tales,* because there's nothing small or big, spiritual or material, either in the higher worlds or in the lower worlds, that does not have its root in the book *Shivkhey* or in *The Tales.* Examine them and you will see wonders* -- how in tales that appear to us as simple things, great and awesome things are alluded to[1] -- and through this you will achieve faith

---

[1] "In this tale there is not a word in which there is no mystical intention, and he who is expert in [understanding] books can understand a few clues." *Sipurey Mayses* 111:4.

"You will see in amazement how in every subject wondrous things are alluded to, and the awesome wonders of this tale are impossible to speak of at all.... How very fortunate is he who merits even in the world-to-come to know the tiniest bit of it. Whoever has a brain in his skull, the hair of his flesh will stand on end and he will understand a little bit of the greatness of the Creator, praised be He, from the greatness of the real *tsadikim* when he looks carefully at the story of this awesome thing." *Ibid.,* 112:2.

"Who can praise, who can recount, who can appreciate, who can imagine even one tiny part of thousands of thousands and ten thousands of ten thousands of the sparkling of a very few of the allusions of the greatest wonders of the most awesome and sublime mystical meanings of this awesome tale, which is full of the deepest mystical meanings from beginning to end, and he who thinks

in *khakhomim*, for without faith in *khakhomim* you will not accomplish anything, and all your *toyre* and good deeds won't count.

From me,

....

---

deeply about the matter will succeed in finding the sparkling of some allusions according to his worth." *Ibid., ibid.*, col. 3, after the tale of the king and the only son and the beggars.*

#14

From Reb Zelig Letitchiver
To Reb Zaynvl Verkhievker

The moment I got your letter [#12] I sent a special messenger to Pulshtin. By the merit of our holy *rebe* and the members of our fellowship, I was sure they would bend over backwards there so no harm would come to us, G-d forbid!, and that's how it was.

The *melamed* is right now by an *arendar* in the village of Bilke near the holy community of Pilshtin, and he came with his *arendar* to the fair. On his way into town, he went by the market where they sell the horses. Your prince's servant recognized the *melamed* and ran straight to the wagon and grabbed hold of the horses' reins.

It was our good luck the healer, Yankl, of Pilshtin, had gone with the servant at the request of our Faithful, and never left his side.* As soon as the servant grabbed hold of the horses' reins, the healer began urging the servant not to make a big commotion on market day in a place where there are lots of people, but to say in plain view of those who were already gathered by the wagon that he wants to buy from the *arendar* some horse harnessed to the wagon, and to go with him and the *melamed* to the tavern where he could do, really, whatever he wants.

The servant did what the healer asked. He went with the healer and the *melamed* to the tavernkeeper, Reb Khayim Khalodivker, who is one of our Faithful, and he gave them fish and a few glasses of mead. They ate and drank to their heart's content, and while the servant was drinking, the *melamed* fled to the cellar and from the cellar to the outside.

The servant started shouting. He said he knows which village the *arendar* was from, and the prince of that village is a relative of his prince, and he also knows the tavern. But the healer began pleading with him and he really begged him. He told him he should remember he once cured him of venereal disease, G-d save us!, and he kept it quiet and didn't reveal it to his prince, and that *he* is obliged to do *him* a favor too, to keep a secret *too,* because if he reveals this to his prince, then harm will come to *him* -- that is, the healer -- too.

The tavernkeeper, Reb Khayim, gave the servant from the alms box of Rabbi Meyer Balanes two rubles and the servant promised to keep quiet and not tell his prince a thing about all that happened to him with the *melamed.* We're confident he won't let word get out, because you can bet the prince is sure to be angry at him -- why did he go to the tavern and start drinking and on account of that didn't buy horses for him or have the messenger arrested?

But all the same, I'm notifying you of this so you'll keep an ear out for what the servant says when he gets home, because the healer informed us the servant will go from Pilshtin to the village of Zaluzin to the local prince on some errand from his lord and four days later he'll come back to Pilshtin and from there he'll go home. So you should know this.

From me,

....

#15

From Reb Zaynvl Verkhievker
To Reb Zelig Letitchiver

Even without your letter [#14] I'd want to know how it went in Pilshtin. Since I had news that last Monday the servant was due home from Pilshtin, on Sunday night I went to Yankl Rudniker who runs the local mill 'cause I heard that Tuesday is the time for payment of the lease installment for the mill. I asked him to do this for our holy *rebe* -- to pay the installment on Monday and to send the payment with me directly to the prince.

Even though Yankl's a very crude man, he has a healthy respect and fear of our holy *rebe* and he promised me to do this. But when he counted his cash he seen he's still short two hundred Polish zlotys and he said Monday afternoon they'll bring him that amount for grain he sold to the local flour dealers. So I went to Sholom Kaziner who runs the distillery in Zolik and asked him to give the miller two hundred zlotys for grain on account of I knew that Sholom is a little wealthy and he'll do it for me, and that's what happened.

With G-d's help the installment was complete, and Monday before daybreak I went to Reb Yankl Rivke's our grocer, whose little shop the road from Pulshtin to the manor goes by. I told him when the servant passes by his shop [on his way] from Pilshtin to the manor, he should start talking with the servant and ask him about the fair in Pilshtin, take him into the shop and treat him to good vodka, and in the meantime let me know the servant arrived. And when I send word to him I'm on mine way to the manor, he should stop talking with him so he'll go to the manor.

That's what he done. I went to the manor and sent word to the grocer he should let the servant go. When I came to the vestibule of the manor I waited and looked out the window to see if the servant was coming and when I seen the servant coming I went to the prince. A servant wouldn't let me into the room where the prince was but I gave him a *grivne* and said I have an urgent matter for the prince.

Inside, the landlord heard someone intruding right into his room. He came into the foyer and says to me, "Who are you?" I bowed low to him and I says, "I have brang the installment for the mill." The prince says to me, "Wait here awhile." When our Freyda heard mine voice, she came into the foyer too and I wished her good morning. The prince asked her if she knew me, and the clever girl, she should live to a hundred, says, "Why wouldn't I know him? He's a relation of mine and a member of the local community." The prince says, "I thought he's the miller's FAITHFUL SERVANT,"* and I says, "G-d forbid, sir. I am, thank G-d, an important man, and compared to me he's a common and crude man. But he had no money to pay the installment and he asked me to lend him the money. I thought, 'Who knows, maybe he'll take the cash for something else and won't pay the installment and mine lord will take away from him the mill and he won't have the means to pay me back the money.' So I came mineself with the payment."

The landlord says, "In that case, why haven't I seen you even once about hiring some business from me?" I says to him, "I can't compete with other men to lease a business and to ruin one another. If it is mine lord's kindness to lease me the mill I'll lease it, only it shouldn't become public until the time comes for taking over the mill." The prince says, "Why not, especially since you're a relative of my Freyda? In three months Yankl's contract runs out and I'll lease it to you." I kissed his boot, and the landlord called to his servant in a loud voice he should go immediately to call his secretary to accept from me the money. **He took a pipe to smoke tobacco** and I ran **to the kitchen and took a glowing coal and put it to his pipe**. He was pleased with me and told me very GRATEFULLY, "I like you -- you're a good man."

Meanwhile the servant [returning from Pilshtin] arrived at the house and the prince asked him, "Did you buy horses?" The servant says, "No, because there were no good horses that appealed to me. There was one horse I wanted to buy from an *arendar* but he didn't want to sell it. He told me, '**Don't ask me for the horse, because he's my very favorite, because in every difficult time and place where three good horses can't pull the carriage, he pulls it all by himself. This has happened to me several times, so love for the horse is engraved on my heart.**'"

When the servant told this, the master broke out laughing and says to the servant, "Are you making fun of me or is this the horse that was a reincarnation of a debtor and the Besht forgave him the debt, on account of which the life of the horse was ended?[1] You would have been a fool to buy this horse even for a high price because the horse would have up and died, as a result of which the *khsidim* would have accepted you as *rebe* over them like their Besht!"

---

[1] **Once, when the rabbi (the Besht) was on a journey he stayed overnight in a village with one of his people who made a great feast in his honor, during which the rabbi spoke with him as people do about his affairs -- whether he was making a living and how his situation was, and he told him of his good situation** ALL IN ALL.

The rabbi said, "You have good horses? Let's go have a look at your horses," and they went to the stable. The rabbi liked a pony and asked the householder to give him the horse as a gift. He replied to him, "Sir, don't ask me for this horse because he's my very favorite, because in every difficult time and place where three good horses can't pull the carriage, he pulls it all by himself. This has happened to me several times, so love for the horse is engraved on my heart."

A while later they spoke again of his good situation -- how he also has many debts due from people. The rabbi said, "Please show me your IOUs," and he showed him all the IOUs. When he saw a certain IOU the rabbi asked him to give him the IOU as a gift. He replied, "Why does the rabbi want this IOU, since it's been several years since the debtor died and nothing was left to repay the debt?" The rabbi said, "I want it anyway," and he gave him the IOU as a gift. He took the IOU, tore it in two and completely forgave the deceased the debt.

After this the rabbi said, "Now go have a look at how the horse is doing." He went and looked: The horse lay dead! And he understood that it was not a coincidence. The rabbi said, "Because the man whose creditor you were was unable to pay you, he was sentenced to work off the debt to your satisfaction and he was transformed into a horse. That's why he worked so hard to satisfy you. Now that his servitude has been forgiven, he has returned to his former place, the horse's life has ended and so the man has really died." *Shivkhey ha-Balshemtov* 30:3 [Mintz, 218f.].

When I heard this I almost went out of mine mind. Freyda asked him, "I read this tale, but how does my lord know it?" The landlord says, "You read the book?! -- I forget its name..." -- and he ran to the bookcase and took out the infamous *bukh* and looked at it and says, "The book is *Shivkhey ha-Besht** and you must have it in Judeo-German,* the Austrian or Lashtchuv edition."

When I heard this I started shaking all over. On account of the shaking, the installment money fell on the ground and when I bent over to pick up the money from the ground, the holy book *Seyfer ha-Mides* of Our Teacher the *Rov,* Rabbi Nakhmen, fell from mine breast pocket. I grabbed *it* first and kissed it and put it back in mine breast pocket and then I picked up the cash.

While the prince's secretary was coming to receive the money, the prince looked in his *bukh* and says, "Your book must be *Seyfer ha-Mides* of Rabbi Nakhmen, the great-grandson of the Besht. You're a *khosed* too! In that case I won't lease you the mill because in that book it says you're allowed to cheat us."

"Perish the thought!" I cried. "It don't say that in this book!" He looked in his *bukh* and says to me, "On page 14, paragraph 6, doesn't it say this explicitly?!"

I took the holy book and looked at it and cried, "Perish the thought, sir! He wrote here that it's okay to cheat *idolators,* that is, worshippers of stars and planets, but not *you!"*

When I said this, he went through the roof and he says, "I know you say this, and there's even a Notice about this at the beginning of this book, as all the Jewish authors have,* but I know very well that in the Talmud and in all the Jewish books, when they speak of idolators they aren't speaking only of worshippers of stars and planets, because they're even commanded to pray for the well-being of the government. In fact, in your books (he looked in the *bukh* and says), every place where it says "nations," "foreigner" or "non-Jew," it refers to *us.* Even though you say about, 'Pray for the well-being of the government,'* that it refers to fear of G-d with *dveykes,*[2] why did that Rabbi Nakhmen write in *Kitser Likutey MohoRa"N* that it's a *mitsve* for the *tsadek* to give a bribe to the idolator?[3] Maybe he also meant 'to give a bribe to idolators who lived eighteen hundred years ago'?!"

"You thought it was a fool who wrote this *bukh*? He's a fool like you! He knows you and your *tsadikim* very well. I wouldn't trade one page of his *bukh* for all your foolish books! The *Seyfer Mides* you carry in your

---

[2] *Mevaser Tsedek* 29:4.

[3] See note 2 to letter 3.

breast pocket at the behest of Rabbi Nakhmen[4] and that you kissed -- isn't *this bukh* more worthy of being kissed?" As he said this he ran to me and shoved the *bukh* at mine mouth to kiss it.

I almost fainted, but a great miracle happened for me 'cause Freyda was there and she saved me by her cleverness. She pleaded with the prince and told him we don't kiss [just] any book, only a book by a Jew. The prince says, "He's not worthy of kissing this *bukh.* The *bukh* will be defiled by his unclean lips!" He screamed at me to pay the money and get out of his house at once and he says, "I'll give the receipt for the installment to the miller himself," and pushed me out of the manor.

I went home melancholy but when I got home I drank a big glass of vodka* and I composed mineself. Why should I be melancholy? Didn't I do all this for the sake of our holy *rebe,* his light should shine? And what's it to me if such a *goy* speaks evil of the *tsadikim*? Surely if our holy *rebe,* he should live, wishes, he'll CUT HIM DOWN TO SIZE. Indeed, our *rebe,* with G-d's help, has the power to humble the celestial prince of any nation.[5]* To humble such a *goy* is a mere trifle and if the prince wants to do us or me mineself some harm, G-d forbid!, our holy *rebe* is sure to make him die.[6]

But I was afraid maybe the prince will send for the miller to give him the receipt and he'll find out that the money was his very own and he didn't borrow from me a thing and *I* asked to go with the installment. He'll make inquiries about this -- "Why did I want to go with the installment?" The miller's a very crude man -- when they'll take him for interrogation he'll reveal I told him the matter concerns our holy *rebe.*

So I went straight to the miller and said I had to tell him an important secret only he should swear to me holding a holy object* not to tell no one what I'm telling him 'cause on account of this I could fall, G-d

---

[4] He wrote it himself (the *tsadek,* Our Teacher the *Rov,* Rabbi Nakhmen) in a very small pamphlet and said that his intention was that everyone would be able to carry it near him always, because the virtues *(mides)* are the foundation of the entire Toyre. Introduction to *Seyfer ha-Mides* of *MohoRa"N.*

He who has the privilege to look at that holy book with clear eyes will understand that truly the virtues recorded in that holy book are the foundation of the whole Toyre in its entirety that has been bequeathed to us by the real *tsadikim* who are in every single generation, may their memory be blessed with life in the world-to-come, may their merit protect us and all Israel our brethren.

[5] "The *tsadek* is able through his worthy acts to bring about the downfall of the celestial prince of a nation so that, of its own accord, it too falls." *No'am Elimelekh* 74:2.

[6] "Sometimes a person dies before his time on account of the complaints of a *tsadek.*" *Mides* 52:80.

forbid!, into mortal danger. He didn't want to swear by a *Seyfer Toyre* so he swore to me by *tfiln.*

I says to him, "Look, for the *mitsve* you done today for our holy *rebe,* he should live, by sending me to the landlord with the installment, G-d has given you a part of the reward immediately in this world, in addition to a reward He'll give you in the world-to-come. 'Cause when I entered the foyer of the manor, I asked a servant if the prince is home and he told me he was in the other room with someone else. I gave the servant a zloty to go tell the landlord I brang the installment from the miller. The servant went to the other room and came back and told me, 'The prince says to wait until he comes to this room,' and the servant went away."

"I thought, 'Who is this person who's in there with the prince?' So I went quietly to the doorway and looked through the keyhole and I seen the wicked slut Freyda Reb Isaac's (here I spat on the floor and says, 'Her name and memory should be wiped out!') with the prince on the bed. I actually **seen a little something**!*

"When I heard them mention your name I put mine ear to the keyhole to hear what they were saying. The slut says, 'The miller earns a lot of money from my lord's mill,' and the prince says, 'In fact, someone else used to hold the lease and he didn't make the payments on time and was always asking for an extension. *He* pays me just as much money as the first one used to and he always pays regularly and promptly. The payments are due tomorrow and he sent the installment today.'

"'And why not?' says the slut. 'Don't he earn double what he pays for the mill? Grain used to be cheap and now it's dear. And what's more, because of the mill he has a large quantity [of grain]. From my lord's mill he has become very wealthy.'

"The prince says, 'What can I do? He still has three months to go. If some [other] lessee happens my way, then I'll lease *him* the mill for three more years.'* The wicked one said *she'll* get him a dependable and faithful man who'll lease the mill. In the meantime I seen the landlord get up from the bed and I backed away quietly 'til I reached the doorway of the foyer and stood in the doorway.

"The prince came into that room and asked me, 'Did you bring the installment?' I bowed low and says, 'I did.' He asked me, 'Are you the miller's trustee?' In the meantime, the adulteress, Freyda-Her-Name-Should-Be-Wiped-Out, came in from the outside through a different doorway into the foyer and pretended like she just now came to the prince.

"I says to the prince, 'No sir. I'm a member of the local community, but the miller didn't have the money to pay the installment. He was still short six hundred zlotys and I lent them to him. Since he didn't have time to come himself with the installment -- 'cause he had to go to the holy community of Litin to sell grain on contract to the steward of the contractor who lives there -- he asked *me* to go, and here I am.' The prince asked me, 'Why doesn't he have the money? Doesn't he make a lot of money from the mill?'

"I says to him, 'Sir, surely everyone knows he was very rich at the time he leased the mill but now he's lost a lot of money. But since he's a very faithful and good man, he didn't want to ask mine lord for a break. He always pays what's coming.'

"When I says this, the prince turned his face to the Slut-Her-Name-Should-Be-Wiped-Out like he wanted to ask her if what I says was true, but she winked at him and he kept quiet. The prince went and pulled the cord tied to the bell in the little room where the servants stay. The bell rang and the servant came to him. He ordered [the servant] to call his secretary to receive the installment and he went to the fourth room to get from there the account book and the contract to record the payment of the installment.

"Me and that slut were left in the foyer and I couldn't restrain mineself. I went over to her but I didn't look at her brazen face, G-d forbid!, and I says to her, 'I seen and heard everything you done with the prince in the other room and I'm going to write everything to our holy *rebe* and to your husband and to your whole family. I'll tell everything!' She began to tremble, especially when she heard the name of our *rebe* the *tsadek,* he should live, and she says to me, 'For cryin' out loud! What do you want to do to me -- take away, G-d forbid!, my livelihood?'

"I says to her, 'And what do *you* want from the miller? He's a worthy and good man. I wouldn't take your whole body in exchange for one of his toenails!'

"She says to me, 'You'll see, I'll make it so everything will be okay and he'll keep the mill. Just don't do nothing bad to me.' I says to her, 'Will you swear to me you'll make it so everything will be okay?' and she says to me, 'As soon as you leave here, go to my house. I'll swear to you about this there.'

"In the meantime the secretary and the landlord came and accepted the installment and the prince said you should send for the receipt 'cause he didn't have time to give a receipt at the moment. But I stayed while he wrote everything in the account book and he also wrote the receipt on the contract.

"Since I said you'll travel to the holy community of Litin to sell grain, so leave home at once and send your servant to the manor for the receipt in two hours. I'll go to the wicked Freyda so she'll swear to me to fix everything -- not just to fix what she spoiled but to make it even better then it was, so the prince will give you a break for years to come."

When the miller heard all this he says, "Now I see that there is none on earth but the *tsadikim*," and then and there he returned to me the zloty I told him I gave the servant, and for mine trouble he promised to send me today a bushel corn flour and a quarter bushel wheat flour and half a bushel buckwheat cereal. He also ordered his right-hand man then and there to **send** our holy *rebe*, he should live, **a gift of a wagon with all kinds of flour and fowl**, and since the servant is one of our Faithful, you can bet, of course he'll pick out the best and very nicest flour and, of course, the very fattest fowl.

When I finished that business with the miller, I went to our Freyda to ask her if after I left there the prince spoke with the servant about the messenger he ordered [him] to search for in Pilshtin, but on the way I met the bearer of this letter and he's in a hurry to be on his way. So I decided to let you know quickly the whole story. Please tell our holy *rebe*, he should live, that *I* brang about this gift of assorted flour and fowl for him and that *I* brang the miller under his wings[7] and from here on in, of course, he'll be among our holy *rebe*'s people. He's a simple man and very rich so our holy *rebe*, he should live, should keep me in mind at the very least when he smokes a pipe.

Since the wayfarer before me is in a big hurry, I got to be brief. G-d willing, when there'll happen to be from here to there* a traveler, I'll write you a clear report what the prince talked about with the servant with regards to the messenger, I mean, the *melamed*.

These are the words of
....

---

[7] "He who brings an ignoramus under the wings of the *tsadek* receives a reward for this." *Mides* 51:64.

#16

From Reb Zelig Letitchiver
To Reb Zaynvl Verkhievker

I got your letter [#15] and yesterday the **wagon** arrived **with all kinds of flour and** the best and nicest **fowl**. When the wagon came I put in for you a good word with our holy *rebe*. I told him you managed all this with the miller because you did him a favor with your prince.

Meanwhile, the wife of our *rebe*, the *tsadkones*, she should live to be a hundred, came in and asked whether to accept the assorted flour and fowl.[1] Beaming, our holy *rebe* said with pleasure, "Do so, but you know you must send thanks for this to our Reb Zaynvl of Kripen." The *tsadkones* answered in her wisdom, "*You* can send thanks, not me." Our holy *rebe* said, "Well spoken," and at the same moment our *rebe,* he should live, began smoking the tobacco furiously and lots of smoke went up from the pipe. He must have had you in mind at the time.

When I saw this was a good time and the right moment to speak with our *rebe,* he should live, I told him good things about Freyda Reb Isaac's too -- that many times she did us and you big favors. Our *rebe,* he should live, said she has a great soul -- that her soul was taken from Yo'el, wife of Khever the Kenite.* I asked him if your prince was a reincarnation of Sisera and he answered me angrily, "Why must you ask about what's not permitted to you?"* and stopped smoking the pipe. I wanted to take the stem and the pipe from him and set them by the window but he didn't let me. I realized this was my punishment for asking him and spoiling the mystical intention in the smoking of the tobacco. On account of this he didn't want to privilege me with the *mitsve* of serving.

I really regret this question, but G-d knows the truth -- that my whole intention was to know if your prince is a reincarnation of Sisera and is sure to be defeated, so our group would be rid of such an archenemy. But if G-d knows my intention, our holy *rebe* must also know my intention.[2] The fact that he didn't want I should take the pipe must've been so as to humiliate me for my own good[3] and for this alone I'm obliged to cast myself into the fiery furnace for our *rebe.*

---

[1] Whoever has a brain in his skull will understand that this custom to ask the *tsadek* whether to accept the gifts that are brought is a worthy and good and lovely custom.

[2] "The *tsadek* resembles the Creator, blessed be He, who is unique among the higher beings and the lower beings. So too the *tsadek,* in his devotion and in his unity with all Jews, is similarly regarded." *No'am Elimelekh* 81:4.

"When the *tsadek* hears some utterance he is able to comprehend it to know the root of the thoughts of the person through his speech." *Ibid.,* 72:2.

[3] "Sometimes the *tsadek* of the generation, by the anger he expresses towards you, tempers the judgment." *Mides* 19:95.

"We must accept their reproof (of the *tsadikim*) in order to receive mercy thereby....For just as their reproof sometimes comes by way of deprecation...for they suffer great sorrow from us....The prayer that from our perspective is nothing but good, is bad for the *tsadikim,* in the sense of, MY PRAYER IS AGAINST THEIR EVIL DEEDS." *Likutey MohoRa"N* 50:3.

"Sometimes the *tsadek* elevates someone and afterwards lowers him. This is for the benefit of the person." *Mides* 52:93.

"When G-d is the *tsadek,* ANGRY EVERY DAY below, then G-D'S MERCY IS ALL DAY (on high, because 'when there is judgment below there is no judgment on

So I'm notifying you your letter caused me awful aggravation. I don't know what's going on. Your prince didn't used to be so very wicked. I remember once he was traveling through our community and he asked about our holy *rebe,* and now I see from your letter he's an enemy and a foe of all our Faithful and of all the *tsadikim* and it seems this is all on account of the *bukh.*

I don't know what's going on here. At first I thought one of the *goyim* composed it. I was surprised at this too, because, thank G-d, it's been several years since the *goyim,* too, in our country began respecting us -- especially our *rebes.* Some of them sent *pidyens* in the thousands and tens of thousands and some of them came and begged our *rebes* to help them in their affairs.

Even as recently as a few months ago when I was in Galicia, I saw a *goy* from Wallakhia* who traveled for something he needed to a fellow from Kalashke named Yokltse, who the Galician *khsidim* call *"rebe."* You can imagine what a *rebe* he must be if the foolish Galician *khsidim* call him *"rebe."* You can bet, of course, he's merely "Yokltse."* Some of them call him "Reb Yokltse the Prophet." Did you ever in your life hear such a thing -- nowadays to call a *rebe* a prophet? I don't envy neither the *rebes* of Galicia or their people. All the same, even *goyim* make pilgrimages to him.

The Wallakhian that I mentioned to you made a pilgrimage for the sake of his beloved, because it seemed to him his beloved Wallakhian *goye* didn't love him like she used to, but loved someone else. The Wallakhian told me, when I saw him passing through the holy community of Butchatch, that when he came to that "prophet," he [the "prophet"] told him immediately why and wherefore he had come and advised him what to do. When the Wallakhian spoke of that "prophet" he spoke with fear and reverence. When he mentioned his name, he always said, "May G-d give him life."

I bit my lip so as not to laugh openly. The foolish Wallakhian didn't have the sense to understand that that man back home in Wallakhia who advised him to travel to Kalashke must've been one of Yokltse's people and he sent word ahead to Yokltse that the Wallakhian would come to him and what matter he would come to him about. You can bet he must have written him all the Wallakhian's words and affairs. *All* Yokltse's operations must've been done this way.

I got lots to tell about this Yokltse but let's leave this and return to our subject -- that a few months ago the *goyim* were still traveling to Galician *rebes,* and how very much the more to *our tsadikim,* and now all of a sudden they started more and more to mock and one of them openly wrote a

---

high'*)." *No'am Elimelekh* 85:2.

bukh and published it. I was amazed at that. But now I seen from your letter that that *bukh* contains a number of things from our holy books, so a *Jew* must've written it, and my amazement reached to high heaven! How can it be nowadays that a *Jew* could defy our group openly??!!

Clearly, it's been several years now that our circle has spread as far as the community of Pest in Hungary. The Jews in Ashkenaz, who our group's divine light didn't yet shine on, don't know our people. What's more, there's not one among them who would know our customs as they're described in the infamous *bukh.* As for the people of Poland, Wallakhia, Moldavia and part of Hungary -- they're almost all of them among our Faithful. Even if there's one in a thousand who don't love us in his heart, he's afraid, of course, of the wrath of the *tsadikim* and the members of our fellowship, because they seen many opponents who dared to rise against us suffered a crushing defeat.[4] Some of them died a strange death, some became paupers and some had their homes and all their possessions burnt. Some remained desolate because their wives and all their relatives left them and some died in captivity.

The wonders were so very numerous that in Lithuania -- where our chief opponent, Elijah of Vilna, who excommunicated the whole group,* lived -- and in Minsk and the other small towns, they devised against us there conspiracies and decrees, as you'll see in the wicked *Seyfer ha-Vikuakh.** Nevertheless, nowadays there too they all belong to our faction and the holy book *Shivkhey ha-Besht* was published for the first time in Kopust, which is in *Lithuania!** So I don't know where this particular Jew comes from who knows our people and knows the great power of the *tsadikim* and their disciples and their disciples' disciples,* and who can BE SO BRAZEN and write openly such words of *apikorses* and heresy!

So it's up to us to do everything possible, to risk our lives to get hold of the *bukh.* I hope to G-d, by the merit of our *rebe* the *tsadek,* he should live, that when we get hold of it we'll figure out, of course, who the

---

[4] "Whoever challenges the *tsadek* ends up being caught in a bad trap." *Mides* 56:185.

"[That is] the one who speaks about the *tsadikim* and bad-mouths them with abuse and vilification,* which is considered in the sight of the Creator, praised be His name, as if he were speaking, as it were, about Him, blessed be He. Regarding this, Scripture doubled SHE WILL BE CUT OFF CUT OFF *(HIKORES TIKORES),* to refer to the two cases of *kores* [the biblical punishment of being 'cut off' from one's people] mentioned above, which concern actual idolatry, like the final conclusion of the *Gemore,** and for the one who defames the *tsadikim,* which is only out of haughtiness. Therefore he will be cut off from place to place and he will be a wandering fugitive exile on the earth." *No'am Elimelekh* 76:3.

author is and where he lives and then we'll do with him whatever our heart desires.

From me,

....

The main thing I forgot. Let me know as soon as possible if your prince spoke with the servant about the *melamed,* and if the miller in his innocence still thinks you'll manage to get for him the mill for three years at a discount.

#17

From Reb Zaynvl Verkhievker
To Reb Zelig Letitchiver

I hereby send you a thousand thanks that you put in for me a good word with our holy *rebe,* he should live. And I was so pleased when I read in your letter [#16] that our holy *rebe* said to the *rebetsn,* the *tsadkones,* she should live, she should send me a thank-you for the **wagon with the assorted flour and fowl** and the *tsadekes* answered that this our holy *rebe* could do, not her.

But I'm disgruntled on you. When our *rebe,* he should live, began smoking the tobacco quickly, why did you spoil the mystical intention by starting to talk with him about the prince? In mine humble opinion, even though I got no business with mysteries,* all the same, in mine worthless and contemptible opinion, it seems to me that our *rebe* the *tsadek,* when he started smoking the tobacco, had me in mind, and with his intense *dveykes* made a unification of The Holy One, blessed be He, and His *Shkhine.** And on account of you mentioned to him the name of that sinner -- I mean, mine prince, who's a big crook and wallowing in money-lust -- and caused a menstrual flow to the *Shkhine,** in the sense of, THEIR GOLD [SHALL BE] AS SOMETHING UNCLEAN, by mentioning the name you also caused a separation between The Holy One, blessed be He, and his *Shkhine*[1] and you ruined everything!

---

[1] Through their iniquities the wicked cause a separation between the Holy One, blessed be He and His *Shkhine* because they cause Her (the *Shkhine*) a menstrual flow*...and for this reason the wicked are called MEN OF BLOOD because the 365 prohibitions depend on the 365 sinews where the blood vessels are...so it is necessary to temper this blood, that is, to rectify the [transgressions of] prohibitions,

I'm not saying this is certain 'cause who am I TO FOLLOW THE KING? I know I can't reach what the little fingernail, the toenail of the little toe of the foot of our *rebe* the *tsadek,* he should live, can reach, but I'm saying this *could've* been one thousandth or one ten-thousandth of the mystical intentions our holy *rebe* had to direct in this [matter].

So please, if I should have such a privilege again, don't say a thoughtless word and don't even make any slight movement. Just stand still in fear and reverence and watch very, very closely the sweet movements of our *rebe* the *tsadek,* he should live.[2]

As for the servant, I asked our Freyda and she told me the prince asked the servant if he seen the messenger. He answered that he didn't see him, that once he seen a Jew from a distance and thought he was the messenger but when he got close to him he realized it was someone else.

The prince says to Freyda, "I would give I-don't-know-how-much for this messenger because I know for certain that the letter was written by the sect of the *khsidim.* I know very well what they do in their affairs concerning their *rebes* and their sect in general. Did you know that they permit bloodshed and such? The author of this *bukh* knows them quite well. Everything he wrote in his *bukh* he reproduced from their books and he copied everything from their own words."

From the words of that scoundrel you can see the author must be a Jew. So even more it's up to us to find out who he is so as to pluck him up by the root. For G-d's sake, urge all our Faithful to do all what they can, and me and our Faithful around here will also do all what *we* can, of course -- we *here* and you *there.*

We had already bigger concerns then a *bukh.* How many grave battles we had since we began being a holy fellowship! How many slanderers and accusers we had! How many adversaries rose up against us! How

---

which are the sinews, and to whiten them in the sense of 'The turbid blood is decomposed and made into milk [by a nursing mother]'*...so it is necessary to rectify the totality of the sinews [*gidim*] as in the verse, HE DECLARED [*VAYAGED*] TO YOU HIS COVENANT,* and then by means of this rectification of the covenant, which is the totality of the sinews...and based on this the totality of the sinews is called *'Shaddai'* because it fires *(shadey)** and shoots restorative whiteness like an arrow...." *Likutey MohoRa"N* 47:1-2.

He who looks there will find spiritual gratification for it is a great *drush,* that is, great on high and extensive, AND THE FEAR OF THE L-RD IS HIS TREASURE.

[2] "Because of this the movements of the *tsadikim* are sweet and good to those who see them because the movement is from the power of the soul and the soul is part of God on high, in whom all is good. For this reason when anyone makes the movements of his fellow it is not acceptable for any person because it is not his own...and it is, G-d save us!, like idolatry..." *No'am Elimelekh* 61:4.

many composed books against our group! How many of them traveled from community to community to preach against us openly! But we, by the merit of the *tsadikim,* took revenge against some of them and some of them died, and our group endures and in every generation our people increase.

In the days of the Besht, he should be remembered for life in the world-to-come, there were many who disagreed with him, but now who would dare, G-d forbid!, to speak against him? With all the *tsadikim* it was the same. People would always praise only those *tsadikim* in the generations before them. But the *tsadikim* we got *now*adays -- everyone, including their contemporaries, praises them and admits they're the pillars of the world. So certainly in their merit we'll get sweet revenge against the writer of the *bukh* too and everything will be alright again.

These are the words of

....

#18

From Reb Zelig Letitchiver
To Reb Zaynvl Verkhievker

I hereby inform you in great haste you should travel at once, for G-d's sake, to you-know-which place where the *melamed* is because you know the healer from Pilshtin is a big drunk and he spilled the beans about what happened in Pilshtin on market day in front of one of the *misnagdim,* who revealed it to the sheriff, who wrote an order to the bailiff of the rural police to put the *melamed* in iron chains!

So for G-d's sake, don't be lazy about this. We were lucky that when the lord sheriff's scribe brought the order to the sheriff to sign, the sheriff asked the scribe, "What order is this?" and the scribe said, "To have the *melamed* arrested." The sheriff signed his name and said to the scribe, "Post the order at once because you know it's an urgent matter."

When he said these words, Reb Aharon Lozer's, our wineseller, who happened to be by the sheriff at the time, was standing there. He immediately informed me of everything and I sent the postmaster's agent with a gift to the postmaster, who opened the order and read it right in front of the agent. It said there to put the *melamed* who delivered a letter to your prince in iron chains and to present him here. The agent begged the postmaster to delay the thing. The postmaster took the order, put it in his box and promised to send it a few days later.

So in the meantime, take the *melamed* and bring him to another district or come up with some other plan, just so everything'll be alright. I'll also do whatever needs doing around here.

From me,

....

#19

From Reb Gedalye Balter in Aklev
To Reb Gershon Koritser in Nigrad

Your letter with six and thirty zlotys' worth of silver money that you sent for a *pidyen* for your only son, I received. Be advised that last *Shabes* at *shaleshudes* our *rebe*, our *tsadek*, may he live, told us that two *pidyens* would arrive this week. Concerning one he saw judgments, but he didn't say who it would be from or which the judgments pertain to. Yesterday when they brought him six red ducats from Reb Pinkhes Lubinker he made a *pidyen* and said, "With G-d's help, even though red represents the quality of strict justice, I tempered them in the sense of, AND THE GOLD OF THE LAND IS GOOD." I supposed that these were the judgments that our *rebe* foresaw, and when the messenger came from you and brought silver coins I was filled with joy that the *pidyen* was sure to be effective, because silver is whiteness in the sense of mercy.

But afterwards I saw that I hadn't understood at all. When I set the money before our *rebe* he was absolutely astounded and he almost wouldn't accept your *pidyen* had I not urgently implored him. I told him that you risk your life for him, as in the renowned case of the pearls.* Then he closed his eyes and smoked the pipe very rapidly. He sent up lots of smoke and worked himself into a sweat and became very agitated. He cried out, "Return, return!" and cried out further, "THE LIVING, THE LIVING SHALL THANK YOU."* When he said this the *pidyen* was complete.

When he regained his composure he said, "How very wise is Reb Gershon. It appears that he must be a little bit of a kabbalist for he knew to send twice eighteen zlotys."* Afterward I asked our *rebe* the *tsadek* what caused our *rebe*, may he live, to cry out, "Return, return!" He told me that when he closed his eyes he saw the Angel of Death descending to earth very joyfully. He understood that he would go to your only son and he almost didn't know what to do. At that instant he remembered the *kavone* of the smoke of the incense that stops the plague* and he meditated on the *kavone* of the heat and so he began to puff furiously. When the Angel of Death saw that his evil was cut short, he started quarreling with him and said, "*I* am sent of the Omnipresent," and our *rebe* replied to him, "*I* received the payment for the *pidyen.*" So he made a compromise with him that your son would be sick twice and the second time he would be laid out **in a coma**,* which is a kind of death, because right now he doesn't have the strength to survive **a coma**.

I understood that this was the reason he said, "THE LIVING, THE LIVING SHALL THANK YOU," as if to say, he'll be sick twice and thereafter he'll live many years and he'll be, G-d willing, truly a servant of the L-rd -- and this was the reason he said, WILL THANK YOU. And for this reason he also said, "Return, return!" as if to say, twice the Angel of Death will return from him. Because I know, of course, that our *rebe* doesn't utter a word in vain.

Our *rebe* said further that because of the coin of silver he was in terrible danger, because even though silver *(kesef)* is mercy, still there's silver and there's silver. There's silver in the sense of "yearning" *(kosef)* -- this is mercy -- and there's silver in the sense of "bread of silver."*

You can see from this what our holy *rebe* did for you, so my advice is that you should also be sure to do something substantial for our *rebe,* may he live. In my opinion here's what you should do. In your community there's a certain Talmudist named Moyshe Fishl's. He's a simpleton. He knows nothing but to go from his house to the *besmedresh.* I know that he's well-respected by all the people in your community. Be sure to make his acquaintance so that through you he'll join up with our Faithful. I know for certain that if he's on our side all the people of your community will become followers of our *rebe* the *tsadek* and it will be to our HONOR AND GLORY. Be well.

From me,

....

#20

From Reb Zaynvl Verkhievker
To Reb Zelig Letitchiver

The moment I got your letter [#18] I went to the marketplace to see about a wagon. This was on Friday. I **seen a boy standing in the marketplace with a wagon with three horses and I asked him, "Where**

are you [coming] from?" He says, "From Pilshtin," **and it was really true that he had left a merchant somewhere and come home with the empty wagon.**

I hired the driver and got to the town of Pilshtin an hour past noon. In the town of Pilshtin I found the *melamed* 'cause he came there to buy stuff for *Shabes.* I went with him straight to his village of Bilke and told the *arendar* the *melamed* had to hide out for a few days in another district. On *Shabes* the *melamed* stole away to another village a parasang* from his village so on Sunday he could go from there to another district. I stayed in the *melamed*'s village over *Shabes.*

I asked the *arendar* **if it was possible for him to get fish around here and the householder told** me **that it was just plain impossible to get.** I asked him if there were ponds by him and he said **that he had two ponds.** So I **took a stick and tied a string to it and cast into** the pond, and I **brang up from the pond a big fish.** I gave it to the householder and he made it for *Shabes.*

I had great pleasure on this *Shabes* on account of some young men from Pilshtin came to spend *Shabes* with me in that village 'cause in Pilshtin there's still not no *rebe.* The healer of Pilshtin also spent *Shabes* there 'cause that village's prince was sick, and I drew the healer close in every way possible 'cause he's a man who can help us in lots of ways. Also a steward of the contractor Kalmen Bisinger of Koven spent *Shabes* in the same village, but him I didn't see. Since he's very respected in the eyes of that village's prince, he [the prince] gave him an apartment in the manor and from the *arendar* they sent him food and drink at the manor.*

On account of the pleasure I had I couldn't sleep. I got up very early and when I got up I went straight to the woods by the inn. I strolled around in the woods with great pleasure. All of a sudden I heard some wailing sound. I followed the sound and came to a very old tree and I heard someone wailing inside the tree. I asked, "Who are you?" and he says, "I am the demon that the Besht imprisoned in the forest."[1] I says to

---

[1] I heard from my father-in-law and also from the rabbi of our community that when the Besht was still living in an inn in the village they once needed rain and he prayed for rain. There was a witch there who had a demon and she worked a magic spell so that rain would not fall but the Besht foiled her magic with his prayer....

The witch went to his mother and said, "Tell your son that he should leave me alone or I'll put a spell on him." His mother thought that the quarrel with her concerned a debt for vodka and his mother said to him, "Son, let this *goye* be, for she's a witch." He told his mother, "I'm not afraid of her," and he went right on praying for rain.

The witch came to his mother a second time, after which she sent her de-

it, "Wasn't the Besht a tavernkeeper around here?" And it says to me, "It's true that the Besht was once a tavernkeeper a few parasangs from here. He imprisoned me in the woods around there but the lord of that there forest later ordered the forest should be cut down. Since this village, Bilke, belonged to the same lord who owned the village where the Besht was a tavernkeeper, and so as not to wrong the [heavenly] prince of the village where the Besht lived and had a good name, and so as not to steal from this lord a single tree and also so as not to put me in captivity under the power of a lord other then him under who the Besht had placed me -- they decreed in Heaven, with the agreement of the Besht, that the heavenly prince of the forest would take me and bring me here to the village of Bilke."

The demon began begging me in tears to put in for him a good word to our holy *rebe,* he should live, 'cause our *rebe* "has the power to free me." I says to it, "What will you give me if I do this for you with our holy *rebe?"* The demon says, "I'll give you a gift far more valuable then any fortune." I says, "I don't believe you 'cause many times you didn't keep your word, not to mention that you lied to our rabbi the Besht, his memory should be blessed with life in the world-to-come.[2] So give me the gift right now and I'll certainly keep mine word and do mine part."

At that moment a little piece of glass fell out from the tree and the demon says to me, "This is a piece of the window pane through which I injured the *goye*-witch who sent me against the Besht."[3] I put the piece of glass in mine pocket and even though there was no *eruv* there,* all the same I thought, "For such an important matter it's a *mitsve* to desecrate the *Shabes."* Now I carry the piece of glass in mine *tales-kotn.*

At the *shaleshudes* I said very broad *toyre* with G-d's help, and I know that the piece of glass that was broken on account of the Besht, his memory should be blessed with life in the world-to-come, brang all this about for me. Last Saturday night the Besht came to me in a dream and says to me, "Your time to reveal yourself in the world is not yet come, but be assured that on account of the piece of glass you got in your *tales-kotn,* you'll be very famous." I woke up and couldn't sleep no more.

---

mon against him. But when it came to him it couldn't get within four cubits of him. The Besht said to it, "How dare you come to me?! Go at once and injure the *goye* through a small glass window!" And it did so. Afterward he imprisoned it in the forest and it can never move from there.

When the Besht had emerged into public view, he was traveling with people by way of the forest. He stopped and went into the forest. He peeked at it sitting in captivity and laughed a lot. They asked about it and he told them this tale. *Shivkhey ha-Besht* 17:1 [Mintz, 123].

[2] *Shivkhey ha-Besht* 28:1 [Mintz, 200] and many more places there.

[3] See above, note 1.

I got up Sunday morning and traveled with the healer to the holy community of Pilshtin. The healer went to the bailiff and gave him a gift and he [the bailiff] promised to take care of everything. On Sunday the order arrived from the sheriff and the bailiff went into the village of Bilke where the *melamed* was and didn't find him, and when he came back he wrote a report of all this.

So now, you do whatever's needed to keep the sheriff quiet, 'cause at the moment I can't do nothing 'cause I'm moving with tremendous *dveykes* in the upper worlds,* since the piece of glass carries me from one world to another, from one sanctuary to another, and constantly mine senses and substance become less and less. Proof of this is that for four nights now I didn't sleep. Every night I see the Besht and other *tsadikim.* Their souls are in the celestial treasure-houses on high that come to me and, G-d willing, you'll see soon what will become of me!

From me, your friend and soulmate,

....

#21

From Reb Zelig Letitchiver
To Reb Zaynvl Verkhievker

Before I got your letter [#20] I already knowed about what happened to you in the woods with the demon because that steward who spent *Shabes* there in the village of Bilke on the *Shabes* when you were there too was the wicked and worthless Mordekhai Gold. He was in the woods -- you can bet he had some slut in the woods -- and his assistant told him Friday night that at the inn there was a *khosed* with some young men. When he saw you *Shabes* morning in the woods he thought you must be this *khosed* who's spending *Shabes* at the inn. So he went by himself and hid in a hollow tree in the woods and said what he said to you and tossed you the piece of glass that some hooligans had thrown at the tree or at a bird. First thing Saturday night he sent a special messenger to his father-in-law the *misnaged* wineseller and wrote him everything. Right now they're making of you a laughingstock. Even our holy *rebe,* when he heard this, laughed and said, with a shake of his head, "Zaynvl Verkhievker dreams of being a *rebe!*"

So for G-d's sake, don't tell another soul about this and get rid of the piece of glass at once! The moment you see this note, write *me* a letter that when you was spending *Shabes* in the village of Bilke, in the morning you went to the woods near the inn to relieve yourself and there you saw the sinner Mordekhai Gold with a lecherous *goye* performing a filthy act in the woods, and you went with two of the men who were with you in the village and grabbed him and the *goye* but he ran straight to the manor and hid there, so you let the *goye* go too.

Also write in your letter he spent *Shabes* by the lord of the manor and ate *treyf* food by the lord that he stayed with. Be sure to discuss this with the *arendar* there and tell him when anyone asks him about this incident, he should say, "What do I got to do with such things? I live [here] by the grace of my prince and he loves Mordekhai Gold. What do I need this for? I don't know from nothing." And when he says this, he should shrug his shoulders. Also discuss this with the men who were there with you on *Shabes* so they'll say they know about this incident and that two of them went with you to the woods and grabbed the wicked and worthless fornicator, his name and memory should be erased.

As for the sheriff, we already done what we had to. Reb Aharon Lozer's, our wineseller, is very respected in the sight of the sheriff and other nobles. He spoke with the sheriff and gave him a gift of a dozen bottles of good wine. He [the sheriff] promised not to do nothing at all in this matter, but Reb Aharon told us the sheriff told him to make sure the *misnaged* Mordekhai-May-His-Name-Be-Erased Gold should also keep quiet, because he said, since the matter has got around a bit, he himself is even afraid that he [Mordekhai] shouldn't spill the beans to the lieutenant governor and get the sheriff in hot water over this.

We had to tell our *rebe* a little of the story, but not the whole story, and our holy *rebe* got angry at us -- why were we afraid? -- because of course everything will be alright. The merit of our holy *rebe,* he should live, stood us in good stead, because last night the brother of the *misnaged* wineseller came from Galicia with merchandise and the *misnaged* took the merchandise to his cellar by himself.* His brother, who's named Reb Borukh Dubner, is a member of our fellowship and our holy *rebe* always befriends him in every way possible. That night he even spent the night by our holy *rebe* and while he was by our *rebe* a great miracle happened for us from Heaven because the sheriff found out about the thing and went with his men to the home of the *misnaged* and declared it [the merchandise] contraband. The *misnaged* gave him lots of money but all the same the sheriff wouldn't let him go until he swore to him and a promissory note was deposited that his son-in-law, the sinner Mordekhai, wouldn't tell anyone on earth about the messenger.

The main thing I forgot. With regards to the *bukh,* our holy *rebe,* he should live, said we're sure to get hold of it, so rest assured that soon we'll get hold of it. So do whatever you can and leave it to the merit of our *rebe* the *tsadek,* he should live.

From me,
....

#22

From Reb Zaynvl Verkhievker
To Reb Zelig Letitchiver

I hereby give you a thousand thanks for notifying me of the act of the sinner Mordekhai-His-Name-Should-Be-Wiped-Out Gold. I'm sending you inside here the letter what you wrote to send you and two men signed on it that the thing happened just like I wrote and they're ready to swear solemnly on a *Seyfer Toyre* about this.

I really remember that while I was speaking with the demon -- 'cause that's just what Mordekhai is -- a real demon -- I seen a *goye* walking in the woods. The two men that signed the letter were also in the woods at that time on account of they spent the whole night in the woods. I talked with the *arendar* and the two men that signed the letter also told him features of the *goye* who was walking in the woods, 'cause I was at that time greatly uplifted when I talked with the demon and I didn't see her this way with all the features like them two men, 'cause they seen her from every angle. The *arendar* recognized her and said she, I mean, the *goye,* is a real whore and that she's a young widow. I told the *arendar* he should keep an eye on the *goye* in case she gets pregnant and to let me know, and the *arendar* promised me. He's one of our holy *rebe*'s people and of course he'll do what I told him.

I sure hope everything will be alright and everyone will know that, with G-d's help, the truth is on our side, especially since the two men that signed the letter are worthy men. One of them collects funds in Pilshtin for *Ertsisroel* and the other is in charge of lighting candles for the soul of Rabbi Meyer Balanes and is very busy with *mitsves.* He's a grandson of Reb Yoyne Kaminker.*

As for the *bukh,* I'm informing you that since the to-do with the messenger, the *bukh* don't see the light of day. If the prince takes the *bukh* he don't go beyond the bookcase with it. He just looks there at what he wants and puts it back in the bookcase. But still I don't got the slightest doubt we're sure to get hold of it. Since you wrote me our holy *rebe* said we're sure to get hold of it, so of course we'll get hold of it! I'm delighted about this 'cause maybe our holy *rebe* will make our prince blind so we can get hold of the *bukh* from him. That way I'll also get revenge on that scoundrel that said he wouldn't lease me the mill 'cause I'm a *khosed*.

The main thing I forgot. I want you should give an explanation for me before our holy *rebe,* he should live, 'cause I understood from your letter that our holy *rebe* thinks about me, perish the thought!, that I want to be a *rebe.* Never did this enter mine mind. But at the time I wrote you the story of the demon Mordekhai-His-Name-Should-Be-Wiped-Out, mine mind was confused on account of I didn't sleep for four nights. I'm not guilty of nothing 'cause The Hidden and Secret Light, Our Teacher the *Rov,* Rabbi Nakhmen, THE SAINT and Holy Man OF BLESSED MEMORY, already charged us to believe even nonsense and lies....[1]

These are the words of

....

---

[1] "It is better to believe even in nonsense and lies in order to believe also in the truth than to reject everything, that is, to reject the nonsense and lies and thereby everything becomes a mockery to him and he rejects the truth too." *Kitser Likutey MohoRa"N,* Book 2, par. 167.

#23

From Reb Zelig Letitchiver
To Reb Zaynvl Verkhievker

You did very good giving you-know-which letter to them two men to sign because they're among those I know very well in our community too. Whoever sees your letter with their signature will believe without no doubt at all that the sinner Mordekhai performed a filthy act with the *goye* in the woods and to save himself he concocted everything he wrote about you with regards to the demon. Even to our *rebe* I showed your letter and he said of you, "Zaynvl Verkhievker is not one of them you'd call 'a loser' *(shlimazl),*" and he felt much better about the situation.

The sinner Mordekhai isn't home yet but when he gets home, for sure he'll be ashamed to show his face in public since all our townfolk already know about this. Because as soon as your letter arrived we wrote lots of notes about what he did in the woods and that very night we put up the notes on the walls of the synagogue and the study halls and the house of his father-in-law the *misnaged,* and more on houses of some of the community members who don't belong to us so much. But on our *kloyz*, on our *rebe*'s house and on the bathhouse we didn't put up nothing. In the morning we went to the bathhouse to hear what folks would say there and we heard everyone who came to the bath talking about the act of Mordekhai-May-His-Name-Be-Erased with the *goye*. They all said, "His name and memory should be erased, this awful sinner!"

Our holy *rebe*, he should live, WHOM NO MYSTERY BAFFLES, said *gimatrie:* * "AND HE FOUND WRITTEN THAT MORDEKHAI HAD TOLD (הִגִּיד, *HIGGID*). '*HIGGID*' plus 2 adds up to '*goye*.'* There's also an allusion in this that Mordekhai-May-His-Name-Be-Erased ate *treyf* meat on *Shabes* by the prince of Bilke at the manor, and of course it goes without saying, also meat with milk,* namely, '*ha-gid*' (הַגִּיד, the sinew),* specifically '*gid*,' since the *gid* (sinew) is nothing but meat."

"And this is the mystical concept of 'meat with milk': 'Milk' is 'IN ITS MOTHER'S MILK' -- this is the part of the mother in a man, namely, the appetites. The *treyf* meat he ate is also '*ha-gid*' (the sinew), so he blemished the covenant of the tongue [הִגִּיד, *higgid*] and the covenant of the flesh [הַגִּיד, *ha-gid*],* which are one and the same mystical concept because in both of them there's nothing but flesh."[1]

Our *rebe* the *tsadek*, he should live, also said this deed is also hinted at in the verse, "THERE WAS A JEWISH MAN IN SHUSHON THE CAPITOL AND HIS NAME WAS MORDEKHAI [SON OF YO'IR SON OF SHIM'EY SON OF KISH, A BENJAMINITE] -- that is to say, Mordekhai *was* a Jew before he became licentious. SHUSHON (שׁוּשַׁן) is a rose (שׁוֹשַׁן, *shoshon*) of red appearance, in the sense of, WHY IS YOUR CLOTHING SO RED? *HA-BIRO* (הַבִּירָה, the capitol) is an expression for speaking -- '*havoro*' (הברה, utterance), because Mordekhai Gold, of course, spoke obscenely, and the sound of his speech (קוֹל הברה, *kol havoro*) is meaningless speech (קל הברה, *kal havoro*). That is to say, Shushon is red, that is, the sins, THOUGH YOUR SINS BE LIKE CRIMSON, namely, the sin of the capitol (הַבִּירָה, *HA-BIRO*)* is the sin of speech (הברה, *havoro*)."

"*BEN YO'IR* (בֶּן יָאִיר, son of Yo'ir) is '*ben ya'ar*' (בֶּן יַעַר, someone in the

---

[1] "This is the meaning of the verse, THE CHOICEST OF THE FIRST FRUITS OF YOUR SOIL, namely: In the days of youth BRING TO THE HOUSE OF THE L-RD YOUR G-D, 'DO NOT COOK A KID *(GEDI)*' -- '*gedi*' has the same letters as '*gid*' (sinew) -- 'WITH ITS MOTHER'S MILK' -- meaning, with the part of the mother in him, namely, the appetites.... In this is also the mystical concept of 'meat with milk' as is stated above, because the sinew contains nothing but meat, and this too is because the covenant of the tongue and the covenant of the flesh are one and the same mystical concept because in both of them there is nothing but flesh." *Likutey Yekorim* 4:2.

Undoubtedly the *tsadek* said the introduction to his *toyre* in the name of the *Likutey Yekorim* but Reb Zelig abbreviated his language.

woods) because *'alef'* (א) and *'ayin'* (ע) interchange, as is known. *BEN SHIM'EY* (בן שמעי, son of Shim'ey) is a term for gathering, from the expression, *VAYESHAMA SHO'UL* (וישמע שאול, Saul gathered),* that is, that he gathers the husks that are nurtured from him. *BEN KISH* (בן קיש, son of Kish) is like, 'A stone in a pitcher goes rattle, rattle (קיש קיש, *kish, kish*).'* *ISH YEMINI* (איש ימיני, a Benjaminite) is an expression of being ready, *VAYEMAN* (וימן, AND HE READIED), meaning that he was ready for punishment." MAY HIS LIPS BE KISSED.*

What you asked of me -- to make an excuse for you to our holy *rebe* -- rest assured I'll certainly do this, but I didn't have a chance to do it since our holy *rebe,* he should live, is at the moment very busy. When I discuss this with him I'll let you know every single thing he says in every detail.

From me,

....

#24

From Reb Zaynvl Verkhievker
To Reb Zelig Letitchiver

You can imagine what great joy I had from what you wrote me -- that everyone in your community is talking about the act of the sinner Mordekhai-His-Name-Should-Be-Wiped-Out. Also everybody around here, they're all talking about it 'cause I told them the whole story in great detail, especially of the *toyre* of our holy *rebe,* he should live. We see plainly that the *Megile** refers in no uncertain terms to this sinner His-Name-Should-Be-Wiped-Out, who eats *treyf* and fornicates and uses filthy language and of course commits all the sins in the Toyre, and I'm sure when he comes to our community, for sure there'll be no recovering for him 'cause people will kill him with their tongues. For who [ever] saw by us such a terrible sinner?! He sure won't have the urge to stand in a tree and make fun of worthy people next time!

But I don't know why you keep silent towards him. If he was in our town he would be already finished. It's nothing to us, with G-d's help, to finish off such a terrible sinner. I don't ask more then that he should live in our town, and I assure you in less then half a year it'll be over with him and he'll be one of them who do the bidding of our holy *rebe.* I know you can do what you want with him too, but maybe our holy *rebe* don't want to and that's why you won't do nothing. So would you please let me know so I'll know how to act with him, 'cause I heard one of these days he's coming here 'cause he wants to do some business with our prince.

These are the words of
....

#25

From Reb Zelig Letitchiver
To Reb Zaynvl Verkhievker

I'm surprised at you you ask me why we keep silent towards the sinner Mordekhai. Don't you know that with G-d's help we got the power to pluck up such a Mordekhai by the root in a twinkling? But his time didn't come yet. First we got to uproot his father-in-law. Even though he's a simple man and never opposed us openly, all the same he's first to fall. Thus our holy *rebe* told us and we see this is the truth, because last *Shabes Koydesh* our holy *rebe* didn't say no *toyre* at the *shaleshudes,* he just rested his head* on his right hand and laid it on the table. This went on for about half an hour and after that he raised his head once suddenly and said, "Wolf, son of Rokhel, father-in-law of Mordekhai Gold, will be undone." We were overjoyed by this. We sang *zmires* and danced in a circle with tremendous *dveykes* and the dances were like those in the days of the Besht.[1]

On Sunday when I was at the *mikve* I heard something new, that Wolf Dubner's maid is pregnant. No doubt it's by his son-in-law, the sinner

---

[1] **Once on *Simkhes-toyre* the men of the holy fellowship, the disciples of the Besht, were dancing joyfully in a circle and the *Shkhine* was ablaze around them.* During their dancing the shoe of the junior member of the company tore. He was a very poor man and HE WAS VERY UPSET about his being prevented from dancing with his companions to rejoice in the festivity of this *mitsve*.**

The daughter of the Besht, the *tsadkones* Odel, was also in the house, standing at the side to see their Rejoicing at the Water-drawing. She said to that disciple, "If you promise me that I'll give birth to a baby boy this year, I'll give you good shoes right now," because she had shoes in the store. He promised her that she'd certainly have a baby boy and so it was that the rabbi, Our Teacher the *Rov*, Rabbi Borukh of the holy community of Tultchin, was born to her. *Shivkhey ha-Besht* 31:2 [Mintz, 223f.].

Mordekhai-May-His-Name-Be-Erased. I also heard the *misnaged* Wolf sent the maid away from his home and the attendant who he had for the wine left him too. Since Reb Aharon Lozer's is our wineseller, he took the attendant who left Wolf Dubner for *his* wine.

I know our Reb Aharon is a bitter enemy of Wolf Dubner and I made up my mind to go to Reb Aharon Lozer's, because through him we can check it out thoroughly. I went to Reb Aharon and we talked with the attendant, and he promised to tell us where the maid went. Everything is sure to be alright, like our holy *rebe,* he should live, said at the *shaleshudes.*

Soon I hope to let you know lots more about this affair because they're sure to suffer a mighty big defeat soon and you're sure to be delighted.

From me,

....

#26

From Reb Gershon Koritser
To Reb Gedalye Balter in Aklev

Yesterday I went to Moyshe Fishl's in our community as you directed me in your letter [#19] and I didn't find him home. The people at his house told me he was in the old *besmedresh* and I went looking for him. I found him busy with the *mishne,* "He was riding on the back of an animal,"* and struggling to explain it to some *yeshive bokher.* He reviewed it over and over again.

I waited 'til he took a break from his teaching because I know it's his custom not to interrupt in the middle of the subject on any account. First off I asked him why he was exhausting himself so to make this *bokher* understand. "He's obviously the son of a pauper and he certainly has nothing to pay you your tuition fee."

To this he answered me, "Since I was not privileged with male children, I made up my mind to study Toroh with my pauper friend's son. Our sages OF BLESSED MEMORY have already said, 'Whoever studies Toroh with his friend's son, the Toroh considers as having borne him.'"*

I asked him why His Exalted Eminence* don't go to some *tsadek* and ask him to pray for him for male children. He showed me the letter you wrote him [#13] and I told him the case of the *pidyen* our *rebe* performed for my only son and the case of what happened with Reb Shloyme of the holy community of Ramishl, which is by us common knowledge. All the while he stood bewildered like he believes and he don't believe. Since I knew he don't know me very well, I didn't want to swear before him about this because I thought, "LET ME NOT BECOME CONTEMPTIBLE in his sight so he won't believe me some other time."

It looks to me he never had a taste yet of *Kabole,* since he mostly keeps the laws of the *Shulkhen Orukh** -- praying *minkhe* before the stars come out, and in the morning praying *Vatikin.** He don't have the least inkling about the new holy books because mainly he sits in the old *besmedresh.* I found nothing but a few tractates [of Talmud] there and four *Shulkhen Orukhs* and *Duties of the Heart,** and he spends all his time with them.

A few times he asked me if it was true that he [the *rebe*] kept my son alive and he wondered how it could be in this day a mortal could stop the Angel of Death with the smoke of a pipe. He argued with me about this in particular. "Surely we shouldn't imitate Aharon the priest with the fire-pan of incense,* because it's holy and it was [only] at the command of Moyshe Rabeyne he did it, and as our predecessors said, 'If the ancients were human beings, we are like asses...,'* and how much the more so we."

That's how he spoke with me. I STARTED SHUDDERING he shouldn't lead me astray too, G-d forbid!, from the way of truth. So I changed the subject and asked him if his wife is impatient about this, and he answered me that against his will she already sent to several *rebes* for a *pidyen.*

So my advice is you should send him the holy book *Shivkhey ha-Besht* as a gift, and to me you should also send that book in Yiddish, which I'll give to his spouse. I'll make sure in the process to persuade his wife about a trip to our *rebe,* because just as he listened to his wife's advice many times, he'll listen to her now too. For now I'm informing you his name is Moyshe, son of Rivke. Perhaps our *rebe,* he should live, will have to pray for him to G-d that He incline his heart towards us. Be well.

From me,

....

#27

From Reb Zaynvl Verkhievker
To Reb Zelig Letitchiver

I'm sending you some good news* -- with G-d's help we already succeeded in discovering the whereabouts of your community's *misnaged* wineseller's maid, and we already know where she is! The *misnaged* sent her to Pilshtin to her father. Her father, of course, you know -- he was an attendant by our holy *rebe,* he should live, and he's named Leybele Khedve. He's a good and worthy man. The *misnaged,* of course, wanted the healer Yankl to make for her a remedy.* I made a special trip to Pilshtin to the healer to treat me for **hemorrhoids**. I stayed there a few days and I befriended the healer in every way possible [even] more then before and every time he was by me I gave him lots to drink.

Once, when I seen he was good and drunk, I started talking with him about the maid and I realized he knew everything. He told me that Yehude, who used to be the attendant by Wolf Dubner and after that Reb Aharon Lozer's took him, was once here and told the maid's father, I mean, Leybele Khedve, he wants to marry the maid 'cause she was pregnant by him. When I told him this must be a lie and the wineseller must've paid him for this -- that he should say that the maid was pregnant by him but she was really pregnant by Mordekhai Gold, the wineseller's son-in-law -- he told me this couldn't be 'cause Mordekhai was by the doctor of the holy community of Minkovits a number of times to cure him so he could have children, on account of he's childless, and the doctor said he can't help him right now.

But I told the healer that when he [Mordekhai] was by the doctor, he couldn't help him 'cause at that time our holy *rebe* didn't make yet for him a *pidyen,*[1] but later on he made for him, I mean, for Mordekhai, a *pidyen* so that he won't be childless, and this *must've* helped him. I also told him our holy *rebe* sent him some sick people, that he's respected by our holy *rebe,* and also that our *rebe* told me distinctly that only *he* could do something effective for hemorrhoids. The healer was very pleased by this and he said soon he'll be in your community, so be sure to befriend

---

[1] It follows that it is impossible for a doctor to heal except by means of a *pidyen* in that it is necessary to perform the *pidyen* first to temper the judgment and only then the doctor has authority to heal, as mentioned above. That is, HEALING HE WILL HEAL (ורפא ירפא, *VERAPEY YERAPEY* [the numerical value of whose letters total 578]) (with the addition of 2 [corresponding to the number of words]) is the numerical equivalent of "redemption of a life" (פדיון נפש, *pidyen nefesh* [the numerical value of whose letters total 580]) because the essence of healing is by means of a *pidyen,* precisely by virtue of the fact that it tempers the judgment.

This is what our rabbi of blessed memory said: "From here on in, authority is given to the doctor to heal -- precisely from *here on* in, that is, after the *pidyen,* only then does the doctor have authority to heal -- because before the *pidyen* the doctor does not have authority to heal...only after the *pidyen* and the tempering [of the judgment] does he have authority to heal, as mentioned above." *Likutey MohoRa"N,* Book 2, 6:4.

him, and I sure hope he'll give you testimony the *misnaged* Wolf Dubner came to him to do something so the maid would abort the fetus.

These are the words of

....

#28

From Reb Zelig Letitchiver
To Reb Zaynvl Verkhievker

Three days ago the healer from Pilshtin was here. He ate by me supper and some of our men were also by me. I gave him lots of mead to drink and he gave us written testimony that the *misnaged* Wolf Dubner sent to him to give a remedy for the maid so she would abort the fetus. He would've given testimony that Wolf Dubner himself asked this of him but we considered maybe the *misnaged* would testify he wasn't in Pilshtin, or on the day the healer was in our community the *misnaged* wasn't home or he was the whole day by some lord in our community, so it's better he [the healer] said he [the *misnaged*] sent someone to him for this. If we have to clarify this, one of our people will say he sent *him* and talked with him in secret so no one else saw them, or in another way as it appears necessary.

But we didn't do nothing yet with the testimony because it's better to wait 'til the time is ripe. No doubt this ripe time will come soon because our holy *rebe* said the *misnaged* will be undone, so of course he will be. So for G-d's sake, be sure to stay on the lookout. If you make any more good discoveries, notify *me* right away too so we'll know what to do.

From me,

....

#29

From Reb Zaynvl Verkhievker
To Reb Zelig Letitchiver

Just as our holy *rebe,* he should live, said, so it was. The lord of the village of Slabudshik bought a barrel of grape wine by the *misnaged* Wolf

Dubner and when he brang home the wine he told his *arendar,* Reb Peysekh, who used to work by Reb Aharon Lozer's and is also a relation of Reb Aharon, to pour the wine out of the barrel into bottles. When the *arendar* started to transfer the wine in the cellar, he came up from the cellar to his landlord and began shouting he's not transferring the wine 'cause there's deadly poison in this wine, G-d save us! The lord took a bit of this wine and gave it to his little dog and the dog fell down dead!

The landlord wanted to send the *arendar* with the wine straight to the authorities but the *arendar* begged the lord not to do that 'cause he would take away the wineseller's livelihood. He told the lord it'll be better for him to send the case to our holy *rebe* to give a ruling about this. At first the lord wouldn't, but when the *arendar,* Reb Peysekh, begged the landlord and pretended to have compassion for the wineseller and even promised the lord that for him, I mean, for the lord, it would certainly be better by our *rebe* then by the authorities, the landlord agreed to this.

I'm notifying you of all this quickly 'cause tomorrow or the day after, Reb Peysekh will go with the wine to our holy *rebe* 'cause the landlord is taking prior testimony from the judge in his village and from other people who were at his house at the time the incident happened so in case the wineseller don't want to accept the ruling of our holy *rebe,* he'll file a complaint against him to the authorities. So you know what to do.

These are the words of

....

#30

From Reb Zelig Letitchiver
To Reb Zaynvl Verkhievker

I'm hereby notifying you that yesterday the *arendar,* Reb Peysekh, came to our holy *rebe* with the barrel of grape wine sealed with the seal of the lord of Slabudshik. When the *misnaged,* Wolf Dubner, found out about this matter, at first he started crying out that the *arendar,* Peysekh, must've thrown the deadly poison into the barrel of wine. But afterward he reflected that if the case comes before the authorities it'll be worse for him because a bad rumor will spread about him that he sells poisoned wine and the noblemen won't want to buy from him no more wine. Also with the authorities he'll have large expenses for bribes and such. Right away he sent a special messenger to his brother, Reb Borukh, he should come to him to help him by our holy *rebe* because his brother's an honored man and our holy *rebe,* he should live, loves him dearly.

But in the meantime the police chief found out about the matter. Even though we kept the thing a big secret, he found out about it all the same. He sent for the *arendar,* Reb Peysekh, and questioned him, and since he was afraid to lie since his landlord would say the opposite, he had to tell the story like it was. But the *misnaged* was lucky that before the case was over, his brother Reb Borukh came and begged our holy *rebe,* he should live, to do his brother the *misnaged* a good turn. He promised that his brother would obey our holy *rebe* every which way if only he would save him from the hands of the police chief and keep the thing secret. Our holy *rebe* sent for the police chief's agent and did all in his power to keep the matter quiet. He doled out lots of money to the police chief and his secretary and such and the police chief promised that if he'll smooth things out with the landlord of Slabudshik, then he'll tear up the deposition.

In the meantime I notified Leybele Khedve, the father of the maid in Pilshtin, he too should come to our *rebe* with the testimony of the healer that I delivered to him. He asked our holy *rebe* to force the *misnaged* to compensate him for anguish, healing, loss of time and indignity* for his daughter, since now the time is ripe. Our *rebe,* he should live, sent for Reb Borukh, the *misnaged*'s brother, and said that first of all he has to compromise with his Leybele. Reb Borukh compromised with him and the *misnaged,* of course, gave him lots of money. For the wine, our *rebe,* he should live, ruled that the *misnaged* should lend the landlord of Slabudshik four hundred czerwone zlotys for three years interest-free and also give him a cask of the choicest grape wine as a gift. And to Reb Peysekh, that landlord's *arendar,* he must give for his trouble thirty czerwone zlotys.

The *misnaged* came to our *rebe* and pleaded with him, and gave our holy *rebe* a gift -- a cask of kosher grape wine worth fifty czerwone zlotys. I'm sure he won't soon be opposing our holy *rebe,* and the rest of the *misnagdim* too will see the great power of our holy *rebe,* he should live, and of our faction in general. They'll certainly be afraid to open their mouth against us and, G-d willing, we'll be privileged to take revenge against them few people who still hate us in their heart.

From me,

....

#31

From Reb Zaynvl Verkhievker
To Reb Zelig Letitchiver

You really revived me with your letter [#30] 'cause I had a few days of awful aggravation, since Mordekhai Gold bought from our prince the *arende* of our community and the [nearby] villages. Before he bought the *arende,* our prince had made a franchise.* He sold his vodka to the taverns and gave the tavernkeepers for this some small per cent. When the tavernkeepers of our community seen they can't make a living, they asked that sinner Mordekhai to buy the *arende* since he's a big shot by the prince 'cause he sits by him and studies his *treyf* trash.* He bought the *arende* along with a certain amount of vodka from the prince and he set a price for the vodka with the tavernkeepers for a whole year.

This was very good for them 'cause vodka has gotten expensive nowadays, but he don't take from them more then the price he set with them when he bought the *arende.* On account of this he became a bigshot by them. But to *me* this sinner wouldn't sell vodka. He said that mine brother, who lives in the village of Biltchik, bought by him vodka on credit and when he bought the vodka I vouched for him and afterward he squirreled away four hundred zlotys for himself. I don't remember, maybe I did give my word, but what's one thing got to do with another? I'm a member, thank G-d, just like the other members of our community, and I can be a tavernkeeper like the other tavernkeepers too, so why won't this sinner sell me vodka to [help me] make some money?

On account of this I was very aggravated but when I got your letter I was so pleased that I forgot I was aggravated, especially since I thought, "If his father-in-law, Wolf Dubner, bit the dust, without a doubt this sinner too will bite the dust." But please, if he *does* get overthrown, our holy *rebe* shouldn't do for him nothing -- just bury him ten cubits deep!

These are the words of
....

#32

From Reb Zaynvl Verkhievker
To Reb Zelig Letitchiver

Reb Borukh, brother of the *misnaged* Wolf Dubner, came through our community and I asked him to put in for me a good word with Mordekhai Gold to give me vodka on credit. Reb Borukh asked him and he consented and gave me on credit three hundred zlotys' worth of vodka. I paid him that amount on time and he gave me more vodka.

So I'm hereby sending our holy *rebe,* he should live, every *Shabes* two gallons of vodka. What do I care if later on the sinner Mordekhai Gold will be shortchanged for a few gallons of vodka? What'll he do to me? For a few gallons of vodka he won't take mine house! And in the meantime he's sure to get overthrown, so drink to mine health. When I got time I'll come to our holy *rebe* for *Shabes* and I'll bring with me also plenty of vodka and we'll drink like kings. For now, I don't got no worries 'cause I'm a successful tavernkeeper and I make a good living.

These are the words of
....

#33

From Reb Zelig Letitchiver
To Reb Zaynvl Verkhievker

I'm sending you a special messenger because the matter is very urgent. The *arendar* that lived in the village of Bilke near Pilshtin was here and he told me your prince wrote a letter to his prince to question the *goye* that was in the woods at the time you was there keeping *Shabes,* and to do all he could to find out what man she got pregnant from at that time. Since the prince of Bilke kept the matter a big secret, the *arendar* couldn't do nothing about this because they took the *goye* suddenly for questioning. She said there she got pregnant from two men that were in the woods. As evidence she had stole from one a letter [#126] that was in his pocket and she handed over to the landlord the letter she stole.

The *arendar* himself tried every trick to get hold of the letter or at least see it but the landlord wouldn't even show it to him. He said he didn't trust him. Only when Mordekhai Gold will come to him, then he'll give *him* the letter to translate it for him into Polish so as to know who were the men that fornicated with the *goye* in the woods and to send them to Siberia! So you can see that this is no trifle because the *arendar* came to me literally scared to death and told me that as soon as he found out about the matter and saw that his landlord wouldn't even trust him to show him the letter, he hurried over here because he's terrified about this, that nothing bad should happen to him neither, G-d forbid! He asked me to speak with our holy *rebe* on his behalf and he also gave as much as he could afford for a *pidyen*.

So for G-d's sake, do all you can to get hold of some of the sinner Mordekhai's handwriting and send it to me. I'll show the writing to Reb Yosl Fradel's the scribe so he'll write a letter in Mordekhai's handwriting. I hope that by the merit of our holy *rebe,* he should live, G-d will do for us a miracle so the *arendar* can steal the letter the *goye* handed over and put Mordekhai's letter in its place and when the case comes before the commission they'll see Mordekhai was the only fornicator, as becomes him, and not only will we rescue the two men from Pilshtin but we'll also take our revenge against the sinner Mordekhai. For G-d's sake, don't be lazy about this, because who knows what tomorrow will bring?!

From me,

....

#34

From Reb Gedalye Balter in Aklev
To Reb Gershon Koritser in Nigrad

A hearty thank you, my brother, for your sound advice to send the simpleton Moyshe and his wife the book *Shivkhey ha-Besht.* YOU HAVE PERCEIVED WELL, but first we also need to understand whether he's a vessel prepared to receive it. Perhaps his soul isn't rid of his father's filth* or his teacher's *toyre.** It may be that when he sees it he'll make fun of it and not only will we not be able to get hold of him but he might, G-d forbid!, make mischief on account of it, and by virtue of the fact that he's considered in his town something of a Talmudist, he might cause others to stumble too because they'll believe him when he says that he found something unseemly in it.

Even though I knew him, that in his youth he was a worthy and honest man, all the same I saw in the one letter he wrote me that a spirit of *apikorses* flickered in him, G-d save us! Because what he wrote me was that his wife sent for a *pidyen* to some *rebes* "even though I know that there is nothing of substance in them." So it seems to me that you should take this copy of *Shivkhey ha-Besht* and lend him one pamphlet this week and then see how things go and keep me up to date. A word to the wise....

What a great celebration there was last night* by our *rebe* the *tsadek,* he should live! A few times he said, "OPEN FOR ME THE GATES OF RIGHTEOUSNESS,

I WILL ENTER INTO THEM...,"* and the *Rov*, Rabbi Yoysef, danced before him. IT CAME TO PASS AT MIDNIGHT* that our *rebe* stood up suddenly, **his face aflame like torches**, and washed his hands from the jug of water in front of him and said with dread and fear, "Blessed be the Omnipresent, who has drawn me near to His service, praised be He, blessed be He."* He also danced a little. Then he ordered those around him to be silent and he said before us words of Toyre, crying and shouting, though not a word was heard from him until he concluded a second time, "Blessed be the Omnipresent, who has drawn me near to His service...." Then he recovered and lay down on the bed to recuperate a bit, and he ordered that everyone in the group be given two shots of vodka.

As for me, the moment I saw that that vodka from the tavernkeepers wasn't good, I hurried home to bring some of the vodka you sent me. When I brought it to our *rebe*'s house, the *Rov*, Rabbi Shloyme, and the elder, Reb Moyshe, tasted it and recommended it to our *rebe*. He asked me to tell him the truth how I came to have it, and I had to let him know the truth. Truly, our *rebe*, may he live, was very surprised -- why didn't you send *him* vodka too? -- and I was terrified our *rebe*, G-d forbid!, shouldn't become angry and on account of this utter something not good about you. I know already that every word he utters when he's angry is like an angry sword[1] and I immediately began making excuses for you -- that you must not've had the best vodka and when you'll have it, of course you'll send him -- so make sure to send our *rebe* the *tsadek*, may he live, the finest vodka you can.

In the meantime, here's money for you for two casks of vodka, which you should send me not later than next Sunday because that's market day by us. Thank G-d there was no harm done, perish the thought!, with the vodka you sent me last week, because no one from the *arende* saw it.* Be well.

From me,

....

---

[1] It is not just the *tsadek* of Aklav who is like this, but all the real *tsadikim*. I remember when the *tsadek* known as The *Tseyrey* came to the holy community of Dishpol after the passing away of the *tsadek* Rabbi Koppel* of blessed memory. At the first *shaleshudes* we spent with him he spoke to us as follows: "I'm informing you that I'm not like the great saintly *Rov* who has passed away. He was a very great Light. He had the power to curse someone and then, when that person rectified what he had spoiled, he could turn the curse into a blessing because he had power to do whatever he wanted. But not I. If I should curse someone, I can no longer renounce the curse. So I'm informing you of this so that you won't be surprised later on when you see that I don't have the same power as the saintly *Rov* who has passed away, because he was a very great Light."

#35

From Reb Zaynvl Verkhievker To Reb Zelig Letitchiver

When I read your letter [#33], I BEGAN TO TREMBLE 'cause I seen this is literally a matter of life and death, especially since I asked around among people who come to our prince and they said the prince is very angry about this affair 'cause the sinner Mordekhai got hold of one of them notes you fastened to the walls of some houses. He translated it into German and showed it to the prince and told him you done all this and he knows that two men from our group spent that night in the woods and must've fornicated with the *goye.* That scoundrel, our prince, got furious at us and he said, I mean, our prince, he wouldn't give a hoot about his whole fortune if he could solve the case, and right off he sent a messenger to the village of Bilke to the prince there to do whatever he done.

All the noblemen tremble before our prince since it's rumored soon he'll be appointed lieutenant governor, 'cause the current lieutenant governor will be governor. A few days ago our prince got a letter from Peterburg from a friend of his that the czar already signed his lieutenant governorship. I go around on account of this like a real *meshuge,* 'cause you don't know what a villain he is. If he gets -- G-d forbid!, Don't tempt the devil!* -- into the government, then all the noblemen who were up 'til now our friends will become our enemies. 'Cause he's our sworn enemy, and like I heard in confidence, he said he'll write the authorities to take the *goye* there for questioning to investigate the matter thoroughly. So it seems to me [we got] to reveal the whole affair to our holy *rebe* and ask him to perform some noteworthy act for the two men from Pilshtin. 'Cause you *know* that they're certainly worthy men. Even if they *did* commit this act in the woods, what of it? Should they really be condemned for such a trivial act?* At least they're worthy men and very hard workers and, G-d forbid!, if you don't make some special effort at once in this affair, then they're sure to lose their living, G-d forbid! And me and the *arendar* of the village of Bulke will be also in terrible danger.

In mine opinion, we got to make sure first of all with the healer from Pilshtin to give the *goye* some remedy she should abort the fetus. First of all let there be no fetus, 'cause if there'll be a fetus it'll be worse 'cause they'll want the men to pay for food, first of all, for the *goye* and the child, and it'll be also a big humiliation for *us.*

So write me your opinion about this, and if you agree to it I'll go mineself to Pilshtin. Just send me money for expenses 'cause in a few days it'll be time to pay the sinner Mordekhai-His-Name-Should-Be-Wiped-Out for the vodka, plus I'm short the cash for the vodka I sent our holy *rebe.*

Some other time I wouldn't be so scared but right now I'm terrified to start with this sinner 'cause he must be very angry on me. This sinner will be overjoyed if I don't pay him, so he could complain against me to the prince and that crook would give the order to take all I got. I'll see about borrowing me some cash by pawning stuff to pay the sinner Mordekhai what I owe him, and when I give him the money I'll make special sure to get from him a receipt in his handwriting, and I'll send you the receipt so you'll see the handwriting of that sinner. Even though in mine opinion you shouldn't do this, since in any case our prince is very angry at Reb Yosl Fradel's 'cause he [the prince] said that *he* [Yosl Fradel's] must've written the letter for the *bukh* in the name of the lieutenant governor, all the same I'll send you Mordekhai's handwriting, 'cause if you do do this it'll obviously be on the advice of our holy *rebe,* he should live, so of course it'll be okay.

These are the words of
....

#36

From Reb Zelig Letitchiver
To Reb Zaynvl Verkhievker

I got your letter [#35]. What you write me -- to reveal the matter to our *rebe,* he should live -- I didn't know what to do. We consulted around here, and to a man everybody said to still keep the matter secret from our holy *rebe.*

But I don't know what to do with regards to the affair itself, because it's no trifle this business. Our hope [pinned] on the arendar of Bilke is kaput, because I had a report, and you must've known about this too, that the lord of the village of Bilke even had the arendar arrested because the goye said at the questioning it was him, that is, the arendar, who put her up to speaking against the sinner Mordekhai Gold in the first place, since he's very wealthy and she'd get for this lots of money from him. On account of this the prince of Bilke got very angry and had the arendar arrested and took everything he owned for the lease payment.

There was also more bad luck that among his things they took to the manor they found a receipt the *arendar* prepared for the lease payment, which Reb Yosl Fradel's wrote for him. Since on the date written on the receipt, as well as for eight days before that date and eight days after that date, the landlord wasn't home because he was by another lord a few parasangs from his home, he had proof this receipt is counterfeit.

So let's not take any further action based on Mordekhai's handwriting, even though I had a report that the landlord of Bilke is embarrassed to talk about this receipt because he's afraid they'll say he took the rent money from the *arendar* and denies he made the payment so he said the receipt is forged -- so he'll keep this whole matter of the receipt secret.

Even so we agreed not to do nothing else through Reb Yosl Fradel's, and there's nothing else we got to do right now but speak with the healer of the holy community of Pilshtin to make sure the *goye* won't have the child. Because first of all let there be no child, and afterwards we'll figure out what to do, and the merit of our holy *rebe* will help us.

For the expenses to Pilshtin take a loan from Yankl Rudniker. Talk to him in the name of our *rebe* and he's sure to give it to you. But for G-d's sake, do everything quick.

From me,

....

#37

From Reb Zaynvl Verkhievker
To Reb Zelig Letitchiver

I'm on mine way at once for Pilshtin to the healer, Yankl, 'cause I heard our prince wrote the Bilke prince he should make sure to do what he could so his *arendar* would confess who asked him to put the *goye* up to saying Mordekhai fornicated with her. He promised him if he'll confess he'll forgive him everything, so I'm afraid if they'll stand the *goye* face-to-face with the *arendar* and she'll tell him face-to-face he put her up to speaking against Mordekhai, he'll be forced to confess.

So I'm going there and I'll see the healer gives her something so she'll abort, and on account of she'll abort she'll be of course sick, and she won't be able so soon to say to the *arendar* face-to-face he put her up to it, and in the meantime by the merit of our holy *rebe* we'll get some help from somewhere else. Since I got to get going I made it brief.

These are the words of

....

#38

From Reb Zelig Letitchive:
To Reb Zaynvl Verkhievker

Since THE L-RD CAUSED the bearer of this letter, who's going to your community, TO HAPPEN MY WAY, I'm writing you you should write me through him what you did in Pilshtin and whether you concluded everything there okay. The bearer of this letter is one of our holy *rebe*'s people and you can write through him whatever you want, because we're terrified around here even though the authorities don't know yet about the matter. All the same, we're afraid the matter shouldn't become a federal case, especially since it's also rumored around here the prince of your community became lieutenant governor.

When our *rebe* heard about this, he said, "The prince of the holy community of Kripen will be lieutenant governor?!" Although he said this with an expression of surprise -- and it follows, of course, that he don't *got* to be lieutenant governor[1] -- even so we're afraid because maybe our holy *rebe* intended something else by this astonishment. So we want to hear whether you did your part in Pilshtin, and what the healer said about this affair.

These are the words of

....

[1] "For the *tsadek* who brings abundance discusses with human beings their need and intends with his words to ordain for them enough for their need by means of his speech." *No'am Elimelekh* 69:4.

"Through faith in *khakhomim*, by believing that all their words and deeds are not simple and there are mystical meanings in them, by this the judgments are tempered." *Kitser Likutey MohoRa"N* 29:254.

#39

From Reb Zaynvl Verkhievker
To Reb Zelig Letitchiver

I was overjoyed when I got hold of your letter [#38] through the bearer of this letter and I seen from it that our holy *rebe* said with surprise that our prince will be lieutenant governor. You're in doubt about this astonishment, but I'm not the least bit in doubt that our *rebe* meant by this astonishment he *won't* be lieutenant governor. Even though our holy *rebe,* he should live, must've intended by this astonishment lots and lots of mystical meanings that I can't imagine or understand, all the same, in mine opinion this must've been one of the meanings too, 'cause you don't know what a villain and crook this prince is.

I was in Pilshtin and I done there all what needed doing. The *goye* got very ill and since the healer of Pilshtin is healer also for the landlord of Bilke, he sent for him, I mean, the landlord sent for the healer. The healer said the *goye* needs to stay home and not drink nothing, but remedies he's afraid to give her since she wouldn't take care of herself as would be necessary and it'll be worse for her. I had a report through the wife of the *arendar* of Bilke that the *goye* is every day sicker and certainly won't be able to confront the *arendar.*

Soon I'll let you know what's happening with her, 'cause I told the wife of the *arendar,* when the *goye* wants vodka, to give her as much as she wants for free. So even the thing that the healer gave, the *arendar*'s wife gave the *goye* in a flask of vodka, which she [the *goye*] drank by her. I told the *arendar*'s wife I'll give her back as much vodka as she'll give the *goye* 'cause the healer said that for the *goye,* right now vodka is a real death potion.

These are the words of

....

#40

From Reb Zelig Letitchiver
To Reb Zaynvl Verkhievker

What can I tell you? You brought us back to life with your letter [#39], because we were almost like the walking dead around here. A few days ago a councilman's agent told us he heard by his gentile they're talking about this business in the village of Bilke. Even though they said the matter didn't reach the authorities yet, even so we're afraid the matter shouldn't become, G-d forbid!, a federal case, because your prince must be exaggerating this affair and you can bet he must've written about this matter to government officials. We can't count on the *arendar* because he's a very coarse man and when they'll take him for questioning face-to-face with the *goye,* and she'll, of course, tell the whole story, he'll tell everything too.

So it must've been a great miracle the *goye* got sick and from this we see plainly our holy *rebe,* he should live, must know of this and must've taken action concerning this, particularly since on *Shabes Koydesh* we heard him say important judgments are pending[1] and all-out efforts must be made to annul them. Thank G-d, we see it's a trifle for him to do whatever he wants.

Because after he arranged the compromise between the landlord of the village of Slabidshik and Wolf Dubner, that landlord came to our *rebe,* he should live, and stood before him like a slave before his master,* and wouldn't sit down until our *rebe* directed him several times to be seated. He told our *rebe* that by his relative, the prince of Kripen, there's a *bukh* in which is written nonsense about the *tsadikim* and about all our people in general, and his relative, that is, the prince of Kripen, ridicules and makes fun of the *tsadikim* and of the group, but he [the landlord] doesn't pay no attention to him [the prince] because he [the landlord] likes everyone who holds to his faith, whether *goy,** Ishmaelite,* Jew or Tartar. Our holy *rebe,* he should live, responded to him sweetly about this. My landlord's relative is still young. The time will come when he'll see who to side with and who to laugh at.

The lord, that is, the lord of Slabudshik, paid our holy *rebe* for a *pidyen* and told our holy *rebe* he was very pleased he had the privilege to see him and talk with him and when he'll speak with the prince of Kripen he'll tell him some big liar wrote his *bukh,* and he went away from our holy *rebe* in high spirits.

Surely if our holy *rebe,* he should live, wishes, he'll turn your prince too into our friend, because when the prince of Slabudshik will tell your prince about our *rebe,* he should live, he's sure to become a changed man. So be sure to keep an eye out when the prince of Slabudshik comes to your prince. In case he forgets to discuss this with your prince, then tell his *arendar,* Peysekh, he should remind his landlord about this, since we know for certain the prince of Slabudshik will do anything for our holy *rebe,* because two days ago the *arendar,* Peysekh, bought from a merchant three pounds of tobacco and brought it to his prince and said our holy *rebe* sent the prince this tobacco and that this tobacco was brought as a gift for our holy *rebe* from The Holy Land.

---

[1] "For the *tsadikim* see beforehand when judgments are pending." See in *Keser Shem Tov,* fol. 18, and in *Igeres ha-Koydesh* in the holy book *No'am Elimelekh* 112[:4] and in all the holy books you will find this and comparable statements. There is no need of proof.

The tobacco was really very good. We saw it because Peysekh also brought our holy *rebe* three pounds of this very same tobacco and it was really wonderful stuff. The prince of Slabudshik was very pleased by this gift, and the *arendar*, Peysekh, told his prince he should at least do this for our holy *rebe* -- read the *bukh* that the prince of Kripen has and see who's the author and where does he live and all what's written in the *bukh*. The prince of Slabudshik promised the *arendar*, Peysekh, to do this, and said he'll be soon in Kripen to tell your prince *mazl tov* on his lieutenant governorship.

So for G-d's sake, don't forget what I wrote you.

From me,
....

#41

From Reb Zaynvl Verkhievker
To Reb Zelig Letitchiver

I'm sending you special one of our men, 'cause the matter is very urgent. All the efforts we made here with the *goye* didn't accomplish nothing. The healer said he'd have to start all over at once. By now it's already old and it won't help no more. The *goye* started getting better and the situation's very bad 'cause soon when the *goye* will be all better, our prince wants to send her to the authorities. But now, by the merit of our holy *rebe*, he should live, just as I wrote you that by his merit we'll have help from another quarter, there happened for us a great miracle the likes of which was never heard.

The *arendar*'s wife told me she spoke with the *goye*'s father when he was drunk and he told her he was thinking of running away from here to Galicia. The *arendarke* began talking with him whether he'll take also his daughter there. He said he's afraid to take her 'cause she'll slow him down on the way since he has to run away on foot on account of he has no horses. The *arendarke* says, "And if a wagon and a few zlotys for expenses were given to you, would you take her?" And the gentile, the *goye*'s father, says, "If they'll give me a wagon and eight zlotys, I'll take also my daughter to Galicia."

Today that gentile came to the *arendar*'s wife and told her what'll be -- "Give me a wagon and eight zlotys." And he wasn't drunk when he said it. The *arendarke* says to him, "I don't know, I'll see. I'll ask someone and

I'll get back to you." The gentile says, "Good, I'll wait. If you'll give me a wagon and eight zlotys, I'll certainly take my daughter to Galicia."

So we made up our minds to send the *goye* to Galicia, but we're afraid to hire a wagon so the matter shouldn't be revealed later on by the driver. So now I'm sending you the bearer of this letter to send us the carriage of our holy *rebe,* he should live, with his coachman, 'cause only on the carriage of our holy *rebe* can we rely in a matter like this. And in case you don't want our holy *rebe* should know about this matter 'cause maybe you still didn't tell him this story, tell him you'll send the wagon with Reb Leybush Shifre's to bring the *Ertsisroel* and the Rabbi Meyer Balanes money from our community and from the nearby communities, and we'll send on the wagon the gentile and the *goye* to Galicia.

By the help and merit of our holy *rebe,* we'll bring everything to an end once and for all, but for cryin' out loud do everything quick, 'cause when the *goye* will be all better there won't be time no more to do this on account of the prince will send her to the authorities.

These are the words of

....

#42

From Reb Zelig Letitchiver
To Reb Zaynvl Verkhievker

Even though it was very hard work urging our holy *rebe,* he should live, to give permission Reb Leyb Shifre's should take his carriage with his coachman to travel to your community and to the nearby communities for *Ertsisroel* and Rabbi Meyer Balanes money, nevertheless I was very happy with your plan because it's a very wonderful plan, since we'll get rid of the *goye* once and for all.

But for G-d's sake, make sure to do everything lickety-split and make sure to send them to the village of Kavrifke near the border, because the local *arendar,* Reb Moyshe Hamernik, is very submissive to our holy *rebe* and he's respected by those stationed at the border there. He'll do, of course, everything for our benefit, and I got confidence you'll, of course, do everything in the best way possible. For G-d's sake, don't hold on to the wagon long because our holy *rebe* ordered it should be back by next *Shabes Koydesh.* Because of the urgency I was brief.

From me,

....

#43

From Reb Gershon Koritser in Nigrad
To Reb Gedalye Balter in Aklev

I did like you ordered me. I took one pamphlet of the book *Shivkhey ha-Besht* you sent me and put it in a book in the old *besmedresh.* On Monday when I came to that *besmedresh,* I found the pamphlet on the reading stand by Moyshe Fishl's and in it, next to several subjects, were small ink notations on the paper. I understood that this Moyshe Fishl's had obviously studied it but I didn't know what these notes were -- whether to interpret them as praise or criticism.

In the meantime, I played dumb and asked him, "What's that in your hand?" He said, "This pamphlet is called *Shivkhey ha-Besht.* I found it in a book in the *besmedresh* but I don't know what it is or who its author is or what this word 'Besht' means -- whether it's the name of a person or an angel or an acronym. Sometimes it seems he's a human being, eating and drinking and sleeping with his wife in one bed like a peasant,[1] and I marked those places. And at other times it seems to me he's an angel, because angels and *meshiekh* and dead people spoke with him. My friend Reb Gedalye of Aklev already wrote me that whoever recites it, his prayer doesn't go unanswered -- like with Psalms. A few times I wanted to write him to send me that book but no traveler happened my way."

I answered him at once that through me he can accomplish whatever he wishes and I'll certainly be his faithful servant in this, but I didn't explain to him anything about that holy book. So be sure to write me a friendly letter and write in it that you're sending this book to the both of us. That way I'll be able to learn with him out of the book -- perhaps I'll be able to find out what he really thinks* -- and I'll write you everything clearly. For this undertaking please tell our *rebe* the *tsadek,* he should live, that he should pray for me this Moyshe shouldn't make me stray from the way of truth, and G-d should help us bring him in and draw him close under the wings of our *rebe,* our Light, he should live, because someone as eager and as ignorant of all the books by the *tsadikim* of our days as he is, I never seen.

And please, please inform our *rebe,* our Light, he should live, that the fool Shmuel of Saklufke is coming to test him. If our *rebe* knows what the prince answered him [Shmuel] about the petition, he'll give our *rebe,* he should live, what he promised him, but if not he won't give it to him. So be advised that I went to his prince myself and I bought from him a

---

[1] *Shivkhey ha-Besht* 6:2 [Mintz, 45] and more in other places.

hundred bushels of barley just so I might learn what the landlord answered him. So it happened that the landlord told me he promised to give him a concession on what he owes and for the future he'll even give him a gift over and above the contract.

So make sure the moment he comes in the door our *rebe* reproaches and humiliates him that he came to test him,[2] so he won't suspect our *rebe,* he should live, from now on. Also, when the self-taught Moyshe Fishl's hears our *rebe* knows secret things, his heart will faint, and the aforesaid Shmuel is sure to believe because he's Moyshe's mother-in-law's brother and very close with him. There's nothing more [to say].*

From me,

....

---

[2] "Whoever tests the *tsadek* is like one who tests the Holy One, blessed be He." *Mides* 54:127.

#44
From Reb Zaynvl Verkhievker
To Reb Zelig Letitchiver

Since I knew you'd want very much to know what happened with the wagon, I'm hereby informing you that as soon as Reb Leybush Shifre's got here towards evening, I took the *goye* and had her dressed at night by the *arendarke* of Bilke in Jewish-style clothes, and she sat down with one of our Faithful in the wagon. The *goye*'s father sat on the coach-box like a coachman and they traveled like husband and wife with a gentile wagon driver. Dovid, the coachman of our holy *rebe,* he should live, also went along as an attendant, 'cause I thought maybe they'll have, G-d forbid!, some mishap on the way, and he's very brave and can rescue them.

I told the man that went with them -- I mean, that man who sat with the *goye* in the wagon -- they should go to the village of Kavrifke like you wrote, and tell the local *arendar* in your name to help him they should leave him at the border, but all the same I told him not to reveal the story to the *arendar* there 'cause what do we need alot of people knowing about this business for? I told him he should say his wife -- I mean, the *goye* who the *arendar thinks* is his wife -- was struck dumb all of a sudden ('cause in any case I ordered the *goye* should act like she's dumb so no one will recognize she's a *goye*)* and he was by our holy *rebe,* he should live, to do something for her, and since our holy *rebe* is his relation and loves him dearly, he made for her a *pidyen* and gave him his carriage and his coachman as an attendant and a Canaanite slave* for a coachman and told him to go to Lvov* to the doctor, on account of our holy *rebe* looked* and said only the doctor in Lvov can help her.

Since the *arendar* of Kavrifke is very submissive to our *rebe* like you wrote me, when he'll see the carriage and our holy *rebe*'s coachman, he'll be scared out of his wits and it goes without saying, of course, he'll do everything possible to leave them at the border on foot, 'cause I told them they should go on foot to the border and say our holy *rebe* didn't give them the carriage except as far as the border. I done this 'cause you wrote me not to keep the carriage long.

The eight zlotys for the gentile, the *goye*'s father, I got from Reb Leybush Shifre's. I gave them to the *arendar*'s wife to give the gentile and I hope, by the merit of our holy *rebe,* he should live, soon he'll return the wagon and everything will be alright.

Believe me, from this event I seen what is faith in *khakhomim.* I, who wasn't yet privileged to have perfect faith, but still on account of the tiny bit of faith I do got, had strength to do a thing like this, and had confidence that of course I got nothing to fear 'cause of course I'll succeed[1] -- but someone else who isn't among our Faithful and don't got faith in the *tsadikim* would've surely been afraid to do things like this. But I know for certain the merit of our holy *rebe* will stand me in good stead. Especially since I'm sending them with the carriage of our holy *rebe* I wasn't the least bit afraid and I knew for certain everything will be fine, and I done this very happily even though I know it's really a matter of life and death. And even now that I done it and the carriage still didn't come back, still I'm not the least afraid, so I see now what is faith in *khakhomim.* Please, at the right time, mention me to our holy *rebe,* he should live, to help me to have more and more faith in *khakhomim.*

These are the words of

....

---

[1] "Through faith in *khakhomim* comes success." *Mides* 23:19.

#45

From Reb Zelig Letitchiver
To Reb Zaynvl Verkhievker

You made me feel a little better by your letter [#44] you wrote me informing me that you sent the *goye* and her father to Galicia. I was especially pleased by the plan you came up with to dress her in Jewish-style clothes and I sure hope they reach the right place without no hassles, because from what I hear these days it's very easy at the borders and the merit of our holy *rebe,* he should live, is sure to help us so everything will be just fine.

Rest assured I'll certainly mention you to our holy *rebe,* he should live, when the time is ripe, but up 'til now the time wasn't ripe since our *rebe* didn't speak yet of this affair, even though I don't got the slightest doubt our holy *rebe* must know the whole story because if he didn't know he certainly wouldn't've given his carriage. Especially since he once said in no uncertain terms, "If my driver Dovid wasn't home, I wouldn't have gave them my carriage because another coachman couldn't drive my horses like he does." And of course, by what he said -- that another driver couldn't drive the horses like he does -- he was referring to the *goye*'s father, who sits on the coach-box like a coachman and drives the horses, like you wrote, and this was what he meant by "another driver." So there's no doubt our *rebe* must know the whole business.

Especially since he gave up his carriage just when he really needed it, because this week was *Legboymer** and it was always his custom to go on *Legboymer* to the countryside to shoot a bow,* which is called "archery." He told us once, in his boundless humility, that he does this because a Jewish custom is *toyre,** but we know, of course, that he must really be shooting with the bow against the devil and there isn't a shred of doubt that every year he kills him.

This *Legboymer,* too, he wanted to go to the countryside. Since our holy *rebe*'s carriage wasn't home, we sent to Mendele Odele's to lend his wagon for our holy *rebe,* he should live, and even though we don't consider him one of our Faithful, still we thought he wouldn't defy us because in any case there wasn't 'til now no one opposing us openly -- but still he was defiant and wouldn't lend his wagon. He said he couldn't lend it since his horses are transporting provisions for soldiers. From Heaven it happened at that moment Reb Moyshe Slafkvitser came to our holy *rebe* on *Legboymer* and gave our *rebe,* he should live, his wagon.

We transported our *rebe* with exceeding honor to the countryside. In front of the carriage went the musician Reb Yehude with the fiddle, and his brother Reb Yoysef went with him, beating the drum and cymbals. We went -- a very big crowd around the carriage and following the carriage -- singing very lovely melodies, with our holy *rebe* sitting in the carriage with Reb Moyshe Slafkvitser and a few more of his young men. Whoever didn't saw *this* celebration *never* saw celebration.*

We came to the countryside and our holy *rebe* gave the order to stop. We stopped and took him from the carriage. He took the bow to shoot and he shot, and the arrow landed far away. Everybody wanted to wave the arrow but I couldn't run after the arrow because I wanted to look at our *rebe*'s face when the arrow was shot, and what he'll do with the bow without an arrow.

I saw that before he shot the arrow he waved his hand upward and when the arrow was shot he put both hands down. At first he held the bow in his left hand and the arrow in his right hand, but when the arrow was shot he took the bow in his right hand. By this, too, he must've intended profound and lofty meanings because ordinary people think it should be the other way around, as people say, "Ever let the left hand drive away and the right hand draw close,"[1] but he shot -- that is, drove away -- the arrow with the right hand. So I thought, "The mystical meaning in this must be VERY DEEP -- WHO CAN DISCOVER IT?" I had great pleasure from this, the kind of pleasure those who brought the arrow to our holy *rebe,* he should live, had.

I'm also informing you that today our holy *rebe* changed his custom, because he never used to shoot the bow but once. You know that, with G-d's help, for many years I had the great privilege to be around our holy *rebe* and he never shot the bow more than once. But today, when they gave him back the arrow, he turned in the direction where your community lies and shot the arrow in that direction. It seemed to me, in my humble opinion, that he intended by this to kill the demon in your community,[2] and a word to the wise.... So I'm informing you all this so you'll enjoy it because everything is sure to be alright.

Furthermore, I'm informing you we had splendid revenge against Mendele Odele's because on the very night after *Legboymer,* the horses were stolen from him, namely, them horses he wouldn't lend our holy *rebe.* I got no doubt his wagon too will soon be smashed or burned and

---

[1] I know that some fools will make fun of this and say that Reb Zelig is an ignoramus and did not know that this expression is in the *Gemore,* as I heard about one scoffer [who] said that it's in *Sanhedrin* where it says, "Ever let the left hand push away and the right hand draw close, and let it not..." and Reb Zelig didn't know this and he wrote, "As people say." But our holy *rebe,* Our Teacher, Rabbi Nakhmen, has already said in *Seyfer ha-Mides* 52:81, "It is possible that a man can be a great *tsadek* even though he has not learned much." Also in the holy book *Keser Shem Tov,* fol. 22, you will find, "The soul declared to the Rabbi (the Besht), may he be remembered for life in the world-to-come, that the reason he was privileged to have revealed to him supernal matters was not because he had studied many Talmudic tractates and codes of law but rather because of prayer." If great *tsadikim* can be without Toyre, how much the more so those who serve them.

[2]When I spoke with Reb Zelig he told me that he was aiming at the landlord of Kripen.

everyone will see -- even the sinners -- what our holy *rebe,* he should live, and our group are capable of.

I wanted to send you at least the arrow that our holy *rebe* killed your devil with so you'll have pleasure from it, but when he shot the arrow a second time the arrow landed in the carriage. In my opinion the thing is an omen that the devil will be humbled under the seat of our holy *rebe.* When it landed in the carriage, the driver took the arrow and said he won't give it to no one because it's his good luck charm.

The driver sold the arrow to a young man from Graidik who came to our holy *rebe* on *Legboymer,* and the bow our holy *rebe* gave to the brothers Reb Yehude and Reb Yoysef who were making music on the instruments. They were standing at the time near our *rebe,* he should live, and the brothers wouldn't give the bow to no one in the crowd. Since the bow, of course, belonged to the two of them and each one wanted to hold it, our holy *rebe,* he should live, said that on the way back they shouldn't play the instruments.

So the two brothers walked all the way from the countryside to the home of our *rebe,* he should live, both of them holding on to the bow. When they came to our holy *rebe*'s home, they began arguing among theirselves who should hold the bow. One said to divide it up by lot -- one will take the bowstring and one will take the bow. But the other said the bowstring is worth more than the bow since it's by the power of the bowstring the arrow flew. Reb Khayim Kaliner made a compromise between them by drawing lots -- the one who gets the bowstring will pay the other one who gets the bow a certain sum.

And that's what they did. They drew lots, and Reb Yehude got the bowstring and Reb Yoysef got the bow. Reb Yehude took the string and tied it around his fiddle and Reb Yoysef took the bow and wrapped it around his drum AS AN EVERLASTING MEMORIAL. We saw plainly in this the providence of the Creator, because the bow he couldn't've wrapped around the fiddle and the string wouldn't go nice on the drum neither, but this way everything was just fine.

But what do we need signs and proofs? All the goings-on and all the stuff that happens by our holy *rebe,* he should live, are all miraculous events. Indeed, every instant, every single moment, we see such signs and wonders, and we got to rejoice and relish the privilege we have to be among the followers of our holy *rebe,* he should live. So BE STRONG AND COURAGEOUS in your actions for our communal welfare, and be strong of faith in *khakhomim,* for without faith nothing else matters.

We see when a bird flies from its nest when it wants to eat -- clearly, if it didn't have faith it wouldn't fly, for it don't know if it'll get something to eat or not, and it would've been better for it to stay safely in its nest.

Why should it fly, especially when it's raining or cold outside? But the faith it has gives it the desire and strength to fly, because it knows when it'll fly it'll have something to eat. And if a bird has faith, shouldn't *we* a thousand times more have perfect faith?!

From me,

....

#46

**From Reb Zaynvl Verkhievker
To Reb Zelig Letitchiver**

I got your letter [#45] and let me tell you -- by the merit of our holy *rebe,* our *rebe*'s coachman came back with the carriage and with our man, and the *goye* went with her father on foot to Galicia without a hitch, but the Jewish-style clothes the *goye* was wearing she kept with her. At first she said on the other side she'll give them back, but on our side she can't give them back 'cause they wouldn't let her cross the border. But when she got to Galicia, the bitch* wouldn't give back the clothes no more. She said the men that were with her in the woods can pay for the clothes. Our man that went with her to Galicia was scared to make there a commotion over this on account of the people of Galicia, 'cause even though the *arendar* that lives at the border in Galicia is one of Moyshe of Shreg's people, all the same our man was afraid to talk with him about matters like this 'cause you already wrote me about the Galician *khsidim,* especially the people of Moyshe of Shreg, who was always a peddler and all of a sudden became by the Galician *khsidim* a *rebe,* making *pidyens* and making money.

The *khsidim* of Galicia say of him he's a very great expert in *Shimesh Tilim.** Isn't this a riot? Yokltse of Kalashke they call a prophet and Moyshe of Shreg a great expert in *Shimesh Tilim!* I don't know if they're really fools and really think there's some substance in their *rebes,* and imagine that a *rebe* does his stuff through the use of psalms or other things, or if they really know there's no substance in them at all. But since there's no choice, I mean, since they don't got this privilege of having in Galicia *rebes* and real *tsadikim* like in our country, they got to take whoever happens along and wants to be by them a *rebe* -- even one of the liars.[1]

---

[1] "Since there exist real *tsadikim* who are very exalted in degree and it is their way to speak great and wonderful things, because they can really do great things and

But why should I speak of such fools? Let's return to our subject -- the *goye* and her father are already, by the help and merit of our holy *rebe,* he should live, in Galicia, and *now* what will our thieving prince do?

From our holy *rebe*'s trip to the countryside on *Legboymer* I had great pleasure and aggravation. I was pleased you had the privilege to see such joy and celebration, especially how our holy *rebe,* he should live, shot the arrow toward our community to kill our demon so he'll be humbled under the seat of our holy *rebe,* he should live. And I was aggravated 'cause *I* wasn't privileged to see that celebration. But I consoled mineself with the fact that I done something important for the good of our people and for the good of our holy *rebe,* and our *rebe,* he should live, will surely have from this act pleasure.[2]

I LOOK TO THE L-RD He should strengthen mine heart with faith to do also in the future even greater things for the good of our *rebe*[3] and to guard our holy *rebe* so he won't have no aggravation, G-d forbid![4] Surely the merit of our holy *rebe* will help me in all matters. *Omeyn.* This should be His will.

These are the words of
....

---

serve the L-rd through everything in the world, even through eating and drinking and such, and there are *tsadikim* who can perform a *pidyen* by their eating -- since there are *tsadikim* like these, on account of this there exist liars who also boast of great and wonderful things like these." *Kitser Likutey MohoRa"N,* Book 2, par. 109.

[2] "Sometimes by virtue of one small pleasure one performs for the *tsadek,* one merits the world-to-come." *Mides* 53:107.

[3] "Whoever wishes to benefit the *tsadek,* The Holy One blessed be He gives him strength for this." *Mides* 53:110.

[4] "Whoever guards the *tsadek* so that no aggravation befalls him will merit honor and will enjoy the [reward for] the *tsadek*'s righteousness." *Ibid.,* 54:139.

#47

From Reb Zelig Letitchiver To Reb Zaynvl Verkhievker

I'm informing you Reb Leybush Shifre's came home from the journey safe and brought from this trip lots of *Ertsisroel* and Rabbi Meyer Balanes money. Our holy *rebe* was very pleased he saw Reb Leybush get home safe with his carriage. When this Reb Leybush saw that our *rebe,* he should live, was in total bliss, he began bragging about you to our holy *rebe.* He told him -- that is, Reb Leybush told our holy *rebe* -- you helped him very very much in all respects. I too said you always knock yourself out to do everything possible for our good, even risking your life.

Reb Leybush said you're right now at a loss for a living because the sinner Mordekhai-May-His-Name-Be-Erased stopped giving you vodka. Our holy *rebe* said in amazement, "Reb Zaynvl Verkhievker don't make a living?!" and he raised his eyes when he said this. I was very pleased by this because I knew for certain soon you're sure to make a living. First of all, I advise you every morning after easing nature twelve times you should say[1] the passage from *Shivkhey ha-Besht,*[2] **The angels said to the Besht, "Why do you keep still while the rabbi of the holy community of Rashkov don't make a living?"** because I heard from our holy *rebe,* he should live, that this passage is very effective for making a living.

For now, be sure, for G-d's sake, to remind the *arendar,* Peysekh of Slabudshik, he should remind his landlord when he'll be by your prince, to have a good talk about our holy *rebe,* he should live, because I got no doubt your prince will become a changed man for a few reasons -- since our holy *rebe* shot the arrow there and the arrow landed in the carriage that our holy *rebe* traveled in, also since your prince must see now that G-d does what our *rebe* wishes. Why should he need more proofs than he saw plainly that when the landlord of Bilke wanted to question the *goye* in the infamous affair and your prince also wanted to send her to the authorities, she left the village of Bilke with her father and the prince of Bilke was punished by losing two [taxpaying] subjects.

It follows, when the landlord of Slabudshik will tell him of the sweet actions and movements of our holy *rebe,* of course he'll start being humble before our holy *rebe,* and in my opinion on account of this a good living will come your way, because then he's sure to listen to everything our holy *rebe* tells him and he'll drive out, of course, the sinner Mordekhai, and give you the *arende* and the mill and all his business.

So for G-d's sake, get moving on this!

From me,

....

---

[1] Corresponding to the twelve words in this saying.
[אמרו המלאכים להבעש״ט: למה אתה שותק והרב דק״ק ראשקוב אין לו פרנסה?]

[2] *Shivkhey ha-Besht* 28:3 [Mintz, 204].

#48

From Reb Zaynvl Verkhievker
To Reb Zelig Letitchiver

I give thanks to you and Reb Leybush Shifre's for the favor you done me, mentioning me to our holy *rebe,* he should live, and praising me to him. I see plainly that this, and also the advice you gave me to recite the passage from the holy book *Shivkhey ha-Besht,* helped me a lot in making a living, 'cause Yankl Rudniker, the miller here, leased the mill for three more years and since he knows I helped him in this he took me as [his] right-hand man, on account of the trustee he used to have just bought the *arende* in the village of Ivanik -- so now I make a living. Even though I still don't make a *great* living, all the same I hope that as soon as I get to know the bakers and flour-dealers and contractors that grind at the mill, I'll make sure to do for them sometimes favors in the mill, and in return they'll do for me favors too, and I'm sure to make a good living.

Right now, please give me advice what to do with the *arendarke* of Bilke, 'cause she's demanding her clothes the *goye* took to Galicia 'cause she -- I mean, the *arendarke* -- gave the *goye* the *Shabes* clothes she had and now she's crying to me she don't got nothing to eat 'cause her husband is still under arrest. The prince took all his things and just his wife's clothes he left her out of compassion. Right now she don't know where her next meal is coming from and if she had the clothes she'd sell them. So please, for cryin' out loud, give me advice what to do!

Also, please let me know where the rumor started that Mendl Odele's found his horses in the town of Akhziv* and showed with clear evidence that Khayim Leyb of our Faithful and a relation of the *tsadkones* -- our holy *rebe*'s wife -- stole them and they took him to jail. Even though I know for sure this must be a dirty lie, all the same I want to know how the rumor got started, so I can tell people who talk about it that it's a lie and tell them what really happened and save our holy *rebe,* he should live, from a bad reputation.[1]

Again I'm asking you shouldn't be lazy about this -- let me know right away if not sooner the whole story 'cause I'm having awful aggravation from this. I heard some people talking about this affair openly.

These are the words of
....

---

[1] "Whoever loves the *tsadek* must keep the *tsadek* from getting a bad reputation." *Mides* 52:69.

#49

From Reb Zelig Letitchiver
To Reb Zaynvl Verkhievker

I was very, very pleased by your letter [#48] because I saw from it you're making a living. You're sure to make a good living too, because the fact that you're still not making a good living yet is only because our holy *rebe,* he should live, didn't say nothing but, "Reb Zaynvl don't make a living?!" -- therefore you're making a living. If he'll say, "Reb Zaynvl don't make a *good* living?!," you would certainly make a good living.

So if the time will be ripe to talk about this again with our holy *rebe,* I'll tell him you're not making a good living, and if G-d allows our *rebe,* he should live, to say in surprise, "Reb Zaynvl don't make a good living?!" -- then you're sure to make a good living, because in my opinion the saying from the book *Shivkhey,* "**The angels said...**," also must not work for more than just a living -- and not for a *good* living -- since the angels too only said to the Besht, **"The rabbi of the holy community of Rashkov don't make a living,"** and they didn't say, "He don't make a *good* living." What a shame the rabbi of the holy community of Rashkov didn't make a living at all! -- because if he made a living but not a good one, then the angels surely would've said to the Besht, "The rabbi of the holy community of Rashkov don't make a *good* living...," and then this passage would work for a *good* living and it would be very good for you.

But in any case don't worry a thing, because when the time will be ripe I'll be sure to mention you to our holy *rebe,* like I wrote you above. Also I spoke with Reb Leybush Shifre's about this and he'll also do whatever has to be done, and it's sure to be fine.

As for the *arendarke*'s clothes, we consulted around here and decided to send Reb Khayim Kaliner through the nearby communities [to collect] for ransoming captives.* We'll make sure to discuss this with our holy *rebe,* he should live, because folks don't know yet so well why the *arendar* of Bilke is still under arrest, and of course they suppose he stays put because of the installment he can't pay, so Reb Khayim is sure to make lots of money when he'll have permission from our holy *rebe* to make a trip for ransoming captives, and then you'll pay out of this for them clothes.

As for Mendele Odele's' horses, I'm informing you witnesses already testified Mendele Odele's sold the horses to Khayim Kaziner. But Mendl boasted he'll present evidence -- three noblemen who were by him at the time we sent to him to lend the horses for our holy *rebe,* and that he went right off with them noblemen in the wagon of one of them to the village of Mutnitse to buy grain from the landlord there and they never left him, and he was by the landlord of the village of Mutnitse the whole night, that is, the same night on which the horses were stolen from his home. He went to that village to talk with them nobles about this testimony.

A renowned miracle happened for us -- when he left home, that night his house burned to the ground. When he came back he saw plainly his punishment, since he wanted through the testimony of liars to have some people, namely, them men who swore he sold the horses, he wanted to have them sent, G-d forbid!, to Siberia. When he saw this, he sent to our *rebe* and then he came himself to appease our holy *rebe* and promised not to take any further action against Khayim Leyb, but the court still won't let Khayim Leyb out of jail. But soon we hope to get him out of there.

From me,
....

#50

From Reb Zaynvl Verkhievker
To Reb Zelig Letitchiver

I give you a thousand thanks for promising me to talk with our holy *rebe* about a good living for me, and when our holy *rebe,* he should live, says in amazement like we want, it'll be, of course, fine. For now I'm sending our holy *rebe* corn flour and wheat flour and semolina and barley, and also for you I'm sending half a bushel corn flour. You can be sure that when our holy *rebe* helps me, I'll send, of course, much more, and I'll be done with gloom and doom, and that way I'll also subdue the enemies,[1] which I got right now lots of.

About the clothes, *pleeease* take care of this right away 'cause yesterday the *arendarke* was over here and cried she has nothing at all to eat and she and the children will starve to death 'cause from the tavern the

---

[1] "Whoever is melancholy should give a gift to the *tsadek* often." *Mides* 44:11.

"310 immersions* annul fear. He should also give a gift to the *tsadek.*" *Ibid.,* 46:18.

"Through a gift one brings the *tsadek,* one subdues the enemies and does away with the evil spirit that settles on the person." *Ibid.,* 55:172.

"Whoever brings enjoyment (to the *tsadek*) from his belongings is as if he brings enjoyment to all Israel, and he is saved from death." *Ibid.,* 56:181.

just to some nearby communities, and brought back, thanks to our holy *rebe*, lots of money. We sent you the bearer of this letter to pay the *arendar*'s wife for the clothes according to the settlement you'll make with her. We really ransomed captives too, because from this money Reb Khayim Kaliner brought, we ransomed Khayim Leyb from jail. We really spent lots of cash on him because the judge is a miserable money-grubber, and also the other court officials we had to give lots of money. For anyone else they would've taken even less dough, but for Khayim Leyb they wouldn't settle for chicken-feed since they know he's a relation of the *tsadekes*, the wife of our holy *rebe*, he should live. Thank G-d we finished this business too before it reached the authorities, because we see plainly that every single day the hatred against our holy *rebe* and against our group grows stronger among the princes of the province.

This must all be because of your prince and this *bukh*, so be sure, for G-d's sake, when the lord of Slabudshik and his *arendar*, Peysekh, will be with you, to remind the *arendar* his landlord should at least read the *bukh*, like he promised him already, because at least we got to know the name of the *bukh* and who's the author and then we'll know what to do. Also, the prince of Slabudshik should ask your prince where he bought this *bukh*, and when we have information about this, we'll buy there all the *bikher* they got and burn them up because we see this *bukh* is no trifle and we got to risk our lives in this matter that affects our entire group.

From me,

....

#53

From Reb Zaynvl Verkhievker
To Reb Zelig Letitchiver

I got your letter [#52] through the bearer of this letter and I made with the *arendarke* a settlement for the clothes. The bearer of this letter paid her off and I thought the whole world was mine now that I'm free of this *arendarke*, 'cause she wouldn't let me be. Every single day she was following me and crying and I was even terrified she shouldn't go to the sinner Mordekhai to ask him he should help her by the prince and reveal to him the whole business, and he, of course, would tell the prince and it would be, G-d forbid!, very bad.

'Cause in any case the prince is now worse then what he was, 'cause ever since the *goye* fled with her father he goes around like a real scoundrel. One of our merchants who was by him told me he heard the prince say, "I know for a fact that it was the sect of *khsidim* who arranged that the *goye* fled, but what can I do? At the moment I still don't have proof of this, but when I get proof then I'll pluck them up by the root!" -- don't tempt the devil!

It would be better in mine opinion to kidnap the *arendar* from jail and see he goes with his wife to another province, 'cause as long as he'll be in our province I'm terrified of this thieving slave driver, 'cause for sure he won't rest until he does all what he can to see the thing through.

The lord of Slabudshik arrived today, but he left at once for another lord not far from here, and in three days he'll come back and hang around by our landlord ten or twelve days. I wrote today to the *arendar*, Peysekh, he should come here too to remind his landlord about the matter of our holy *rebe*, and I'll be sure, of course, to spare no effort so our landlord will become our friend.

These are the words of
....

#54

From Reb Zelig Letitchiver
To Reb Zaynvl Verkhievker

Today the rabbi of the holy community of Latke in Galicia came to our holy *rebe*, he should live, and he told me that when he was traveling through the holy community of Greater Tsidon he had to go to the local district with his passport and he heard the district officials saying a *goye* had come to them from our country with her father, and the *goye* is pregnant and said she's pregnant by two Jews. The district officials had a good laugh over this and so did a Jew who's important in the district there. Some of the officials said to ask the *goye* the names of the two Jews by who she got pregnant, but their boss said, "What business do we got with such matters?"

That rabbi told me all this on purpose, because it's clear to him the *goye* got pregnant from *misnagdim*, since it's well-known the *misnagdim* are fornicators. He said to me, "Maybe this story will help you around here." When I heard this, IT SHOOK ME UP and I decided to let you know all this so you'll keep your eyes peeled in case some letter arrives from the district of Greater Tsidon for your prince in connection with this.

We also consulted around here and decided to send someone special from our Faithful to Galicia, so he'll stay there and move around in that district so as to make there inquiries. But we got to send someone who has family in that there district so if he'll run into any trouble, the members of his family will go running to the district officials not to harm him, G-d forbid!, and he also has to be someone who can put on an act so the local folks don't find out he's from our faction and so he can speak with the people there. Because you must've heard that in the city where the district seat is there are lots of people who they call there "experts in the sciences."* They're really only common *apikorsim* as we long since heard and as we knew -- that all them so-called "experts" are just common *apikorsim* -- and even the rabbi of the holy community of Latke told us they are.

So be sure to look for someone who'll have all those qualifications and we'll send him to Galicia. Also, we'll have from his mission many other benefits besides this, because he'll inform us regularly of the news in Galicia, and he'll also make sure to attract people from there under the wings of our holy *rebe.*

To cover expenses, we'll give him some of our holy books to sell there because right now it's very easy at the border to bring the books over there. Not only will we do something important by spreading the holy books in Galicia where it's forbidden to print them, but we'll also make a big profit, because I heard that in Galicia they sell our holy books at high prices. I heard that for the holy book *Toldes,* they pay two silver rubles and even more. So make sure to send us someone like that because the matter is very urgent.

From me,

....

#55

From Reb Zaynvl Verkhievker
To Reb Zelig Letitchiver

In keeping with your letter [#54], I'm sending you the bearer of this letter, Reb Meyer Yankev of Zaslav.* He has a draft card* and he even has a family of big shots in the holy community Nakhal Hamotsa, which is near the district seat.*

His relations there aren't from our group. Even this is an advantage 'cause in that district such men are the powerful ones. He's also a very good mixer, and he can talk with the local people, of course, 'cause he was born in Galicia and it isn't ten years since he came to our country. He also knows the *rebes* of Galicia and also the merchants of the holy community of Akhziv, on account of he bought from them a few times merchandise. With the border guards he's a wonder, 'cause since he carried packets of contraband* a few times, he gave them lots of money and got to know them very well. I'm sure that through him we'll be able to do in Galicia whatever we want.

But in mine opinion you should give him also some letters from merchants in your community 'cause they're very well-known in Galicia. Let them write that they're sending him to Galicia to buy for them merchandise. It would be best to give him a letter from Reb Aharon, your wineseller, 'cause in the holy community of Greater Tsidon, where the district seat is, there's plenty of wine to sell and Reb Aharon buys there all the time wine. Even if Reb Aharon don't need right now wine, what will it hurt him if he'll give him a letter? In any case he [Meyer Yankev] won't buy wine 'cause he'll say the wine isn't up to his standards or the price is too high, but at least that way he'll have freedom of movement and an excuse to stay in the holy community of Greater Tsidon for a few days. And meanwhile, of course, he'll get to know there the local big shots and also the common people, 'cause he's someone who can speak with everyone, no matter who.

These are the words of

....

#56

From Reb Zelig Letitchiver
To Reb Zaynvl Verkhievker

I was very pleased with Reb Meyer Yankev who you sent us. In heaven we couldn't've picked ourselves a better man than him. Today he left here for Galicia, and since Reb Aharon our wineseller needed wine, he sent one of his assistants to the holy community of Greater Tsidon, and we sent Reb Meyer Yankev with that assistant as trustee. Reb

Aharon ordered the assistant he should choose the wine and Reb Meyer Yankev will pay for it, and in this way, of course, he'll get in good there with the local wine merchants. It's well-known that district officials and other noblemen come to wine merchants to drink wine and while drinking they talk alot about things that should even be kept secret. Reb Meyer Yankev will find out in this way everything we'll need, especially since Reb Aharon told us the wine merchants in the holy community of Greater Tsidon are among the prominent men of the community. So if he'll have there, G-d forbid!, some trouble, of course the wine merchants will go to the district officials and won't let them do him no harm, G-d forbid!

We also gave Reb Meyer Yankev authorization from the printer of the holy community of Mezhebush, the rabbi, Our Teacher the *Rov,* Rabbi Yankev Pinkhes, to sell there the holy book *Toldes Yankev Yoysef,* which is newly reprinted. In the authorization it says distinctly that it's forbidden for anyone to sell this book in Galicia. Only Reb Meyer Yankev has authorization to sell them in their country. The authorization's not handwritten, but it's printed in the print of that holy community, and in my opinion even the big *apikorsim* of Galicia must be afraid of words that were printed in Mezhebush, where the Chief of all the *rebes* always stays.* Because this at least they can't deny -- that the Chief who stays always in Mezhebush is certainly something. Also for the rabbi, the printer Reb Yankev Pinkhes, you can bet they must have very great respect.[1]

We also gave Reb Meyer Yankev a letter from our Faithful to the merchants and dignitaries of the holy community of Akhziv who belong to our faction, because, thank G-d, we got there lots of people, and almost the whole town belongs to us even though many government officials live there.

We hope that through Reb Meyer Yankev we'll be able to do everything in the best way in all the business we'll have to do in Galicia, and I don't got even the slightest doubt about this.

From me,

....

---

[1] Those people who don't know the above *Rov,* I inform them that he's the son-in-law of the *tsadek,* Rabbi Borukh Tultchiner, and his wife is named Odel after the mother of the *tsadek,* Rabbi Borukh. Therefore, of course, he is something great even though he is seemingly a very simple man and a peerless ignoramus and does not comprehend even one word of the holy tongue.* Nevertheless, he is something great.

#57

From Reb Zelig Letitchiver To Reb Zaynvl Verkhievker

The rabbi of the holy community of Latke, who's still staying by our holy *rebe* because he wants our holy *rebe* should appoint him rabbi in the region of Ibarisev, spoke a few days ago with our holy *rebe,* he should live, and complains alot about the people in Greater Tsidon because he had there from the district awful aggravation. One of the district officials in particular did stuff to him -- called him names and said to him harsh words -- and the rabbi said all this is because the people around there are big opponents of our faction.

Our holy *rebe,* he should live, said to him, "You yourselves are responsible for yourselves. Why don't you do nothing about that community? There must be men there who you can do whatever needs to be done with. I remember on last *Rosheshone* there was by me two young men from there and they told me in their community there are really few *khsidim,* but all the same they said they got a special *minyen* in one of their homes and they also said many local community members and dignitaries and Talmudists, when a *tsadek* comes there, go out to him to greet him. Even the local rabbi, although he isn't one of our people and maybe even in his heart he hates us, still goes out to a *rebe* who comes there. What more do you want?"

"When I was still in Galicia, I remember at that time all the *tsadikim* who would come to Greater Tsidon had awful aggravation and terrible disgrace and humiliation. What did they do to the *tsadek* of Hanipoli, to the *tsadek* of Tcharna Ostra, to the *tsadek* of Prshevorsk?!* They never let anyone from our faction make for himself a *minyen* or pray before the Ark* or even hang around there a few days. The *tsadek* of Prshevorsk wanted to give them ten czerwone zlotys to let him pray before the Ark in their synagogue because he saw a bright light over the synagogue,[1] but they wouldn't let him.

"Some of the *tsadikim* they drove out of town. The Elder (*Der Zeyde,* The Grandfather),* remembered for eternal life, who had there even relatives, was forced to flee from there on *Motse Shabes,* and some of the

---

[1] The *apikorsim* from there said that he wanted to pray in the synagogue in order to acquire a reputation for himself that he had prayed there in the synagogue, and also thereby to draw some people from there close to our circle, but no one is fool enough to believe their words!

members of the community say the one who informed against The Elder to the local officials had been many years very sick and from then on became FIT AS A FIDDLE. And they say this was because of this *mitsve,* because by them this was a great *mitsve.* They even wanted to drive out The Elder on *Shabes Koydesh,* but some people interceded for him so they let him be until *Motse Shabes.* He had to flee from there at night on *Motse Shabes,* and that same year The Elder died.

"What more proofs do we need? Indeed, Our Teacher the *Rov,* Rabbi Dov, son of Our Teacher Rabbi Shmuel, *shoykhet* of the holy community of Linits, told me some tales of the Besht, remembered for eternal life, that he didn't want to print in the holy book *Shivkhey ha-Besht* for certain secret reasons,[2] and I saw that the *Rabbon,* the Besht, also had there awful aggravation and terrible humiliation even though he spared no effort to bring the local people under his wings."

When the rabbi of the holy community of Latke heard all this, he began pleading with our holy *rebe* to tell him these tales. Since that rabbi is highly respected by our holy *rebe,* he should live, because that rabbi was a very wealthy man in Galicia and he's a wonderful creature and was in Galicia always a contractor, which is called there a "warehouseman," even though he was a rabbi, and still he was always one of our circle -- so our holy *rebe* loves him very much and our *rebe* told him these tales that happened to the Besht in the holy community of Greater Tsidon.

First he began to tell the attempts the Besht made there to draw the local people close to him, and here's what happened. When the Besht was in the holy community of Greater Tsidon, a silver vessel and valuable objects were stolen from a householder there. That householder went to the Besht because there they regarded the Besht as a common wonder-worker *(balshem).*[3]* When the householder told the Besht of the

---

[2] See *Shivkhey ha-Besht* 5:4 [Mintz, 41]. He wrote as follows: **I did not wish to write the substance of the story for a secret reason...and therefore the root of the story I did not wish to reveal.** And we see plainly that he didn't write all the stories of the Besht. He just selects the food from the rubbish, or maybe the opposite.

[3] There's no reason to be surprised at the fact that in the holy community of Greater Tsidon they thought of the Besht, may he be remembered for life in the world-to-come, merely as a common wonder-worker, for he who looks at the holy book *Shivkhey ha-Besht* will see that in many places -- and almost everywhere at the time -- they didn't think anything of the Besht, and some reverent and faithful people made fun of him. Even in Mezhebush where he lived for some years they thought nothing of him, as you'll see there, 6:2 [Mintz, 44] and col. 4 [Mintz, 48]; 10:3 [Mintz, 77] and col. 4 [Mintz, 79]; 11:1 [Mintz, 81f.]; 14:1; 18:1 [Mintz, 129]; 23:1 [Mintz, 164]; 24:2 [Mintz, 173f.] and col. 3 [Mintz, 175] and in many more places, and of course, it had to be so, as is known.

theft, the Besht asked him who he suspected and the householder said he suspected his attendant. The Besht said to the householder, "I order you to send me next *Shabes Koydesh* a hundred and sixty almonds, twice a hundred and sixty raisins and three times a hundred and sixty pistachio nuts, but don't tell a soul how many you're sending me."

The day of *Shabes Koydesh* arrived and the householder took the almonds and raisins and nuts and sent them to the Besht on a large tray by way of his attendant, as the Besht ordered. When that attendant came to the Besht, the Besht asked him in a loud voice, "From who are you?" The attendant said, "I'm from So-and-So son of So-and-So," that is, he said the name of his master. The Besht cried in a louder voice and made very strange movements, as was his way, "Why did you steal from the almonds, raisins and nuts?" and the attendant said, "I didn't take a thing!"

The Besht said, "You wait here while I go to a special room to do there something." The Besht went to another room and took with him all them things with the silver tray so the attendant wouldn't run away in the meantime from the house. And the Besht began to count in the special room the almonds and raisins and nuts. Then he came back to the first room, grabbed the attendant by the wrist[4] and said in a very

---

[4] **Once some famous doctor came to the duchess of the town. The duchess regaled him with praise of the Besht -- that he was a great man and also an expert in healing. The doctor said, "Send for him to come here." She said, "It is not in keeping with his Honor except to send a fine carriage for him as is done for lords, for he is a great man." She sent for him and he came before them.**

The doctor asked the rabbi if it was true that he was an expert in healing, and he answered him, "It is true." He asked where and which expert he had studied with, and he said, "G-d taught me." It was a laughing matter to the doctor, and he asked him further whether he understands about the pulse.

The rabbi said, "Look, I happen to be sick. See what you can tell from my pulse, and I'll see what I can diagnose from your pulse." The doctor took the rabbi's pulse. He understood that there was a sickness but he didn't know what it was, for he [the Besht] **was really lovesick for G-d -- something that was beyond the doctor's understanding. Then the rabbi grabbed the doctor by his wrist and turned to the duchess and asked, "Were such-and-such valuables stolen from you?" "Yes," she said, "They were stolen a few years ago. I don't know where they are." The rabbi said, "If you send to his inn and open his chest, you'll find all the valuables intact." She sent straightaway and found just as he had said, and the doctor left there in terrible disgrace (and the reason is that the back part of** [the Divine countenance, or configuration of *sephirot* called] **"Father"* is numerically equivalent to one hundred and eighty-four, as is the sum of the letters of the Hebrew word for "pulse," and therefore the**

loud voice, "You stole twenty-five almonds!" And he waited a little and pretended like he was taking his pulse and then said in a strange voice, "And you also stole thirty-two raisins!" And he waited a little more like before and said, "And you also stole fifty-one nuts!" And he ordered that the attendant be searched and they found on him all the above, just as the Besht had said, no more and no less.

The attendant started shaking in his boots because he saw this is no joke. The Besht started to roll back his eyes and make strange movements and he shouted in a very loud voice, "Sinner! Confess you stole valuables from your master or else I'll pluck you up by the root!" The attendant shook even worse and he confessed he stole and told where he hid them and returned everything he stole. The Besht was very pleased by this because he imagined from now on all the people in the holy community of Greater Tsidon will belong to him, but this very householder by who the theft happened, who owed the Besht a favor, told all his townfolk what trick the Besht used to expose the theft, and all the people around there began making fun of the Besht worse than before.

The *Rov*, Our Teacher, Rabbi Yehude Leyb,* who came back from The Holy Land and was living there, invited him deliberately for the midday meal. The Besht thought that rabbi wanted to do him an honor, but then he saw he did this just to make fun of him some more because after the meal, that rabbi's valet came and said to the Rabbi [the Besht], "I found a dairy spoon in with the meat spoons you ate with," and all the people who were at the time in the home of the rabbi started to poke lots of fun at the Besht and said, "What's this? You're the Besht and you didn't know a dairy spoon was in with the meat spoons?!"

Also, when he prayed there in the *besmedresh* they called him up to a *Seyfer Toyre* and he recited the blessing before it and after it, and afterward, when they began reading with the man they called up after him, they found a defect in the *Seyfer Toyre* and they all began making fun of him. He had to flee from the *besmedresh* and he lost a shoe when he fled from the *besmedresh.*

I'm writing all this to you on purpose so you'll see how the power of our faction and the *tsadikim* nowadays grows greater and greater, so that even in the city of Greater Tsidon where the Besht was disgraced and humiliated, there are now, thanks to the *tsadikim,* some members of our Faithful, and I got no doubt that soon the other people there will also belong to our circle. It's only because the *rebes* of Galicia don't do nothing that there's still people opposed to us there now. So in a little while, when we exert ourselves, we're sure to bring all the people around there

---

***tsadikim* could recognize in the pulse all the sins, as is written in the holy *Zohar* and in *Tikuney Zohar*).** *Shivkhey ha-Besht* 35:3. [Mintz, 253f.]

under the wings of our holy *rebe,* he should live, because what our holy *rebe* said to the rabbi of the holy community of Latke, "Why don't you do nothing about that community?" he certainly didn't say for nothing.

From me,

....

#58

From Reb Zaynvl Verkhievker
To Reb Zelig Letitchiver

Last week the *arendar,* Reb Peysekh, from the village of Slabudshik, arrived here and stayed a few days and got his prince to talk with our prince about our holy *rebe,* but he said it didn't help nohow since our prince is a sworn enemy of our holy *rebe* and our whole group.

I told Reb Peysekh about the *bukh,* and he told me his prince asked our landlord to lend him the *bukh* to take home and he wouldn't, but he was allowed to read the *bukh* in his [the landlord's] house. When he started reading the *bukh,* the *arendar* asked him what it says in the *bukh* and who's the author. He told him he didn't yet read nothing but the title page and Introduction and the author's name isn't written there, but he did say he knows for sure the author is a Jew and he wrote this *bukh* in Galicia by some *rebe* there.

I thought, "This could be true -- maybe the *rebes* of Galicia done this deliberately against our *tsadikim* 'cause they're afraid one of our *tsadikim* might show up in Galicia and make them [seem by comparison] like garbage and they'll die of starvation."

All the same I was delighted the Slabudshik prince read the *bukh* 'cause I thought when he'll read it then he's sure to say the author is a big liar -- 'cause he was by our holy *rebe* and knows our group, so he knows that what it says in the *bukh* is all a worthless lie. But a few days later the *arendar* asked him -- I mean, the *arendar* of Slabudshik asked his lord -- if he read the whole *bukh,* and the lord answered him, "I read it all," and said he'll write to the town of Akhziv to send such a *bukh* for him too, since he thought the *bukh* was terrific.

The *arendar* asked him what he [the author] wrote in the *bukh,* and he told him lots of wickedness from the *bukh* and began talking about our whole group and all the *tsadikim,* especially our holy *rebe.* He said through this *bukh* he found out about everything what happened with the wineseller Wolf Dubner.

In a nutshell, what can I tell you? The *arendar* told me mine landlord was fit to tear out his [the *arendar*'s] tongue through the back of his neck!

Also, the *arendar,* Reb Peysekh, told me when his landlord got very angry on account of what it said, he told the *arendar,* "Peysekh, up to now I forgive you what you did, but from here on in, if you'll be among the sect of the *khsidim,* be advised that I'll throw you out of the *arende.*"

The *arendar* left him in despair* and came to me and told me all these things. When he told them to me I BEGAN TO TREMBLE 'cause I see we can't rely no more on the Slabudshik prince and the matter is no joke, don't kid yourself! So for cryin' out loud, write Reb Meyer Yankev he should be sure to take some action in Galicia about the *bukh!*

These are the words of
....

#59

From Reb Zelig Letitchiver
To Reb Meyer Yankev, Emissary in Galicia

I don't know why you didn't write us yet even a single word from Galicia. Surely you know it's very urgent for us to know what you did there!

I'm also informing you you should be sure to do whatever you can to get to the holy community of Akhziv because there's many prominent men there who belong to our circle, and even though they're in Galicia, still they do for us what they can to the limit of their small brains* and, of course, they'll be your help and support in whatever you'll need there.

So make sure to go there at once to speak with them, and also make sure to buy up all the infamous *bikher* available there, because I heard that in that holy community there are some merchants with their *treyf* trash, and even Jewish merchants there with trashy books, so of course you can bet this *bukh* will be for sale there, especially since the prince of the village of Slabudshik said distinctly he'll write to the holy community of Akhziv they should send him from there this *bukh.* So for G-d's sake, don't be lazy about buying up all the *bikher* you find there and not leaving them even one *bukh,* and sending them all to us.

Also make sure to discuss this with the *rebes* of Galicia *they* should take action too concerning this matter. Even though the *rebes* of Galicia are no big deals, all the same since there's no choice we got to join up with them for now so as to do whatever possible to shush up the thing with the *bukh,* because the wickedness goes every day from bad to worse.

And also write us what's new there about the two people that fled there from our country, because I'm afraid the clothes you-know-who took shouldn't make some impression. So for G-d's sake, send us the lowdown as soon as possible.

Also write us about all the news you hear there and let us know about the people in Galicia what kind of people they are? Especially about the people in Greater Tsidon -- if they're really big *misnagdim,* or if all this is because the *rebes* of Galicia are among those we call "losers" *(shlimazls).*

From me,

....

#60

From Reb Gedalye Balter in Aklev
To Reb Gershon Koritser in Nigrad

Here's news for you of what's going on, that is, what happened hereabouts. Last *Shabes Koydesh* after the *Musef Kdushe,** I went home to make *Kidesh* over the wine because I felt faint, but the *gabe* of our *rebe,* may he live, came and said our *rebe* ordered [him] to summon me to come to ameliorate the dream* he dreamt. When I arrived at his home I found him sitting on his chair by the table, with our Faithful sitting at his right and at his left with three full bottles of vodka standing before them.

Our *rebe,* may he live, sits in a *tales* and a white gabardine like an angel of G-d, and his face is turning different shades. Then he began little by little to get excited and his face got so red I was afraid to look at his face, and then he started to tremble and GET ALL EXCITED and he began in a loud voice, "A good dream have I dreamt" -- three times, and we responded to him as it's written in the prayerbook* -- to the end.

And then he added some more verses of his own, but he didn't calm down and he said they should perform the amelioration again.

Still he didn't settle down and he began a third time.

Afterward he calmed down a little but a deep melancholy came over him. When we saw all this, and he turned white as stone -- who knows what he saw? -- the members of our group turned their eyes to me because they had confidence in me that surely NOTHING WOULD BE TOO WONDROUS FOR me. I remained stupefied too, at his not telling me beforehand!* I thought to myself, "He must have seen some verdict against me -- may it never be worse! -- so he kept the matter hidden from me."

Afterward he gave the order to notify all our Faithful that they should convene after noon to recite the whole *Shivkhey ha-Besht* from start to finish. At this I was really frightened because surely for a minute matter he wouldn't move heaven and earth so.

They all turned homeward sadly, without tasting the vodka and the *TSAPIKHIS* WITH HONEY that were laid out for them, AND I REMAINED ALONE I didn't go home. I ate breakfast by our *rebe,* may he live, but I didn't know what I ate. Right afterward all our Faithful gathered and we began reciting *Shivkhey ha-Besht* with dread and fear of G-d.

When we finished three folios, our *rebe* rapped on the book with his hand and we all fell silent. Our *rebe,* THE GLORY OF OUR STRENGTH, rose to his feet and said, "HOW LONG WILL YOU REFUSE TO OBEY my words? Was it in for nothing I summoned you to recite this holy book? Don't you know that not just one has risen up against us and against all the members of our fellowship to wipe every trace of us out of existence, but rather, in every single generation...."*

"Now someone has risen up against us who has the power to cut our faith out root and branch and give the upper hand to the Talmudists who don't believe in nothing but *Gemore* and *Poskim* and *Tosfes** and the rest of the commentators in their plain meaning. When they come to some miracle like the legends of Rove bar Bar Khone that can't be explained in a plain sense, then they say, 'In this there must be some deep mystical meaning, but we have no business in mysteries.'* And when they see one of our holy books like the *Toldes, Likutey MohoRa"N* and the holy *Shivkhey* and the rest of the books by *tsadikim,* they despise them and lay them with books by heretics.

"These *apikorsim* don't believe neither in the Besht or in the other *tsadikim* of our time -- not in the miracles and wonders the *tsadikim* can perform and not in the thing all Judaism depends on, namely, to make a pilgrimage to a real *tsadek.* On account of this they don't believe in no *tsadek* and when some *tsadek* comes to their town they don't ask how he's feeling. Just the opposite -- when they see that our Faithful go to welcome him, they laugh and make fun of them: 'How they have pulled the wool over their own eyes -- to believe that this is a *tsadek* and the holy spirit rests upon him and he can do miracles!'

"And they bring them proofs from the *Gemore.* For example, they ask, 'Is the present generation better?',* and the saying of the *Medresh* that the *Shkhine* didn't rest on Moyshe Rabeyne in Egypt because he was outside the Land,* and they only interpret these statements in their plain sense.

"What are we to do about this? Many times this happened to us. When they wanted to burn the holy book *Toldes Yankev Yoysef,* they wanted to wipe out the memory of *us* too. If it wasn't that our father the Besht fought against them from on high, as you can see in this book, *Shivkhey ha-Besht,* folio 36, column 4,* we would all be dead already.

"Now, too, I want to rouse up our Besht to stand in the breach before us, but *you* recite his book like you're asleep. Come on now! Wake up! Beg the Besht he should rise up to help us!"

Immediately we started the book *Shivkhey ha-Besht* over with wonderful *hislayves* and *dveykes* and when we got to the tale that took place with the aforementioned *Toldes,* our *rebe,* our Light, stood before the Ark himself and began reciting it.

And when he got to that matter when the heavenly court acquitted Rabbi Yoysef, son of the holy *Rov,* Our Teacher Rabbi Mikhel of Zlotchev, and the people ordered that he enter a carcass etc.* -- and he saw that the printers of the holy community of Barditchev had left this out,* he shrieked, "Vey, vey! If our *Faithful* did this, what will the *misnagdim* do?! Indeed, this is a signed and sealed case, yet they dared to leave it out!"

When we finished the book *Shivkhey,* we stood the three bottles of vodka on the table and our *rebe* gave the order to bring a silver goblet. He filled it and drank most of it and afterward let each one of us drink from that very goblet.

When they all went home, and only I ALONE REMAINED to serve our *rebe,* may he live, he went to his room to rest a bit and I followed him. I took off his gabardine and his shoes and he lay down on the couch. I asked him what was this vision that our Master, our Light, saw. And he told me he saw an old man sitting in his house and in front of him was *Seyfer Likutey MohoRa"N* and a few other holy books by the real *tsadikim,* and that old man took some grammar book and laid it on those holy books.* Come see* where his words lead.

Be well.

From me,

....

#61

From Reb Zaynvl Verkhievker
To Reb Zelig Letitchiver

Let me inform you on the run we got high hopes our prince will become our friend! I wrote you already that also the Slabudshik prince became our enemy from the day he read the *bukh,* so we couldn't rely on him no more, but there happened for us by the merit of our *rebe* the *tsadek,* he should live, a very great miracle. Freyda Reb Isaac's who was widowed for a few months now, got pregnant after her husband's death and she don't know what to do. Not a soul found out about it. Only the prince, of course, knows, 'cause it was from him she got pregnant.

She came to me on the Q.T. and revealed to me the whole affair and asked me to help her and give her some advice so at least she won't give birth in our community 'cause it'll be for her very shameful, and I advised her she should pretend to be sick and say she wants to go to our holy *rebe,* and you can bet, of course, her family will let her go, and you should make sure there to get her some place by one of our Faithful to give birth there to the child hush-hush and, of course, not only will the prince give us as much money as we want for this, but he'll even have to side with us so the secret shouldn't get out and it would be for him on account of this very humiliating. And if we'll see he'll be our enemy any more like he is now, then we'll spill the beans and they'll remove him on account of this as lieutenant governor 'cause this is by them a serious offense to father a child with a Jewess and that the child should remain among the Jews. Before Freyda travels your way, I'll talk some more with her and if I'll see it's better to talk about this with the healer Yankl, I'll tell him he should give her something so she'll abort the fetus and the prince will be on account of this *more* indebted to us.

These are the words of someone writing in a terrible hurry,

....

#62

From Reb Zelig Letitchiver
To the Rabbi in the Community of Kolne

It's been a long time now I didn't wrote you news even though, with G-d's help, our holy *rebe,* he should live, constantly comes up with lots of novel interpretations* and DOES GREAT THINGS BEYOND NUMBER and reveals SIGNS AND WONDERS by the thousands and tens of thousands, because I was harassed from every side and I didn't have time even to scratch myself, because every single day visitors come from far and wide, both from our kin and also -- not to be mentioned in the same breath -- Wallakhian *goyim* and the like, to our holy *rebe,* he should live, with their affairs. You know I'm always by our *rebe* to see to it no one should enter his room where he holds court if our *rebe* don't give the order to let him. Sometimes I got to speak with the visitors before they go to our holy *rebe* and sometimes I go to their inn to tell them whatever our holy *rebe,* he should live, orders [me] to tell them. And aside from this, it falls to me to do many things, and to serve our holy *rebe*'s Honor with every kind of service and to talk with him about whatever business people ask of him and stuff like that.

So I couldn't write you. But for the moment, our holy *rebe,* he should live, is secluded in his meditation room* and he don't let no one into his presence. Even *I* don't have permission to come before him if he don't call for me,* so I'm writing you this letter to keep the promise I made you when you were for the *Yomim Neroim* by our holy *rebe,* to write you regularly.

First of all, I inform you our holy *rebe* loves you deeply. Every time he prays before the Ark he always takes the *pushkele* he has from you, and on *Motse Shabes* after *Havdole,* when he walks back and forth about the house and sings *zmires,* he wears your Turkish shawl over his shoulders, and when I mention your name he always asks if I had any letter from you.

Last week, when I got your letter through your *mekhutn,* the dignitary Reb Avrohom Shatser, who you brought near under the wings of our holy *rebe,* I told our *rebe* what you wrote me and he was delighted. When your *mekhutn* asked our holy *rebe* for advice about his business and gave him lots of money for a *pidyen,* our holy *rebe,* he should live, said to him, "Rest assured everything will be alright because your *mekhutn* recommended you." When your *mekhutn* left and I saw our holy *rebe* was greatly uplifted, I told him you asked me to write you something of the *toyre* our *rebe* comes up with. He told me he gives me permission to write to you -- to *you* specifically and not to nobody else -- so you can say the *toyre* in his name in your community at the *shaleshudes,* but still he didn't permit me to write nothing but the *toyre* of the *shaleshudes* I heard on the *Shabes* before the writing of the letter -- whereas the *toyre* that was already a week old I wasn't allowed to write so I shouldn't spoil the mystical intent. And obviously, you know, of course that what's not allowed is forbidden to write, because the case of the one who wrote the *toyre* of the Besht is familiar to you.[1]

---

[1] I heard from the rabbi of our community that once some man wrote down a *toyre* of the Besht that he had heard from him. Once the Besht saw some demon walking and holding a book in his hand. He said to him, "What is this book you are carrying in your hand?" He replied to him, "This is the book that you composed." Then the Besht understood that there was someone who was writing down his *toyre*. He assembled all his people and asked them,

Our holy *rebe* ordered to pay special attention to the list of reasons our *rebe* gives for Jewish customs, because at first it seems they're obvious and reasonable but our holy *rebe* told me they're very, very subtle and profound matters and not everyone is privileged to understand them. Ever since our *rebe* gave me this order, I see always more and more that the words are ancient and profound and exalted above and beyond.*

So I'll write you some of them we were privileged to hear from our holy *rebe,* he should live, at the last *shaleshudes.* But I'll write you everything with striking brevity, because a word to the wise is sufficient.

When the jester interrupts the discourse of the bridegroom,* it's in the category of "the fragments of the Tablets [broken by Moses]."[2]*

The reason we throw hops at the bridegroom at the time of the *badekns** is it's an allusion to THE WHEELS (האופנים, *ho'ofanim* -- the letters of האפען, *hopn,* hops)* WENT WHEREVER THE SPIRIT (*ruakh*) IMPELLED THEM TO GO,* and a bridegroom is like spirit *(ruakh).*[3]*

The crouching dances[4] we do at dancing time are in the category of, I SHALL GO *DOWN* WITH YOU TO EGYPT *AND* I SHALL BRING YOU *UP*.[5]*

This will do you for now.

G-d willing, soon I'll write you broader *toyre* of our holy *rebe,* because I just started writing our holy *rebe*'s *toyre* with the authorization of our *rebe* SO IT WON'T BE ABSENT FROM OUR MOUTH AND FROM THE MOUTH OF OUR POSTERITY FOREVER.

"Who among you is writing down my *toyre?"* That man confessed and brought him his manuscripts. The Besht examined them and said, "There is not even one word here that I said." *Shivkhey ha-Besht* 25:1 [Mintz, 179].

[2] Perhaps it is for this reason that we give a wedding gift, for Moses became wealthy from the fragments [that fell during the hewing out] of the [second set of] Tablets [from a sapphire quarry].*

[3] Perhaps it is for this reason that at the time of the veiling, we anoint the forehead of the bride with honey, because from honey and hops we make mead and through mead we enter [a state of] *hislayves,* as is known from *Likutey Yekorim* 31:4.

[4] Dancing in which we go up and down like the Cossacks dance.

[5] These three reasons I have seen also in *Likutey MohoRa"N,* Book 3, fol.13,* but G-d forbid that one should think that the *tsadek* of Zalin heard this from Our Teacher, Rabbi Nakhmen, or vice versa, for why would they say *toyre* that is not theirs, G-d forbid?! Indeed, it is known, thank G-d, that by every one of the *tsadikim* of our time the *toyre* gushes forth more than with a source of water. But of course both of them were attuned to the truth according to the Besht's explanation of the statement, "The whole world is sustained for the sake of *(bishevil)* my son Khanine."* *Shevil* is a path. When he revealed a *shevil* it was easy for others to understand it too. *Keser Shem Tov,* Part 1, fol. 1. But which of the two of them revealed the path for the reasons stated above I was not privileged to discover.

If I'm privileged to know the reason for our holy *rebe*'s present seclusion, I'll inform you of this as well.

Please write me often about how you are and what's happening around there, especially about Mendl Barer,* the follower of the fake *rebe* of Dishpol,* and if he's drawing anybody from your community close to his fake *rebe.*

Be well.

From me,

....

#63

From the Rabbi of the Holy Community of Kolne
To Reb Zelig Letitchiver

His lovely letter* [#62] SPARKLED BEFORE ME and I REJOICED AS OVER ANY TREASURE when I heard of the well-being of our *rebe* the *tsadek,* may he live, and of His good health.* MAY G-D GRANT THIS AND MORE -- to hear of your* well-being always until the coming of our *meshiekh.*[1] *Omeyn Selo* forever.

May His Eminence* accept from the hand of the bearer of this letter a long Turkish pipe stem with an amber mouthpiece, which a merchant from our community here brought me from the holy community of Yasi. I request that they be presented to our *rebe* the *tsadek,* may his light shine, for it is a piece suitable for presentation.* I have consulted experts here and they valued them at ten czerwone zlotys.

Soon the aforementioned merchant will arrive in your community to consult our *rebe,* may his light shine, about the matter of the debts for which he remains responsible in Yasi to Jews and -- no comparison intended -- Wallakhians, of about three thousand czerwone zlotys. If he pays them, he will not have even a *prute*'s worth of cash left, but he is a very honorable man, a generous and G-d-fearing man. He intended to travel directly to our *rebe,* may his light shine, but some business matters

---

[1] Some scoffer said that he never saw written in this sense, "until the coming of our *meshiekh,*" but whose fault is it that he never saw in the holy book, *Or Peney Moyshe* 15:3, "It was blurted out by the holy fellowship of the Rabbi of all the Exiles, 'the *Go'on,* Our Teacher the *Rov,* Dov Baer, may he live until the coming of our *meshiekh,*'" and if the *tsadek* and scribe for Toyre scrolls, *tfiln* and *mezuzes* of Prshevorsk so wrote, it must be a *mitsve* to write so always.

delayed him. But soon, G-d willing, he will definitely go and will bring with him for our *rebe* the *tsadek,* may his light shine, treasures from the commodities of Yasi, in addition to which he will, of course, give our *rebe,* may his light shine, a proper sum for a *pidyen,* as is fitting.

The meanings of the customs His Eminence wrote to me refreshed my spirit, for never in all my life had I heard this. From Heaven they have given our *rebe* an opportunity to distinguish himself.* Please write me always at least a bit of the holy *toyre* of our *rebe,* may he live. May His Eminence accept from the hand of the bearer of this letter a very fine Turkish *tales-kotn,* which I obtained from Yasi, and may it be a remembrance for Him.

From me, His friend **who sends Him* regards always,***

....

I have overlooked something essential. Mendl Barer, the adherent of the fake *rebe* of Dishpol, is sparing no effort to draw the people in our community close to his *rebe.* But His Eminence may be certain that none of his attempts will succeed because, with G-d's help, the people in our community now almost all submit to my authority and will not do anything small or large without me.

Let it also be known to His Eminence that last Friday the rabbi of the holy community of Koven, the capitol -- who was one of the fake *rebe* of Dishpol's people -- died. One of my friends from there wrote me that some prominent men in that community who are adherents of our *rebe* the *tsadek,* may he live, would agree to accept me as rabbi, but I would not do anything without the approbation of our *rebe* the *tsadek,* may he live. Indeed, I know that the fake *rebe* of Dishpol's people would spare no effort against me, but if our *rebe* the *tsadek* approves, then surely THE MATTER HAS PROCEEDED FROM THE L-RD.

These are the words of the aforesigned.

#64

From Reb Khayim Gavriel in Koven
To Reb Yankl Pulnaer in Dishpol

I'm hereby informing you that last Friday the rabbi of our community passed away and I been informed that the rabbi of the holy community of Kolne, who's a follower of the fake *rebe* of Zalin, wants very much to be by us rabbi. He wrote about this matter to friends of his around here and they already started talking this up with the contractor Kalmen Bisinger who got lots of influence by the authorities. Also with the other notables of our community they talked about this.

But we wasn't silent neither and we done our part too. With G-d's help, we have on our side the lady Khaye, that contractor's wife, because her only son is one of our *rebe* the *tsadek*'s, he should live, people. He's a dear boy and his mother's darling and he nagged her so much she promised him to persuade his father he should be on our side. I believe this only son will go out of his way for us because he's still tender in years and has no will or understanding at all of the ways of the world -- only what we tell him in the name of our *rebe* the *tsadek* is his fondest wish.

Since I already knew he'll always be able to help us I took pains to lure him under the wings of our *rebe* the *tsadek,* he should live. And this wasn't easy because he's very learned and he was a follower of **the judge Mikhal*** Kahane here who he studied with.

I still remember what I did after all the fruitless efforts and labors to lure him to our *rebe* the *tsadek* and to distance him from that judge, who you know, of course, is a big opponent. What I did was this: Reb Leybele the flour-dealer, a relative of the only son of the contractor, was by our holy *rebe* on a *Shabes Koydesh.* When he got back from there, I spoke with him and told him to talk with that only son and tell him that our holy *rebe* -- in the middle of the *toyre* he said at the *shaleshudes* -- laid his head on the table and was silent for about a quarter of an hour and then suddenly lifted his head* and cried out in a loud voice, "Eyliohu, son of Khaye of Koven, has a new and very lofty soul and I see a bright light upon him."*

So this Reb Leybele went and told all this to that only son, and when the only son heard this from his relative he started to side with us and every single day he becomes more devoted to us. Afterwards I drew him even closer to our circle through great exertion and he's sure always to be a help and support to us in all our affairs.

Now eight days ago I gave him the holy book *Shivkhey ha-Besht,* and when he read it he asked me to get him some of the precious relics mentioned in that holy book because all he cares about is to have such treasures as these that not everyone deserves or can get, and since his father's filthy rich he's willing to squander a fortune to get them. I told him since our *rebe* is the grandson of the Besht, he has in his possession several of the things he wants, and also some of the things are even in the possession of members of his holy family and, of course, when he wishes, our holy *rebe* will get them, and even them things that are still hidden our holy *rebe* will get hold of when he wishes.

So make sure to send me some things. Here's a partial list of things he wants to get -- I copied them from the list of all the things that only son handed me in his very own handwriting -- namely:

- the **good strong stick** that the Besht, when he was a *melamed*'s assistant, struck the werewolf, or at the very least a piece or a splinter of this stick;[1]
- a few ashes from the conflagration of **the town of Okup** that was burned by the Prince of the Toyre,* and an ember plucked from the fire is even better;[2]
- the short fur jacket and broad girdle that the Besht came to the home of the *Rov,* Our Teacher Rabbi Gershon Kutiver in;[3]
- the axe, or at any rate the axe handle, of the scoundrel who wanted to kill the Besht, and if there should be a little of the scoundrel's blood on it, all the better;[4]
- a few feathers from the bedding that the Besht slept together with his wife on when the disciple, Our Teacher the *Rov,* Rabbi Gershon Kutiver, spent *Shabes* by him;[5]
- one of Reb Sender Shoykhet's fingernails that fell because he slapped the cheek of the spirit;[6]
- a piece of the Besht's silk gabardine that the *tsadekes,* the Besht's wife, made for him from the money she got for the marten pelts, and a piece of the silk dress of the *tsadekes* herself is even better;[7]
- a little of the grain that was trembling at the prayer of the Besht, and barrels of grain are even better;[8]
- a piece of the watch the Besht fixed when the dead came in droves to Rabbi Gershon Kutiver to rectify them by means of *kavones* the Besht taught him;[9]
- a few ashes from the conflagration of the holy community of Sharigrod on which was the decree that it would be consumed all at once, but the Besht managed to give the conflagration an extension of time so the whole town was burned fitfully in the course of twenty years.[10]

---

[1] *Shivkhey ha-Besht* 1:4 [Mintz, 13].
[2] *Ibid.,* 2:3 [Mintz, 18].
[3] *Ibid.,* 3:1 [Mintz, 21].
[4] *Ibid.,* 3:2 [Mintz, 23].
[5] *Ibid.,* 4:2 [Mintz, 30].
[6] *Ibid.,* 4:3 [Mintz, 33].
[7] *Ibid.,* 6:1 [Mintz, 43].
[8] *Ibid.,* 7:2 [Mintz, 52].
[9] *Ibid.,* 8:2 [Mintz, 61].
[10] *Ibid.,* 9:1 [Mintz, 67]. He who wishes to give himself spiritual delight and physical pleasure should study those awesome and wonderful tales alluded to in that holy book, and he will also understand from them that anyone who has

In case none of these precious relics is available by our holy *rebe,* let me know and I'll write you the other things Eyliohu, that only son, included in the list he handed me, and maybe you can find some of them other things he listed.

These are the words of
....

[even] a little fear of Heaven is really obliged to do everything in his power to acquire at least one of these precious relics.

#65

From Reb Yankl Pulnaer
To Reb Khayim Gavriel in Koven

I got your letter [#64] and I talked with our *rebe* the *tsadek* about the matter of the rabbinate of your community. He ordered me to write you to spare no effort, to do everything in your power not to let the rabbi of the holy community of Kolne become in your community rabbi, and he said you should make absolutely certain it won't be as he [the rabbi of Kolne] wishes. Our *rebe* also ordered to write to all who submit to his authority they shouldn't spare no effort in this neither. Our *rebe* said explicitly this rabbi is one of the sages who are called lepers[1] and one of the Jewish demons.[2] Rest assured we'll certainly do our part.

I also talked with our *rebe,* he should live, about Eyliohu, the contractor's only son, who you lured under our *rebe*'s wings. Our *rebe,* he

[1] "There are sages who are learned even in the holy Toyre but who have no faith (in the holy books by the *tsadikim* of our time and in the *tsadikim* themselves). These sages are called 'lepers' and one must keep far from them and from their vicinity in every way possible, just as our sages of blessed memory warned [us] to keep far from actual lepers, because what comes out of their mouth is highly injurious to an honest man, who can fall into carnal passion, G-d forbid!, on account of what comes out of their mouth, because these sages are for the most part notorious fornicators." *Kitser Likutey MohoRa"N,* Book 2, par. 174

[2] [Talmud] sages are Jewish demons. They receive their *toyre* from the demons who have a double *toyre*...and this is [the meaning of] WHO HAS CONTENTIONS? WHO HAS TROUBLE? *(LEMI MEDONIM? LEMI SIYAKH),* that is, on account of trouble *(SIYAKH)* (an acronym), on account of ***Kh**okhem **S**heyd **Y**ehudo'ey* (a [Talmud] sage is a Jewish demon), on account of him there are contentions, on account of him there is opposition. *Likutey MohoRa"N* 46:1-2.

should live, said he'll be able to accomplish alot through his mother, but our *rebe* the *tsadek* ordered to make sure to distance him however possible from the judge Mikhal Kahane who was his teacher, because our *rebe* knows the judge is also one of them Jewish demons, and the husk can't bear any scent of holiness and is sure to spare no effort against us.

As for the things you wrote to send for the contractor's son, now's not the time because if you'll give him now any of them things you won't be able to get from him money for them. Since we'll need him in the matter of the rabbinate of your community, so it's better to wait with them things 'til the matter of the rabbinate is settled, and afterwards we'll be able to get from him a small fortune for the stuff he wants. All the same, if you see that it's a matter of life and death, write to me, and also write me some more things from the list he gave you and I'll make sure to send you some things that maybe I can find easily.

So as to assign some rabbi to your community, our *rebe* the *tsadek* said to accept Reb Shmerl, the son-in-law of Reb Yankev Leyb of your community. Our *rebe,* he should live, said explicitly, "Even though this Reb Shmerl has a few small shortcomings in matters of stealing and fornicating, all the same he has a good and great soul and he'll be good for us." We see Reb Shmerl is certainly no trifle, because our *rebe* the *tsadek* always draws him close in every way possible, and also his father-in-law is a very wealthy man and a common boor and important in all the councils. I already wrote this Reb Shmerl in the name of our *rebe* the *tsadek* that our *rebe* the *tsadek* and all our Faithful want this. Make sure you talk with him about this too.

From me,
....

#66

From Reb Zelig Letitchiver
To the Rabbi of the Holy Community of Kolne

Your pure letter [#63] arrived in my hands last week by way of the bearer of this letter, and also the pipe stem with the amber mouthpiece I received and I delivered it to our holy *rebe* in your name. I see you are very lucky because at the time I delivered this to our *rebe,* he should live, he was in total bliss, and he took the pipe stem at once and inserted it in the pipe he has from Reb Moyshe of Pest. Whoever didn't see our holy *rebe* smoking a pipe with your stem never in his life saw beauty.*

When he smoked that way for about a quarter of an hour with intense *dveykes,* he asked me, "What did the rabbi of the holy community of Kolne write to you?" I told him everything you wrote, and also about the rabbinate of the holy community of Koven, I told him that you don't want to be rabbi there without the knowledge and approval of our holy *rebe,* he should live. He was silent for about five minutes and then he ordered me to write to our Faithful in the holy community of Koven they should talk with Reb Kalmen Bisinger, the local contractor, about this matter.

I already wrote them and got from them a favorable answer. I told our holy *rebe* the contractor promised our Faithful to arrange the rabbinate for you with the authorities. Our holy *rebe* was silent and then he said, "I just said to speak with *him* because it was necessary to speak with him, but efforts with the authorities we don't need so much." So I'm informing you of all this so you should know what happened.

And I hereby send His Toyre Eminence thanks for the *tales-kotn* you sent me because it's very nice. Be well.

From me,

....

#67

From Reb Khayim Gavriel
To Reb Yankl Pulnaer

I got your letter [#65] and I REJOICED LIKE ONE WHO FINDS GREAT SPOIL when I seen our holy *rebe* calls the rabbi of the holy community of Kolne and the judge Mikhal Kahane of our community "Jewish demons" and "lepers," because I can't stand them nohow in no way whatsoever, and I'm absolutely certain now they won't accept that rabbi for our community. But for cryin' out loud, send me some of the famous things for the contractor's son, because I know for a fact the contractor already promised the opposition to convince the authorities the rabbi of the holy community of Kolne should be by us rabbi, and if his wife and son won't help us we won't accomplish nothing, G-d forbid!

About Reb Shmerl, son-in-law of Reb Yankev Leyb of our community, who our *rebe* the *tsadek,* he should live, said to accept as rabbi by us, we talked already with his father-in-law about this and he's not willing because he's a simple and peaceful man and he's afraid of the *misnagdim* -- the issue shouldn't become a big to-do -- but it seems to me if we promise to pay the expenses he'll have to spend on this business, of course he'll agree to this matter because he's a real cheapskate. And in my opinion everyone will certainly be happy to make a contribution because it's a big deal, but without paying money I really doubt we'll be able to bring it off Reb Shmerl should be rabbi, and [then] of course, don't tempt the devil, G-d forbid!, the rabbi of the holy community of Kolne will be by us rabbi, and then all the folks in our community here will be followers of the fake *rebe* of Zalin like the people of the holy community of Kolne. So don't be lazy about this. Do all you can.

These are the words of

....

The main thing I forgot. I'm hereby writing you some more things on the list I got from the contractor's son. Why I'm not writing you all the things on the list is because he listed so many things they need a whole sheet of paper. Also I don't got enough time to write everything so I'm writing you for now just some of them things, namely:

- a piece of **the inside-out wolf fur** the Besht **was dressed** in when he recited before the Reprover sayings from a book, and **he laid** the Reprover **curled up on the bed** and the Reprover **heard thunder and saw lightning and awesome torches for about two hours** because **it was the receiving of the Toyre** like at Mount Sinai;[1]
- **the pillow of the Besht** that **Reb Tsvi**, his **scribe, buried his head** in when **two demons came to the house and made fun of the Besht** and **sang *Lekho Dodi*** * in the Besht's *nign;*[2]
- a branch of the tree where **the Besht imprisoned the witch's demon**, and if it's possible to send lots of branches to make a small besom for the bathhouse,* all the better;[3]
- a piece of the **stick that the Besht took in his hand and said to Reb Shmerl's wife, "See that you give birth to a boy or else I'll break your bones with this stick,"** **and that's what happened;**[4]
- a piece of **the shoe strap the Besht ordered to hit a certain dead man** with and then to shut the corpse up **in the house three weeks until the festival of *Peysekh* and on *Peysekh* night to seat him at the table and support him with pillows**, and the corpse **fled at the third** of the four **cups;**[5]
- a **plank** from **the house of Reb Moyshe, Chief Judge of** the Court

---

[1] *Shivkhey ha-Besht* 11:2-3 [Mintz, 83].
[2] *Ibid.*, 14:4 [Mintz, 107f.].
[3] *Ibid.*, 17:1 [Mintz, 123]. See above, Letter #20, note 1.
[4] *Ibid.*, 18:2 [Mintz, 132].
[5] *Ibid.*, 22:3 [Mintz, 160].

of **the holy community of Kutiv**, who **saw pigs walking on the ceiling** because there was **a demon** there, and the Besht went to sleep in the house of the Reprover where **the demon knocked on the wall and windows** and when they told the demon, **"Yisroel ben Eliezer is here," it didn't knock no more**;[6]

- a piece of the **stick** that **Rabbi Gershon** Kutiver **knocked on the** heavenly **gates** with to plead before **the** heavenly **court** for the Besht and the gates **were opened** on account of the knocking with that stick, and he pleaded there and the Besht was saved from the penalty of death, and if it's possible to get the whole stick, of course, even better;[7]
- the *tsadek*'s candlestick in which **the candle** that had been burning **told the Besht that** the *tsadek* **had intercourse by that light**, and if it's possible to get hold of the snuff of the candle, all the better;[8]
- **the lintel of the passageway of the *arendar*'s house** in a village **a short parasang from the town of Brezne, which raised itself on its own with the whole building** so **the Besht's wagon could enter** the passageway, **and twenty years later Reb Eliezer Brezner saw that** lintel **and it still wasn't back in its former position**;[9]
- the pipe of the Besht that he traveled with **and soldiers took it** on the way because **the stem was very long** and **the pipe stuck out of the wagon, and an hour later the Besht told his attendant, "Take a horse and ride until you reach the soldiers and take the pipe from them," and he did, and when he reached them and saw them sitting on their horses asleep he took the pipe and went his way.**[10]

These are the words of the aforesigned.

---

[6] *Ibid.*, 25:2 [Mintz, 180f.].
[7] *Ibid.*, 26:2 [Mintz, 188].
[8] *Ibid.*, *ibid.*, col. 4 [Mintz, 190].
[9] *Ibid.*, fol. 29:4-30:1 [Mintz, 214f.].
[10] *Ibid.*, fol. 30:4-31:1 [Mintz, 220f.].

#68

From the Rabbi of the Holy Community of Kolne To the Judge Mikhal Kahane in Koven

I am surprised at you for not having written to me for an entire month now. Why have you NOT LIFTED A FINGER? DO YOU NOT KNOW, HAVE YOU NOT

HEARD the efforts that the opposition is making to install there in the rabbinical post the Shmerl fellow, son-in-law of Reb Yankev Leyb of your community? They are boasting that the contractor, the *gvir,* Our Teacher Kalmen Bisinger, has promised to help them in every way possible.

Although I know the man and his way of speaking, his nature and his temperament, and it is literally contrary to human intelligence that he would agree to accept as rabbi the aforementioned Shmerl -- a man known to everyone as a thief and a fornicator, about whom Dovid, king of Israel, may he rest in peace, said, WHAT RIGHT HAVE YOU TO TELL OF MY LAWS...? -- nevertheless I thought, THERE IS NOTHING NEW UNDER THE SUN and it has ever been thus. Perhaps the Dishpoler *rebe*'s people SWAYED HIS HEART. Consequently, I ask that you inform me of all the particulars so that I may know WHICH WAY TO TURN.

I am confident that in the strong friendship between us, you will stand AT MY RIGHTEOUS RIGHT HAND* and not be casual about this, and you will be certain to discuss this with the *gvir,* Our Teacher, the aforementioned Kalmen, that they not SWAY HIS pure HEART, for I know that what you say matters to him.

I also ask that you not murmur against me for having sought help from the *rebe* of the holy community of Zalin and from his subordinates. DO YOU NOT KNOW, HAVE YOU NOT HEARD that nowadays the notorious sect has become as mighty as Heaven and in their sight all the men of Toroh ARE CONSIDERED AS CHAFF and the masses are strongly attracted to them, and men of my age, unless they have some support from a *rebe* of the sect, will not find sufficient sustenance and will literally die of hunger, as has already happened, because of our many iniquities, to many eminent, keen, G-d-fearing and upright Talmudists who did not follow their ways?

What could I have done? You know my situation. My children in particular depend on me and I was compelled to do my utmost to ingratiate myself with the aforementioned *rebe* and his secretary. I have already sent them gifts and they have promised me to do all they could for me. So I ask that you judge me kindly.*

I am sending you enclosed herein some reasons for Jewish customs, which the secretary of that *rebe* sent me [Letter #62] in the name of his master. In his opinion this was a gift WHOSE VALUE NO FORTUNE COULD EQUAL and I know that you will find it as favorable as do I. But for Heaven's sake, let the matter be known to no one, for although in your community the notorious sect is not yet as powerful as in other communities, nevertheless there too they can find a pretext to hurt me, for WHO CAN HIDE from their presence? And they are sure to give notice hither as well, where the RULER'S SCEPTRE is in their hand.

Be well. From me, your friend, **sending you regards always**, with a willing heart and soul.*

These are the words of
....

#69

From Mikhal Kahane
To the Rabbi of the Holy Community of Kolne

I have received your lovely letter [#68] and it has revived me. For I had already despaired of you and considered you among the notorious sect who are all, in my opinion, literally idolators (and I shall demonstrate this with clear proofs for all to see in my treatise, which it is my intention, G-d willing, to publish.[1]) Now, however, I have seen that it is only your pain and the stress of having to make a living THAT HAVE BROUGHT you TO THIS POINT and you are still far removed from them, so I love you as ever. But I entreat you -- take care you do not genuinely follow their ways for they are really out to ensnare people.

With reference to the rabbinic post here, rest assured that I have already spoken with the *gvir*, Reb Kalmen Bisinger, and he promised me to pay no attention to the counsel of your opponents and to do everything WITHIN HIS POWER for you, and I have also spoken with the other notables of our community and done everything in my power, so do not be at all concerned. Even though the Dishpoler's men have already laid their hands on the aforementioned *gvir*'s son, who is my disciple, and he nagged his mother to persuade his father to side with them, nevertheless I know that *gvir* and I guarantee that he will not go back on his word,

[1] I was in the home of the judge Mikhal Kahane when I was invisible. I went there in order to see whether there is anything of substance in this treatise, and to take it from there to burn it up. I saw it several times and I even read in it a number of proofs he brings to substantiate his words of heresy and *apikorses*. He is delighted with them because his proofs are from the *Gemore* and *Poskim* and other ancient books. I realized that it would have been appropriate to take the treatise away from him but this sinner didn't let go of the treatise. He wouldn't even set it on the table, and [even] when he held the treatise in his hand he was still afraid all the time. While he was writing his nonsense and heresy and *apikorses* I couldn't take it, and when he stopped writing he always went directly to the bookcase and hid the treatise in the bookcase and closed it immediately.

particularly since he is in anguish that they have corrupted the soul of his dear son and he will take his revenge on them by extirpating them from here in our community.

From me, your friend since youth,
sending you regards always and
desiring your success,

....

#70

From Reb Yankl Pulnaer
To Reb Khayim Gavriel

I hereby inform you it wasn't possible to get hold of any of the precious relics you wrote me to send you for the contractor's son, because our holy *rebe* is right now very busy and I couldn't talk with him about this at all. But last week we started digging a well by the home of our *rebe** the *tsadek,* he should live, because we saw plainly it's a big thing there should be a well by the home of our *rebe* the *tsadek* and to name the well after our *rebe,* he should live, like the well near Mezhebush named after the Besht, remembered for eternal life.[1]

---

[1] Who doesn't know the miracles that the *tsadikim* of our time perform by means of [water from] the well of the Besht, may he be remembered for life in the world-to-come, which is about half a short parasang from Mezhebush! It's about three years now since this well began having a reputation. The *Rov,* the *tsadek,* Our Teacher Rabbi Borukh of Tiltchin, remembered for eternal life, didn't think much of this well. But thanks to the current Chief *Rebe,* the well has become AN ENSIGN FOR THE PEOPLES* because he performs very great and wondrous things with [water from] the well.

I know that the scoffers say there's nothing great about this well and the whole matter of this well is that the Besht, who would order, like the other wonder-workers and exorcists, to take still water* for cures, would always order to take it from this well -- as other wonder-workers do, to associate some well with still water. But why should we speak of their heresy?! Some of them even say that our group is starting to designate wells as holy, like other nations do. Clearly, it's not worth responding to such words, especially since the marvels themselves that the Chief *Rebe* performs by means of the well stop up the mouths of those who speak heresy.* Let them go to Mezhebush and see [for themselves] and be silent!

Also, since our *rebe*'s house needs a whole lot of water -- during the past year I paid for water alone almost sixty rubles -- so we dug the well, and when the gentiles dug they found in the ground a very old clay pipe. I took from them the pipe and now I'm sending it to you. Give it to the contractor's son and tell him this is the pipe of the Besht and our *rebe* the *tsadek* sends it to him, and he'll believe what you say since the pipe is very old and also they really found it on the grounds of the house of our *rebe* the *tsadek,* he should live. This must be Divine Providence, because how did such a pipe come to be so deep in the ground and remain 'til now whole, especially since we found it [just] when we needed it? So this pipe must be something important and it was lying so long in the ground [just] so we could send it at this very time to the contractor's son.

To emphasize the point I'm writing you another letter [#71] enclosed with this letter, so you'll show it to the contractor's son and for sure without a doubt he'll believe you everything. But for G-d's sake, make sure to get from him lots of money for this, because our *rebe* the *tsadek,* his light should shine, has enormous expenses. Believe me, this year I paid just for chopping firewood more than a hundred twenty rubles, because almost a thousand wagonloads of wood our *rebe* needs for heating the rooms in his royal residence and for his kitchen, because the visitors become every day more numerous, and you can imagine how many visitors there are when every week almost three hundred pounds of onions are required!

What's more, the well we're digging now will be also a great expense, and it must've been Divine Providence to find just now the pipe, so through it our *rebe* the *tsadek* will be granted the expenses he spends on the well, since our *rebe* needs at the moment lots of cash.

Even though our *rebe* the *tsadek,* he should live, is, no evil eye!, very rich -- anyhow the cash he receives is substantial -- he lends it out immediately by way of "transaction permits,"* and the interest I receive quarterly from the debtors, I lend out to middlemen on pawn for weekly payments. People even think this money I lend out on pawn is mine, and really it's the money of our *rebe,* he should live. But what do I care? On account of this I have credit. So make sure to send from the contractor's son lots of money and I'll pass it on to our *rebe,* he should live, and I'll put in for you when you do it a good word before our *rebe* the *tsadek.*

As for expenses for the matter of Reb Shmerl being rabbi in your community, I didn't talk with our *rebe* because HOW CAN I BRING MYSELF to talk with our holy *rebe,* who would insist a contribution be made for this matter, when I know our *rebe* has right now himself great expenses? You know that if folks give a contribution for some cause, they give at the same time less money to our *rebe* the *tsadek.*

But we're expecting the collectors of *Ertsisroel* funds and Rabbi Meyer Balanes funds will arrive presently and they're sure to bring lots of money from this quarterly period. So I'll see, if there'll be a good time I'll talk with our *rebe* about this. And if the matter is urgent and you can't wait, see that you collect among the people you're close with, or give Reb Yankev Leyb, Reb Shmerl's father-in-law, an IOU for whatever he spends on this matter, since later on we can easily repay him, because then of course our holy *rebe* will come to your community and he'll make there and thereabouts lots of dough, because I heard the Zaliner's people always make lots of money from the local villagers there for their fake *rebe,* and our *rebe,* he should live, is sure to make much more. Or else later on we'll figure out another plan to come up with the cash.

These are the words of

....

#71

The Letter Enclosed with the Preceding Letter

I'm surprised at you, my bosom friend, that you asked me to send you precious relics from the vaults of our holy and awesome *rebe,* which he inherited from his grandfather, The Light of Israel and its Holy One, the Besht, remembered for eternal life. Don't you know that a piece as small as [a grain of] sand of them items is worth more than all the riches and TREASURES OF KINGS in the whole world? I almost couldn't raise this issue for discussion with our holy *rebe.*

But I see plainly that the exceptional young gentleman, Our Teacher Reb Eyliohu, the contractor's son, is a very lucky fellow, because last *Motse Shabes* I was with our holy *rebe* in his room and he was smoking a pipe with intense *dveykes* as usual, but such *dveykes* as he was smoking with at the time I never ever saw, and I didn't have the good fortune to see anything like it ever since I have the privilege to be around him. All of a sudden our *rebe* said to me, "I see that Eyliohu, son of Khaye, will forsake all the *toyre* he learned from the Jewish demon, the judge Mikhal Kahane, and will be a pillar of the world as he approaches the true *Toyre* from a literal perspective (see in the Prologue), but he still needs support."

When I heard this, I said with great joy and anxiety, "Our *rebe,* who will support him if not our holy *rebe,* he should live?"

And our *rebe* the *tsadek,* he should live, took the pipe he was smoking and said to me, "Take the pipe I inherited from my grandfather the Besht, remembered for eternal life, and send it to Eyliohu, son of Khaye -- but he shouldn't smoke it -- and it will be to him a help and support." At once I washed my hands and accepted the pipe near a *mezuze* fastened to the window. I placed it in a case within a case until the next day, and now I'm sending you that pipe to deliver to the young scholar, Our Teacher Reb Eyliohu.

Let it be known that this pipe is that very same pipe that the holy and awesome Besht **smoked on the road. The stem was so long that the pipe stuck out of the wagon and as they were traveling this way, an officer and two soldiers came riding toward them on horseback and took the pipe from him and went on their way. The rabbi also traveled on and an hour later the rabbi stopped and said to his attendant, "Take a horse and ride until you reach the soldiers and take from them the pipe," and so he did. When he overtook them and saw them sitting on their horses fast asleep, he took the pipe and went on his way.**

After the Besht passed away, the pipe became part of the inheritance of his daughter the *tsadkones,* Mrs. Odel, remembered for eternal life, who was a real fire, because the Besht took her name from the verse in the Toyre, LIGHTNING FLASHING AT THEM (*ESH DAT LAMO,* אש דת למו),* which ODeL[1] is a acronym for. Because of this she was a real fire, as is known from the shoes she gave to a certain student, the youngest of the fellows.* And as a result of them very shoes, the *tsadek* Rabbi Borukh of Tiltchin was born.[2]

From that *tsadkones,* the pipe came by way of inheritance to our holy *rebe.* So you can see this is a very important item and I really envy the young gentleman, Our Teacher Reb Eyliohu, this gift. You know I'm not rich, but still, I myself would give for it my house. But apparently our holy *rebe* knows why he gave him -- specifically *him* -- this pipe, and in my worthless opinion it seems to me one of the reasons our *rebe* the *tsadek,* he should live, sent him this pipe could be because this pipe has the power to put the wicked to sleep. And the value of a pipe for acts of righteousness is well-known, especially *this* pipe that the Besht smoked.[3]

---

[1] *Shivkhey ha-Besht* 19:1 [Mintz, 137].

[2] See Letter #25, note 1.

[3] **The Talmudist and sage** whom **Rabbi Yekhiel, the Chief Judge of the Court of the holy community of Kovle, sent to probe the character of the Besht, thought that Rabbi Gershon** Kutiver, **the Besht's brother-in-law, was the Besht. He asked him, "Are you the Besht?" Rabbi Gershon Kutiver replied to that Talmudist and sage, "Ay, ay, am I the rabbi? If only I could have** [the portion in] **the world-to-come that our rabbi** (the Besht) **earns by smoking one pipe!"**

It follows that the pipe will have the effect, in my opinion, of making the judge Mikhal Kahane fall asleep, and the young gentleman, Our Teacher Eyliohu, will be aroused to wonderful *hislayves,* which is the essence of devoutness. Please let me know as soon as you delivered it into the possession of Our Teacher, the aforementioned Reb Eyliohu.

From me,

....

And that *Rov,* Rabbi Yekhiel, became a follower of the Besht. *Shivkhey ha-Besht* 14:3 [Mintz, 105]. From this you can see the great and awesome power of the pipe, so take care not to make fun of a pipe, G-d forbid!

#72

From Reb Khayim Gavriel
To Reb Yankl Pulnaer

I got your letter [#70] **and saw a piece of evidence in the first two lines where it says** our *rebe,* he should live, is very busy at the moment. I was very pleased by this because I know all his busyness is only for the sake of our Faithful, to bring them all the abundance they need -- children, life and sustenance* -- since the obligation to do it is on *him* and not on The Holy One blessed be He.[1]

Of course, since he's busy, no doubt he'll get for us every benefit. And I saw it turned out just as I thought, because when I delivered the pipe to Eyliohu the contractor's son and showed him your letter [#71] enclosed with the letter you wrote me, it seemed to him LIKE HE FOUND A GREAT TREASURE. And when I saw he was beside himself with joy, I told him that it was proper to send our *rebe* the *tsadek* in return for this some suitable gift too. "It's true," I told him, "that there's nothing in the world as valuable as the pipe, but at least you got to send him what you can because The Merciful One desires the heart,"* and he promised to give me some article for our *rebe,* he should live. I went to him last Thursday

---

[1] "That is, 'the shopkeeper is absolved and the householder is liable,'* meaning that the essence of the obligation is on the *tsadek,* who is obliged to attain everything. He is called 'the householder' for he brings abundance to the world, like the householder who brings abundance to the members of his household. The Holy One blessed be He, as it were, has no obligation on Him since the *tsadek* alone, through his holy acts, is able to attain everything." *No'am Elimelekh* 22:4.

and he gave me a large and very fancy goblet, which must be worth maybe fifty czerwone zlotys or more. But he asked me not to tell this to nobody because the goblet belongs to his father, and that I myself should go to our *rebe* to hand over to our *rebe* the *tsadek* himself that goblet.

I told him, of course, I'd be very glad to go but I don't have even enough to hire a wagon, and he said he'll pay me for the wagon and expenses. But he said right now he's got no money, but he heard from his father he'll be receiving money for delivery [of goods], so when his father will get the money he'll give me what's needed. And that's what happened. Yesterday he sent for me and gave me two banknotes of five rubles each. I went home and gave a thousand thanks to our *rebe* the *tsadek*, he should live, because I saw plainly it was only on account of him I had this money -- and I didn't have yet *matses* for *Peysekh*.

I told the contractor's son I'm going straight to our *rebe*, he should live, with the goblet, but I'm afraid to travel because maybe the contractor will find out about the thing, G-d forbid!, and when he finds out I went at this time to our *rebe*, he'll have suspicions about me and our *rebe*, he should live. So I left my house so Eyliohu would think I went to our *rebe*, and I went to the village of Khaluvnik where I bought by Reb Aharon *shmire* wheat.* So make sure if one of our Faithful should come here to our community to direct him to collect from me the goblet.

These are the words of

....

#73

From Reb Yankl Pulnaer
To Reb Khayim Gavriel

The bearer of this letter, Reb Dovid Tsere's, is going to your community. Please hand over to him the right vessel wrapped and sealed and he'll deliver it to me. I'm surprised at you you didn't write me even a single word about the rabbinate of your community. So write me by way of the bearer of this letter all the particulars.

These are the words of someone very busy,

....

#74

From Reb Khayim Gavriel
To Reb Yankl Pulnaer

I hereby send you by way of the bearer of this letter the important vessel for our *rebe* the *tsadek.* Please mention my name before our *rebe,* he should live.

As for the rabbinate of our community here, I talked with Reb Yankev Leyb, Reb Shmerl's father-in-law, and he answered me "Yes," and "No," and wavered. When I saw he's a very crude man and there's no talking with him, I went to his sister Soro Reb Meyer's, and persuaded her she should make sure to prevail on her brother in that matter because it's an honor for her whole family if her brother's son-in-law would be here rabbi. She went to him and talked with him about this at length and he promised her he'll agree if his son-in-law is willing.

I told her she should go herself to his son-in-law and she went to his son-in-law too, but he's not willing no way nohow. He answered her he's afraid the judge Mikhal Kahane shouldn't make for him trouble because he [Mikhal Kahane] is a great scholar and very sharp-witted.

So I'm informing you all this because I don't know what to do. I talked with some of Reb Shmerl's friends and they really urged him to accept the rabbinate, but he's not willing on no account to listen to them, and I know for sure that if he won't be by us rabbi, they're sure to wind up with the rabbi of the holy community of Kolne. So make sure to talk about this with our holy *rebe* and write me what to do about this.

These are the words of

....

#75

From Reb Yankl Pulnaer
To Reb Khayim Gavriel

A certain vessel that you sent I received, and I delivered it to our *rebe* the *tsadek* himself, he should live, last *Shabes Koydesh* eve. Our *rebe,* he should live, was overjoyed **and he walked back and forth about his house in an exalted mood** and with *dveykes* **and sang** *Azamer Bi-*

*Shvokhin** **and made the Great *Kidesh**** from this vessel **in his customary manner** with wonderful *hislayves* as usual. When I saw our *rebe* the *tsadek,* he should live, so very uplifted, and at *Kidesh*-time didn't take his eyes off the vessel,* especially when he sang, "At the wine in the cup...,"* I thought to myself, "This vessel must no doubt be one of the goblets of Rabbi Odom that **the kaiser took from a table setting** to **conceal in his breastpocket** when he was by him at the banquet,[1] and now this goblet must've come to our *rebe* the *tsadek* to rectify it, and for this reason the goblet had to be lost by the contractor."[2]

On *Motse Shabes* after the *Havdole,* I told our *rebe,* he should live, I had a letter [#74] from you, and I told him what you wrote about Reb Shmerl, Reb Yankev Leyb's son-in-law. He ordered me to write you you should tell this Reb Shmerl in his name to accept the rabbinate of your community and he shouldn't be at all afraid of the judge because he has from him nothing to fear.

So tell him all this, and of course he shouldn't be afraid at all, because obviously our *rebe* the *tsadek* himself will come on the first *Shabes* they accept him [Reb Shmerl] as rabbi for your community, and when the judge defies him, then our *rebe* the *tsadek* will take away from the judge his *toyre* just like the *Rabbon,* the Besht, took away the *toyre* of Rabbi Mikhal, judge in the holy community of Horodni, when Our Teacher Rabbi Yekhiel Mikhel became rabbi there and the judge was giving that rabbi trouble.[3] And, of course, everything will be alright.

From me,

....

---

[1] *Shivkhey ha-Besht* 2:1 [Mintz, 15].

[2] "Know that all objects that a person has -- everything comes so that the portion of holiness in it may be rectified. For this reason, sometimes when he has already raised them [the holy sparks], they [the objects] get lost." *Darkhey Tsedek,* par. 64.

"Therefore it happens that he will lose that thing when he has already finished rectifying all the sparks in that object that belong to his soul-root. Then G-d takes that object from him and gives it to another because the sparks remaining in that object belong to the root of another who is of his soul-root." *Likutey Yekorim* 15:1.

[3] **When the Besht wanted to go on his way he was afraid lest the judge make trouble for the rabbi, so he took his *toyre* from him and he** [the judge] **became an ignoramus. It was his custom to arise at midnight to study...and when he opened the book he didn't know a thing and he thought that his mind was not clear....In the morning, after prayer, he was studying his daily portion. He took the book and opened it, and he didn't know a thing. He understood that the Besht had done this to him. He came to the Besht and said, "My master, return to me my *toyre*."** *Shivkhey ha-Besht* 26:3 [Mintz, 189].

The main thing I forgot. You wrote me the contractor's son gave you two banknotes of five rubles each, but I know for certain each one was for a hundred rubles. When I first found out about this I wanted to go straight to our *rebe* and tell him what you did, but I had mercy on you and I thought maybe at the time you actually received them you didn't know what amount they were.

I'm giving you notice now you should see to it at once to send me the balance of them two banknotes, that is, a hundred and ninety rubles, so I can hand them over to our *rebe,* he should live, because a sum of two hundred rubles the contractor's son certainly didn't give you for expenses for your*self.* He obviously gave them to you so you would deduct from them ten rubles for expenses, like you wrote, and the rest you would give to our *rebe* the *tsadek,* for accepting the vessel.

If you don't send the money, you'll be very sorry, because the truth is, even *ten* rubles aren't coming to you because you didn't travel with the vessel. And don't suppose you can deny the matter, because Reb Hirsh, a wineseller from our community, arrived from your community, where he received money from the contractor for wine. This Reb Hirsh owes our *rebe* money, and he brought me the interest in large banknotes and told me Reb Kalmen Bisinger the contractor gave him these banknotes. When he asked him to give him small banknotes, he told him the cashier didn't have small bills, only big ones of a hundred rubles.

Reb Hirsh told me the contractor made an error with the cashier, because as soon as he got home and put the banknotes on the table and started counting them, he was short two bills. There was no one else in his house besides him and his wife and his only son. He ran straight to the cashier and told him he was short two banknotes. The cashier yelled at him and said he counted them carefully into his hand and someone must've stole the two banknotes from him.

So I'm warning you to return the balance of the banknotes to me, or else you'll be -- don't kid yourself! -- very sorry for this.

These are the words of the aforesigned.

#76

From the Rabbi of the Holy Community of Kolne
To the Judge Mikhal Kahane

Greetings and salutations! Your* pleasant words SPARKLED BEFORE ME last Friday on the eve of *Shabes Koydesh.* I have long known that you have not withheld anything I have asked of you, but now you have revived me* by your pure speech. Because you have judged me generously, may The Omnipresent judge you generously* as well in all your undertakings. And if IT HAS PROCEEDED FROM THE L-RD that I be privileged to be in your holy camp to delight with you as we did in the days of our youth in the house of Our Teacher the *Rov,* The Great Light, Rabbi of All The Exiles, Our Teacher the *Rov,* Rabbi Elijah, remembered for eternal life, then you will see that his pure teachings are inscribed still ON THE TABLET OF my HEART.

But what to do in these distressing times? I have heard that you always openly declare your opinion against the notorious sect, but not everyone is privileged to be on such a level as that on which you stand. You are in a big town and among aristocrats and knowledgeable people, and all the people, GREAT AND SMALL ALIKE, LISTEN TO YOUR VOICE, and THE L-RD HAS GIVEN you A LEARNED TONGUE and a proud spirit. You can really stand up to them.

NOT SO I, WHO DWELL AMONG A PEOPLE OF UNCLEAN LIPS, A PEOPLE THAT DOES NOT KNOW THE WAY OF THE L-RD, a people all of whose ways are only to devote [themselves] to their *rebe,* to recount his praises, to sanctify him and to adore him,* and if one dares to utter the slightest word against them, he thereby endangers his life.[1] Indeed, permitting bloodshed comes easier to them than killing a fly. Such a man is considered among them a heretic and an *apikoros* even though his righteousness REACHES THE VERY SKY. Concerning this, you find in their *Seyfer ha-Mides,* "One should not pray for anyone to die, even a heretic, for it is preferable to kill him by human agency rather than by Divine intervention."[2]

Anyone with common sense will understand to what end they wrote this in *Seyfer ha-Mides,* and because of our many iniquities the power of the sect has now grown so considerable that even those who are not of the sect, when they hear from members of the sect that someone is a heretic and an *apikoros,* they believe them thoughtlessly, whether they checked and discovered this fairly and truthfully or simply undertook of their own accord to SPREAD AN EVIL RUMOR ABOUT worthy people.

From every sound that issues from the mouth of the *tsadek,* they say an angel is created,[3] and more beloved to them are the words of their

---

[1] "My eyes have seen that some departed this world in an untimely fashion, because of our many sins, on account of controversies like these, AND WAIT BUT A MOMENT and you will see wonders." *Igeres ha-Koydesh* in *No'am Elimelekh* 111: 2. This statement is truly profound.

[2] *Seyfer ha-Mides,* 36:103.

[3] "As for the *tsadek,* from every sound that comes out of his mouth an angel is created." *No'am Elimelekh* 73:2.

tsadikim than the Toroh of Moshe.[4] The whole people, SMALL AND GREAT, are attracted to their *rebes*, because IT IS EASY IN their VIEW to acquire eternal life simply through the word of the *tsadek*,[5] and not to see hell by virtue of going out to greet the *tsadek*.[6]

So DO NOT BE SURPRISED that I am now an adherent of the *rebe* in Zalin. If they had lashed [Khananye, Misho'el and Azarye, they would have worshipped the image].* The worry and anguish of earning a living is worse than a physical affliction, especially for a man like me whom G-d has given a worthy wife and six children.

Believe me,* my friend, my whole objective in aspiring to the rabbinical post in your holy community is just so as to remove there my filthy garments* and show in plain view that only my pain and sorrow led me to SIN WITH MY TONGUE. Since your letter [#69] reached me, I have been reminded of the days of our youth when THE TOROH OF THE L-RD WAS OUR DELIGHT and the doctrines of Our Teacher were free of any dross or falsehood. While still there we heard no unseemly word, Heaven forfend -- and now, when I look at some "book" of the aforementioned sect, I see that it is full of filth and obscenity that the mind cannot endure.[7] The fire of passion burns hot within me to cast the *toroh* of the sect behind me.

---

[4] "The words of wise *tsadikim* are more beloved than words of Toyre and Prophets. One must heed and obey them even though they do not show you any miracle." *Mides* 51:60.

[5] "The *tsadek*, by his word, can assign this one to paradise and that one to hell." *Ibid.*, 51:54.

[6] "By virtue of going out to greet the *Rov*, one will not see hell." *Ibid.*, 52:65.

[7] "And this is [the meaning of]: THE FIRST FRUIT OF YOUR SOIL --YOU SHALL BRING TO THE HOUSE [OF THE L-RD YOUR G-D]. DO NOT COOK A KID *(gdy)* -- the letters of sinew *(gyd)* -- IN ITS MOTHER'S MILK, that is to say, even sexual craving should be for the sake of Heaven, for the craving in the male is from the power of the female that is in the male, for everything is emanated from male and female and even the male is inclusive of male and female." *Likutey Yekorim* 5:1.

"Just as physical intercourse does not eventuate in a child unless one performs his marital duty with a vital organ and with desire and joy, so too in spiritual intercourse, that is, speaking Toyre and prayer, when it is [performed] with a vital organ [i.e., tongue]." *Keser Shem Tov*, Part 1, 1:2.

"Prayer is intercourse with the *Shkhine*. Just as in the beginning of intercourse there is rocking, so too one must rock himself in prayer at first, and afterward he can stand motionless." *Likutey Yekorim* 1:2.

"They are called male according to the way of the male who disrobes from top to bottom and the female in the opposite way." *Ibid.*, 30:3.

"TO KNOW YOUR WAYS ON EARTH. 'To know' is like ODOM KNEW -- an expression for intercourse...; TO KNOW ON EARTH means 'the *Shkhine*'; YOUR WAYS is an expression for the connection of intercourse, which is called 'a way.'" *Likutey Amorim* 2:3.

"KNOW THE G-D OF YOUR FATHER AND SERVE HIM. KNOW is a term for intercourse from the expression, ODOM KNEW." *Tanye,* fol. 57.

"WHEN A MAN SEDUCES A VIRGIN. SEDUCES *(yephateh)* is an expression of adornment *(yipuy),* that is, the *tsadek* who adorns *(yeyape)* the *Shkhine* to be called a virgin...; AND LIES WITH HER, is an allusion to The Holy One blessed be He and His *Shkhine* ...; TO HIM AS A WIFE, meaning that he brings the female into him, meaning, into the male." *No'am Elimelekh* 46:2.

"'For if he had a claim as to her virginity,'* meaning, if you really find such *tsadikim,* who have ways of making the *Shkhine* a virgin again...." *Ibid., ibid.,* col. 1.

"IN ORDER TO RAISE UP HIS COVENANT *(BRIS),* the raising up of the covenant *(BRIS)* is an allusion to intercourse." *Likutey MohoRa"N,* Book 2, 56:2.

"It is possible to bring, G-d forbid!, abundance to the forces of evil, that is to say, lying with the concubine of our heavenly Father." *Or Ha-Meyer* 18:4.

"There are two [kinds of] *tsadikim* -- one whose words are like plowing and the other whose words are like reaping, [in other words,] one whose words are the raising of the *bris* for intercourse [i.e., erection], and the other whose words are what draw forth the seed and bring the embryo into being in its mother's womb and make it grow [i.e., ejaculation]. So when there is a controversy between these two *tsadikim,* let no outsider mix into their conversation when they are speaking with one another, so as not to spoil the mystical intent." *Mides* 92:18.

"I AM ALIVE BECAUSE OF YOU *(BIGLOLEYKH)* is an expression for dung *(glolim),* in the sense of, AS THE EXCREMENT *(HA-GLOL)* BURNS, meaning that the Divine essence could enter excrement too."* *No'am Elimelekh* 5:4.

"The complete *tsadek* who wants to bring him [the as-yet-incomplete *tsadek*], too, to a high rung, says to him, PUT YOUR HAND UNDER MY THIGH, meaning that he should connect with him. Alluding to this is MY THIGH, called *'yesod,'** which is sexual connection, as is known." *Ibid.,* 10:4.

"MAKE FOR IT FOUR GOLDEN RINGS. RING is the ring of betrothal for the *Shkhine." Ibid.,* 48:3.

From everything stated above, you can see how the rabbi of the holy community of Kolne, with full malice aforethought, blinds himself. Everyone knows that young men, who would not have studied any book, study the holy books by the *tsadikim* of our time, because in them they can find tranquillity for themselves* when they read things that breathe life into their spirit and their soul. On account of this they study the holy books mentioned above with intense *dveykes* for its own sake, precisely for its own sake in fact. Of this the prophet said, AND ON THE COMPANY *(SOD)* OF YOUTHS TOGETHER, that is to say, the study that is mystical*(sod)* is precisely *sod* (for *sod* (mystical) and *yesod* (genital) are one and the same); YOUTHS TOGETHER, meaning, gathering themselves together; YOUTHS, that is, young men, to study and to teach, to observe and to do, and without *sod* (mystical) or *yesod* (genital), as mentioned above, they would not study at all. So who can't see the great usefulness of the *toyre* that is in the holy books by the *tsadikim* of our time, which is in the category of *sod* or *yesod?* Who indeed?! Concerning the above rabbi and those like him it says in the preceding

So I implore you, for the sake of the love between us, to act to bring me out of this filthy prison, for there is no greater *mitsve* than this. Our sages of blessed memory have already said, "Whoever saves one Jew, [Scripture credits as having saved an entire world]."*

These are the words of your friend who looks forward to seeing you soon,

....

---

verse, SEE, THEIR EAR IS UNCIRCUMCISED SO THEY COULD NOT HEAR. BEHOLD THE WORD OF THE L-RD BECAME A REPROACH TO THEM. May G-d, in His great mercy, make our eyes shine with the *toyre* of the real *tsadikim. Omeyn Selo* and so may it be His will.

#77

From the Judge Mikhal Kahane To the Rabbi of the Holy Community of Kolne

I already informed you that the *gvir*, Our Teacher Reb Kalmen Bisinger of our community here, promised me to do everything in his power for you. Now his spouse, the *gvire,* out of her boundless love for her only son, has asked him not to take any action in the matter of the rabbinate and he, even though he has never gone back on his word, was nonetheless temporizing and has not taken any action either against you or for you. He is hoping that the day will yet come when his spouse too will agree with him.

It is now five days since he saw a little craziness in his son, who has begun to become something of a *khosed.* This *gvir* asked me to have a heart-to-heart talk with his son and to convince him to forsake his wicked ways. I did as he requested and went to his son's room. When I entered his room I saw a book in his hand. When he saw me he wanted to hide the book, but it was too late to conceal it and I saw that it was the book *Shivkhey ha-Besht.* As I had never seen it, I had wanted to have a look at it ever since it was published. When I opened it I saw in it that the Besht was expecting to ascend in a tempest like Elijah of blessed memory, but he didn't ascend because his wife died on him and he became **half a man**.[1] When I read this, I WAS AGHAST and I said to my student, "Can you believe such heretical things?" He replied to me that he believes it with perfect faith* since he read in this book some wonders

---

[1] *Shivkhey ha-Besht* 23:3 [Mintz, 169].

that the Besht had performed during his lifetime, and all the wonders that Elijah performed, the Besht too performed -- MORE SPLENDIDLY:

- "ELIJAH BENT OVER AND PUT HIS FACE BETWEEN HIS KNEES so as to bring rain upon the earth, whereas *he* by his prayer alone brought the rain.[2]
- "ELIJAH STRETCHED HIMSELF OUT OVER THE dead BOY AND CRIED TO THE L-RD to RETURN THE BOY'S LIFE TO HIM, whereas *he* returned the life of the boy who had died a few days before. By his word alone he sustained this boy.[3]
- "Elijah said in the name of the L-rd, THE PITCHER OF MEAL WOULD NOT BE FINISHED AND THE JAR OF OIL WOULD NOT BE DIMINISHED, whereas *he* provided Reb Motl Pulnaer by means of the oxen drivers **the sum of thirteen hundred zlotys**, though he started out with just **two quarts of vodka**.[4]
- "Elijah was VERY ZEALOUS FOR THE L-RD OF HOSTS and he cried out to the L-rd to answer him with fire SO THAT IT WOULD BE KNOWN TO all THE PEOPLE THAT THE L-RD IS G-D IN ISRAEL, whereas ***he*** **touched a tree with his finger and the tree was enkindled**, and all this was just so his men might warm themselves, and **the servant dried the rag that was on his feet**.[5]
- "Elijah feared for his life because of Izevel AND HE WENT TO THE WILDERNESS AND WANTED TO DIE, whereas *he* was not afraid of a certain squire who **hated him and** who **said when he saw him he would kill him with a gun**, and he went to the commissioner in his town when the squire was there but the squire didn't see him and when the squire found out about it **he said: Since he is such a person I must appease him.**[6]
- "When Elijah was in the wilderness and he didn't have anything to eat, AN ANGEL brought him A CAKE BAKED IN ASHES AND A JAR OF WATER, whereas *he* set a big feast with many kinds of delicacies before his disciples *without* the help of an angel.[7] Furthermore, even when the *angels* desired that the rabbi of the holy community of Rashkov should earn a living, they said to him [the Besht]: **Why do *you* remain silent?**[8]
- "Elijah was obliged to eat twice of the foods the angel had brought

---

[2] *Ibid.*, 5:1 [Mintz, 36].
[3] *Ibid.*, 35:3 [Mintz, 252].
[4] *Ibid.*, 24:1 [Mintz, 172].
[5] *Ibid.*, 18:2 [Mintz, 131].
[6] *Ibid.*, 27:1 [Mintz, 193].
[7] *Ibid.*, 35:2 [Mintz, 251f.].
[8] See Letter #47, note 2.

him in order to go forty days on the strength of the meal,* though the trip was without contemplative prayer, whereas *he* --although he didn't go for forty days, but an angel didn't bring him food -- *he* didn't eat at all and he went without eating for **three days *in* contemplative prayer**.[9]

- "Elijah prophesied in the name of the L-rd, THE DOGS WILL LICK UP AKHAV'S BLOOD AND THEY WILL DEVOUR IZEVEL, whereas *he* permitted his wife **to buy marten furs** from a caravan **because they would all be killed by robbers.**[10]
- "Elijah said in the name of the L-rd, THE BED WHICH Akhaziohu IS LYING ON he WOULD NOT RISE FROM, whereas *he* said of a healthy tax-collector who had not gone to bed at all that **today or tomorrow he will die**, and so it was.[11]
- "Elijah STRUCK THE WATER with his MANTLE AND IT PARTED RIGHT AND LEFT* so he could cross on dry land, whereas for *his* sake **the mighty mountains moved closer to him and became level ground** and afterward they moved back, and this **happened several times.**[12]
- "And several signs and wonders appear in this book of the Besht that Elijah didn't perform, so he must not have been *able* to perform them."

I asked him: "Who guarantees us that all the things found in *Shivkhey ha-Besht* are true? Does *he* know the ritual slaughterer of Linits,* or is it signed by witnesses and a court? And why didn't they publish the book *Shivkhey ha-Besht* while the Besht and his generation were still alive? Why did they wait until the whole generation who knew and saw his deeds and acts had died? Indeed, our rabbi, our Light, the *Rov,* The Great Light, Our Teacher Rabbi Elijah,* told me and my companions that he had known the Besht well. He told us that in his generation he was like the rest of the wonder-workers and he wasn't even learned but was even more of an insolent man and a swindler than the other wonder-workers of his generation."[13]

When I said this, a jealous rage came over my student and he started berating me and the *toroh* that he learned from me, in the manner of all

---

[9] *Shivkhey ha-Besht* 3:3 [Mintz, 24].
[10] *Ibid.*, 6:1 [Mintz, 43].
[11] *Ibid.*, 5:2 [Mintz, 38].
[12] *Ibid.*, 3:2 [Mintz, 22].
[13] Who could believe that in this era there could be so ruthless a sinner as this judge, may his name be erased! All this is on account of the *toyre* that he learned. As it is written in *Likutey MohoRa"N* 20:3, "When the *Shkhine,* who is called 'the Oral Toyre,' enters into a Jewish demon Toyre sage, this is called 'the exile of the *Shkhine,*' and then he has the audacity to speak arrogantly about a *tsadek."*

the members of the sect. "You're a heretic and an *apikoyres!*" he screamed. In rage he ran to the chest, took out a dirty pipe and kissed it, and said to me, "See this pipe? I'll have you know that I wouldn't exchange it for all your *toyre* and that of all the rabbis in the world!"

The noise was audible in his father's room and he, too, came to us, but the son did not let up from his harangue. He ran around his room with the pipe in his hand like a *meshuge* and he screamed and abused me and his father and SPOKE DISPARAGINGLY of all the rabbis and worthies of our time who are not of the sect. We stood horrified at the sight for we saw plainly that HE WAS OUT OF HIS MIND.[14]

His father, in terrible anguish, wanted to strike him with his fist, but I stopped him. I took him [the father] by force and went with him to the other room, where that *gvir* said to me, "Now the time has come to accept the rabbi of the holy community of Kolne as rabbi of our community here, but I heard that he too is of the sect of the *khsidim* and is subject to the *rebe* in Zalin." I told him what I know of you -- that you are of the "forced converts",* many of whom, because of our numerous iniquities, are hiding in caves -- and he believed me.

So I thought to inform you of all this so that you might rest assured, for in a few more days I hope to send you, G-d willing, a copy of the permit concerning the rabbinate* of our community here.

Be well.

These are the words of your bosom friend,
sending you regards always,
....

---

[14] Whoever has read Letter #71 will know that he took the pipe in his hand so that he would enter a state of *hislayves* and the judge would fall asleep, but why he entered a state of *hislayves* and the judge did *not* fall asleep -- I have not been privileged to discover the reason.

#78

From the Rabbi of the Holy Community of Kolne To the Judge Mikhal Kahane

I received your epistle and saw from it that you have no interest in esoteric matters.* Had my [own] eyes not seen your handwriting, I would not have believed that in this exalted generation there are still people who have not read the book *Shivkhey ha-Besht,* which has already been printed five times now, and more than six thousand copies have been disseminated among our kinfolk in the course of two years. Of you and those like you, the prophet said, MAKE THE HEART OF THIS PEOPLE FAT....

For I know for certain that if someone would only read the Author's Introductions to *Shivkhey ha-Besht,* he could not keep himself from reading the book in its entirety. As the author explicitly states there: **"Therefore let everyone who reads it know faithfully that I have not written this as folktales or chronicles, but rather so that the reader should pay attention and really consider with insight* every one of G-d's awesome deeds, and should draw for himself a moral lesson from this, to adorn his heart with fear of G-d or with faith in the power of our holy Toyre that emanates from the story...."***

You must not have read even the Introduction and you do not know that he who is occupied with the praises of the *tsadikim* is like one who is occupied with *Mayse Merkove* -- and who would not wish to be occupied with that *Mayse Merkove* which is permitted to us? I GRIEVE FOR YOU, especially for your soul, which has been placed in such crude matter.

As surprising as it is to you that the Besht is more important to the group than Elijah, that is how obvious it is to me. And if G-d gives you the privilege of reading the holy books, you will see that he was greater even than G-d! And not just the Besht specifically, but even the *tsadikim* of our generation too are more important than The Holy One, praised be He,[1] the patriarchs[2] and Moyshe Rabeyne, may he rest in peace![3]

Be so good as to read the Author's Introduction to the book *Shivkhey ha-Besht,* published in Kopust,* and you will see that the *tsadek,* Rabbi Menakhem Mendl, testified **in these words: "The word of G-d was in**

---

[1] "The *tsadek* teaches The Holy One, praised be He -- using *His* Toyre -- how He should act towards us." *Mides* 54:131.

"This is the meaning of, THE EYES OF THE L-RD BELONG TO THE *TSADIKIM*: It is in the power of the *tsadikim* to provide eyes for G-d to watch over Israel." *No'am Elimelekh* 11:3.

"ALL YOUR CHILDREN SHALL BE TAUGHT OF THE L-RD, meaning that the complete *tsadikim,* who are called YOUR CHILDREN, are taught of the L-rd because they teach, as it were, The Holy One, praised be He, how He should act with us." *Mevaser Tsedek* 2:4.

"OPENING YOUR HAND.... This refers to the *tsadek,* because the *tsadek* is the one who opens the hands of the Creator blessed be He, as it were." *No'am Elimelekh* 103:3.

[2] "At will, the *tsadek* can bring abundance and accomplish something by means of his own activity, even without the merit of the patriarchs, that is to say, that the prosecution -- have no illusions! -- is great, and the merit of the patriarchs is of no use alone. It is necessary to hold fast to a rung higher than the rung of the patriarchs." *Ibid.,* 88:2.

[3] See in the *Prologue,* footnote 1.

the power of The Balshem. He was unique. None of the ancients were like him, NOR WILL THERE EVER BE ANY [LIKE HIM] ON EARTH." And is there anyone greater than Rabbi Menakhem Mendl? Indeed, the Besht himself testified concerning him that he mentioned him by way of the *tfile,* and he let him use his house of meditative seclusion.[4]

This will be utterly baffling in your coarse sight,* for you know what the Ramban, remembered for eternal life, said about the verse, HE UNLOADED THE CAMELS -- that he was incredulous that the *khsides** could be greater in the house of Rabbi Pinkhes ben Yo'ir than in the house of our father Avrohom,* may he rest in peace.[5]

But you and all the ancients who predeceased the Besht study the Toroh as it is written -- with garments -- while the *tsadikim* of the generation to whom the Toroh has been handed down[6] study it after the stripping away of the garments. Therefore, only they know the way of truth,* and we have only to listen to them, to obey them, and to cast away our reason and our knowledge -- just to rely on them, even though it appears to us that they are acting against the Toroh.[7]

G-d willing, when I come to your community I shall teach you the new Toyre and make known to you THE PATHS OF RIGHTEOUSNESS without

---

[4] *Shivkhey ha-Besht* 21:3-4 [Mintz, 154].

[5] The Preacher, The Holy Light, Our Teacher Rabbi Dov Baer of Mezeritch, sensed this surprise and said with his golden eloquence, "It is known that whatever ascends higher contains more intelligence and clarity. So we find with Rabbi Pinkhes ben Yo'ir's ass *(khamor)* that he had intelligence to distinguish between tithed and untithed.* The reason was that Rabbi Pinkhes ben Yo'ir had attached himself to G-d with total *dveykes* to the extent that He was even on his material things *(khomriuso)* and He caused this same intelligence to enter into them. And so we find with Avrohom, may he rest in peace, HE PURSUED AS FAR AS DAN -- for in reality how could he fight against five kings? Rather, he fought against them with contemplative prayer in that he brought them to judgment...And Avrohom DEPLOYED *(VAYEIKHALEYK)* AGAINST THEM BY NIGHT, meaning that he separated *(vayekhaleyk)* *'H'* (from) *'LaYLoH'* (night) and *'LaYiL'* (darkness) remained, which is in the category of judgments, and with this he pursued them."* *Likutey Amorim* 12:3.

[6] "The essential principle is that he have faith in *khakhomim* and be attentive to their honor and revere them greatly. Even if it appears to him that they are acting, G-d forbid, against the Toyre, he must believe that they must be acting correctly according to the Toyre, for the Toyre was handed down to the sages of the generation to expound it in accordance with what they know. Therefore, one must cast off his reason and knowledge, only to rely on them [the sages of the generation]." *Kitser Likutey MohoRa"N* 43:431.

[7] "The *tsadek* is permitted to breach the fences of others for his path." *Mides* 53:119. Also see note 6.

which WE GROPE ABOUT LIKE BLIND MEN, and I shall thereby SAVE YOU AND YOUR SOUL from hell,* as is the wish of

Your friend, **sending you regards always** with a willing heart and soul,

....

#79

From Reb Khayim Gavriel
To Reb Yankl Pulnaer

I got your letter [#75] and I did like our *rebe* the *tsadek* ordered me through you. I talked with Reb Shmerl to accept the rabbinic post in our community and he shouldn't be afraid of the judge, but all my words were for nothing because he's not willing nohow. I see plainly this is just because his father-in-law is a very crude man, and he's afraid he shouldn't have to spend lots of money for the rabbinic post.

If you'd send me money then of course I'd be able to convince him to accept the rabbinic post. So I'm writing you you should make sure, for God's sake, to send me cash for this business. The Zaliner's people in our community already did their part and the deal was already done, but I'm still holding things up. I promised to pay cash and you know I don't have right now even a *prute*'s worth, because our people around here are few and they're almost all of them paupers and beggars.

Believe me, the two hundred rubles a certain somebody gave me -- I didn't know at first and I really thought each one was for just five rubles, but Reb Aharon in Khalivnik told me each one was a hundred rubles. I spent eighty rubles of it for *Peysekh* because I thought, "Why should I stint for *yontef* with this? If G-d helped me to get money by the merit of our *rebe* the *tsadek,* he should live, why shouldn't I honor such a holy *yontef?*" And the rest I gave as a bribe for the rabbinic post to an official of the council chamber. If it weren't for that, the rabbi of the holy community of Kolne would've been already accepted as rabbi here.

So for cryin' out loud, make sure to send money because I promised some more people cash. If you don't send it -- don't kid yourself! -- it sure won't be good, and you'll see in a little while the liar of Zalin will come to our community and wield his authority in his usual arrogant way.

These are the words of

....

#80

From Reb Yankl Pulnaer
To Reb Khayim Gavriel

I saw from your letter [#79] it's very urgent to spare no effort in the matter of the rabbinate of your community, and since the collectors of *Ertsisroel* funds and Rabbi Meyer Balanes funds arrived last week from the communities that belong to our *rebe* the *tsadek,* he should live, I thought now would be a good time to talk with our *rebe* about this. But when I wanted to go to his room, along came the *rebetsn,* the *tsadkones,* she should live, and went to the house of meditative seclusion of our *rebe,* he should live. I wanted to hear what our holy *rebe* would discuss with the *tsadkones,* she should live, because the things he discusses with her in his house of meditative seclusion must be ancient and secret* and exalted above and beyond,* because at such time no one's allowed to enter there.

So I stood near the room for about a quarter of an hour and I didn't hear nothing. Then I heard our *rebe* the *tsadek,* he should live, say, "In my opinion, fifty is enough."

And the *tsadkones,* she should live, says, "You're always stingy just to me. How many people eat and drink by you who you get nothing from! For this you're not stingy, but when it comes to *me* you're always stingy!"

Our *rebe,* he should live, says, "You don't understand this. It just has to be that way. *I* know, of course, why I don't begrudge them eating by me." Our *rebe* also says, "After all, I didn't promise you more than fifty!"

The *tsadekes,* she should live, says, "What *is* this? You didn't promise me because you didn't know so much money would be coming to you, but now that they brought you plenty, why won't you give me at least seventy-five?"

And our *rebe,* he should live, says, "What can I do with you? You're so stubborn!" And I heard him counting her out money.

When the *tsadkones* came from the house of meditative seclusion, she told me to go to Rivke Peyse's, who deals in pearls,* and I followed her. The *tsadekes* bought from her a hundred czerwone zlotys' worth of pearls. She put seventy-five czerwone zlotys down and twenty-five czerwone zlotys remained on account.

I realized this wasn't the right moment to go to our *rebe,* so I went the next day and told our *rebe* all that happened, like you wrote me. Our *rebe* was silent at first and then he says, "This fool Shmerl isn't fit to be rabbi in Koven," and I couldn't talk no more about this business.

So I'm informing you of this so you'll know what our *rebe* answered me about this. And as I see it, Shmerl really is a big fool, because how could he not be a big fool if you told him in the name of our *rebe* he shouldn't be afraid of the judge Mikhal Kahane nohow, yet this fool don't want to accept the rabbinic post and said he's afraid of the judge? What can the judge do to him if our *rebe* told him he shouldn't be afraid?!

From me,

....

#81

From Reb Khayim Gavriel
To Reb Yankl Pulnaer

So our holy *rebe* won't, G-d forbid!, complain about me later on, I'm informing you the contractor Kalmen Bisinger of our community was very angry at his only son because he was insolent to the Jewish demon, Mikhal Kahane the judge, his name should be erased. In my opinion he got angry because he looked at the face of this lying judge,[1] and in his anger he gave the order to write the letter for the rabbinic post to the rabbi of the holy community of Kolne. All the big shots of our community signed the letter, not to mention the people who are followers of the liar in Zalin, and there's no one who'll stand up to them.

I'm terrified that if you don't move heaven and earth, then the letter is sure to be confirmed by the council too, and then we'll be among them who cry out and aren't answered.* So make sure, for cryin' out loud, to tell this to our *rebe* the *tsadek,* he should live, and if our *rebe* don't want to do nothing against this, then at least we'll know it's okay as is and that's how it has to be.

These are the words of

....

---

[1] "Whoever looks at the face of a liar gets angry." *Mides* 28:21.

#82

From Reb Yankl Pulnaer
To Reb Khayim Gavriel

I got your letter [#81] and I told our *rebe,* he should live, everything you wrote me. Our *rebe* said to me, "Didn't I already tell you this fool Shmerl isn't fit to be rabbi in Koven and the rabbi of the holy community of Kolne isn't one of them we call losers?" I didn't talk no more about this business because I saw the matter obviously has to be as is.

So make sure to cozy up to the rabbi of the holy community of Kolne as soon as he arrives in your community, because what our *rebe* the *tsadek* said about him -- that he's no *shlimazl* -- he didn't say for no reason. Our *rebe* must foresee he'll distance himself from the liar in Zalin and draw close to *our rebe,* he should live.

So the moment that rabbi arrives in your community, be sure to write me whether the fake *rebe* of Zalin comes with him, and what the rabbi is doing there, and what *you* did. Also, if he comes to your community by himself without the Zaliner, all of you go out to greet him and honor him. Thus has our *rebe* the *tsadek* commanded.

From me,
....

#83

From the Judge Mikhal Kahane
To the Rabbi of the Holy Community of Kolne

I wanted to send you a copy of the permit for the rabbinic post here but I saw that it would only be redundant, because in three more days, G-d willing, the messengers of our holy community here will travel to you with the permit to bring you hither. All the local dignitaries have already signed the permit and it has also been confirmed in the council chamber. Only some of the Dishpoler's people were unwilling to sign, but don't be afraid of these firebrands because in our community they have no REPUTE* among the worthies.

So be sure to prepare yourself for the journey and, G-d willing, when you arrive here, I shall be your student* to learn from you the new *Mayse*

Merkove, which I have neither heard nor seen except in your lovely letter [#78] of the twenty-eighth of last month.

These are the words of your friend, who looks forward to seeing you here soon, G-d willing,

....

#84

From Reb Zelig Letitchiver
To the Rabbi of the Holy Community of Kolne

This very minute I got a letter from the holy community of Koven and I was very pleased because I saw in it His Toyre Eminence will be accepted as rabbi of that holy community. Let it be known to His Toyre Eminence that the fake *rebe* of Dishpol's people did everything in their power not to let His Toyre Eminence be accepted, but a lie don't fly.* I wrote you already that our holy *rebe* said His Toyre Eminence will be rabbi in Koven. So praised be our holy *rebe!*[1] See, NOTHING REMAINS

---

[1] The rabbi of the holy community of Kolne got very angry when he read this letter because Reb Zelig had written, "Praised be our holy *rebe.*" He said that soon they would say to the *tsadek,* "Praised are You, O L-rd...." I'm very surprised at this man. How has he forgotten what is written in the book *No'am Elimelekh* 11:3, "That blessing that we recite every day -- '[Praised are You, O L-rd our G-d, King of the universe,] who opens the eyes of the blind'* -- means to open eyes on high to watch over Israel...It is in the power of the *tsadek* to provide eyes for G-d." Therefore it follows that every day we are blessing the *tsadikim* for providing eyes for The Holy One, praised be He, and we are saying to the *tsadek,* 'Praised are You, O L-rd our G-d, King of the universe' -- that is, the *tsadek* -- 'who opens the eyes of the blind' -- namely, that he, the *tsadek,* opens the eyes of the blind -- namely, G-d, as it were.

And there is no reason at all to be surprised at this, for we have found that the *tsadek* is called "Praised" *(Borukh)* , *No'am Elimelekh* 5:2, and is also called "You" *(Atoh). Ibid.,* 24:2. He said, YOU BRING LIFE TO THEM ALL..., which refers to...the *tsadek,* as if to say, the *tsadek* is called "YOU," in that he is part of You (of G-d)...and he meant that the *tsadek*...brings life to all the worlds, and "G-d" -- that is, "G-d of holiness" -- he is certainly called. See Letter #16, note 3.

Accordingly, why should it not be said of the *tsadek,* "Praised are You..." *(Borukh atoh...)* and all the blessings, just as of G-d? Nor do I have the slightest doubt that soon, when no one will dare to speak against our faction even in secret, and when all Israel will belong to us as we hope, in the merit of the

UNFULFILLED of all HE HAS SPOKEN and all THE EFFORTS the Dishpoler's side made WERE IN VAIN, and we see plainly only his holy words have brought all this about.[2]

Our holy *rebe* instructed me to write you as follows: "When **you arrive in the community** of Koven **they will show you great honor. If, G-d forbid!, you do not resist, you will lose everything that has come about thus far.**"[3]

I'm also informing His Toyre Eminence our *rebe* spent on the matter of the rabbinic post of His Toyre Excellency a lot of money. You know our *rebe* don't have funds of his own at the moment and he went into debt for you. So when you arrive in Koven be sure to speak about this with the local dignitaries they should send immediately for our holy *rebe* to spend there *Shabes.* For His Toyre Excellency too this will be a great benefit, because I heard there's a judge there who's a big troublemaker and you're sure to have aggravation from him, but if our holy *rebe* is there he certainly won't be defiant. And if he *is* defiant, then our *rebe* will order him to produce his *tfiln,* and they'll be, of course, ritually unfit,

---

tsadikim, the *tsadikim* will convene to formulate prayers explicitly about the *tsadikim,* for whose sake alone our physical and spiritual necessities come to us and without whom G-d could not, as it were, do anything, as we have explained in several notes from the holy books of the *tsadikim* of our time. And then we will not need to pray, as in the past, to G-d.

[2] "When human beings come to the *tsadek* concerning their necessities -- for example, that he should achieve something for them by a landlord or government -- then the *tsadek* says to this man, 'The government will fulfill your requests and it won't be any other way.' And it is like a commandment from the mouth of the *tsadek* that it won't happen any other way." *No'am Elimelekh* 34:4.

[3] **Once the Besht went to the holy community of Brod and stayed overnight somewhere near Brod. During the night the Besht became frightened and his knees knocked together until he awakened Reb Tsvi, the scribe, from his sleep, as a result of the sound of the knocking. The scribe said to him, "What is this trembling?" And he told him that "My rabbi came to me (that is, Akhiye the Shilonite) and asked me, 'Who is more worthy -- you or Avrohom our father, may he rest in peace?' I asked him, 'What is the point of this question?' He said to me, 'You will go to the holy community of Brod and they will show you great honor. If, G-d forbid!, you do not resist, you will lose everything that has come about thus far' -- and I became very frightened."**

When he arrived at the holy community of Brod, the dignitaries came to welcome him in splendid attire. He began to play with the horses and to stroke them and pet them with his hands in the manner of those familiar with horses. Now you know the extent of the Besht's fear of sin. *Shivkhey ha-Besht* 15:3. [Mintz, 112]

and the judge will flee from town in humiliation,[4] and His High Toyre Excellency will rest easy there.

Since the people in the holy community of Koven will certainly come out to greet you, and His Toyre Eminence will have to say before them *toyre,* so I'm writing you some of the *toyre* of our holy *rebe* so His Toyre Excellency will say this *toyre,* which is very, very far-reaching, even though I'm writing you the *toyre* in abbreviated form, because you know our holy *rebe* is of them *tsadikim* who say *toyre* below with the utmost brevity, but on high it is very, very great and far-reaching:[5]

> ZIMRI SON OF SALU, CHIEFTAIN OF A SIMEONITE PATRIARCHAL HOUSE *(NESI BEIS AV LESHIM'ONI)* is the same as, "If this contemptible character encounters you, drag him to the *besmedresh."** This refers to ZIMRI -- an expression for "cutting off." SON OF SALU is the evil inclination, in the sense of PRICKLING BRIERS *(SILON MAM'IR),* and that is ZIMRI SON OF SALU. When you want to cut off the evil inclination, which is called SON OF SALU -- *NESI BEIS AV,* take or carry it to the father's house,* that is, to the house of the *tsadek,* who is like a father, and thereby, *LESHIM'ONI,* that is, thereby you will succeed in making the evil inclination obey *(tishma)* Me, and that is *LESHIM'ONI, NI* -- specifically *NI,* that it will obey *Me.*
>
> ACCORDING TO [literally, TO THE MOUTH OF] THE TOYRE THAT THEY WILL TEACH YOU... *(AL PI HA-TOROH ASHER YORUKHO),* meaning, we wouldn't know what a man who can't be occupied with Toyre is supposed to do. To such a person He said, "You got a remedy -- to sustain the *tsadek."* This is precisely TO THE MOUTH OF *(AL PI),* and he is literally the mouth of the Toyre *(PI HA-TOROH)* -- that is, to give to the mouth of the Toyre, namely, to the mouth of the *tsadek.*[6]
>
> AND TO THE SONS OF KEHAS HE DID NOT GIVE ANY; [SINCE THEIRS WAS THE SERVICE OF THE SACRED OBJECTS], THEY WOULD CARRY BY SHOULDER *(VELIVNEY KEHAS LO NOSAN...BAKOSEYF YISO'U).* It is known that the *tsadek* must bring abundance down to the world. Therefore the *tsadek* must cleave even to the sinner and even commit sin in order to bring the abundance to the wicked. That is why AND TO THE SONS OF KEHAS *(VELIVNEY KEHAS),* who were *tsadikim,* the sacred

---

[4] *Ibid.,* 16:3 [Mintz, 119].

[5] "There are those who say very extensive *toyre,* who stretch it out and blow it up, but nevertheless, on high it is very brief....But, conversely, there are *tsadikim* who say *toyre* on earth with the greatest brevity, but on high it is extensive and very, very great. Blessed are they." *Kitser Likutey MohoRa"N* 59:587.

[6] *Or Peney Moyshe* 199:3.

service fell upon them. And what *was* the sacred service they carried by shoulder? -- that they had to bring down the abundance, which is called *koseif.*[7]

I explained you this *toyre* with the intention that on account of it the people there will send for our holy *rebe* to give him sustenance, and so he'll bring abundance to them too, as stated above. A word to the wise....

You'll see, by the help of our *rebe,* when our holy *rebe* will be there everything will certainly be for His Toyre Excellency just fine, and also for the members of the community it'll be very good, because of course, obviously His Toyre Excellency knows the *tsadek* comes for wanderings, so when he'll arrive in the world-to-come he'll remember all the places where he was, and in this way benefits will come to these places.[8]

From me,

....

---

[7] ["The *tsadek* who wishes to bring abundance to human beings must attach himself to them... for whoever wishes to bring about some benefit for his fellow cannot fully perform this benefit for him except by attaching himself in total unity. If so, the *tsadek* must attach himself to all Israel in order to benefit them. And how does he act with a sinner, G-d forbid!? Clearly, even though he is a sinner, he still needs abundance and a livelihood, and how can the *tsadek* connect himself with him? Concerning this the *Gemore* said, 'Great is a sin committed for its own sake,' so that the *tsadek* also commits some sin but it is for its own sake, and thereby he can connect himself with the sinner, too, and benefit him too."] *No'am Elimelekh* 70:1. The meaning is that one *tsadek* says *toyre* that another *tsadek* has already said. See Letter #62, note 5.

[8] *Mides,* fol. 81, the word "wandering *(tiltul),*" par. 3.

#85

From Reb Khayim Gavriel To Reb Yankl Pulnaer

I'm hereby informing you the new rabbi came to our community and the public welcomed him with great honor. The fact is, to our *rebe* the *tsadek* they don't show greater honor. All the big shots of our community went to greet him at the village of Brest, more than a parasang away from our community. They hung around by the *arendar* there more than two hours and ate and drank, and the rabbi said before them *toyre,* and afterwards they traveled together with him to our community.

Still another crowd **came out to greet him, and when they met each other they all went down to a place in the woods and made a throne of tree branches and seated him on it and installed him as rabbi over them. He said before them words of *toyre**** and the crowd was very pleased. This is understandable since they never heard *toyre* from the mouth of our holy *rebe.*

Still now they're treating him with great honor. With all the affairs they come to him and he resolves them, and the two sides are satisfied with him because he explains the decision well. Two days ago I went to him like you ordered me. I couldn't talk with him much since he had many cases, and I saw plainly here too that all the words of our holy *rebe,* he should live, are the Toyre of Moyshe, because he [the rabbi] is really no *shlimazl.* But for this same reason I'm terrified everyone will become attached to him and he'll lure them to the fake *rebe* in Zalin.

But who am I to think thoughts against the will of our holy *rebe,* he should live? Of course our holy *rebe* knows what he did, especially since I see already two *Shabosim* passed and the Zaliner didn't come to our community, and I even heard a few times he made fun of the Zaliner. It follows, obviously, of course there's not a shred of doubt he'll distance himself from that liar and draw close to our holy *rebe,* he should live, and everything will be alright.

These are the words of
....

#86

From Reb Zelig Letitchiver
To Reb Zaynvl Verkhievker

I was very happy when I read your letter [#61] because I saw plainly it's a great miracle for us Freyda Reb Isaac's is pregnant. I hope your prince sees this punishment came to him because he made fun of our holy *rebe* and our Faithful.

Your advice to send her to our community is very good. When she arrives, our *rebe,* he should live, will tell her she should stay here a few weeks to recover, and I'll give her to Itsik Avrohom's, who lives in

Krasne. I already talked with him and he's very willing. Even though he's rich, all the same I know he's a miser who would die for less than a *prute*'s worth,* and for a few rubles he'd sell his wife and children.

She'll give birth there hush-hush because I made up with him if he reveals the matter I won't give him nothing. By him a ruble is a lot of money -- for one ruble he would kill himself. All the more so for the right amount he'll make sure, of course, not a soul finds out about it. Especially since his wife is right now pregnant, he said he'll say later on his wife gave birth to two children (twins) and he'll keep the thing secret forever. He just wants the prince should give him a note for a fixed sum for child support. Through this affair we'll have your prince by the balls and he'll always be afraid of us.

What you wrote, that you want to talk with the healer before you go to our *rebe,* is total nonsense. For G-d's sake, don't do that! Because what good is it to us she should abort? On the contrary, as far as we're concerned, better she should have a live, HEALTHY, STRONG child, because if she'll abort, then later on the prince will deny the whole thing and he'll be to us a worse enemy.

From me,

....

#87

From Reb Zaynvl Verkhievker
To Reb Zelig Letitchiver

Before I got your letter [#86] I talked with the healer about you-know-what, but I didn't tell him who I need the remedies for. He gave me remedies and you-know-who took them, but they didn't do nothing for her. She has just lots of bleeding as a result from them, and there's no way she can travel right now 'cause she's very sick. I'm going around like a *meshuge* 'cause I'm afraid she shouldn't die, G-d forbid!, and not only won't we have no more hope the prince will be on our side, but he'll surely be even worse of an enemy then he is now, 'cause maybe she told him she got the remedies from me, and when he'll see she got sick from the remedies and she'll die, he'll take away mine livelihood -- don't tempt the devil! So please make sure, for cryin' out loud, our holy *rebe* makes for her a *pidyen,* or orders someone else should die for her so she'll stay alive.[1]

These are the words of

....

[1] "Sometimes they decree from on high that a number of persons will die and there is one among them whom the *tsadek* likes. The *tsadek* has the power to pray for him and save him and to designate another in his stead." *Mides* 53:120.

#88

From Reb Zelig Letitchiver
To Reb Zaynvl Verkhievker

I'm hereby sending you specially by way of the bearer of this letter a quart of wine sealed with my seal. Have Freyda drink from it right away because this wine is from the very wine our holy *rebe,* he should live, looked at,[1] so she's sure to get well from this.

I couldn't tell our *rebe* to make a *pidyen* for Freyda since you didn't send money for the *pidyen,* and you know for a *pidyen* you got to give money.[2] But as luck would have it, somebody from Lavitch sent to our holy *rebe* for a *pidyen* and our holy *rebe* was at the time in his room of meditative seclusion. I took the *pidyen* money with the note they sent from there from the hand of the messenger to deliver them to our *rebe,* he should live, and I took the note they sent and hid it, and gave our holy *rebe* another note with the names of Freyda and her mother, for profuse bleeding and that she shouldn't abort.* Our *rebe* made a *pidyen* and, of course, on account of this everything will be alright. For G-d's sake, write me by way of the bearer of this letter how she's doing, because I'm also sorry she's sick.

From me,

....

[1] "Therefore a woman whose bleeding is profuse though it is not her period, despite the fact that wine is harmful to her as mentioned above, in the sense of WINE THAT REDDENS *(YAYIN KI YIS'ADOM),* the ending of which is *DOM* (blood) in the sense of, 'The wine enters, that which is hidden, exits,'* nevertheless she may be cured by means of wine that a real *tsadek* has looked at." *Likutey MohoRa"N* 48:3.

[2] "One must pay money for a *pidyen.*" *Mides* 18:66.

"Empty hands cannot appease the demand of justice." *Mides* 76:10.

The main thing I forgot. For G-d's sake, if any of the wine is left over, so send it back to me because it's priceless. Just once, when our holy *rebe* was in total bliss and was extremely pleased with me, he gave me as a gift four quarts of this wine he looked at, and who knows whether I'll have this good fortune [again] for the rest of my life?

These are the words of the aforesigned.

#89

From Reb Zaynvl Verkhievker
To Reb Zelig Letitchiver

The wine you sent me Freyda wouldn't drink. She said she heard from a big doctor wine is for a sick person very bad. So I'm sending you back three quarters of this wine by way of the bearer of this letter and a quarter I took for me. What would you do if Freyda drank the whole quart or if I wrote you she drank a quarter? But I'm telling you the truth, and I'm sure you'll forgive me for taking a quarter. Who knows, maybe some of this wine will be needed for some woman from our Faithful.

Freyda started, by the merit of our *rebe,* he should live, and on account of the *pidyen,* to get better, and soon she'll travel to our holy *rebe,* 'cause I told Shloyme Umner, her relation and a follower of our *rebe,* to talk with the family she should go to our holy *rebe* on account of her illness, 'cause except for Shloyme, the family don't know she's pregnant.

He talked with them and they all agreed once she gets better a little she should go to our *rebe,* he should live. Maybe I'll go with her too, 'cause I got nothing to do at home right now anyways since that crude Yankl Rudniker fired me as trustee in the mill, on account of the sinner Mordekhai-His-Name-And-Memory-Should-Be-Wiped-Out Gold. Now I don't got *no* livelihood! For the trip I'll get something for mine trouble, and also I'll be respected by the prince that I went with her and repaid him good instead of bad what he done me at the time of the to-do when I brang him rent for the mill and he kicked me out of the manor.

So let me know when you got everything ready to receive her, 'cause in mine opinion it's better she shouldn't hang around in your community nohow -- just she should be by our *rebe,* he should live, and go straight to Krasne so not a creature in the world finds out about it.

These are the words of
....

#90

From Reb Yekusiel Klinkvitser To Reb Zelig Letitchiver

When I was last month by our holy *rebe,* his light should shine, you promised to help and support me by our *rebe,* he should live, in the matter of a livelihood. Now I got a source* to get a certain job but everything depends on you. If you're willing to help me, I'll for sure have an honorable living.

Here's the story. You know Yankl Rudniker hired Reb Zaynvl Verkhievker as [his] right-hand man at the local mill and Reb Zaynvl made from this a good living. But last week Reb Yankl Rudniker fired Reb Zaynvl as trustee. When I talked about this with Yankl, he told me Reb Zaynvl pulled a swindle with all the bakers, flour dealers and contractors who would grind at the mill. When someone ground, for example, a hundred bushels of grain at the mill, Reb Zaynvl recorded only seventy bushels in the account book, and he charged them for thirty bushels half the price of milling.

Also with the grain he skimmed off the top he made a big swindle. When he sold a hundred bushels of grain for milling, he recorded in the account book only eighty bushels, and the rest he split between him and the contractors who bought the grain from him on contract. Even with the millers and the mill assistants he was in cahoots, and they stole flour from the bins at the mill and split it among theirselves.

Yankl Rudniker found out about this through Mordekhai Gold, because Mordekhai accepted a contract and his steward who he got from Galicia finagled with Reb Zaynvl what the other stewards were finagling with him at the mill. But since this steward acts honestly toward Mordekhai Gold, he didn't take the profit from what he did with Reb Zaynvl for himself -- he just wrote it on his receipt for the transaction. When Mordekhai Gold saw this he got furious with his steward and said he don't want to profit from stolen goods and who gave him permission to steal? -- don't he know the mill don't belong to Reb Zaynvl but to Reb Yankl Rudniker? And he sent straight to Reb Yankl Rudniker and informed him all this. Yankl began checking everything and it all turned out to be evident.

That's what Yankl Rudniker told me, and even though I don't believe a word of it -- because Reb Zaynvl is by us a revered man and very devoted to our rebe, he should live -- but be that as it may, Yankl Rudniker already fired him and I know Yankl will listen to you. So please, sustain me* and my household and write this Yankl he should hire me as trustee. Of course I'll give you a reward for your trouble, as is right and proper.

These are the words of

....

#91

From Reb Zaynvl Verkhievker
To Reb Zelig Letitchiver

The bearer of this letter, the lady Mrs. Freyda, is leaving right now for our holy *rebe,* he should live, to perform for her some cure. I had a mind to go with her but mine wife wouldn't let me. Also her family said she should go by herself so she shouldn't have lots of expenses. So I didn't go, but I want to be to her a help and support in all what she'll need there, because you know already she done us lots of favors around here and she's a respected and wonderful creature -- there's really no one like her in the whole world -- and she'll be able in the future too to do for us big favors all what we'll need, so speak with our holy *rebe* for her 'cause she's very shy around our *rebe,* he should live, and she won't be able to speak with him herself about her condition. I'm sure you'll give consideration to these words of mine and do all what you can.

Also I'm asking from you something else. I heard Reb Yekusiel Klinkvitser was bragging you're going to help him by Yankl Rudniker to accept him as [his] right-hand man at the mill in mine place. True, I see I can't be no more by him trustee, 'cause he's a very crude man and he heard lies about me from the sinner Mordekhai-His-Name-Should-Be-Wiped-Out Gold, so as far as I'm concerned, of course, better he should accept Reb Yekusiel in mine place then he should accept someone else as trustee.

But at least it's proper that if he should take Reb Yekusiel, Reb Yekusiel should give me for this some gift, whatever it might be. After all, the trustee job was mine, and I left that job, and it's not right I should leave it without nothing. Isn't it just on account of I left it he can accept Reb Yekusiel? Everybody around here knows if I wanted now to speak with this crude Yankl he would take me back with open arms, but I don't wish to. So why shouldn't Reb Yekusiel give me for this some gift of cash or at least grain? So please, if you do something for Reb Yekusiel, remember me too, 'cause I'm right now flat broke.

These are the words of

....

#92

From Reb Zelig Letitchiver
To Reb Yekusiel Klinkvitser

I got your letter [#90] and of course I think it's terrific Yankl Rudniker should take you as [his] right-hand man at the mill. But to tell you the truth, the right thing is you should make some arrangement with our Reb Zaynvl, because the rumor Yankl Rudniker spread about him is false, of course, and he must've made up this rumor about him because Reb Zaynvl didn't want to be by him no more, or because the sinner Mordekhai Gold misled him. So it's fitting and proper you should give Reb Zaynvl a few zlotys as a buyout for this, or else earmark for him in the future some grain. That's always the way of the world.

And if you'll do this, I'll write Yankl Rudniker for you, and when the time is ripe I'll even talk with our holy *rebe* about this so our *rebe,* he should live, will give instructions to write to Yankl in his name and he's sure to accept you, because the words of our holy *rebe* one must fulfill.[1]

From me,

....

---

[1] "Whoever disregards the instructions of the *tsadek* -- his prestige is diminished." *Mides* 27:17.

"Whoever rejects the words of a *tsadek* is as if he had consulted sorcerers." *Ibid.,* 56:182.

#93

From Reb Zaynvl Verkhievker
To Reb Zelig Letitchiver

I give you a thousand thanks you wrote Yekusiel Klinkvitser to make with me a deal for the trustee job at the mill. He showed me your letter

[#92] and made with me a deal that when Yankl accepts him, to give me each month for a whole year half a bushel corn flour and a quarter [bushel] wheat flour and a quarter [bushel] barley -- even though the thing didn't materialize on account of the crude Yankl struck up a close acquaintanceship with the sinner Mordekhai-His-Name-Should-Be-Wiped-Out and he don't do nothing without Mordekhai-His-Name-Should-Be-Wiped-Out. When he wanted to take Yekusiel as trustee, he must've asked Mordekhai for advice and Mordekhai didn't agree. 'Cause you know that sinner -- how can he bear that one of our Faithful should have a piece of bread through him or through the people he has a prejudice against? This sinner advised him to hire somebody who came to him from Galicia and Yankl hired him.

What can I tell you? I see plainly this sinner lies in wait against our community. He himself holds the *arende* and his people he even settles in our community. And all this is by the power of the prince, 'cause otherwise he certainly wouldn't dare to settle his people by us.

I don't know what you yourselves think. I'm telling you this is no small matter. Every single day he gets better known around here with the local community members. Some who were simple people and would always kowtow to us don't pay me no attention at all now, and they don't pay attention even to none of our Faithful, and sometimes they make fun of us even. And all this on account of this sinner His-Name-Should-Be-Wiped-Out and his people and by the power of our prince!

I got to do mine part and let you know about all this, and you got to see to it to take some action about it, 'cause I'm telling you over and over this is no small matter!

These are the words of
....

#94

From Reb Zelig Letitchiver
To Reb Zaynvl Verkhievker

I don't know what [kind of] person you are! You wrote me *how* many times Freyda was pregnant by your prince, and now I see you don't know your ass from your elbow! Because three days ago she started having labor pains. She was having very hard labor and she sent a special messenger for me I should come to her to Krasne. When I got there she was very sick and I was afraid she shouldn't die, G-d forbid! She broke out sobbing in front of me and I told her she should confess who she got pregnant from. I deliberately said this to her when Itsik Avrohom's was in the house too, so if she should die, me and Itsik would be witnesses she was pregnant from the prince. She told me and Itsik Avrohom's she got pregnant from Hirtsele, son of our holy *rebe!!!**

When she said this I BEGAN TO TREMBLE because I know that miser [Itsik] -- if he sees he has no hope of getting a lot of money from the prince, he'll tell everyone the whole story. On the spot I told him not to believe what she says because she said this out of shame, since it's more shameful for her to be pregnant from the prince than to be pregnant from the son of our *rebe,* he should live. And I told Itsik Avrohom's he should leave the house because I had some things to talk about with Freyda.

When he left I told her if I help her give birth she shouldn't say she got pregnant from the son of our holy *rebe,* and she should tell Itsik Avrohom's it was only out of shame she said this. I showed her with clear proofs it isn't good for her she should say this in public, especially since our *rebe* the *tsadek* would have grievances against her. She promised to do like I said, and in return for this I promised to help her. I ordered [her] to wash in front and in back[1] with the wine I brought with me, and then and there she gave birth to a stillborn child.

Yesterday Shloyme Umner was here by our holy *rebe* and he asked me about Freyda -- where she is and whether she already gave birth? -- and I told him she gave birth to a stillborn child. He was overjoyed and said to me with great glee, "Zelig, my brother, you're good for a big gift from me because I'm delighted by this news."

While I was speaking with him, he too told me she was pregnant from Hirtsele, our holy *rebe*'s son. I said to him, "But *I* heard she was pregnant from your prince?" He broke out laughing and said the prince never had an affair with her[2] because the prince isn't that sort. He likes Freyda just because she's very clever and because her father once helped the prince in an important matter, so he's forever grateful to his

---

[1] "A remedy for a woman having hard labor is that she should wash in front and in back with wine. 'The wine enters; that which is hidden comes out.'"* *Mides* 97:2.

[2] See Letter #16, that when Reb Zelig asked the *tsadek* of Zalin if the landlord of Kripen was a reincarnation of Sisera, the *tsadek* responded to him with complaints, "Why do you ask about what is not permitted to you?" Now you'll understand from this sharpsightedness of the aforementioned *tsadek,* and [from the fact] that he can see from afar, that he would know that the aforesaid landlord had no affair with a reincarnation of Yo'el.

[Freyda's father's] children. He also told me the prince don't even know she's pregnant, and if he *would* know he'd be very angry at her and wouldn't even let her into the manor.

So I'm amazed at you! How could you write so many times she's pregnant from the prince? I thought you heard this from Freyda. Now I see what a miracle it was for us she gave birth to a stillborn child. Clearly -- don't kid yourself! -- if she had a live child, the matter would never have remained secret from the prince and he would've been angry at us. Especially at our holy *rebe* he would've been very angry, and he would've been a worse enemy to us than before. Also the disgrace before the whole public that she got pregnant from our *rebe*'s son and we kept her at Krasne would've been humiliating. So see for yourself what could've happened on account of what you wrote, as you must know. You should know from now on how to behave in affairs that concern us.

From me,

....

#95

From Reb Zaynvl Verkhievker
To Reb Zelig Letitchiver

What can I say? Of course you're right for being mad at me in your letter [#94] 'cause the truth is I didn't talk with Freyda about the notorious affair. I thought without a shred of doubt she must've got pregnant from the prince 'cause I knew she always goes to him. Also, since I seen this could be a big help to us, it seemed to me the thing must be so.

But now I see what a miracle it was for us that at least she had a dead child. 'Cause when I got your letter, I deliberately sent our grocer, Reb Yankl Rivke's, to our prince's housekeeper, to cozy up to her and talk with her about Freyda. He told me the housekeeper told him Freyda was by the prince and told him she'll travel to one of her relations a few parasangs away from here and stay a few weeks there because she still had to wrap up the matter of some inheritance. I realized from these words the prince don't know nothing about whether she's pregnant or where she went.

It was mine good luck you wrote me everything right away, 'cause I'm right now flat broke. When I didn't have even for *Shabes,* I wanted to go to the prince and tell him I risked mine life for him in Freyda's affair.

I wanted to ask him he should give me at least some bushels grain and I had no doubt he would for sure give me. But now I see the great miracle what happened for me -- that I got your letter before I went to the prince -- 'cause for sure this scoundrel would've killed me dead, G-d forbid! So I'm giving you a thousand thanks you notified me all the particulars.

Please tell Shloyme Umner when you see him he should give me a few zlotys at least, 'cause right now I literally don't got what to eat. 'Cause however it turns out, I done their family* a very big favor in this affair. Even though mine intention was regarding the prince, all the same a big benefit came to them through me and they got to do *me* favors too. I'm sure you'll do this for me.

These are the words of

....

#96

From Reb Meyer Yankev in Galicia
To Reb Zelig Letitchiver

I got your letter [#59] by way of a visitor from your community. For the time being, I can't write you more than that of a certain two people who fled to this country, in the holy community of Greater Tsidon they know nothing at all. Maybe that fellow who's important in the district and who the rabbi of the holy community of Latke saw knows something about this, but the particulars he doesn't know, and even if he *were* to know there's nothing to fear from him because for the most part he stays home and has no extensive dealings with the other locals. Furthermore, it's not his nature to tell what he saw or heard in the district, so we have nothing to fear from him even if he *were* to know, especially since he surely doesn't know anyway. So far, no one knows *anything* about those two people.

But a few days ago I was at a wineseller's in the holy community of Greater Tsidon whose acquaintance I made by purchasing wines for Reb Aharon, wineseller in your community. A lord stayed at this wine merchant's as a house guest for several days because he had some business in the district, and that lord's servant came from his village with a letter from his wife, in which she wrote him to send her some things from town. The lord asked the servant what news there was from home and the servant said, "The *goye* who came to our village gave birth to two children." The lord started laughing and said, "Very good, now we'll have four more souls -- the *goye,* her father, and two children she gave birth to."

While the lord was having this conversation with his servant, the wineseller was in the house with the members of his household, but they weren't paying attention to it. I was listening carefully, and I promptly started speaking with the master and the members of his household of other things so they wouldn't hear what the lord was discussing with his servant and so they wouldn't start speaking with the lord.

Later on I asked the wine merchant, "Who is this lord? It seems to me I've seen him." And the wineseller told me the lord is from the village of Pankievits. The next day I went to that village, where I said I wanted to travel to Lvov to buy wool so I'd have some profit for expenses, and there I made the acquaintance of an *arendar* by the name of Reb Yisroel Dov. He's among our Faithful and we also realized we're relatives, but all the same I didn't want to reveal to him anything of the affair. But when I sat with him at the tavern, I heard a *goy* there recounting some devotional practices* and stories from our country and I listened carefully to what he was telling. I would imagine he must be the father of the infamous *goye.*

I said to the *arendar,* "I see this gentile is from our country," and the *arendar* said, "That's right. He ran away from your country and a little while ago he came to our village with his daughter."

I asked him if it's allowed in this country to accept people who flee from our country and he said, "It sure *is* allowed." I asked him, "And if they write from our government to send those people back to them, do they send them back?" The *arendar* said, "G-d forbid! Only if the fugitive committed some theft or other foul deed there and they send word here, then they send him back. Several weeks ago our district office sent back a servant who stole a lot of money from his master there and who also fled to our village. But if he didn't steal anything there or commit any foul deed, they don't send him back even if they write a hundred times."

I immediately began discussing another matter with him, and about an hour later I said the wool was too expensive for me and I returned from there to Greater Tsidon. I was overjoyed that I found out where the gentile with the *goye* is, especially since I knew they didn't steal anything at home except Jewish-style clothes and our government doesn't know about *that,* and the *arendarke* doesn't complain about the clothes because you paid her for them, so I know for sure they won't send them back from this country.

Since I had nothing to do in the holy community of Greater Tsidon, I traveled to Nakhal Hamotsa* to the local rabbi whose name is Shlemiel ben Lemekh.* I was with him and I saw that although he's nowhere near the stature of our *rebes*, all the same he's a very down-to-earth man. He's no longer like he used to be, because he didn't used to involve himself in affairs but now his son-in-law showed him he has to become involved in all the affairs of the community* and he did what he was told because his son-in-law is from our country and he knows that's how it has to be.[1]

Since so far I've only been in the holy community of Greater Tsidon and in the holy community of Nakhal Hamotsa, therefore I haven't had anything to write you until now. Now I intend to travel soon to the town of Akhziv* and to some other places, and I hope to write you from there lots of news about the people of Galicia and their *rebes*.

These are the words of

....

[1] "The *tsadek* of the town -- all their affairs depend on him." *Mides* 51:62.

#97

From Reb Zaynvl Verkhievker
To Reb Zelig Letitchiver

Last Monday Freyda came back. When I seen she was all better I went to Shloyme Umner he should give me a gift for mine trouble what I had. He gave me a pittance and I says to him, "What's this for mine trouble?" and gave it back to him. He got very mad and says to me, "If you know what's good for you, get out of here fast or else I'll finish you off but good so you'll have what to remember me by!" and he really let me have it.

I went to Freyda and she promised me to do me a favor. She finagled it that the sinner Mordekhai gave me more vodka on credit and I found out how she done it. She begged the prince he should talk with the sinner Mordekhai about this and the prince told her I'm not worth it she should stick up for me. But still, since she begged him he done it for her sake, and now I got me a respectable living pouring drinks.

Please help me with this 'cause I know, of course, soon this sinner won't want to give me no more vodka, but if you write Freyda and Shloyme, of course they'll do for you all what you want, 'cause when I was by them I heard how they sing your praises as a good man and so bighearted since they think everything you done was just for them.

These are the words of

....

#98

From Reb Meyer Yankev To Reb Zelig Letitchiver

At first I had in mind to write you the news from Galicia all at once, but as I see that I'll have quite a lot to write you from this country, I decided to write you a few things at a time.

First let me inform you that people in Galicia are really just like our rabbi -- The Hidden Light, Our Teacher Rabbi Nakhmen, THE SAINT and Holy Man OF BLESSED MEMORY -- wrote,[1] but the *rebes* are worthless. If only there were two, or at least one, of our *rebes* here, then before long they'd all be transformed because they're really all set to be our Faithful. What more do you want? We surely don't need bigger *apikorsim* than those in

---

[1] The reason they tell wonders about the *tsadikim* in the land of Kiro [Austrian Galicia] is because their people are worthy people and they believe in the *tsadikim,* for through faith that they have in the words of the *tsadek,* wonders are revealed. Because the *tsadek* is really full of wonders, and when one has faith in the *tsadek* and sets his eyes and his heart on the words of the *tsadek,* on every single word, because he believes that all his words are true and just and with mystical intent -- afterwards, when he [the believer] comes home, he looks carefully at everything that happens to him and understands in retrospect the words of the *tsadek,* which he [the *tsadek*] spoke with him when he was by him, that this was the intent of the *tsadek,* which he implied to him within words that he spoke with him. Thus every single thing that happens to him, everything that he implied to him would be so, he finds retrospectively in the words of the *tsadek.* It follows that the wonders are performed and revealed by this means. *Likutey MohoRa"N* 100:1.

Unworthy one that I am, I have thus far not been privileged to hear from some *tsadek* the reason why Our Teacher Rabbi Nakhmen, THE SAINT and Holy Man OF BLESSED MEMORY, said this about the people of Galicia. Why are we worse than they? Is not the faith in the *tsadikim* in our country much greater than that in Galicia? Perhaps G-d will yet privilege us to know the profundity of this matter.

Greater Tsidon! True, they're renowned as prominent *misnagdim,* but nevertheless, believe me, soon enough they'd become our Faithful. But the point is, the *rebes* in Galicia aren't worth a damn.

When I was in the town of Akhziv, they told me some stories of the *Rebe* Yokltse of Kalashke*, and I'll write you a few of them in particular.

Animal dealers from Wallakhia kept oxen* in the pasture in Zurovne, and some German merchant from Olmits* came to the pasture and wanted to buy the oxen from them. He offered them a good price so they'd have a profit of four hundred fifty czerwone zlotys, but the fools didn't want to wrap up the deal without permission from their *rebe.* However, since they were ashamed to tell the German they wanted to ask the *rebe,* they told him they couldn't sell because they had one more partner a few parasangs away and they had to ask him too. The German thought this was the truth and he said he'd wait a few days.

So one of the partners went to the *Rebe* Yokltse and asked him whether to sell the oxen, and the *rebe* told him not to sell and to go themselves with the oxen to Olmits. And so they'd be confident that they'd be sure to earn lots of money in Olmits, Yokltse said to them, "I am a partner in this transaction (that is, [an] inside [partner])."* They shook hands the way merchants do when they wrap up a deal and the merchant gave the *rebe* thirty czerwone zlotys for this advice. He came to Zurovne and told the German the partner didn't agree to the price.

So they went with the oxen to Olmits where they had a loss of a thousand three hundred czerwone zlotys of principal, in addition to the [loss of the] profit of four hundred fifty czerwone zlotys that the German would have given them. On account of this loss they became fugitives from their home and they're hanging around here in Galicia. The fools didn't know that this *rebe* gives them the advice not to sell the oxen because he supposes that if a German travels from Olmits to Zurovne to buy oxen, it stands to reason that oxen must be more expensive in Olmits, but he doesn't know that in Olmits at one market they sell oxen at a high price and at the other market they can be very cheap -- but he's among the *rebes* who wouldn't know what's going on in Olmits if their life depended on it!

One more. A lord was sick with gout and he took cures by many doctors, but they didn't help him at all. His *arendar,* who was among Yokltse's people, told him to send to his *rebe* for a *pidyen,* and the landlord listened to the *arendar.* He sent to Yokltse for a *pidyen* and said to the *arendar,* "If the *pidyen* works, I'll give the *rebe* my two good horses as a gift." The *arendar* went with those two horses to the *rebe* and paid him for the *pidyen.* When Yokltse told him the *pidyen* was very good, he immediately gave him the two horses -- because the *arendar* had no doubt at all that his landlord would get well -- and the *rebe* sold the horses to a horse trader from Akhziv for thirty-six czerwone zlotys.

A few weeks later, when the landlord saw he was as sick as ever, he told the *arendar* to return the horses to him or he'd file a complaint with the district against his *rebe.* The *arendar* went to the *rebe* and told him this, and the *rebe* was scared out of his wits and told the *arendar* he already sold the horses and would make sure to compensate the landlord for the horses. It took an all-out effort on the part of the *arendar* until he compromised with the landlord for seventy czerwone zlotys, and Yokltse's people made a contribution and paid the seventy czerwone zlotys.

Are there *rebes* like this in our country? Our *rebe,* and even the least of the least, wouldn't have taken the horses unless he asked first whether the lord was giving him the horses conditionally, and then he wouldn't have taken them. This fool didn't ask anything -- he just took them. Even if I forgive him that he *took* them, why did he *sell* them? Would our *rebe* sell horses some prince gave him as a gift? A fool like this Yokltse doesn't know what it's worth when a *rebe* travels with horses and his people tell everyone, "See these horses? Prince So-and-So gave these horses to the *rebe* as a gift and he even sent to him for a *pidyen* etcetera," but this fool Yokltse sold them and grabbed thirty-six czerwone zlotys.

Also the remedies this *rebe* has* are very wonderful as well. Someone from the town of Akhziv consulted him about his little boy who was wailing and having convulsions -- which is called whooping cough -- and Yokltse gave instructions to beat the boy with *heshaynes* and to write the name of the child and his mother three times on the beam of the house. The father did so. Every time the boy would wail they would beat him and the boy always blacked out, but they paid no attention to that. They went on beating him like this for a long time until the boy stopped blacking out. Since convulsions don't last more than half a year in a child, and they beat him more than half a year, the blackouts stopped of their own accord.

Furthermore, one of the local people gave Yokltse two thousand Rhenish gulden for his -- that is, the *Rebe* Yokltse's -- short sheepskin coat and high fur hat and bedsheet, but when a big commotion was made about this, Yokltse's people spread a rumor throughout the country that the *rebe* returned a thousand zlotys to that man and a thousand zlotys he distributed to the poor as soon as he received them, and for what he received and returned he must have had a reason.

To another *rebe* in Galicia two men came for children. I knew both of them. One was the rabbi of Tilaks and the other a fellow from Bakizov. The *rebe* ordered that they should make a match between them -- the rabbi would have a daughter and the other would have a son. The rabbi of Tilaks started to ask the *rebe* to give *him* the son and let the other have the daughter, but the *rebe* wouldn't. He said, "If you should have the son then you won't want the match, so you will have a daughter," and the rabbi of Tilaks had to agree to this too. They wrote an engagement contract and broke pots* and paid the matchmaker's fee. In a nutshell, they did everything people do for a real engagement contract because as far as they were concerned this too was a real engagement contract. Because the *rebe said* -- therefore, of course, it must be so! But now they don't have children! The *rebe* has already died and neither of them has any children!

I have lots to write about the *rebes* of Galicia but the wagon driver wants to leave and I have to be brief for now.

These are the words of
....

#99

From Reb Zelig Letitchiver
To Reb Zaynvl Verkhievker

Last night a councilman's agent came and informed me your prince wrote he had information which village the *goye* and her father are staying in and he wrote [to our authorities] to send word to the authorities in Galicia to send them back to them because they committed a certain criminal act in our country. By their regulations they have to return people like that who committed a criminal act. So for G-d's sake, make sure to check this out -- where'd he get this information where they're living? -- so we'll know from now on who to protect ourselves from.

I'm also writing Reb Meyer Yankev he should go straight to the city of Greater Tsidon to the village of Pankievits and investigate there all the particulars of the case. You do whatever you can do from there too. For G-d's sake, don't sleep on this! And also around here we'll do everything we can to keep the case here so they won't send so quickly to the authorities in Galicia, so in the meantime Reb Meyer Yankev will do there what needs to be done there to help the situation. But we can't rely on this alone because maybe he won't be able to accomplish there what's necessary, since he's in a foreign country.

So it's forbidden for us to sleep, G-d forbid!, just to do everything in our power. Also, for G-d's sake, write me regularly what's new there!

From me,

....

#100

**From Reb Zelig Letitchiver
To Reb Meyer Yankev in Galicia**

I don't know where the bad luck came from that the prince of Kripen found out where the *goye* and her father are living, and that he wrote our government to write the authorities in Galicia to send back them two subjects because they committed a criminal act here, and by their regulations they say they have to send such people back to them. So for G-d's sake, go straight to Greater Tsidon to the village of Pankievits. And in the city, where the authorities are, make sure to do what you can, and notify us promptly what's new there and what you did for our communal welfare, as well as with regards to the above affair.

I'm also informing you I sent you yesterday ten copies of the holy book *Toldes Yankev Yoysef,* which is newly reprinted. I sent them to an *arendar* who's at the border in Kavrifke and he'll send them to Galicia* by way of one of his people. You'll be able to make a contract for several hundred copies, because even though around here they grab them books from your hand, all the same we want to send at least six hundred copies to Galicia so the people over there will become more and more familiar with our books. Also, if we see they buy a lot of them there, then the publisher of the holy community of Mezhebush will publish more holy books, and we'll be privileged to disseminate the holy books endlessly.

I'm also informing you the son of our holy *rebe* divorced his wife, so maybe a nice match will come along for him in Galicia, because our holy *rebe,* he should live, has a strong wish to make himself a match from Galicia with some rich man, whereby we'll have big backing in Galicia. In many ways it would be good to arrange himself a match from Galicia.

From me,

....

#101

From Reb Zaynvl Verkhievker
To Reb Zelig Letitchiver

When I got your letter [#99] I almost fainted. I ran like a *meshuge* straight to Freyda and Yankl Rivke's and cried my eyes out in front of them, and I also told them I'm really in hot water now. They went straight to wherever they had to go and made a few inquiries and found out the particulars.

Here's what happened. By a landlord from the village of Lifnik who's a neighbor of our prince, a servant stole lots of money and valuables and fled with a subject from Lifnik to Galicia. The servant went to the village of Pankievits 'cause he has there his brother, an official in that very village. The landlord of Lifnik sent envoys to Galicia and they made a thorough investigation about the servant and found out he's in Pankievits, so he wrote to the Pankievits prince that the servant had stole from him lots of money and stuff. The lord of Pankievits gave orders to search the servant and they found the stolen goods. He wrote the whole matter to his district and the district ordered to send the servant back to our country.

When they brang the servant back to Lifnik, our prince was also there by the Lifnik prince. As soon as they brang the servant, the lord of Lifnik slapped him* around and was very angry at him. He says to him, I mean, the landlord of Lifnik to the servant, "Tell me this instant where the subject is who fled on the same night you fled." The servant starts swearing he didn't know about the subject 'cause when they crossed the border they split up -- he went to Pankievits to his brother and the subject went a different way and he didn't see him no more.

The landlord starts screaming his head off and says, "I'll send to Pankievits and if I find the gentile there, I'll beat you to death!" The servant starts swearing again up and down he didn't see no other gentile from our country in the village of Pankievits -- just a *goye* and her father who ran away from the village of Bilke.

When our prince hears this he starts asking the servant nicely whether the *goye* that came to Pankievits had a child, and when she came there, and if she stayed there or wanted to go somewhere else. He promised to give him a gift if he'll tell him the truth, and the servant says, "I'm definitely telling my lord the truth, because that very *goye* works for my brother, the official in Pankievits, and I heard from her and her father that they want to stay in the village of Pankievits. They also told me that when they left home the *goye* was pregnant and two children were born to her in Galicia. I don't know any more about them."

Our prince says, "I don't need to know more," and he was overjoyed. He gave the servant a gift and asked the lord of Lifnik not to do the servant no harm. He traveled straight home and done what you know.

So for G-d's sake, through Reb Meyer Yankev do whatever you can, 'cause this is literally a matter of life and death, G-d save us!, 'cause you can't imagine what a wicked fiend our prince is. I wrote you already that in our community, almost every single day our people grow fewer on account of the wickedness of the prince and Mordekhai-His-Name-Should-Be-Wiped-Out Gold and his people. The proof is I didn't know the prince wrote to the authorities about the *goye.* It used to be when the prince said in his house a word concerning us, I would know at once. But now I don't know nothing 'cause almost all of them follow the sinner Mordekhai-His-Name-Should-Be-Wiped-Out and lots of people are afraid of him and the prince.

I wrote you already about this and you didn't do nothing. I'm urging you again twice and three times and I'm urging you again a thousand times -- if you don't make a special effort about this so it'll be okay, then it'll be -- G-d forbid!, don't tempt the devil! -- very bad, especially since a few days ago the sinner Mordekhai-His-Name-Should-Be-Wiped-Out managed to get the prince to give the householders around here privileges with regards to their houses,* 'cause up 'til now they didn't have no privileges with regards to the houses.

When the prince got the proclamation from Peterburg that he was made lieutenant governor in our province, Mordekhai-His-Name-Should-Be-Wiped-Out went with some community members to the prince to tell him *mazl tov.* Mordekhai made a speech with his nonsense in the German language -- 'cause he really must've said outright nonsense since he's also certainly a fool and the proof is he's tall[1] -- and in the middle of the speech he presented the petition to give people privileges with regards to the houses. The prince was very pleased with the nonsense and the flattery what he told him in this speech, and he promised to give them privileges -- and he did.

And from that day on, almost all of them, especially them who got houses, became devoted to this sinner, and on account of this the wickedness in our community grows stronger every single day, and there's almost no bearing the wickedness. Only a few of the wretched and poor people in our *kloyz* still really hold to the truth with us, and even among

---

[1] "Tall people are generally fools." *Kitser Likutey MohoRa"N* 53:538.

them there are some people who got favors from the sinner Mordekhai 'cause he really does favors for everybody, no matter who.

I know for sure he don't do this out of fear of G-d or wholeheartedness, but in order to boast and snatch people. But others don't see this and they suppose his actions are sincere and become very devoted to him. This is very not good. So I'm informing you all this so you won't say later on it's my fault for not writing you nothing about this.

These are the words of
....

#102
From Reb Meyer Yankev
To Reb Zelig Letitchiver

Your letter [#100] reached me when I was in the holy congregation of Kalaktsig. I traveled straight to Akhziv where I spoke with some prominent men who I thought we could depend on. Here's how I told them the tale of the *goye:*

That a *misnaged* in our country fornicated with a *goye* who became pregnant by him, and when he realized that the situation wasn't good, he asked that *goye*'s prince, who was his friend, to persuade the *goye* to accuse an old-timer who never [even] looked at the shape of a woman, let alone at the shape of a *goye.* But when they wanted to take the *goye* for interrogation and the *misnaged* saw that the case had come to the jurisdiction of a judge who was very upright and didn't take bribes and was also a very perceptive man, the *misnaged* got very frightened and gave the *goye*'s father money through his trustee's wife, whose husband was one of our Faithful. The trustee's wife persuaded the *goye* -- and also the *goye*'s father persuaded her -- to flee with him to Galicia.

Eventually this judge went to another district and the *misnaged* also removed the trustee from the post, and when the *misnaged* saw that in place of the judge who left us there came another judge who took payoffs and was a friend of his, he decided it was better to write for the *goye* now while his judge friend was here and wrap up the case now through a written verdict so he wouldn't have anything to be afraid of later on -- whereas if he wouldn't settle the case, when the former judge would come back later on, maybe he would write to Galicia to send the *goye* back, and it might come off badly for him.

So he went and informed against the trustee's wife that she had persuaded the *goye* to flee. Because of this they thought in the court that the *goye* must've been made pregnant by the old-timer who the *misnaged* had spread rumors about, since the *misnaged* himself informed against the trustee's wife, and also since the trustee is one of our Faithful. And even though the trustee and his wife will say that they did this by order of the *misnaged* when they were serving him, they won't believe them and they have no proof. So they've sent word from our country to the authorities in Galicia to return the *goye* to them with her father.

That's how I recounted the whole case to the dignitaries of Akhziv. I asked them to help us in this affair because if they bring the *goye* and her father back home, the old-timer and the trustee and his wife are sure to be in terrible danger, since even if the *goye* doesn't accuse this old-timer, the judge will write that she did, so it's a great *mitsve* to help them.

The notables of Akhziv believed me in all of the above. They told me that they already heard about some injustices our judges do, and they solemnly promised to help me. But once I had gone to them several times, I saw there's no substance in their words and everything that comes out of their mouths is a lie. They don't know anything but how to flatter and pretend to be *khsidim.* The majority of them are big hedonists and side with our faction just for the sake of appearances, so people will say of them they're good and G-d-fearing men. But they're utterly empty, there's no *toyre* in them and no fear of G-d and no virtues. The *apikorsim* in Galicia are at least for the most part honest in business, but those make-believe *khsidim* -- even in business they're rogues, thieves and robbers, and for the sake of appearances they side with our faction because they know very well that the *tsadikim* befriend such people and accept money from them and tell them they're doing good, as is known from our holy books,[1] whereby they have at least some respect from people.

So I decided it's better to go to the holy community of Greater Tsidon where I hope I'll accomplish more by the *misnagdim* than what I would accomplish in Akhziv by those who side with our faction. I'm going there today, and from there I'll write you a clear report of everything.

---

[1] "They [the *tsadikim*] accept gifts from sinners so that they [the sinners] should return in repentance." *Mides* 49:3.

"When a sinner does some evil and comes to the *tsadek* and asks him if he acted properly, it is permissible to say to him, 'You acted properly,' in order to save him." *Ibid.*, 53:114.

"Sometimes there is someone who is an ardent adherent of the *tsadek* and he does not feel in himself any fear of Heaven. He should know that were he not an adherent he would not deserve to live at all." *Ibid.*, 56:198.

The ten copies of the holy book *Toldes Yankev Yoysef* I received. I gave them to the *rebe,* Rabbi Asher Don in Kalaktsig, because I made a contract with him for six hundred copies and I received a down payment of a hundred fifty silver rubles. So be sure to send me the books no later than this coming Teyves* at Radvil, and I'll pick them up there.

These are the words of
....

#103

From Reb Zelig Letitchiver
To Reb Zaynvl Verkhievker

When I got your letter [#101] I sank into despair, but it was my good fortune to be called immediately to our holy *rebe.* Of course our *rebe,* he should live, saw I was despondent, so he called me deliberately. The moment I entered his room and looked at his shining face, my melancholy[1] went away and I was filled with joy -- and I forgot to tell our *rebe* what happened in your community.

When I left our *rebe,* he should live, I realized it was a good thing I didn't tell him nothing about this because we consulted around here and decided not to reveal nothing of this to our holy *rebe* yet. But this we all of us agreed -- that Hirtsele, the son of our *rebe,* he should live, should be matched up with Freyda Reb Isaac's of your community. This is sure to be a great benefit for us because we saw from your letter [#97] that Freyda persuaded the prince to have Mordekhai Gold give you vodka. We know for certain that your prince can't stand you, but Freyda still managed this in her cunning. So when she marries our holy *rebe*'s son, how much the more, of course, will she undoubtedly achieve every benefit for our *rebe,* he should live. Because the prince never knew our *rebe,* he should live, well, and the fact is that even though the prince hates our group, he don't harm us at all -- because we seen many people who are prominent *misnagdim* and enemies of our group and nevertheless they like some *rebe,* or all the *rebes,* and some say that the *rebes* are really good but the assistants are no good.[2]

---

[1] See Letter #4, note 3.

[2] "There are sinners who are ashamed to stop believing in the *tsadek,* so they berate those who are under the *tsadek.*" *Mides* 54:137.

It follows that whatever the case, even though the prince is right now an enemy of our group, it could be that through Freyda he'll become a friend of our holy *rebe.* And if he'll only be a friend of our *rebe,* and our *rebe,* he should live, will speak with him just once, he'll turn him into a friend of our whole group, and everything will be, of course, okay.

So make sure to discuss this with Freyda. If you would tie up the match, everything is sure to be alright and it'll be very good for our holy *rebe* and us and you and our whole group. We already discussed this with our *rebe,* he should live, and he didn't say expressly he wants this, but you know our holy *rebe,* he should live -- he don't quickly say, "I want," because if he would say he wants then it would have to be so,[3] and in this situation Freyda has to agree to this matter of her own free will and not because of the word of our *rebe,* since if Freyda does this just because our holy *rebe* said so, obviously it wouldn't be good. Also it's not in the nature of our holy *rebe* to say immediately, "I want," and by his word to force people to do it, but from his sweet movements we saw that he wants this match.

We discussed this with the *tsadekes,* she should live -- our holy *rebe*'s wife -- and she said, "I agree, if Freyda's family gives me a proper gift, at the very least a hundred czerwone zlotys' worth of pearls," and we told her okay. So be sure to discuss this with Freyda's family. If they're willing to give the *tsadekes* pearls* -- that's fine, of course. If not, we'll speak with the *tsadekes* further -- maybe she'll accept less than a hundred czerwone zlotys, and we'll make a contribution ourselves toward this amount so as to finalize the match, because there's nothing more important than to quiet all the accusers, because only through Freyda can we silence the whole thing, especially since I remember, and you'll remember too, that once our *rebe,* he should live, said Freyda is a reincarnation of Yo'el. So in my puny understanding, the meaning in this was that the accusers would be stilled by her, as THE LAND WAS STILLED through Yo'el.

So don't be lazy about this. I expect you won't need Mordekhai's favors neither, but soon he'll need *your* favor.

From me,

....

---

[3] "(The *tsadek*) can rectify and achieve everything by his word alone, that is to say, effortlessly, without any effort or bother. Just as he speaks [it], so it comes to pass." *No'am Elimelekh* 44:2.

#104

From Reb Meyer Yankev
To Reb Zelig Letitchiver

I did as I wrote you [#102] and traveled here to Greater Tsidon. Through the winesellers, I made the acquaintance here of someone who's respected in the district, and he promised me to do all he could. When I had spoken with him at length, I asked him if the local authorities send back our people who have run away from our country. He said to me, "G-d forbid! Only if he stole or killed someone there or [committed] similar criminal acts they extradite, but otherwise they don't extradite." And he told me some stories of such cases when they would write from there a hundred times yet they didn't extradite. I'm here now about two weeks and so far not a hint of the notorious case has come here.

I'm informing you on my honor that the local people -- even though they have the reputation that they're prominent *misnagdim* -- all the same they're better than the people in Akhziv. Now I understand a few of the things you told me in the name of our *rebe* -- when the rabbi of the holy community of Latke was by him -- who said, "You yourselves are responsible for yourselves," because I see plainly that all the people in Greater Tsidon are ready to belong to our group. As clear proof, I'm sending you a letter [#105] that a local judge wrote to the prominent *rebe*, Rabbi Nekhoray, son of the rabbi of Rektsits, about a ritual slaughterer.* You'll see from the letter, which was written with the knowledge of the rabbi and of all the dignitaries, and what more proofs do you need? I got hold of the letter itself, but since I know that whoever hears this won't believe me, I hid the actual letter in order to show whoever wants to see it. So I'm just sending you a copy.

I have no doubt at all that I'll accomplish here whatever needs to be done. Since for now I don't have anything to do around here -- because the moment one word comes from the government to the local district, they'll certainly let me know all the particulars -- so I'll write you some more stories of the *rebes* of Galicia, and you'll see that only they are responsible for the fact that there are still *misnagdim* to be found around here, because they don't know how to speak with such people.

In the holy congregation of Akhziv, they told me that a hedonist came to a certain *rebe* in Galicia and the *rebe* said to him, "You don't have THE IMAGE OF G-D."* The *misnaged* replied to him, "It's written, THE FEAR OF YOU AND THE DREAD OF YOU SHALL BE UPON EVERY CREATURE ON EARTH. Every Jew knows that the animals are afraid of man because he has THE IMAGE OF G-D.

The reason it sometimes happens that a wolf or other beast of prey eats a man is when he has removed from himself THE IMAGE OF G-D and then the animals aren't afraid of him."

"But it happened to me a few days ago that I walked by the home of a gentile and a dog attacked me and bit me. I thought, 'The fact that the dog bit me must be because I don't have THE IMAGE OF G-D now, for if I had had THE IMAGE OF G-D, he wouldn't have bitten me.' But when I left there I saw that a gentile walked by the same dog, and not only did the dog not bite him, but the dog even played with him and was wagging his tail.

"It was very difficult for me [to understand] at first. Surely this gentile doesn't have THE IMAGE OF G-D, yet even so the dog didn't bite him and even played with him. But afterward I decided that the fact that the dog doesn't bite this gentile must be because he gives him something to eat. I asked the gentile if he feeds the dog and he said that he fed him several times. I thereby resolved for myself the difficulty that I had always had, and also the difficulty that assails me now as well.

"I've always seen that *Rebe* befriends total sinners, whom I know and *Rebe* knows are very, very grave and awful sinners. Now, when *I* come to *Rebe*, *Rebe* tells me that I don't have THE IMAGE OF G-D, and this problem really perplexed me. But the real reason is that sinners who are befriended by *Rebe* give *Rebe* [something] to eat, that's why *Rebe* plays with them and befriends them.[1] But as for me, since I haven't yet given *Rebe* anything, you said that I don't have THE IMAGE OF G-D."

So said a man in Galicia to a *rebe* there! Have you ever heard such a thing of our *rebes* -- that they would say to a hedonist whom they know is not of our people that he doesn't have THE IMAGE OF G-D? Hedonists who come and want to draw close to our *rebes* and know for sure that they won't backtrack -- our *rebes* sometimes tell them harsh things, reproach them and curse them. But those hedonists or total sinners who are still far removed from our *rebe*, our *rebe* certainly doesn't tell him

---

[1] "You do not have to chastise your disciple and dismiss him from your presence when he does not want to follow the straight path. Befriend him instead, for this will benefit the other disciples, and eventually he will heed." *Mides* 52:79.

"A person from whom you once received benefit -- do not spurn him." *Ibid.*, 43:3.

"The fact that the *tsadek* accepts money from the sinner, even though this money is suspect of [having been gotten through] robbery, it is still permissible to accept it from him, so that the sinner does not acquire for himself some wicked [Talmud] sage and say of him that he is a *tsadek* and give *him* the money so that he takes issue with the true *tsadek*." *Ibid.*, 43:1.

I have written this here so that people will not be surprised and so that this problem will not be difficult for them as it was for that hedonist.

anything bad, G-d forbid! On the contrary, he [our *rebe*] honors him in every way possible. As a result of this, the believers have multiplied in our country, because even the hedonists and absolute sinners side with our faction because the *rebes* give them honor, and not one *[rebe]* says to him, "Why do you do such and such?" and so on.

But those fools in Galicia must have heard that our *rebes* sometimes reproach and curse people, and they imagine that this is good so they do it too. They don't discern that our *rebes* do this only to those who come to draw close and to do *tshuve. Them* the *rebes* reproach so that they'll be terrified of them, and also so that through this the hedonist will tell him his whole heart and such -- or those who the *tsadikim* see have a bit of haughtiness and such.

But for everything our *rebes* have a reason and they know why they do it. But the fools of Galicia say harsh things to everyone, because they conduct all [their] affairs without common sense -- like the monkey who performs acts that he sees a man do* but doesn't have the sense to discern when one should perform these acts and when one should not perform them. That's what the *rebes* of Galicia are like.

So I'm not at all surprised if there are still *misnagdim* to be found among them. The local people are not the least bit at fault in this and here's proof. A few days ago I was sitting in the home of a wineseller around here and someone who's considered a local came to that home. He didn't know me and he started speaking with the people who were sitting there. The conversation turned to the instrument that arrests the thunder or the lightning, if I recall correctly, and the people asked him, How does the instrument work?* He started to explain the thing to them with his logical arguments and nonsense, which seemed to them to be profound insights and discoveries.

I pretended I wasn't listening, and when this clever creature went away I said to the people who remained, "I don't know why we have to search for farfetched and contrived reasons. In my opinion, this matter is very straightforward. It's known that the thunder strikes a place where there's a husk, and it's also known that before the present era they would lay iron on foodstuffs and such. This was because the iron is capable of driving away the husks,* as is known, for the letters of 'iron' *(**B**a**RZ**e**L**)* are an acronym for **B**ilha, **R**okhl, **Z**ilpa, **L**eya. It follows that it's a very clear and straightforward matter -- that because of the iron that we insert in the roof of the house, the husks won't come to the house and therefore the thunder doesn't strike there."

One of the people who was sitting there said, "In my opinion this reason is the absolute truth. The proof is that I heard that at the time the (cholera) epidemic was here -- G-d save us! -- every day a very large black dog ran among the people, and this was the husk of the epidemic. When they killed that dog with an iron spade, the dog fell dead and from that time on the epidemic ended. We see, therefore, that the dog -- that is, the husk -- died because they struck her with the *iron* of the spade."

One of those people who was sitting there said, "Maybe the dog was really a dog?" and the others started ridiculing him and said, "Obviously! Fine dog this was!"

And the other said, "Haven't we seen that we can also strike the husk with a *wooden* rod, for it's known to us from the book *Shivkhey ha-Besht* that the Besht, of blessed memory, struck the werewolf, which was certainly a husk, with a good strong rod."[2]

And the other replied to him, "From this there's no proof because in *Shivkhey ha-Besht* it's not written that the rod was wood, so maybe it was iron.[3] And even if the Besht's rod *was* wood, it's still no proof because the *Besht* could do this but not someone else. And what is there to be surprised at this? When I was in the holy community of Tlust where the Besht used to live[4] and where his *mikve* still is,* the householder where I stayed the night told me he heard from an old liquor distiller who said he had known the Besht personally, and who told the householder that one winter in very bitter cold, the Besht was in the *mikve* before daybreak and the bath attendant was giving him light for the *mikve* with a little piece of candle. The Besht was staying in the *mikve* a long time, and when the bath attendant saw the piece of candle was going out, he said to the Besht, 'Rabbi, get out of the *mikve* because the candle's going out.' The Besht started laughing and said to the bath attendant, 'What of it? So you suppose that only a candle can give light? An icicle can give light too!' -- and when the Besht said this, one of the icicles [hanging]* in the *mikve* started to glow very brightly. It follows that we can't bring proof from the Besht, because he could make it that a wooden rod too would kill the husk just like an iron rod."

I also heard from those people who were always sitting around by the one tavernkeeper there that they spoke once of a lady Tomorl, wife of Reb Berki of Warsaw.* One of them said that he didn't know why the *khsidim* call her -- by order of the *tsadek* of Lublin -- "Reb Tomorl." How does it fit to call a woman "Reb"?

---

[2] See Letter #64, note 1.

[3] From one *tsadek* I heard a wonderful clue that the stick was iron. He said he has this clue in the orally transmitted mystical tradition. The clue is that the words in *Shivkhey ha-Besht* --"In his hand was a good strong stick [בידו מקל טוב וחזק]" -- adds up in *gimatrie* [(2+10+4+6)+(40+100+30)+(9+6+2)+(6+8+7+100) = 330] to "of iron [מן ברזל]" [(40+50)+ (2+200+7+30) = 329] if we add the number 1.

[4] *Shivkhey ha-Besht* 5:1 [Mintz, 36].

And another answered him, "Don't it say explicitly in the Zohar, 'Tomor is male and female'?* It's known that 'Tomorl' is from 'Tomor,' and the Lubliner must have seen that in Tomorl, wife of Reb Berki, there's a spark of Tomor or maybe a reincarnation of Tomor, and on account of this he ordered she should be called '*Reb* Tomorl' because of the male that was in her. People who don't know about this refer to her without '*Reb*,' and this is because of the female."

I'm writing you all this so you'll see what kind of people there are in Greater Tsidon, and you'll understand from this the holy words of our holy *rebe,* he should live, which he said to the rabbi of the holy community of Latke, "You yourselves are responsible in the matter."

These are the words of
....

105

Copy of the Letter of the Judge of Greater Tsidon
To Rabbi Nekhoray in Rektsits*

By the help of G-d
The..........day [of the month of ....]
[In the year............] by the abbreviated era
Greater Tsidon

To Our Master, Our Teacher and Our Rabbi, The *Rov* of Israel,
The Delight of our Eyes, The Joy of our Strength, The Glory of our Generation,*
The Holy Seed through whom Israel is glorified and on whom she relies,*
The Lamp of Israel, The Right-hand Pillar, The Strong Hammer* of holy renown,
His Holiness, Our Teacher, Rabbi Nekhoray son of the *Rov,* may his light shine:

In view of the need to acquire another ritual slaughterer for our community here,* and seeing as there is a ritual slaughterer available in our vicinity who has a slaughterer's permit from the late prominent rabbi of blessed memory, Chief Judge of the Court of the holy community of Butchatch, the prominent *Rov Go'on* of our community here intended to accept him, for he presented his knife to him for inspection* and he appears to be SKILLED IN HIS WORK, in slaughtering as well as in examining.*

But since the emeritus -- Our Teacher Rabbi Shimshon, may his light shine, son of the *tsadek* of blessed memory, the late prominent rabbi of the holy community of Zbariz -- whose authority is diminished,* protested to the *Rov Go'on* of our community here, even though according to the holy law the ritual slaughterer does not give up his prior presumption of ownership* in this matter, the *Rov Go'on* of our community here really does not wish to accept a ritual slaughterer without the consent of all the residents of our community here.

Consequently, it occurred to him, with the approval of the especially wealthy dignitaries here in our community, that I should write to His Holiness and request of him to inform us of his opinion on this, since a sage is superior to a prophet.* If he agrees to accept the said ritual slaughterer, well and good, but if he should not agree, then far be it from us to accept him.

I beseech him to forgo the honor due him* and make known the whole root of the matter so that we may know how to act, for this is urgent for the residents of our community here.

These are the words of
a doormat trampled* before his students
who writes at the behest of the *Rov Go'on*
and with the approval of the dignitaries of our community here
and awaits his holy, pure response,

Rikmoh, son of Our Teacher,
Rabbi Tan Yats Halevi.*

The *Rov Go'on* of our community here sends greetings and felicitations to His Pure Holiness and requests of him all of the aforementioned.

#106

From Reb Zaynvl Verkhievker
To Reb Zelig Letitchiver

When I got your letter [#103], I went bursting with happiness to Mrs. Freyda and told her about the match you wrote me. *I'd* grab this match with both hands, but she said she can't make a match without the knowledge of her family and without the knowledge and agreement of our prince, 'cause all she's got is from the prince and the prince also promised to give her for her wedding two hundred czerwone zlotys in cash. She told me she'll give me an answer about this match in three days.

In the meantime I done everything possible so the family would agree to this. I was just afraid from the sinner Mordekhai-His-Name-Should-Be-Wiped-Out, 'cause I know Freyda's family also has great faith in him. On account of this I didn't want to speak with them about the gift for the *tsadekes,* she should live, 'cause Mordekhai would have thereby an excuse to wreck it.

But later on I found out they also spoke with Mordekhai about this match and Mordekhai said, "What right do I have to offer an opinion about this match? After all, Freyda's not a child. If she wants the match, let her make it. If not, let her not make it."

I was very happy when I heard this, and as far as I was concerned the thing was as good as done. So today I went to ask Freyda the answer, and she told me when she mentioned the groom's name to the prince, he began crossing himself and said, "Freyda, have you gone crazy? In short, I tell you, Freyda, that if you should speak any further of this match, I'll take away the house I gave you and I'll drive you out of town, because I'm telling you that this sect and this *rebe* of theirs aren't worthy of the living," and he started barking about us and about our holy *rebe* like a real dog.

Finally he says, "You'll soon see, G-d willing, that at least from *our* province I'll pluck them up by the root. If I knew that you knew them and still wanted to hook up with them, I would drive you right out of town, but I'm giving you the benefit of the doubt -- that you don't know them. So I'm telling you -- be very, very careful of them, and please don't discuss those people with me again."

"You think it's *you* they really want? I know them very well. They want *you* so that you'll make *me* their friend, for they must know that I'm involved at the moment in an undertaking so as to be able to uproot them and send them to Siberia. They must know this because nothing is secret from them. If you do something against them in the most secret places* they find out about it, because they have spies in every house and corner. Even to *my* servants they must be giving money to inform them of what I do. Everyone in my town -- even if he doesn't side with them -- is a spy for them.

"Sometimes someone who speaks with them doesn't know if he's informing them of something they need, but they deliberately speak with him a lot until they find out what they need to know. And if you want to know for certain that they don't want *you* except because they know that

I'm your friend, tell them that *you* want the match but since *I* don't want it you have to leave my town and have a falling-out with me, and that you'll live in Zalin. And see if they want you *then!*'"

All this and much more wickedness this scoundrel spoke. But why should I write you all the words and all the grunts of this dog? Even what I wrote you of this is enough already for you to see you shouldn't take this matter lightly, 'cause surely if he says he's busy with an undertaking he must not be sleeping and -- don't kid yourself!, don't tempt the devil! -- it won't be good. So for cryin' out loud, rouse the dead! Do all what you can! Isn't it a shame and disgrace to us that we *still* didn't get hold of the *bukh!* G-d knows *what* goes on in this *bukh!*

It sure is no joke that one *bukh* makes for us so many mortal enemies. At least if we get hold of the *bukh* we'll know what's in it. No doubt some wizard wrote this *bukh.* Right now I'm cursing mine son-in-law a thousand times that thanks to him I returned the *bukh* that was already in mine hand, and the lieutenant governor wouldn't of known about it and neither would we of had all that aggravation what we had from that time on. At the time, I never dreamt the hatred of the nobles would be so great on account of this *bukh. Then* I was pleased mine son-in-law couldn't [read] German, but like I see now, it would've been better for me if he *could've** -- and even *well* -- 'cause that way the *bukh* wouldn't've been around no more, and our Faithful wouldn't've had on account of the *bukh* the trials and tribulations we now suffer thanks to this scoundrel! Who knows what the matter will come to?!

I don't know why you keep silent. In mine opinion, reveal everything to our holy *rebe,* 'cause maybe he has a reason for not doing nothing himself. Maybe first you got to speak with him and ask him he should take in this affair some action.

These are the words of
....

#107

From Reb Zelig Letitchiver
To Reb Meyer Yankev in Galicia

I'm hereby sending you a special messenger because the matter is very urgent and literally of mortal danger. I had a report that the prince of Kripen isn't twiddling his thumbs in the infamous affair, so for G-d's sake, go at once to the local authorities and be sure to keep your eyes peeled there, because they must've already gotten the letter they sent there from our province to send them back a certain two people.

Make sure to discuss this with the notables in the town of Guberske, because even though you write that the people in the holy community of Greater Tsidon are ready to help you, all the same I'm telling you not to depend on the people over there. Even though the Guberske townfolk just belong to the *rebes* of Galicia, still they belong to our faction, whereas the people in the holy community of Greater Tsidon -- even though you write that they're ready to be in our group -- nevertheless LIGHT HASn't yet SHONE ON THEM. They don't got no faith at all in *khakhomim* and we mustn't rely[1] on such people, because even if there's only one among them who's our enemy and wants to harm you, G-d forbid!, the others won't take no action against that one, because as long as they haven't reached the rung of faith in *khakhomim,** they don't got such *hislayves.* Someone who does something for our benefit might maybe please them, but someone who does something against us -- even something serious against us -- is sure to please them too. Maybe sometimes when somebody did us harm they'd have compassion on us and because of this compassion they'd become more devoted to us, but they wouldn't stick up for us as a result of this.

So I'm warning you urgently not to rely at all on the people in the holy community of Greater Tsidon. Just go to the provincial seat and make sure to work it out through the people there that they won't send back the two people in the notorious affair. Make sure also, for G-d's sake, to get hold of the infamous *bukh.*

I heard that a young man from there joined our faction and he knows how to read German *bikher*. So be sure to make his acquaintance and, of course, you'll be able to get hold of this *bukh* through him. Ask him at least to read to you from that *bukh,* so we'll know first of all what's written in it and who the author is. If it's possible there to buy lots of copies of this *bukh,* buy them all, because you'll have money there from [the sale

---

[1] "Whoever does not have faith in the *tsadek,* on account of this his heart is not right with G-d." *Mides* 20:7.

"Before he is an adherent of the *tsadek* he is in the category of FATTEN THE HEART...that is to say, his heart is impenetrable, his ears are closed and his eyes are blind." *Kitser Likutey MohoRa"N* 6:39.

"On account of flawed faith in *khakhomim* he never has perfect advice and he can never give himself advice. He is always doubtful and he doesn't know how to make a final decision in his heart as to how to act, because his heart becomes as filthy as the outhouse. Therefore all his advice is foolish. All this is on account of flawed faith in *khakhomim,* G-d save us!" *Ibid.,* 58:574.

of] the holy books *Toldes Yankev Yoysef,* which I sent you as soon as I got your letter [#104]. But for G-d's sake, don't be lazy about this, because I can't write to you right OUT IN THE OPEN how far the wickedness caused by this *bukh* extends.

From me,

....

#108

From Reb Zaynvl Verkhievker
To Reb Zelig Letitchiver

It's just like I wrote you in the last letter [#106]. Every single day the hatred and the wickedness of a certain scoundrel and murderer gets worse. I'm afraid even to write you or mention his name, so you should know that when I write just "scoundrel," "villain" or "murderer," I'm referring to our prince.

I'm endangering right now mine life by writing you this, and in the future I won't write you no more his name, 'cause the wickedness is getting worse in our community and our Faithful are getting fewer. Every single day less money drops into the *pushkes* for *Ertsisroel* and Rabbi Meyer Balanes funds. I'm afraid that in the future nothing will drop and then the other communities will learn from our community.

Around here the *misnagdim* increase every day. I had also news that in the holy community of Rektsits, the *misnagdim* took a fat man and made him a *"rebe"* as a joke.* They made him a white gabardine with white lace, and just like our Faithful carry the local *rebe* to the bathhouse before every *Shabes Koydesh,* they also carry their *"rebe."* Since they seen that the real *rebe* there has a special cap what he goes to the bathhouse in before *Shabes Koydesh,* they bought for their *"rebe"* too a special cap like this and they carry him in this cap to the bath. Every *Shabes Koydesh* they have the *shaleshudes* by their *"rebe."* They gather there and he tells them *toyre* they call *"khsidishe toyre."* The same with everything they see our Faithful there doing by the local *rebe,* the mockers also do by *their "rebe"* and there's no one to protest this to them. You can imagine the mockery* that's made on account of this.

A few days ago Reb Yekusiel Klinkvitser quarreled with a steward of Mordekhai-His-Name-Should-Be-Wiped-Out Gold, and Reb Yekusiel called the steward *"apikoyres,"* "sinner" and so on -- which was certainly true -- and the *apikoyres* ran to the manor. The prince ordered to hear testimony and afterward he ordered to give Reb Yekusiel thirty lashes. I STIRRED UP the people and several men ran to the manor and begged the prince on Reb Yekusiel's behalf, but they didn't accomplish nothing. Then the sinner Mordekhai Gold went himself with the steward and begged the prince on his [Reb Yekusiel's] behalf, and he done it for *their* sake. He said he wouldn't beat him but only on the condition he should leave town, and Reb Yekusiel had to accept this on himself. So they prepared for him a wagon and they took all the members of his household and the few household goods he had and lead him out of town.

I'm telling you I'm afraid to say one word on account of this murderer, and most of the time now I go about melancholy. I'm lucky the sinner Mordekhai still gives me vodka on credit, so at least I got vodka to drink sometimes, but I can't drink much 'cause mine wife don't let me. I see she's right 'cause if [just] once I don't pay this sinner, then for sure he won't give me no more vodka and I won't have even what to eat. 'Cause now -- even though I don't got *much* of a livelihood -- at least I got a livelihood, since some *arendars* in our vicinity who are still among our Faithful quietly send me now and then a barrel of vodka. I don't pay the *arendar* for it and I have from this a nice profit, but in these times when it costs to live and people aren't any more patronizing me, it's impossible to sustain mineself and the members of mine household in comfort.

So please, when the time is ripe, mention me before our holy *rebe,* he should live.

These are the words of
....

#109

From Reb Meyer Yankev in Galicia
To Reb Zelig Letitchiver

As soon as I got your letter [#107], I traveled to the town of Guberske, which is in this country. When I got here, nothing had arrived here yet from our government. In the meantime, I made the acquaintance of a young man who you wrote me about. Not for nothing did the *tsadek* of Pilza say of him that he has a great soul, because he's a wonderful creature and he has the impudence of holiness,[1] like young men in our coun-

---

[1] "It is not possible to come to the true *tsadikim* except through impudence...and it

try. He's impudent toward his father and his mother, and there's no one around here he's shy of.

Once I had struck up a good acquaintanceship with him, I began speaking with him about the *bukh.* He told me that the truth is he still reads *their* books,* but he doesn't go to *their* trash-sellers because he's afraid to buy from them *bikher* that can harm him, even though he reads nothing but the *bikher* that tell of people's travels, which they call "travelogues," as well as maps of the world, which are called "chronicles."[2] But the other *bikher* he's afraid to read since he doesn't even want to look at books written by important Jews that discuss research.[3]

But he said that since it's badly needed for the benefit of our group, he would go and first get the listing of the *bikher* they have for sale. So he went and brought home a list. I forgot what they call these lists, since the list itself is also printed by them like a *bukh* and bound like a *bukh.* He read the list and said that he found in it this *bukh,* that is, that he found a *bukh* that talks about this subject, namely, about our faction, but he said that he doesn't see from the name of this *bukh* that the *bukh* would be wickedness because the name of the *bukh* is, *On the Nature of the Ḥasidic Sect*,* and is based on this group's books -- thus its name -- and if so it can't be bad for our group.

So he bought the *bukh* and started reading it. He told me first, when he read the Prologue, that the writer of the *bukh* must be a Jew and sides strongly with the rabbis and with the *Gemore,* because in the Prologue he sides very strongly with them and explains to the *goyim* what they judge unfavorably about them [the Jews]. It seems he only complains against *our* faction. But all the same, it appears he doesn't say as much wickedness as you suppose.

---

is not possible to enter into holiness except through impudence." *Kitser Likutey MohoRa"N* 18:160.

"Likewise one must have the impudence of holiness...for it is not possible to enter into holiness except through impudence." *Ibid.,* 19:169.

[2] I know that the fools who think they're experts will make fun of the fact that he calls world maps "chronicles," for in their view world maps are land maps. That's what one of the "experts" in the holy community of Greater Tsidon said to me. But this proves that they don't peruse the holy books of the real *tsadikim* at all, for in the holy book, *Sipurey Mayses* of *MohoRa"N,* 5:1, you'll see explicitly that world maps are called "chronicles." And it stands to reason that Our Teacher the *Rov,* Rabbi Nakhmen, must have known better than the "experts" in Greater Tsidon.*

[3] "Therefore, G-d forbid to look at all at these books that tell of research -- even books written by the great men of Israel -- for there is no evil greater than this." *Kitser Likutey MohoRa"N,* Book 2, par. 42.

When he began to read the *bukh* itself, he said at first that this *bukh* was written by someone who is a friend of our group because he writes, "What is this title *'khosed'?"* and he praises a *khosed* more than a *tsadek.* But when he started reading further he began pulling at his side-curls and cried, "*Vey, vey,* such wickedness I never saw or heard. I even read the books that the Talmudists composed and what some Talmudists and rabbis wrote against our faction, like *Seyfer ha-Vikuakh, Zemir Aritsim, Kivres ha-Taavo* and such, and what the *Rov,* Rabbi Yekhezkl Landau, the rabbi of Prague, wrote in his book *Noda bi-Yehude,* and the rabbi of Pirda, Rabbi Yoysef Shtain Hart, in his book *Zikhron Yoysef,* and the author of *Merkeves Mishne* and such.* But wickedness like this I never saw or heard." And he added, "I'm not surprised the prince of Kripen became a terrible enemy of our group," and put down the *bukh* and didn't want to read it any more.

I started to consult with him about buying up and burning all the *bikher* they have, but he told me that "for *their bikher* this doesn't work like it does with Jewish books, because with Jewish books, when we burn them, then people don't want to buy that book any more since most of the time people don't stick to their opinion. When they hear a book was burned they're afraid to buy that book, because even if one examines the book carefully and sees there's nothing at all harmful in it, still one is afraid and thinks, 'You can bet, if they're burning this book, no doubt some heretic wrote it and it's forbidden to look in it even if there are very good things in it,' and the result is the printers can't print it any more."

"But *their bikher,* if one burns them it's worse, because they buy such a *bukh* more than other *bikher,* because they think, 'This *bukh* must be very good.' Especially when they see we're burning it, they'll think, 'It must be good, so they don't want it spread abroad,' and when the printer sees he sold many *bikher* he'll print it even a hundred times." So he advised me not to do this.

I asked him to buy at least one more [copy of the] *bukh* to send to our country. He went and only found one more copy. The *bukh*seller told him he had had a hundred and fifty copies and sold them all, but since he sees he can sell a lot he ordered two hundred more copies and they wrote back to him that they'll only send him fifty copies because they're sold out, but that they started reprinting it and would send him fifty more copies. So I'm hereby sending you the *bukh* he bought for us, and I'll continue to wait here until the letter arrives from our government.

These are the words of

....

#110

From Reb Meyer Yankev in Galicia
To Reb Zelig Letitchiver

Three days after I sent you a letter [#109] from the town of Guberske, one of the local notables came to me and informed me that the letter had already arrived from our government, and the authorities of this country are sending the case to the holy community of Greater Tsidon to the local district, to take the *goye* and her father to the commission (for interrogation). And since he told me that the matter is still delayed in the government for a few days, I went directly to the holy community of Greater Tsidon so as to do whatever possible there and also to go from there to the village of Pankievits.

In the holy community of Greater Tsidon, I spoke with a man who travels around the district, and he promised to let me know as soon as the case arrives from the government. I went directly to Pankievits and there I discussed with the *arendar,* Yisroel Dov, that when it [the order] arrives to bring the *goye* and her father to the commission, to discuss with them what they should say at the commission. I have no doubt at all that everything will be alright and that they won't send the *goye* back to our country, because they certainly won't be able to establish that she stole or committed some criminal act.

I'll give you a complete report about everything shortly.

These are the words of

....

#111

From Reb Zelig Letitchiver
To Reb Zaynvl Verkhievker

I'm hereby informing you I got a letter [#110] from Reb Meyer Yankev, and I sure hope everything will be alright. I'm informing you as well he also bought a [copy of the] *bukh* for us and sent it to us, because he made the acquaintance in the town of Guberske in Galicia of a young man -- a wonderful creature who can help us there in several matters.

The moment the *bukh* was brought to us, I delivered it to our holy *rebe,* and since then the *bukh* always lies under the rug on the table* of our holy *rebe,* he should live. Sometimes our holy *rebe* looks at the pictures on the page before the title page of the *bukh.* I got no doubt whatsoever everything will be okay.

Because surely you still remember what I wrote you already -- that our holy *rebe* said that of course we'll get hold of this *bukh* -- and here you see we *did* get hold of it, so all the events that happened up to now must've been just so we would send Reb Meyer Yankev to Galicia, so he would make the acquaintance of that young man and buy the *bukh,* so that the command of our holy *rebe,* he should live, would be fulfilled -- to get hold of this *bukh.*

So now, since our *rebe,* he should live, looks at the pictures in the *bukh* -- because there are two pictures in the *bukh,* since apparently two people composed the *bukh* -- of course it's not for no reason that our holy *rebe* looks at them.

Everything is sure to be just fine like before and you'll see that soon everything will take a turn for the better. So don't be at all melancholy -- G-d forbid!

From me,

....

#112

From Reb Gershon Koritser in Nigrad
To Reb Gedalyohu Balter in Aklev

As soon as I started studying with Moyshe Fishl's the holy book *Shivkhey* that you sent me, I realized he's not capable of such exalted things, because with every story he raised objections, and about some of them he said they're against the *Gemore* and its laws. So I stopped studying with him and I took back the book. But because I gave his wife that book in Yiddish, and also talked with her several times and told her some of our holy *rebe*'s miracles, she started urging him to travel to our holy *rebe.* He refused and said that previously he agreed to send to *rebes* for a *pidyen* because he didn't know them and he thought there was substance in them, but since he looked into their books he don't even want to send to them for a *pidyen,* let alone travel to them. I told his wife I saw in him a spark of *apikorses.* She said she saw some *apikorses* in him too, and I showed her with clear proofs he had become a real *apikoyres.*

Once he came home while his wife was studying the book *Shivkhey* and he grabbed the holy book and threw it into the stove. His wife started to have it out with him and his father-in-law quarreled with him too, and he had to divorce his wife on account of this. He didn't take even one *prute.* He left our community and went to Koven because he said the judge there, Mikhal Kahane, is a relation of his. And before he left here, he said about our *rebe,* our Light, he should live, and about you, bad things like I never heard in my life. About you, he said as far as he's concerned you're worse than an apostate, G-d save us![1] So you should know him.

These are the words of

....

The main thing I forgot. There's no greater *mitsve* than that the story I wrote you should be made public in your community and the vicinity so they'll also know this Moyshe and his deeds, because we need this!

---

[1] "Human beings who love one another are permitted to tell one another of something they heard from someone. Moreover, his companion is permitted to listen to what he says, and there is no trace of gossip in it." *Mides* 32:7.

I have written this deliberately so that people will not complain against Reb Gershon that he told gossip, G-d save us!

#113

From the Rabbi of the Holy Community of Koven
To Moyshe Akiva's in Kolne

Indeed, it is true that ever since the day I arrived here I have not had time to think about other affairs that do not pertain to the concerns of the community, for surely you know the custom among our kinfolk that when a new rabbi comes to their community they bring before him all the controversies and lawsuits among them. Everything -- small or large, new or old -- they bring before him. All the heartaches of the members of his community are disclosed to him. They think that he can do everything.

But out of my deep love for you, and because it is fitting for every honest man to keep his word, I shall not permit myself to sleep. So now, at the hour of eleven before midnight, when the members of our community have left me* and gone home, I thought, "Let me keep the promise I made to you before our parting and write to you of my health and my position."

Thanks to G-d WHO HAS NOT WITHDRAWN HIS KINDNESS and truth from me. Even though I AM INUNDATED with concerns* that do not permit me to catch my breath,* at least -- with G-d's help -- I am healthy and whole, SAFE and sound.

As for my position, here too I give a thousand thanks to G-d, praised be He, blessed be He, WHO HAS LED ME ON THIS PATH. For He has brought me here to a town full of sages and knowledgeable men, a town in which the power of the notorious sect has still not prevailed, for there are PEOPLE in it WHO STAND IN THE BREACH AND ERECT A BULWARK AGAINST them. Those few of the sect who are found here are dumb dogs unable to bark and they are split into two factions as well. Some of them are followers of the *rebe* of Dishpol and some of the *rebe* of Zalin. Each side brands the *rebe* of the other side a fake *rebe,* and they are all utterly base, despicable, loathsome and contemptible in the sight of the rest of the members of the community. The great pleasure that I have here in the company of knowledgeable men, particularly in the company of my childhood friend -- the renowned, sharp-witted judge, our teacher Rabbi Mikhal Kahane -- is beyond description. Whenever I enjoy their companionship and I remember the days of my wretchedness when I was in your community restrained by the salvos of the hunters, my pleasure is doubled.

Behold, by the help of G-d, blessed be He, I lack nothing here but your friendship and your company. I beg you to come here at the very least for several days to enjoy yourself in our company and to indulge yourself as you please and as is the wish of

Your friend, **sending you regards always** with a willing heart and soul,

....

#114

From Reb Zelig Letitchiver
To Reb Zalmen Brezner

I come to bring you the good news that yesterday the emissaries of the famous *gvir,* Reb Beyrekh Malke's of Galats, came to our holy *rebe* and told him how their great *gvir* sent them to propose that his [the *rebe*'s] son should marry his [Reb Beyrekh's] daughter. **They presented their words before** our holy *rebe.* **The matter was agreeable to him, and he immediately ordered that the scribe should come to write the engagement contract with *mazl tov.***

When they began to write the engagement contract, the emissaries said, "SIGN [IT] AS YOU SEE FIT REGARDING our *gvir* **but the date of the marriage may not be postponed on any account."** The emissaries wanted to restrict the time of the wedding to the week after *Shvues,** but our *rebe,* he should live, would only agree to the middle of Elul. Since THE MATTER PROCEEDED FROM THE L-RD, the emissaries agreed to this.

I was very pleased by this because the wedding is certain to be drawn out for two weeks until *Rosheshone,* and the father-in-law and his relations that he has will be [in] our province -- even those who always went for *Rosheshone* to the fake *rebe* of Dishpol -- here by our holy *rebe,** he should live, for *Yomim Neroim.* No doubt, when just once they see the king in his splendor[1] and have the great privilege on that account to taste even just once the real taste of *Ertsisroel,*[2] they're all sure to remain followers of our holy *rebe.*

So I'm informing you of this so you'll prepare yourself for the wedding and bring with you a very nice wedding present. You should also notify all our Faithful in your vicinity they should come to the wedding too, and we'll celebrate as befits our Faithful.

I was very sorry I wasn't at [the writing of] the engagement contract because we were all very, very uplifted and the rejoicing was greater than the rejoicing at [the ceremony of] the House of Water-drawing,* so you can imagine how much greater will be the rejoicing at the wedding! Even now I'm getting pleasure from the celebrating I'll do at the wedding.

And just now popped into my mind the *toyre* our holy *rebe* said at the *shaleshudes* before the [writing of the] engagement contract, about the

---

[1] "This is the meaning of WHEN YOUR EYES BEHOLD A KING IN HIS SPLENDOR, namely, when you are privileged to see a king in his splendor -- that is, the *tsadek* in his splendor and his glory -- namely, at the time of the ingathering *(Rosheshone),* which is the time of his splendor and his glory -- through this YOUR EYES WILL SEE A DISTANT LAND, meaning, the Land of Israel *(Ertsisroel)...." Likutey MohoRa"N,* Book 2, 38:1.

[2] "Whoever has tasted the real taste of *Ertsisroel* (for the one learned in other disciplines can also sense the taste of *Ertsisroel* because he perceives the taste of intellect) -- when he encounters a person who was at a real *tsadik*'s on *Rosheshone,* he is bound to notice then the taste of *Ertsisroel,* because on account of this person this air also becomes like that of *Ertsisroel ." Likutey MohoRa"N,* Book 2, 38:1.

verse, THE SONS OF G-D SAW THAT THE DAUGHTERS OF THE LAND WERE PLEASING AND THEY TOOK FOR THEMSELVES WHOMEVER THEY CHOSE. The sons of G-d are the sons of the *tsadikim,* who are called "G-D,"[3] and THE DAUGHTERS OF THE LAND are the daughters of the common people. We see plainly from this *toyre* that our *rebe* already at the *shaleshudes* saw that the emissaries would come to him from the *gvir* of the holy community of Galats to match up the daughter of their *gvir* with the son of our holy *rebe,* he should live.

From me,

....

[3] See Letter #16, note 3.

#115

From Reb Zalmen Brezner
To Reb Zelig Letitchiver

I don't know if you had greater pleasure from [the writing of] the engagement contract than the pleasure I had from the news you gave me that our holy *rebe* wrote an engagement contract with the *gvir,* Reb Beyrekh of Galats! Because I know that he's a very, very great *gvir.* I was with him once last *Shvues* when I was traveling to Istanbul, and in his home I saw silver as [plentiful as] trash. The kaiser don't got as much silver as he does! I saw a silver candlestick there that was standing on the table on *yontef,* and the candlestick was like a tree with leaves and the leaves were green like real leaves. All year long this candlestick lies in a closed and locked chest, and just on *Shvues* they set this candlestick on the table. This candlestick is worth lots of money -- I myself don't know how much -- and for every single *yontef* he has a different candlestick!

For example, for *Sukes** he has a candlestick with *esroygim* and *lulovim* and myrtle branches and *heshaynes.* For *Peysekh** he has a candlestick with *matses* and *morer* and *karpes* and *kharoyses.* For *Rosheshone** he has a candlestick with a *shoyfer,* and for *Shminatseres* and *Simkhes-Toyre** [he has a candlestick with] a flag and braided candles and streamers.* Even for *Purim** he has a special candlestick with *gragers* and *Homen*-clappers and *homentashn* and [a representation of] the hanging of *Homen* with his ten sons. These candlesticks would all be worth several thousand czerwone zlotys. I also saw clothes and jewelry by him [the likes of] which I never saw -- apart from other small things -- which are worth several hundred thousand czerwone zlotys.

Why should I go on at length about his wealth? At the wedding you'll see that what I wrote is only a tiny part of his wealth.[1] So of course I'm very pleased by this -- that our *rebe* matched himself up with that rich man -- especially since through this match our holy *rebe* will take the whole region from Galats to Istanbul under his wings and our circle will spread throughout the land of Turkey. You'll see at the wedding how many wedding presents will drop from the bride's side.

So make sure to write to all our Faithful to bring -- or at least to send -- lots of wedding presents, which will bring HONOR AND GLORY to our holy *rebe,* and I'll write to those of our Faithful located in our vicinity to prepare lots of wedding presents too. I'll also bring a nice wedding present, and at the wedding we'll dance in circles as befits our Faithful.

These are the words of
....

[1] Since I know that people will think that Reb Zalmen is, G-d forbid, given to exaggeration, therefore I inform them that he is the grandson of Reb Eliezer Brezner who saw the lintel of the passageway, as related in Letter #67.*

#116

From Reb Zelig Letitchiver To Reb Zalmen Brezner

I'm hereby informing you that last week a letter came to our holy *rebe,* he should live, from The Holy Land,* that they accepted him there as President* over them. Even though up 'til now a rabbi from Galicia served as their President because all our *tsadikim* wanted to flatter him -- that is, this rabbi -- so that he'd be on our side, because he's rabbi in a large community and is very wealthy, and it was really because of the fact that they made him President that they won him over to our side -- nevertheless, since there were several serious denunciations of that rabbi from the sinners in that country to the government, he gave up the position as President and they accepted our holy *rebe,* he should live. They request of him to receive all the *Ertsisroel* monies -- even from the *kolel* fund-collectors* -- and he should send them to The Holy Land through his in-law from Galats who has very sizable business affairs in Istanbul.*

The letter about the presidency was brought to our holy *rebe* by an emissary of that in-law of his, who also brought our *rebe,* he should live, a very long pipe stem, such as I never saw. This stem was growing on the grave of Rabbi Yose Katnuso, and they gave the pasha alone who's in charge there four money-purses to allow them to cut the stem for our holy *rebe.* I'm under the impression that in one money-purse there are a thousand five hundred lionthalers.*

The reason they sent our holy *rebe* this stem is that one of the men from The Holy Land was at the grave of Rabbi Yose Katnuso to pray, and as a result of the many prayers and petitions he fell fast asleep. In a dream he saw Rabbi Yose Katnuso who told him in the dream -- that is, Rabbi Yose Katnuso told this man who was asleep -- that our holy *rebe* is his spark.[1]* This must be true because our holy *rebe* literally looks like Rabbi Yose Katnuso.[2] For this reason they took the stem to send it to our *rebe,* he should live, because obviously, our *rebe* must have a lot to rectify with this stem.*

Last *Motse Shabes* our *rebe,* he should live, was smoking a pipe with this stem. Whoever didn't see this never in his life saw beauty* and never will. He was uplifting us all with the pipe smoke from this stem. 'Til now no one else has smoked from this stem, and he ordered me to put the stem away in the case that they sent him with it and to put it in the chest. Who knows when our holy *rebe* will order [me] to give him

---

[1] A real *tsadek* revealed to me the reason it says, "Since Rabbi Yose Katnuso died, *khsidim* ceased to exist,"* and why he was named "Katnuso" -- because he was the last* of *khsidim.* That *tsadek* said, "In order to fulfill the *mishne* and still have *khsidim* in our generations, in every single generation, G-d puts the spark of Rabbi Yose Katnuso in some *rebe,* and thereby there can be *khsidim* in every single generation." THE WORDS FROM A *KHOKHEM*'S MOUTH ARE LOVELY. But when I asked another Talmudist, he told me that it is true that this is in the *Mishne* at the end of Tractate *Sotoh,* but in the *Gemore* there,* "Rabbi Abo Yose ben Katnuso" appears instead of "Rabbi Yose Katnuso." Later I asked that *tsadek* which spark was in the Zaliner and he answered me, "Into what is too wondrous for you [do not inquire]."* So I was not privileged to arrive at the truth of which spark is in the Zaliner, or whether since the Zaliner died the spark no longer entered the world [and] *khsidim* ceased to exist, or whether it subsequently entered another *rebe.*

[2] Those of little faith won't be willing to believe that one can recognize the spark from the form, so you'll see in the holy book *Shivkhey ha-Besht* 35:2 [Mintz, 250] that the rabbi, the Great *Maged* of the holy community of Meziritch, recognized in someone that **he really had the form of Rabbi Yokhanen ben Zakkai**, and he had **the spark** of the soul **of Rabbi Yokhanen ben Zakkai.**

this stem to smoke from it? When it enters our holy *rebe*'s mind to smoke from it, it's sure to be something important and I'll let you know.

From me,

....

#117

From the Rabbi of the Holy Community of Koven To Moyshe Akiva's in Kolne

It has been a considerable time since I wrote to you of my good position. Thus far you have not given me the pleasure of your response, which is very precious to me. I know that you have never been indolent in responding to one who requests something of you, and I also know that your affairs do not prevent you from writing me a brief letter -- and I do not know what to make of it. Has, G-d forbid!, your physical health left you, or did you not receive my letter [#113]?

So please, inform me of everything through the bearer of this letter, who is my trusted associate and on whom you may depend in every wise, for he is a discerning and sagacious man. He is the son of my friend -- the renowned, sharp-witted judge, the rabbi, our teacher, Rabbi Mikhal Kahane, may his light shine -- AND YOU WILL SET YOUR MIND AT EASE by speaking with him.

New developments hereabout are few. Only of this I inform you -- that the dignitaries of the holy community of Zalin sent two men to me to inquire whether I would accept the rabbinic post in their community as well. At first I would not because the residence of the infamous *rebe* is there. But now I have heard that soon all the members of the sect there will be dealt a crushing defeat, because there has been exposed there a number of important cases of criminal fraud that they perpetrated. So I intend to write to them that I wish to accept the rabbinic post of their community too. Soon, G-d willing, I shall travel there, because the emissaries who were with me told me that if I should be amenable to this, I could come there and gladly stay several weeks, and in the future too could come to them each year for such a period. Consequently, if you cannot come here to our community, come to the holy community of Zalin next month, so that I may delight in your company there.

Your friend, who looks forward to seeing you soon,

....

#118

From Moyshe Akiva's in Kolne
To The Rabbi of the Holy Community of Koven

PLEASE DO NOT BE ANGRY that I have not written to you for a month now. You know that while you were still here, I was restrained by the salvos of the notorious sect. And since you left here, my friend, my trouble has grown worse.

When you first arrived in Koven, the rejoicing of the sect that you were there knew no bounds, for they thought, "Now we'll take revenge on the SINNERS of the fake *rebe* in Dishpol," for through you they hoped to uproot that *rebe* with all his followers located in your vicinity. They thought that through you the power of the *rebe* of Zalin would prevail there. But when the report came to them from the people there how you ridicule them and their *rebe* and their whole sect, and that your whole effort is to BREAK OFF THE heavy YOKE of the wicked sect FROM YOU and your colleagues, they began to despise you and your friends. And on me -- in that I still DWELL AMONG THEM -- they POURED OUT their WRATH the most.

So I was afraid to write to you, for I know that EVEN IF A MAN HIDES IN SECRET PLACES they will spy him out. But now that G-d has privileged me to see the son of your sharp-witted friend, may his light shine, to enjoy several days with him and to hear from him that there still exist, thank G-d, holy communities that the power of the sect has not touched, my soul has awakened from the fearful slumber that I have experienced until now. I hereby promise you that soon, G-d willing, I shall be sure to come to you, and there I shall take pleasure in your company and in the company of your colleagues, as is your wish and that of

Your friend, **who cleaves closer than a brother,***

....

#119

From Reb Yisroel Dov of the Village of Pankievits
To Reb Zelig Letitchiver

I'm hereby sending you a special messenger on the instructions of Reb Meyer Yankev, to notify you that Reb Meyer Yankev was taken from our district to jail. Here's what happened. As he wrote you [#110] from the holy community of Greater Tsidon, he traveled to my village to discuss with me the infamous affair. Once he discussed with me what he needed to, he decided to go back to the holy community of Greater Tsidon through the holy community of Nakhal Hamotsa. He stayed there for *Shabes* and prayed there at our holy *rebe*'s *minyen.*

Suddenly an official from the district came with men from the town hall and policemen and they surrounded the house during *Shabes* evening prayer. They took the Toyre scrolls and wrote down the names of all the people who were there at the *minyen.* All the community people left for home, but the visitors they took to jail, and among them they also took Reb Meyer Yankev, and they took all his papers to the district. So for G-d's sake, make sure to send me cash and I'll see about rescuing him, but without cash I can't do a thing.

These are the words of
....

#120

From Shmuel Baer in Nigrad
To Moyshe Fishl's in Koven

I feel obliged to notify you of what has occurred here this past week.

When you left here, the members of the notorious sect spread a rumor about you that your wife saw in you some acts of wickedness and *apikorses* and because of this you had to divorce her. Even though you disclosed to me all the particulars before your departure, all the same I wouldn't reveal the matter to any creature on earth.

But some five or six weeks ago now, Gershon Koritser spread a rumor about his wife that she had performed an unseemly act with a young man, and two men from their sect gave testimony to this effect. They compelled Gershon's wife to accept a bill of divorcement from him, and as soon as he divorced his wife he married your wife whom you had divorced. Since all the members of our community who are not from the sect knew for certain that Gershon's wife is an upright and worthy woman, they began complaining loudly about Gershon and about the testimony, and they said that they [the sect] had slandered that woman so that he could marry your wife. When I heard this, I disclosed to some people what I knew of the case of Gershon and your wife, and that you divorced your wife on account of this.

The rabbi of our community sent for one of the witnesses whom we knew had not yet been completely corrupted by the members of the sect. The rabbi of our community began threatening him and explaining to him the seriousness of the sin of false testimony, and he admitted UNDER SOLEMN OATH that he had not seen any unseemly act on the part of Gershon's wife, but that Gershon had badgered him into this -- to give the above testimony -- in return for which he had promised to draw him close to the *rebe* of Aklev, whereby he would have a livelihood.

Subsequently, the rabbi of our community sent for the second witness, and when he [the second witness] saw that the first witness had admitted the whole thing, he too confessed.

And now the whole populace around here GNASH THEIR TEETH at Gershon and at the whole sect, and the rabbi of our community is busy writing a responsum* in this affair.

So I'm informing you of all this since I knew that at the outset the members of that sect also wrote to Koven the reason [they fabricated] for your departure, just as they told it around here.

These are the words of
....

#121

From Reb Meyer Yankev in Galicia
To Reb Zelig Letitchiver

UP TO NOW THE L-RD HAS HELPED US, because now they left me out of jail on bail. But since an official did this without the knowledge of the district, therefore I'm afraid to go in public in the holy community of Greater Tsidon, because I see you wrote the truth that people like those in the holy community of Greater Tsidon won't help us now. When they belong to our faction they'll help us, but now everything's okay by them. If someone does something against us it's okay, and if someone does something for our benefit it's also okay by them, so I'm afraid to show myself in the marketplace. I traveled quietly to the holy community of Nakhal Hamotsa and I'm writing you this letter from there.

Since I know Reb Yisroel Dov wrote you [#119] that they took me to jail but didn't write you all the particulars, so I'm writing you the whole story. In Galicia, no one's allowed to make a *minyen* in his home without written permission from the district.* The overseers from Tutin informed against the local *rebe* and the other men who were making a *minyen* without a permit. As a result of this the district sent an official, who came on the night of *Shabes Koydesh* during evening prayer, took the Toyre scrolls, wrote down [the names of] all the men who were at the *minyen,* let the men of the Nakhal Hamotsa community go home, and just took the visitors to jail. Later on, the district sent the other visitors home under guard.* Only I REMAINED, since they saw in the papers they took from me that I had a correspondence with the *rebe* of the holy community of Kalktsig and with other people there to supply them the holy books *Toldes Yankev Yoysef, Eyts Khayim* and *Pri Eyts Khayim.* According to what I heard, they were holding on to me until they reached a legal decision on this.

You and I were very lucky I didn't have your letters [#59, #100, #107]. I don't know where they are.[1] I only know for certain that the district didn't take them. I don't care what they'll do with me because I accept on myself whatever they'll do, but I *am* concerned that on account of this I can't take any action regarding the *goye.* On Reb Yisroel Dov I can't rely. When I come home I'll tell you what this man is.

I'm also informing you that our people in Galicia spread a rumor throughout their country that one of the *misnagdim* from the holy community of Greater Tsidon committed this act -- that he, with an official of the district and men from the town hall and policemen, fell upon the home of the local *tsadek* with soldiers, and the soldiers cut down the *mezuzes* in the *tsadek*'s house with their swords, and the Toyre scrolls there they dragged with ropes and such -- all this the aforementioned *misnaged* did, that is, he said to do all this. They even spread a rumor that one of the visitors who the district sent home under guard died on the way. This rumor has traveled throughout Galicia, and everyone -- even those who aren't from our faction -- believes it.

And even though I was in the *tsadek*'s house when the incident occurred, and there was no Jew there from the holy community of Greater Tsidon with the official from the district; and what's more, they didn't cut down the *mezuzes* or drag the Toyre scrolls, G-d forbid!; and I also know for certain that not one of the visitors died on the way, because I know all the visitors and I know that they all arrived home safely, and I even know that that visitor who they spread a rumor about that he died

---

[1] I was overjoyed when I saw from this letter that I had brought it about that they didn't find Reb Zelig's letters on Reb Meyer Yankev because I continually took them away from him when I was invisible, so even Reb Meyer Yankev didn't know where they were.

on the way, the *misnagdim* from the holy community of Greater Tsidon sent home with a good wagon; and I also heard with my own ears that while the incident was taking place, the official from the district spoke with the local *rebe* gently and kindly; and it's also clear that the informers were the overseers from Tutin -- all the same I had great pleasure from the fact that the Galician *khsidim* are not *shlimazls* either, and that the people in Galicia believe this rumor that our Faithful spread there, because on account of this even those who don't side with our faction feel sorry for us and have gotten very angry at the *misnaged* who they spread the rumor about that he did this, and the whole population is angry as well at all the *misnagdim* in the holy community of Greater Tsidon!

I expect now that when you send me a passport from my home, the *misnagdim* there will see to it themselves that the district will let me go free, so as to show the populace that they didn't take any action in the affair of the *tsadek*'s *minyen,* so for G-d's sake, send me a valid passport.

These are the words of
....

#122

From Reb Avrohom Moyshe in Zalin
To Reb Zaynvl Verkhievker

Last Wednesday something not good happened to us. In the morning, Reb Zelig Letitchiver was found dead in his bed and we don't know what it was.

I asked his wife and she told me that Tuesday night a messenger from Galicia brought a letter [#119] to her husband. Since her husband was still by our holy *rebe,* she took the letter and told the messenger he should come in the morning for an answer. When her husband arrived home at 11 P.M. she gave him the letter, and when he read the letter he cried aloud, "Strike me dead! Reb Meyer Yankev they took prisoner in Galicia and they took from him all the papers, so they must've taken my letters [#59, #100, #107] too! What should I do, Soroh (that's his wife's name)?! I feel faint -- give me a drink."

[His wife continued:]

"I gave him vodka,* and he drank a little and felt better. He walked back and forth about the house and I laid down to sleep, so I didn't even hear when he laid down himself. In the morning, when the messenger from Galicia knocked at the door to let him in, I got out of bed and went to let him in. When the messenger came into the house he asked me I should give him a drink. I went to the liquor table and saw nothing was left in the flask that stood on the liquor table and I didn't know what this meant. But later on, when the messenger had waited a long time, I went to wake up my husband and I found him dead in bed."

"I suppose that when I was asleep he must've felt faint many times, and on account of this drank all the vodka that was in the flask. And then, when there was no more vodka in the flask and there was also no one to wake him up from the fainting, he must've fainted dead away."

"It was really bad luck that there was no one by him at that time. Even *I* didn't hear nothing because I was fast asleep."

All this the wife of the deceased, Our Teacher Rabbi Zelig, told me. We go about very melancholy on account of this, because our holy *rebe*, he should live, also goes about a little melancholy, since Reb Zelig was his right-hand man. It was even more unfortunate that none of us was there when he received the letter from Galicia [#119], because we would've consoled him and in the meantime he would've gotten the letter [#121] that Reb Meyer Yankev himself wrote to him later on -- that they left him out on bail and that they didn't take Reb Zelig's letters from him because they weren't on him. But what's past is past.

Right now we don't know yet who our holy *rebe* will take in Reb Zelig's place. We put in a word or two with our holy *rebe*, he should live, that he should take *you*, but our *rebe*, he should live, responded to this, "Reb Zaynvl has to to live in Kripen," and we didn't discuss this with him no further. Apparently our holy *rebe* will take Reb Noson Bakilinik, since he is now the one closest to our *rebe*, he should live.

These are the words of

....

#123

From Reb Avrohom Moyshe
To Reb Zaynvl Verkhievker

It turned out just like I wrote you [#122]. Our holy *rebe*, he should live, chose Reb Noson Bakilinik in place of the deceased, Our Teacher Reb Zelig, and through him we found out the reason for Reb Zelig passing away.

Recently by our holy *rebe,* there was a man from Galicia whose name is Reb Yisroel Reb Berish's, who used to be an unrestrained hedonist and committed all the sins in the Toyre. Later on he joined our circle and became a devoted follower of our holy *rebe.* And since our *rebe,* he should live, is very fond of him, our holy *rebe* talked with him for about half an hour. During the talk our holy *rebe* showed him the infamous *bukh* because this Reb Yisroel knows how to read German.

When Reb Yisroel opened the *bukh,* he saw the pictures on the page before the title page. He looked at the *bukh* for about five minutes and said, "Sinners! Their name and memory should be erased!" Our holy *rebe* asked him, "Why are you angry?" And Reb Yisroel said, "The pictures they put on this page are of a *rebe*'s personal secretary greeting a visitor who came to the *tsadek* for *Rosheshone.*"*

When our holy *rebe* heard this he shuddered and said, "Zelig, Zelig," and fell silent. And he began to pace back and forth in the room and said to Reb Yisroel, "Leave me alone."

Reb Yisroel left him and our holy *rebe* was in meditative seclusion for about an hour. Afterward he called to his Reb Noson* and said to him with a radiant face, "Take the *bukh* and throw it in the fire."

When Reb Noson told us all this we pondered over it all and we saw plainly that the matter must've been as follows -- The reason our holy *rebe* would always keep the *bukh* under the rug [on the table] and sometimes looked at the pictures in the *bukh* was that he supposed the pictures were the pictures of the authors who composed this *bukh,* and our holy *rebe* wanted to punish the authors with death by [his] looking, like the late rabbi, the *Maged,* did, as is known. Since the one picture was of a *tsadek*'s secretary, our holy *rebe*'s gaze had an impact, and on account of this looking, Reb Zelig passed away, since *he* was our holy *rebe*'s secretary, and what greater *tsadek* is there than *our* holy *rebe,* he should live, and therefore what greater secretary is there than Reb Zelig? And somewhere a visitor who was by our holy *rebe* on *Rosheshone* must've died too, and Reb Zelig greeted him on his arrival.[1]

So when our holy *rebe* heard from Reb Yisroel that the picture was of a secretary, he understood that on account of his gaze Reb Zelig passed away. At first he was a little melancholy that he caused this to happen to him, so he decided to at least do him the benefit of elevating him[2] and bringing him to a great celestial palace.

---

[1] "The *tsadek* can punish a person with death even on account of his aggrieved feelings, even by mistake." *Mides* 52:88.

[2] "The *tsadek* can elevate the dead to a high rung." *Ibid.,* 50:26.

The Besht taught Rabbi Gershon Kutiver how to elevate the dead, and **the dead came** to Rabbi Gershon **like a great flock of sheep** that he might elevate

So he did what he had to do during his time of meditative seclusion, and afterward he ordered Reb Noson to throw the *bukh* into the fire,* whereby the *tikn* was brought about, because he purified Reb Zelig by means of the fire. It's also in the category of, "He poured out his wrath on trees and stones" and likewise on paper,* and a word to the wise....

These are the words of
....

---

them. *Shivkhey ha-Besht* 8:2 [Mintz, 61].

#124

From Reb Yoysef Aharon in Eshtbuzrak To Reb Shloyme Khayim in Rudke

Last week, when I was traveling from home to the holy community of Greater Tsidon, I went through Kokhartovis. I arrived there on Friday, the eve of *Shabes Koydesh,* before noon, and I wanted to go for *Shabes Koydesh* to the holy community of Greater Tsidon. But when I heard the *rebe, Rebe* Avrohom Yankev, was spending *Shabes* there, I stayed there for *Shabes Koydesh* too and it was a great pleasure for me.

At the *shaleshudes* I heard very, very great and far-reaching *toyre,* and I gave for the *shaleshudes* a barrel of beer. On *Motse Shabes* I went with this *rebe* to a special room he had there, to take leave of him before my trip and to discuss my affairs with him and have him bless me. I spoke with him and he told me about my affairs LOCK, STOCK AND BARREL, and I took a ducat in my hand to give him for the blessing.[1]

But when I asked him to bless me, he began speaking with me about the bad times, and how he needs cash very badly. When I heard this, I understood one czerwone zloty is a small sum* to him, so I took three czerwone zlotys out of my pocket and gave them to him, but he told me that for a *pidyen* I must give him twelve czerwone zlotys. I told him I had several losses this year, and he told me he knows all this but that's how it has to be and that I shouldn't ask any question why I must give

---

[1] "The recipient of the blessing has to give the giver of the blessing a gift." *Mides* 72:1.

precisely twelve czerwone zlotys.[2] I had no other choice, so I gave him twelve czerwone zlotys as he demanded of me.

At first I was a little aggravated by this, but when I arrived at the holy community of Greater Tsidon and went to the man I had business with, I saw it had to be so, because the business I had there was looking very bad. But when I begged the man and gave him a thousand rubles in cash, I achieved -- through the help of our *rebe,* he should live -- everything, and I know for sure that without the help of our *rebe,* he should live, I would've had a big loss.[3]

I saw plainly that our holy *rebe,* he should live, foresaw this from the beginning, and what he said to me about the bad times was his knowl-

---

[2] "One must see that he is not miserly so that no judgments will remain against him, and for this one needs extra wisdom to know how much it is one needs to give (for a *pidyen*) so that no judgments will remain against him." *Likutey MohoRa"N* 94:2.

[3] When I was at the home of Reb Shloyme Khayim when he received this letter, there was some scoffer there who made fun of Reb Yoysef Aharon for believing that *Rebe* Avrohom Yankev achieved the business for him. He said, "Anyone can see from his letter that if he hadn't given the man in Greater Tsidon a thousand rubles in cash, he wouldn't have achieved anything!"

But that is the way of the wicked, I thought, to exchange truth for falsehood, and this scoffer must not yet have been privileged to see the holy book *Shivkhey ha-Besht,* for had he seen it he would have read in it the tale that took place in the holy community of **Zaslov. They found a Christian dead in the field and they wanted to make a libel against the Jews. The people of the town sent to the Besht, who was staying there, and he said that he hadn't heard anything of this in the court. Sometime after *Shabes* he inclined his ear as if he wanted to listen, and he said that they were speaking in the court of this libel. He went to the ritual bath and said, "Don't be afraid." The community sent the intercessor, who heard that the duchess had ordered her doctor to examine the body and to discern whether or not he had died a natural death. But the community was afraid to rely on the Besht, so they gave the doctor thirty zlotys, and thank G-d that there was no libel at all from this.**

Examine this tale in full, *Shivkhey ha-Besht* 10:4 [Mintz, 79] , and you'll have great pleasure. The moral is: Who would be so foolish as to say the community could have accomplished all this by means of the thirty zlotys they gave the doctor, even if the Besht hadn't gone to the *mikve* and hadn't said to them, **"Don't be afraid"**?

So, just as there the miracle is surely the blinding truth, for if not, G-d forbid, they would not have written this tale in the holy book *Shivkhey ha-Besht* -- and we see too that at first the Besht said that he **hadn't heard anything in the court**, and subsequently he heard **and went to the ritual bath and said, "Don't be afraid,"** and why didn't he say this right at the start, and so forth -- so here too, it's forbidden to dispute that it was only the twelve zlotys that accomplished all this.

edge of my business,[4] because our holy *rebe* certainly don't have bad times. So he must've been thinking just about me, and it was only because of the *pidyen* of twelve czerwone zlotys he rectified all this. Although I don't know the reason why precisely *twelve* czerwone zlotys, still, since I see with my feeble eyes what happened, what I don't know must also be right.

So make sure, when that *rebe* of ours comes to your community, to befriend him in every way possible. And if he speaks with you of the bad times, you'll know that judgments are pending against you, G-d forbid!, and you'll see that he'll erase them by what he tells you.

These are the words of
....

[4] See Letter #98, note 1.

#125

From Reb Zaynvl Verkhievker
To Reb Noson Bakilinik

This very minute I had news from somebody who was by our scoundrel, and he told me the crook got a letter in the mail and was overjoyed. As he was reading the letter he kept saying, "This is good!" and when he finished reading the letter he wrote a letter to the Bilke prince on the spot. I sent to our postmaster to find out where this crook had a letter from, and the postmaster said the letter was from Galicia. So of course, you know that the renowned case was decided there not good -- perish the thought!

I'm sending you also a copy of the letter [#126] the *goye* delivered to the Bilke prince before she ran away, 'cause that prince gave the letter to our scoundrel and that crook gave it to the sinner, Mordekhai-His-Name-Should-Be-Wiped-Out, to translate it into German. When this sinner translated the letter, he copied it for himself in the holy script and language as our *rebe* wrote it,* and he put this copy in the drawer of his writing table.

When I was by that sinner yesterday to pay him for vodka -- money and blood are the same* -- he took the papers out of the drawer to make with me an accounting. By and by he left the house to relieve himself. His thieving trustee who was in the house heard some commotion in the marketplace and went to the window to see what was the commotion in the marketplace, and in the meantime I took the letter and hid it in mine pocket. You see from all this that our scoundrel isn't twiddling his thumbs in this affair, and it's sure to be -- don't kid yourself! -- not good.

So I'm leaning towards the opinion you should make all this known to our holy *rebe,* his light should shine, 'cause I wrote several times to the deceased, Our Teacher Rabbi Zelig, that he should reveal everything to our holy *rebe,* but he wouldn't. On account of our many sins he passed away for this, 'cause if he had revealed the affair immediately to our holy *rebe,* we wouldn't of had all this aggravation and we wouldn't of had all the trials and tribulations. We wouldn't of had to send Reb Meyer Yankev to Galicia neither, and the *bukh* would be already by us, and of course we'd know who is the author and we would've plucked him up already by the root, and we wouldn't of needed to bother our holy *rebe* that he should punish the author by looking at the pictures in the *bukh,* on account of which Reb Zelig passed away! The point is -- the deceased should forgive me a thousand times! -- it wasn't good what he done by not listening to mine advice.

So please, at least listen to mine advice and reveal the story completely to our holy *rebe,* and he's sure to help matters. Especially 'cause what will be if we wait longer and later on wind up -- G-d forbid! -- IN DESPERATE STRAITS where we'll have to reveal the whole affair to our holy *rebe,* and our holy *rebe,* when he sees that the matter is very urgent, will perform some furious act and overturn the world -- G-d forbid!

Once more -- please! -- inform our holy *rebe* everything!

These are the words of

....

#126

Copy of the Letter the *Goye* Stole from the Man from Pilshtin in the Woods*

Great peace and blessing to my beloved friends who happily rejoice to do the will of their Creator* with their person and with their substance -- MEN OF TRUTH, PURSUERS OF RIGHTEOUSNESS, whose deeds are recorded in the book*, namely, our Faithful, heads of the distinguished communities and all the members of the community and their fund-collectors, jointly as well as individually, upon whom may all the blessings* be arranged and set. *Omeyn.* May this be His will.

It has been some time since the collector who received the *Ertsisroel* monies from the communities near the holy community of Pilshtin went to The Holy Land. Heretofore, there has not been an opportune time to appoint someone else in his stead. Now I have found ONE WHOM I LOVE WELL, the great, wonderful and distinguished rabbinic sage, the G-d-fearing elder, Our Teacher the *Rov,* Rabbi Aharon Kaliner, one of the residents of the holy community of Pilshtin, a man who, ever since he submitted to our authority, has turned away from all the affairs of this world, and all of whose labors have been only to occupy himself with *mitsves* to the extent of his ability.

Therefore, I HEREBY GIVE AN ORDER to appoint him as collector of all the *Ertsisroel* monies that our brethren, the children of Israel, who dwell in the holy community of Pilshtin and in the towns and villages that belong to the aforesaid community, donate. Consequently, it is incumbent upon all the small collectors in those vicinities to deliver all the pledges and donations that they collect in their communities and villages in accordance with the list in their possession to the aforementioned great sage, Our Teacher the *Rov,* Rabbi Aharon Kaliner. He will record all the collections in the list we have given him, in order to bring us a quarterly accounting of them or to deliver them to the *kolel* fund-collector sent at our behest. I am confident that our brethren the children of Israel will heed these words of ours, which are spoken for the benefit of our brethren the children of Israel who dwell in The Holy Land.

To the truthfulness of my words I have signed below.

These are the words of the one
who speaks uprightly,
....

#127

From Reb Yankl Pulnaer in Dishpol
To Reb Gumpl Kriliver

I heard the Zaliner made a match for his notorious wicked son with the *gvir* Beirekh of Galats and they set the wedding for the middle of this Elul, it should come to us for good. I'm afraid he did this deliberately so all the relations of that *gvir,* who up 'til now have been followers of our holy *rebe,* he should live, will be stuck there for *Rosheshone,* and on account of this won't go to *our* holy *rebe* for *Rosheshone.* So I'm notifying you of this since I know your *gvir* has business affairs in Galats, and you must be well acquainted with all the rich men around there and, of course, with this Reb Beyrekh too. So be sure to spare no effort so he'll renounce the match, especially since you must also know the Zaliner's son is a total sinner and a big hedonist, on account of which he was forced to divorce his first wife, since which he got more wicked. I got no doubt whatsoever that when the whims of that sinner become known to that *gvir* Beirekh, he certainly won't want him as his son-in-law.

Wouldn't it be better for him to match himself up with the son of *our* holy *rebe*? Even though he don't walk the straight and narrow, at least he's the son of a real *tsadek* and he's sure to be promoted soon.[1] But this sinner, son of the fake *rebe,* has no ancestral merit at all, and he'll certainly always remain a total sinner.

So see that you're resolute in this matter, and when you want I'll send you testimony from several people who know them in the holy community of Galats. They'll testify the Zaliner's son is a ruthless sinner, that they caught him several times with out-and-out sluts, and that he committed all the sins in the Toyre. The *gvir* Beirekh is sure to lose the desire to make a wedding, and the followers of our holy *rebe* will come to our *rebe,* he should live, for *Rosheshone,* it should come to us for good as in the past and as of old, and our holy *rebe,* he should live, won't have grievances against them.[2]

These are the words of

....

---

[1] "We promote the son of a *tsadek* when he does not walk the straight and narrow, so that he will walk the straight and narrow." *Mides* 22:4.

[2] "We find that the *tsadek* is aggrieved when one of his disciples draws close to another *tsadek* in order to gain prestige." *Ibid.,* 50:11.

#128

From Reb Yankl Pulnaer
To Reb Itsik Hirsh in Barditchuv

Yesterday I had a report that the Zaliner got a letter from The Holy Land that they accepted him there as President over them, and that he should collect all the *Ertsisroel* and Rabbi Meyer Balanes funds, even from the *kolel* fund-collectors.

You can imagine what aggravation our holy *rebe* will have from this -- that he should send this liar *Ertsisroel* funds and Rabbi Meyer Balanes funds that he collects. So we all agreed to ordain to pledge from now on not for Rabbi Meyer Balanes but for the soul of the Besht. After all, it was just our own people who decreed the custom to pledge for Rabbi Meyer Balanes not long ago. This custom never existed among the Jews and it don't appear in any book.[1]

We still remember when this custom was started in the communities by our Faithful -- that would be some twenty years [ago] -- and it follows that just as at that time we made the regulation to pledge for the soul of Rabbi Meyer Balanes, so now we'll make the regulation to pledge for the soul of the Besht. Folks will, of course, begin to make pledges for him, and the thing is no doubt right and proper, because nowadays, when the holy book *Shivkhey ha-Besht* has been published, people see the signs and wonders the Besht performed, and they'll understand that Rabbi Meyer Balanes wasn't half as great as the Besht, because what are the miracles Rabbi Meyer performed compared to the miracles the *Rabbon*, the Besht, performed, even compared to those we see just in that holy book *Shivkhey*? And it's known that what's recorded in that holy book is the tiniest bit and like a drop in the ocean of what the Besht did, according to what we know orally and according to what's written explicitly on the title page of that holy book.

So be sure to take special pains to institute this in your community where lots of people come to the fairs,* and be sure to institute it in the nearby communities too. I already wrote to all our Faithful who submit to our holy *rebe*'s authority, and I'm sure that by the merit of our holy *rebe* we'll settle this soon. Later on, we'll see about doing something with the *Ertsisroel* funds too. We'll be able to do *this* easily too, because it's known that we can make the air of *Ertsisroel* anywhere.[2]* Then we'll see what the fake *rebe* will do with his letter of presidency! For G-d's sake, don't be lazy at all about this and write me what you done in this matter.

These are the words of

....

---

[1] When he says, "book," he means, "old book," because by virtue of the publication of the holy book *Keser Shem Tov* in the year 5555 (1794-95), we were privileged with the above worthy custom. See *Keser Shem Tov*, Part 2, 23:2.*

[2] "By means of hand-clapping,* one draws in the holy air as it is in *Ertsisroel.*" *Kitser Likutey MohoRa"N* 29:256.

By virtue of someone who was with the *tsadek* on *Rosheshone*, the air becomes like that of *Ertsisroel*. See Letter #114, note 2.

"In all synagogues and study houses there emanates from the Creator, blessed be He, the vitality of *Ertsisroel*." *Yesamakh Leyv* 21:4.

#129

From Reb Gumpl Kriliver
To Reb Yankl Pulnaer

I got your letter [#127] just when my *gvir* wanted to send someone to Galats. Since my wife was very sick I couldn't go, but when I got your letter I thought, "There's nothing more important than this." So I told my *gvir* I'll go myself, and I expect that by the merit of our holy *rebe* my wife is sure to get better, especially since I ordered my wife to send to our holy *rebe* for a *pidyen* twenty-five rubles cash.

Now I'm informing you from the town of Galats that I already spoke with the *gvir*, Reb Beyrekh Malke's, about the match, and I seen he's not pleased with the match. But his wife is the expert and so one must speak with her, and I already spoke with her too. I also spoke with several people who are close to her and I hope soon they'll send back the engagement contract.

Because the truth is, that *gvir* is a very good man, but because of his wife he can't make a good match since everyone complains about her terribly. So the match was very important to them because the Zaliner planted there a rumor that he's a very great *tsadek*. But when I told them the whole to-do with the bridegroom, and when all their friends told them this too, I saw it was making an impression and they'd already lost the desire for this match. If you would send me some testimony or something else to make clearer to them the dealings of the fake *rebe*'s son, they're sure to send back the engagement contract in no time.

These are the words of

....

#130

From Reb Itsik Hirsh in Barditchuv
To Reb Yankl Pulnaer

The matter you wrote me [#128] about the donations for the soul of the Besht is very fair in my opinion, and also in the opinion of all our Faithful it's fair. Everybody around here agreed to institute it, but we figure it'll be hard to institute since all the *rebes* who aren't of the royal seed of the Besht surely won't agree to it. So I decided to handle the matter with extraordinary cunning and deliberateness.

Here's what I did. I told some of our Faithful around here each of them should steal some item from one of the visitors who come to our community for the fairs. Since it's a common practice throughout the Jewish diaspora to pledge for the soul of Rabbi Meyer Balanes for something lost or stolen and such, the visitors who our Faithful stole some things from also pledged for Rabbi Meyer Balanes. When they saw they didn't accomplish a thing with the pledges they went about upset. I gave them advice -- rather, I told one of their friends to give them advice -- that they should pledge for the soul of the Besht, and they decided, "What will it hurt to try?" -- so they pledged for the soul of the Besht. And when they pledged, every one of our Faithful quietly returned what he had stolen to some place in the house where they were staying -- under the trash or on the roof and such.

We did this a number of times here, and the rumor spread from those who pledged for the soul of the Besht -- and already many people have begun pledging, with G-d's help, for the soul of the Besht. In our *kloyz,* we set up a box for the pledges for the soul of the Besht and for the time being we also left the old box for the soul of Rabbi Meyer Balanes. These last two weeks we didn't find even one *prute* in the Rabbi Meyer Balanes box, but in the box for the soul of the Besht there's lots of money.

The visitors who had the items stolen already wrote home the whole story -- that they had a theft and the pledge for Rabbi Meyer Balanes didn't help them at all and only the pledge for the soul of the Besht helped them. Soon you'll see -- in all the communities they'll set up a box for the Besht in place of the Rabbi Meyer Balanes box, and the Zaliner, G-d willing, can put butter on his letter of presidency, because the *rebes* of the royal seed of the Besht certainly won't give him this money that the masses are pledging for the soul of their ancestor.

In any case, we can also finish him off but good if we want, because even according to civil law it's forbidden to take money out of the country* to another land, and the money for Rabbi Meyer Balanes they take *out* of the country, but the money for the Besht will stay *in* the country to keep an oil light burning continually* on the grave of the Besht. It's sure to be okay.

Please let me know if this custom has already spread by you too.

These are the words of

....

#131

From Reb Yankl Pulnaer
To Reb Gumpl Kriliver in Galats

I got your letter [#129] and the twenty-five rubles for the *pidyen* arrived from your wife too. Since your wife's name, Khaye daughter of Rivke, is recorded in our holy *rebe*'s prayerbook, he immediately made a *pidyen,* and you must've already had a letter from home that your wife is FIT AS A FIDDLE, because the *pidyen* was very good.

In the matter of the match, I expect it will be just like you wrote. To make the point stronger, I'm sending you a letter from the Zaliner's son, which he wrote to a slut in the holy community of Kripen. One of our men got hold of this letter from that slut and sent it to me. Since they know that slut in the town of Galats -- because her first husband was from there and he died on account of her -- therefore I got no doubt whatsoever that when you show them this letter in his very own handwriting, which he wrote *after* he made the match, when he should've forsaken his [wicked] ways, and when they recognize his handwriting -- because they must have [a sample of] his handwriting -- then they're sure to send back the engagement contract.

I'm also informing you that now the excellent custom has spread in most of the communities to pledge for the soul of the Besht instead of how they pledged up 'til now for the soul of Rabbi Meyer Balanes. Folks already see the pledges for the soul of the Besht accomplish more than the pledges for Rabbi Meyer Balanes, so make sure to publicize the thing there too and see to it this custom spreads there too, because this is a great benefit for the *tsadikim* who are OF THE ROYAL SEED of the Besht.

From me,

....

#132

From Reb Zalmen Brezner
To Reb Noson Bakilinik

I'm hereby informing you when I came to the town of Galats I went straight to our holy *rebe*'s *mekhutn* and I saw they're not pleased with the match. I checked into the matter and I had a report the Dishpoler's people did all this. One of them lives around here and he showed them a letter from our holy *rebe*'s son that he wrote to a woman in Kripen. They told me they know for sure the letter is his because they recognize his handwriting, and since they know this is an unseemly thing -- because the fact that the *mekhutn* couldn't make a match is because his *wife* has a not-so-good reputation -- so they want to abandon the match.

I was very aggravated by this because this in *itself* -- that our *rebe*'s son is a fornicator -- is just because of the fake *rebe* of Dishpol.[1] Nevertheless his people are singlehandedly spoiling the match. But what can we do? All my hard work to preserve the match didn't help at all, and according to the report I had they'll send back the engagement contract. Even though I told them this is no small matter to send back an engagement contract to our holy *rebe,* still they don't care about this.

So in my opinion, it seems better our holy *rebe* should send back his [copy of the] contract first so we won't be so humiliated, and it's better to spread the word our holy *rebe* don't want the match since rumor has it *they* don't want it. I'll make sure to persuade them they should quietly give our holy *rebe* some specified sum, and I already started discussing this with them. I want to wait 'til I have news from you, so make sure to get a move on and first of all send me the contract, and also write me how much money our holy *rebe,* he should live, will want for the indignity.

I'm also informing you that the guy from the fake *rebe* of Dishpol's people who lives here started a rumor here that in our country they already started pledging for the soul of the Besht instead of Rabbi Meyer Balanes. Since I know for sure that when I left home nothing at all of this was around yet, the fake *rebe* and his people must have some purpose in this. So write me a clear report about this and what our holy *rebe,* he should live, says about it.

These are the words of

....

---

[1] "These are the leaders of the false generation. They intensify -- have no illusions! -- carnal desire in the world." *Kitser Likutey MohoRa"N,* Book 2, par. 55.

#133

From Reb Noson Bakilinik
To Reb Zalmen Brezner

When I got your letter [#132] I almost peed in my pants,* because who ever heard of such a thing -- that one of the crude people would dare to say he'll send back the engagement contract to our holy *rebe?!* But what can we do with these sinners with their fake *rebe?* I know for certain they'll suffer a crushing defeat because the public already knows about their dealings. Even though the matter isn't well-known yet, because there isn't evidence and clear proof yet about their dealings, still I expect soon their exploits will become fully known because many of our Faithful are keeping watch there. One already wrote me he has clear proof about one episode and won't rest until he sees the matter through.

Really, how could they not be sinners if they're always scheming just to harm, G-d forbid!, our holy *rebe?* What does our holy *rebe* do to *them?* Why, their fake *rebe* has a hundred times more people than our holy *rebe!* What does it hurt these sinners that our holy *rebe* made a match with the *gvir* from Galats, or that he got a letter of presidency from the Land of Israel? It's just because they're total sinners they can't bear the real *tsadek* should have some comfort, because how can the husk bear that the holiness should be uplifted and strengthened?* What more proof than this do we need that they and their *rebe* must all of them be total sinners?

But what's past is past. I'm hereby sending you enclosed herein the engagement contract to be returned to the crude *mekhutn,* but on the condition he should give you at the very least two hundred czerwone zlotys for our holy *rebe,* and for the *rebetsn,* the *tsadkones,* she should live, he should give at the very least fifty czerwone zlotys for their indignity. Write me the moment you get the money so we can spread the word our holy *rebe* didn't want the match for confidential reasons.

As for the pledges for the Besht, it's also dirty work on the part of the Dishpol liar's people. They did this deliberately so they wouldn't have to hand over the funds to our holy *rebe,* but none of the *tsadikim* would agree to it and they wrote letters to one another not to allow this thing. The matter has reached the point that all the *tsadikim* decreed with the X* not to set up a box in any *kloyz* or anywhere else for the soul of the Besht.

They gave a very appropriate reason for this, that is, that it's not at all fitting to give donations for the soul of the Besht, because pledges and donations we just give for the souls of those people who died, but the *Rabbon,* the Besht, is still alive and kicking* and every single day is alive and kicking more, especially since the Besht said explicitly, "If the Righteous Redeemer don't come within sixty years, I have to re-enter this world."[1] So if we give pledges and donations for his soul, it's literally a denial of the Besht. For this reason the Dishpoler had to keep quiet too, so his scheme was nullified. So be sure to publicize this thing right away in Galats too so the custom won't spread there, because you know the masses -- when they begin some practice then it's hard later on to uproot this custom from them.

From me,

....

[1] *Shivkhey ha-Besht,* 23:4 [Mintz, 169]. The sixty years have already passed and without any doubt the Besht must already be in the world, but we haven't yet been privileged to know where he is.

#134

From Reb Zalmen Brezner
To Reb Noson Bakilinik

As soon as I got your letter [#133], I went to the *gvir,* Reb Beyrekh, and compromised with him for two hundred and fifty czerwone zlotys like you wrote me. I gave him back the engagement contract and I'm hereby sending you *their* torn-up engagement contract. I couldn't spread the rumor here that our holy *rebe* forsook the match, because around here I'm afraid of that *gvir,* since he and especially his wife are real big shots around here, but if you spread the rumor in our country then word will reach here too on its own.

I'm very pleased that the match has been scrapped because in fact the wife of that *gvir* was a big fornicator. Reb Beyrekh himself is a very good man, but what good is that to me if she's an adulteress? Who knows who the father of the bride is? -- maybe some Ishmaelite or Wallakhian, of course -- so it sure is a good thing we finished off the affair this way.

As for the pledges for the Besht, I told lots of people what the *tsadikim* in our country did about this. This rumor had a big impact around here too, because already here too there were some people who began pledging for the Besht, but when I spread the word that all the *tsadikim* in our country decreed with the X* not to do this, and especially when the people heard the reason for the thing, they stopped pledging for the Besht and started pledging like they used to for Rabbi Meyer Balanes.

I'm also informing you they started around here talking up the match for the daughter of the *gvir*, Reb Beyrekh, with the Dishpoler's son, but when I found out about it I didn't rest until I ruined the thing and nothing will come of it.

These are the words of
....

#135

From Reb Khayim Gavriel in Koven
To Reb Yankl Pulnaer

I'm hereby sending you a special messenger so you'll make sure to hide a certain goblet because this very moment I had a report that our contractor found out he was missing the goblet and made a big stink. Ever since the to-do between the judge and Eyliohu the contractor's son, the contractor hasn't let me into his house, so I don't know what's going on there. I'm afraid maybe it'll occur to him his son took it and his son will confess to him, because since it's been a long time since I talked with him and the new rabbi in our community has talked with him several times, he must've become a follower of the rabbi, and I'm afraid if he confesses the thing, it won't -- don't kid yourself! -- be good.

So for cryin' out loud, make sure to hide the vessel. I'll leave here for a few days and later on I'll see what we should do about this.

These are the words of
....

#136

From Reb Khayim Gavriel
To Reb Yankl Pulnaer

I came back to our community because, thanks to our holy *rebe,* they didn't find out about the matter of the goblet at all, because the contractor don't suspect his son took it. He suspects his assistant and he took him to jail. In the meantime, I spared no effort through our Faithful so the assistant should escape, and since the assistant *did* escape, everyone believes the assistant must've stole the goblet. The contractor already gave up on the wine goblet, so we got no reason at all to be afraid in this matter.

But this I can't stand -- every day the wickedness of the rabbi here gets worse and every day our faction becomes more despised, because he really bad-mouths our group as a whole and isn't afraid to criticize us in his sermons, and every day Eyliohu the contractor's son becomes more devoted to him. From what I heard, every day he studies by him a lesson in *Gemore* with commentators, and I got serious doubts whether he'll still be ours, especially since I heard he even placated the judge already for behaving insolently to him, and literally dissolved in tears in front of him to forgive him what he did. All this the new rabbi brought about.

I tell you this rabbi must be a big wizard, because whoever he speaks with, that person immediately becomes his follower. Even though I'm pleased he's sure to bury the Zaliner -- because he was already made rabbi there in Zalin too, and he already spent several weeks there with his infamous judge, where they became acquainted with the sinner Mordekhai Gold and they all united* against that liar [the Zaliner], and they're sure to bury him good because he already has a good kick in the ass coming to him just for the things he did to our holy *rebe* -- but all the same I'm afraid them sinners won't rest until they also do harm to *our* holy *rebe*, G-d forbid!, since they don't hate the Zaliner because he's a liar, but because he's from our faction, and they hate the whole bunch of us without no distinction.

So my advice is to inform our holy *rebe* of all this, because I tell you this is no trifle and our holy *rebe* is sure to take some action about this.

These are the words of
....

#137

From Reb Meyer Yankev at the Border
To Reb Noson Bakilinik

I heard over here that my friend, Our Teacher Rabbi Zelig Letitchiver, passed away, and you now fill his place by our holy *rebe*. You must know about all the affairs because he was always close with you. So I'm informing you the district of the holy community of Greater Tsidon gave a legal ruling, which they call a *shub pas,* to send me off to the border under guard.* When they summoned me to the district to give me the order of extradition, I found the *goye* with her father there at the district too. The district also gave *them* an order of extradition.

Even though the district was willing to give me a wagon to the border, I didn't want it. I said I'd go on foot, because I thought if I go on foot I'll go together with the *goye* and her father, because they're sure to go on foot since they can't pay for the wagon, and if I go together with them I'll be able to speak with them on the way and tell them what they should say at home at the interrogation.

I was very happy about this because I saw plainly this was [due to] the merit of our holy *rebe,* he should live. But when they gave me the guard with the extradition order and I left the district, I saw two wagons with some men waiting outside the district. I asked who these wagons were for, and they told me the wagons were for the *goye* and her father and the children and for the guards sent from our government to accompany them on the way, because they wrote from there to send them in wagons and they would pay for the wagons.

I almost fainted. I wanted to ask them which border they were bringing them to, but at that moment someone came out of the district and started to get very angry at my guard and ordered him to leave with me immediately. I started to say I would pay for the wagon and they should give me a wagon, and Reb Yisroel Dov was also begging and really endangering his life. He shouted that they should give me a wagon, and he went to the senior official of the district about this, but it didn't help at all. Heartlessly, he ordered to take me immediately and lead me on foot, because when they first asked me, I said I didn't want a wagon.

I realized how good it would have been if I had said I wanted a wagon, because they certainly wouldn't have given me a separate wagon, but [would have sent me] with the *goye* and the other people who went with her, and I would have been able to discuss the notorious affair with her, but I spoiled it myself by saying I'd go on foot. The guard took me and left with me, and I don't even know which border they're taking the *goye* to. So I'm sending you a special messenger, the bearer of this letter, so you'll keep on the lookout there, because the situation could be very bad, G-d forbid! I'm afraid to come home now, so for the time being I'm staying in the village of Kobrin at the border.

These are the words of

....

#138

From Reb Noson Bakilinik To Reb Getsl Meyer in Koven

We consulted around here with all our Faithful and we all agreed to speak with our holy *rebe,* he should live, and ask him to make peace with the fake *rebe* of Dishpol.

At first we were afraid to discuss this with our *rebe,* he should live, but we saw this is no laughing matter -- it's literally a matter of life and death -- so we decided to risk speaking with him. When we saw our holy *rebe* didn't get angry at us for this, we told him this the next day too, especially since we had a report the Dishpoler also wants this, because on account of the *apikorsim* around there he has awful aggravation. We told our holy *rebe* the Dishpoler urgently wanted to approach him and our holy *rebe* said to us, "I agree to this." We were very, very pleased by this, because we got no doubt whatsoever that as a result of the closeness between them all the troubles will be over.[1]

So I'm informing you of all this right away so you'll be sure to talk about this with some of the people in your community who are close to the Dishpoler, so they'll also do what needs to be done. Don't be lazy about this because it's very, very urgent. Give me a report of what you did as soon as possible.

From me,

....

---

[1] I heard from the Zaliner's people that in either case they're delighted that the two *rebes* will become reconciled. For if the Dishpoler is a real *tsadek* and the controversy between the two of them is just for the benefit of Israel, as is explained in *Seyfer ha-Mides,* 35:85 ["The controversy that exists between two *tsadikim* is for the benefit of the Jewish people. Know that also on high there are two angels who are also disputing and their arbitrator is none other than The Holy One, blessed be He, Himself"], then surely when they become reconciled it will also be good. And if the Dishpoler is a sinner, then the reconciliation is certainly good because "when a sinner subjugates himself to the *tsadek,* it indicates that some trouble has been decreed for the *tsadek,* and now the trouble will no longer come upon him," as is explained in the aforementioned book, 54:142.

#139
From Reb Yankl Pulnaer To Reb Khayim Gavriel in Koven

I got both your letters [#135, #136], and you can imagine how scared stiff I was when I read your letters. I got no doubt the Zaliner's people told the contractor about the wine goblet, because a few *Shabosim* ago one of the Zaliner's followers was around here. He saw the wine goblet and was overcome with envy, and he said distinctly there's no such vessel by the Zaliner. We were wondering where he got the desire to come to our holy *rebe* for *Shabes.* When I got your letter, we consulted and we all decided this follower of the Zaliner must've come to our holy *rebe* just for the sake of the wine goblet,* so as to know later on what to say.[1]

He must've told this to the contractor, and we're afraid these trouble-makers* shouldn't take actions in the future with regards to the vessel. Even though you wrote that the contractor don't got no suspicions about his son because he suspects the assistant who ran away, all the same we're afraid, because who knows what they're doing in secret?!

So we all agreed our holy *rebe* should make peace with the Zaliner, and we already discussed this with our holy *rebe,* he should live. We told him the Zaliner sent word to us and very much wants to make peace with our holy *rebe* and wishes to humble himself before our holy *rebe,* and our holy *rebe* told us, "I wish to accept the reconciliation. You'll see I'm not from the world of the female,[2] but the reconciliation won't help the Zaliner at all because it's already too late *(es iz shoyn tsu shpet).*" We were confounded and we don't know what he meant by this.[3]

---

[1] "The liar who comes to see the *tsadek,* his heart is thinking how he will speak afterward." *Mides* 55:114.*

[2] "Whoever has difficulty accepting reconciliation is from the world of the female." *Ibid.,* 35:75.

[3] They really didn't know the meaning, but I know because I was privileged to be by the *tsadek* of Dishpol several times when I was invisible, and several times I saw that he received a letter from some adherent of the Zaliner who was always at the Zaliner's but really was secretly an adherent of the Dishpoler. The Dishpoler's spy was in the Zaliner's home but this was so secret that even the Dishpoler's secretary didn't know it. This spy always informed the Dishpoler by letter how the affairs of the Zaliner stood, and this time this spy wrote that soon it would be very bad for the Zaliner because all his exploits were already known in the government. I listened when the Dishpoler read this letter in his room of meditative seclusion but I couldn't obtain the letter because the Dishpoler

So be sure to discuss this with the Zaliner's people who are by you and see they become reconciled, because in our opinion it could be the Zaliner's not bad, and the fact that our holy *rebe* takes issue with him is perhaps just "so people should not go astray after him,"[4] and on account of this our holy *rebe* couldn't enter serious contemplative prayer,[5] and in any case, even the controversy of *tsadikim* is only for the best.[6]

So be sure to spare no effort they should become reconciled and notify me without delay, because I see plainly our holy *rebe* has enemies, since I saw he has a scratch on his body even though he has no blows or wounds.[7]

From me,

....

---

burned all the letters from this spy as soon as he read them.

[4] "It is permissible not to admit the truth and to take issue with it 'so that people should not go astray after it.'"* *Ibid.*, 36:105.

[5] "For there is [a certain kind of] contemplative prayer that one cannot be privileged with except through very great wealth." *Kitser Likutey MohoRa"N* 56:559.

[6] "This a person needs to know: When there is a controversy of *tsadikim* against him...it is only for the best...for the controversy of *tsadikim* is really only for the best and is not called a controversy at all." *Ibid.*, 59:583.

[7] "When a person feels an itch in his body he knows that he has enemies. Sometimes through blows and wounds that he inflicts on his body he is saved from enemies, because one is exchanged for the other." *Mides* 84:21.

#140

From Reb Getsl Meyer in Koven
To Reb Noson Bakilinik

As soon as I got your letter [#138], I went to Khayim Gavriel and started chatting with him. I changed the subject to the matter of the *rebes* and found him ready to go to the Dishpoler.

He went, and came back today. He brought me the reply that the Dishpoler too agrees to the thing, but said we have to select somewhere the two of them can go because this one certainly won't want to go to that one and that one won't want to come to this one. It would've been better to choose our community, but because of the sinners who are by us we can't choose our community.

The Dishpoler said to select the community of Kolne. In my opinion, our holy *rebe* will also agree to this because there's lots of people there who belong to us, and even those few of the Dishpoler's people, when they see our holy *rebe,* they're sure to become followers of our holy *rebe.* So let me know how to proceed.

These are the words of
....

#141

From Reb Yankl Pulnaer
To Reb Mendl Barer in Kolne

I'm informing you the *rebe* of Zalin sent word to our holy *rebe* he wants to reconcile with him. Our holy *rebe,* he should live, in his boundless humility, agreed to this, but he said the reconciliation would be specifically in your community, and the Zaliner undertook to travel to your community. So make sure to prepare for our *rebe,* he should live, suitably fine lodging, because both for you and for all our Faithful in your community, it's proper our *rebe,* he should live, should have a fine dwelling, because it's known that from the dwelling of the *tsadek* the deeds of the generation are known.[1]

And obviously, of course, you'll also make certain our *rebe,* he should live, will have pleasure and comfort there and the people who come to our holy *rebe* won't come empty-handed.[2] I'm sure the people in your

[1] *Likutey MohoRa"N* 138:2.

[2] "It should not be difficult for you [to understand] why the *tsadikim* derive benefit from others in order to accustom the members of their household to wealth and glory. [You might think that it is] better not to be a leader and not to benefit from others. Don't let it trouble you, for the more the *tsadek* has pleasure and comfort, the larger his soul grows thereby, and then there is a house of repose for the *Shkhine* of The Holy One, praised be He. Consequently, one should not come to the house [of a *tsadek*] empty-handed." *Mides* 50:20.

When I was in the home of the rabbi of Koven and they didn't see me, I heard how he protests against this saying in *Mides.* He said that this saying is the opposite of the *Gemore,* for in addition to anecdotes we find in the *Gemore* about *tsadikim* who didn't have a piece of bread -- like Rabbi Khanine ben Dose and such -- we find a whole statement, "[Do not make of them [the words of Toroh] a crown with which to magnify yourself] nor a spade to dig with."* He also showed what the Rambam wrote about this in his commentary on *Oves,* how the Rambam glorifies the ancients, some of whom were artisans, and Karno, who was a judge in the Land of Israel, used to live by drawing water.* Hillel the Elder used to live by chopping wood, Rabbi Yoysef by carrying wood, and there were many like that. The rabbi of Koven spoke at length about the real *tsadikim* who take a lot of money and collect such great wealth that they and their children are extremely wealthy and they conduct their households like some ruler -- and all this from the wealth of others. He spoke at length in this vein.

But whoever has eyes to see will understand that all the sayings and anecdotes in the *Gemore* were said only with reference to the Talmudists, and G-d forbid to elucidate them with reference to the real *tsadikim,* for we see plainly that the more wealthy they become, the more the wicked return in repentance. The Hidden Light, Our Teacher the *Rov,* Rabbi Nakhmen, has already taught us, "We accept gifts from the wicked in order that they should return in repentance." *Mides* 49:3.

"He whose wealth brings enjoyment to the *tsadek* is as though he had performed the service of the Holy Temple." *Ibid.,* 51:46.

"A sinner who has committed many sins, his remedy is that his activities should be to sustain the *tsadek.*" *Ibid.,* 54:141.

"Whoever brings a gift to the *tsadek,* The Holy One, praised be He, creates pleasure for him." *Ibid.,* 55:171.

"The king (that is, the *tsadek*) collects his expenses from the people." *Ibid., ibid.,* par. 177.

"Whoever benefits (the *tsadek*) from his property is as if he benefits all Israel and he is saved from death." *Ibid.,* 56:181.

"Every place where the soul of his foot treads, the *tsadek* owns." *Ibid., ibid.,* par. 188.

"When the *tsadek* becomes wealthy, on account of this the wicked return in repentance." *Ibid.,* 92:16.

"Great is the act of *tsdoke.* Whoever gives *tsdoke* to the perfect *tsadek* who creates union between the supernal virtues...and then the world is full and satiated with every benefit -- abundance and blessing and mercy and life and children and sustenance and tranquility without end -- which is emanated on account of the *tsadek* who receives the *tsdoke* and through whom the abundance goes to the whole world, to every single one enough for his lack and his need. This is alluded to in the verse, EACH PERSON SHALL GIVE A RANSOM....The word 'ונתנו' (they SHALL GIVE) with the letters reversed is also 'ונתנו' as stated above...and this is the well-known intercourse in which there is intercourse with itself."* *No'am Elimelekh* 53:3.

"There is a *tsadek* who receives *tsdoke* and his intention is also for his own benefit...and even this *tsadek* brings about a union of the two aforementioned virtues by means of his receiving into his hand the *tsdoke* (and also brings abundance)." *Ibid., ibid.*

All the holy books by the *tsadikim* of our time are filled with this. Surely if the *Rabbon,* the Besht, had seen this Rambam, he would have argued with him until

community won't care that there was a fight between the two of them,[3] and they'll do everything as it must be done. Send me a reply by the bearer of this letter so we can get ready for next Tuesday, it should come to us for good, because me and Reb Khayim Gavriel of Koven will come to your community too, and with the help of our holy *rebe,* he should live, everything is sure to be okay.

From me,

....

---

the Rambam were compelled to concede and there would be no allusion to this now in the Rambam's commentary to the *Mishne,* just as the Besht did this another time to the Rambam. See *Shivkhey ha-Besht* 32:4 [Mintz, 233].

But unfortunately, the Besht did not see this Rambam. But truly, so what? We must surmise and believe that if perhaps the Besht *had* seen this Rambam, it would have been so. But for such contemplative prayer one needs great wealth, as explained above, and the rabbi of the holy community of Koven has no wealth. Consider this carefully!

[3] "It is proper not to listen or pay attention to quarrels between the *tsadikim,* just to believe in them. On the contrary, when one hears the quarrels between the *tsadikim,* he should draw for himself a moral that he has an impairment in his brain marrow,* for if his brain were not impaired, he would not have listened to the quarrels between the *tsadikim* and he would not have had any difficulty about them whatsoever." *Kitser Likutey MohoRa"N* 4:18.

#142

From Reb Aharon Khalivniker
To Reb Khayim Gavriel of Koven, Currently in Kolne

I'm sending you a special messenger -- the bearer of this letter -- because it's an emergency! Yesterday, I went to the holy community of Koven where I bought from the contractor Reb Kalmen grain that had spoiled on him for my distillery. When I paid him for the flour with banknotes, there among them was those two banknotes I had from you when you bought by me the *shmure.**

When the contractor saw your two banknotes, he asked me, "Where'd you get these two banknotes?" At first I said I don't know, but when he started to get very angry and said he'd hand me over to the court because he got banknotes from the cashier and when he came home two notes were stolen from him, and he asked the cashier to give him the register of the serial numbers of the banknotes, and since the cashier got the banknotes from the treasury with the register, he handed over to him that very register from the treasury and recorded for him the serial numbers of those banknotes he was missing, and when I paid him for the flour he saw that the two banknotes I gave him, namely, those I got from you, were those very numbers that he was missing, and I saw the matter was no small thing -- I thought to myself, "Why should I get involved in such matters, especially since I know you -- that you, G-d forbid!, didn't steal the two banknotes from him," so I told him the truth -- that I got these banknotes from *you.*

He ordered me not to leave his house, and he sent for his only son and said to him, "I know for certain that you stole two banknotes from me and gave them to Khayim Gavriel, so tell me the truth and I'll forgive you for what you did -- just on Khayim Gavriel I'll take my revenge."

At first his son wouldn't own up to it, but when the contractor sent for the judge and the judge began to speak with the only son, he immediately confessed and started bawling. In between sobs he said, "It wasn't just *this* I stole -- I also stole the goblet and gave it to Khayim Gavriel to give to the *rebe* of Dishpol."

When he said this the contractor literally began to dance with joy. He ordered one of his men to bring me to the court for interrogation, but the judge said to him, "Why should you do this -- won't your son also be culpable in the case?" And the contractor answered him, "Don't worry, because by their laws* there's no punishment coming to my son for this."

When he said this, the judge began to kiss the only son and told him, "You were right to tell the truth, and I love you even more than before. It wasn't for nothing the *rebe* of Dishpol said you have a great and lofty soul, for through you great things will be done in Israel. Through you we shall uproot the wicked *rebe* with his WICKED PEOPLE."

I went with one of the contractor's men to the court, and there too I had to tell the truth -- that it was from you I got those two hundred-ruble banknotes, because there were already witnesses when I said this at the contractor's house.

In the court I heard the judge ordering to send word to Dishpol to look for this wine goblet there by the *rebe.* I would've gone straight to Dishpol, but as I heard that our *rebe* and you too are now in Kolne, I'm hereby sending you a special messenger to let you know all this. You'll know what to do, of course.

These are the words of

....

#143

From Reb Dovid Tsere's
To Reb Yankl Pulnaer

Tonight the sheriff came here from Koven with several of his men. They didn't go to just any house but immediately stationed themselves in front of the home of our holy *rebe,* he should live, and surrounded the house on all sides and started searching. At first, we didn't know what they were looking for and we imagined they were searching for some illegal merchandise. Then, when we realized they were looking for the goblet, we weren't afraid since we knew that several days ago our holy *rebe* ordered that it be hidden. But apparently there was someone from our holy *rebe*'s household who revealed to them how they had hidden the vessel, because the sheriff sent one of his men to the winter stove, where they found the vessel and brought the vessel to the sheriff.[1]

He gave the order to bring chains at once and asked where our *rebe* was so as to put him in irons. We almost fainted when we heard this and we told him our *rebe* wasn't here. At first he wouldn't believe us, but when he rounded up the community and they told him our *rebe* was

---

[1] I heard that the rabbi of the holy community of Koven made great fun of the fact that they were searching for the vessel in the home of the *rebe* of Dishpol. He said that the contractor did this at the behest of Our Teacher the *Rov,* Rabbi Nakhmen, which he said in his book *Likutey MohoRa"N* 100:3, "A person must go back and search for what he has lost....* That which he has lost was with the *tsadek* because the *tsadek* goes out seeking what he [himself] has lost until he finds it," and he said that "one who finds goes back and seeks out what others have lost until he finds their loss too, until he finds what everyone has lost. Therefore one must come to the sage to claim and to identify his loss and to return to retrieve it from him." And the contractor did so, said that rabbi.

Indeed, based on what we hear, our soul grieves at the *apikorses* of the rabbi of Koven, who overturned the living words of G-d,* for he who peruses the aforementioned holy book will see that the *Rov,* Our Teacher Rabbi Nakhmen, THE SAINT and Holy Man OF BLESSED MEMORY, was speaking there only about those things a person loses of the [spiritual] things that were shown to him before he was born, but he wasn't referring at all there to those [material] things that belong to a person in this world. Would he have used the expression "that which he has lost is with the *tsadek?*" Behold, it says explicitly in *Seyfer ha-Mides* 53:121, "The *tsadek* has the power to take from one and to give to another." If so, how much the more so do things that are in the *possession* of the *tsadek* belong to him! Concerning that rabbi it is taught in the Mishna, "He who has studied and then abandoned [the Torah] is worse than all of them."*

definitely not home and had left home a few days ago, he believed them and said, "We'll catch up with him wherever he is."

When this villain began maligning our holy *rebe* and all our people, we were sick at heart. He said, "We know very well what you do and so do the authorities, but be advised that previously you could get away with whatever you wanted, but not now. The lieutenant governor knows you very well. He'll take good care of *you* and nothing on earth will help you, because he knows all your doings and he won't rest until he sends many of the *rebes* and at the very least five hundred of your people to Siberia."

He said many such vile things that we couldn't bear, and some of us covered our ears so as not to hear what this villain was saying. He ordered his men to find out where our *rebe* was and to put him in irons there.

So I'm sending you the bearer of this letter specially -- for G-d's sake, don't delay even for a moment! Run away from there this instant because this villain is sure to find out where you are! Because as I see it, we have lots of enemies around here. Up 'til now they kept quiet -- this was only out of fear -- but now that they see judgments are pending against us, they got no fear or shame and they speak openly AGAINST THE L-RD AND AGAINST HIS MESHIEKH.*

These are the words of
....

#144

From Reb Noson Bakilinik
To Reb Zalmen Brezner in Galats

I'm hereby reporting to you that a few days ago now, the Dishpoler sent word to our holy *rebe* he wanted to reconcile with him. Our holy *rebe,* he should live, agreed to this and they met here in the holy community of Kolne. Last night, after the reconciliation, Yankl Pulnaer -- the Dishpoler's man -- received a letter [#143] from home, and half an hour later -- this was after midnight -- the Dishpoler fled with Yankl Pulnaer and Khayim Gavriel, and no one knows where he ran off to.

During the night we didn't know nothing of this, but in the morning when we awoke we heard this commotion throughout the community. No one knows any more than that a messenger came at night with a letter, and half an hour after they got the letter they took off. In my opinion, they must've fled to Galats, because a visitor who arrived here early today from Galats said that six parasangs from here he came across a covered wagon on the road with three men. Furthermore, from the description he gave of the horses, they're the Dishpoler's horses.

So far no one knows the reason for the flight, but soon folks will find out all the particulars. The few people who sided with the Dishpoler must be ashamed to be seen outside, and there's no doubt at all that they'll all come to our holy *rebe* to be subject to him, and all the villages that were subject to the Dishpoler are sure to come to our holy *rebe* now. I'm informing you of all this for your pleasure, and so you'll see a lie don't fly.*

I'm also informing you in the greatest secrecy that we, of course, know the reason why he ran away, because we knew beforehand it would be so.* Here's what happened: The son of the contractor in Koven began to draw close to the Dishpoler, and he stole a wine goblet from his father and gave it to the Dishpoler. When we had news of this matter of business, we sent one of our people to spend *Shabes* by the Dishpoler, to see whether he still had this wine goblet [see Letter #139]. When this man told us he saw it, we wrote an anonymous letter to the contractor that the wine goblet that was stolen from him was by the Dishpoler. At first the contractor didn't do nothing, and we didn't know if he didn't believe the letter or if he wanted to keep silent until the time was ripe.

Later on we had a report the Dishpoler had hid the wine goblet. It appeared he had notification we knew of it, but we didn't rest until we found out where he hid it.

In the meantime, the contractor found out about another theft of two hundred-ruble banknotes, which he recognized in the possesion of Reb Aharon Khalivniker, who got them from Khayim Gavriel.

The contractor sent to Dishpol to search for the wine goblet. We immediately provided information how he had hid the wine goblet and they found it in the winter stove. Even though this Reb Aharon wrote a letter to Yankl Pulnaer, which would've notified him of what was going on, since Yankl wasn't home, he [Reb Aharon] sent the letter [#142] to Kolne, and in the meantime they searched in Dishpol. Perhaps if Yankl had been home, they would've made sure to send the goblet away from the Dishpoler's house.

I'm informing you of all this because maybe the Dishpoler will come to Galats and not say nothing that he ran away. He'll want to match himself up with the big shot Beirekh from there. So you'll know what to say there, because if he makes the match, even though later on they won't want to go through with it, they'll give him some amount for the indignity.

So make sure not to let this happen, but do everything with cunning because we don't want right now to let them see no enmity.

From me,
....

✉

#145

From Reb Zalmen Brezner
To Reb Noson Bakilinik

I got your letter [#144] a day after the Dishpoler arrived As soon as he got here, Gumpl Kriliver came to me and told me the Dishpoler reconciled with our holy *rebe* and came here because he wants to go to The Holy Land. I was astonished -- how come all of a sudden he's going to The Holy Land? But when I got your letter I understood the matter and I didn't say a word, because I'm afraid when it becomes known it'll be a disgrace around here for our whole group, because the Dishpoler has a fine reputation around here.

So I kept the thing secret, especially since there wasn't even any need to reveal it because his people don't show theirselves in the marketplace, and they're also not letting a lot of people at him -- only a very few of the notables were with him and gave him money for the trip to The Holy Land. According to what I heard, he made two hundred fifty czerwone zlotys around here.

As for the match, they have nothing in mind. Today I heard from Yankl Pulnaer that today or tomorrow they'll all leave here for some nearby community. He didn't say which, but he said in a few weeks he'll come back here because that's when a ship leaves here for The Holy Land.

The main thing I forgot. Please let me know what's new by you, because Gumpl Kriliver told me our holy *rebe* and his people have some false accusation [against them] -- it should never be worse! -- and he said the outcome certainly won't be good. Since you didn't write me nothing about this I'm very frightened. Especially since I saw the Dishpoler had a not-so-good end, I'm very afraid there shouldn't be -- G-d forbid!, don't tempt the devil -- because I saw in the holy book *Likutey MohoRa"N*[1] he

[1] 150:1.

said, "When enemies join together they don't survive -- they fall." So for G-d's sake, write me all the particulars.

These are the words of

....

#146

From Reb Noson Bakilinik
To Reb Zaynvl Verkhievker

I'm hereby sending you a special messenger -- for G-d's sake, notify the right people in Pilshtin to stay light, because the *goye* already arrived here with her father! It's lucky they have a holiday for several days* at this time of year, so they won't take them for interrogation. In the meantime we'll see what can be done.

But the fact is the situation isn't good, because we sent one of our people who knows one of the judges well, and he asked him to help him speak with the *goye.* He spoke with her in the jail, and she told him everything to the last detail. What's more, her father said the *arendar*'s wife persuaded him to flee with his daughter, and his daughter went in the *arendarke*'s Jewish-style clothes to the border, and a man from your community went with them. He said he would recognize the wagon and the driver and the horses, and he told him the color of the horses.

So for G-d's sake, they should stay light in case they got to run away. I don't got time to go on at length since it's a real emergency!

From me,

....

#147

From Reb Noson Bakilinik
To Reb Zaynvl Verkhievker

Woe is us! Fallen is the crown of our head! Our *rebe,* The Light of Our Eyes, passed away last night. **I'll write** you **a little about his passing**

away. When we returned from Kolne, our holy *rebe* was very uplifted in total bliss. We sat by him after the sanctification of the new moon, and he was blissful like we never saw him in our lives. The *tsadkones,* the *rebetsn,* she should live, **went to the cellar herself and brought us as much wine as** we **wanted.** We drank and sang plenty that we had got rid of the Dishpoler from our vicinity.

When we saw our holy *rebe* was in such total bliss, we decided to reveal to him the whole business of the *goye,* because the day before we had news of her that she arrived, like I wrote you.

We told him how the matter currently stands, and he said to us, "Fools that you are. You suppose you're telling me something new? Don't be melancholy." He took the goblet that was standing in the bookcase near him and filled the goblet himself with wine and said, "I drink to the prince of Kripen! You drink to him too!" And we drank and afterward danced in a circle, and the melancholy left us completely. After dancing he drank a second cup to the sinner Mordekhai Gold, and we drank too and danced. In this way we drank four times -- with dancing in between -- and it lifted all our spirits.

Afterwards he gave the order to make tea. He drank tea and took the pipe and **went to the outhouse,** while we danced and sang in the house. At some point it dawned on me our holy *rebe* didn't yet come back from the outhouse, and it seemed to me he had took a very long time, so I went to see what was up.

I saw on one side a candle was burning, and in the middle of the outhouse it was **like a bluish flame.**[1] I forced the door open and screamed, "*Gvald!!*" All our Faithful came out of the house. We took him from the outhouse and saw he was gone.

Aside from this, I was very upset because during the commotion when we were carrying him into the house, the pipe and the shawl he went to the outhouse with were stolen. What more can I tell?! We all go about distraught because we're left as though defiled.[2]

From me,

....

---

[1] **The rabbi** [Rabbi Jacob] **said that Reb Leyb Kesler saw the departure of his** (the Besht's) **soul as a bluish flame.** *Shivkhey ha-Besht* 36:2. [Mintz, 257] From this, Reb Noson understood that the Zaliner had passed away.

[2] "When the *tsadek* passes away, people are left as though [spiritually and ritually] defiled* and their righteousness is contemptible in the sight of The Holy One, praised be He." *Mides* 55:164.

#148

From Reb Yankl Rivke's, Grocer in Kripen To Reb Avrohom Moyshe in Zalin

Early today, Reb Zaynvl Verkhievker's young son brought me the letter [#149] here enclosed and told me his father had sent me the letter and asked me to send it at once by special messenger to His Eminence. The thing seemed very bewildering to me, so I went to Reb Zaynvl's house. I didn't find him home and his wife wasn't home neither, just his two sons and one daughter I found. I asked them about their father and mother, and they told me both of them left home during the night and didn't come back yet.

I realized they ran away from here so I asked one of his relations, who told me Reb Zaynvl ran away out of fear. I asked him, "How could he run away? He didn't even have money for expenses!" He told me that by luck he had about three hundred zlotys for vodka, which he was going to pay to Mordekhai Gold today, and he took that sum with him and left the three children here, because he knew that Mordekhai, out of compassion for the children, wouldn't take the house but would leave it for the children.

Since the matter is very urgent, therefore I'm sending you the letter by special messenger.

These are the words of

....

#149

The Letter Enclosed From Reb Zaynvl Verkhievker To Reb Avrohom Moyshe

For G-d's sake, the moment you see this letter go straight to Reb Yosl Fradel's and tell him our prince was by the Bilke prince, who **was bragging how he built a fine and very fancy inn somewhere. He was praising it to the skies and** our prince **asked him** to go there with him. When they got there, the two princes went into the inn and our prince seen the *melamed* sitting by the local *arendar* and studying with the *arendar*'s children in the inn! The prince recognized the *melamed* and says, "Put him in chains! He's the very one who brought me the letter [see Letter #6] from the lieutenant governor who's now governor!" Then and there they took the *melamed* and sent him to the court. It was just lucky a servant was there with our prince, and when he came home he told this story to one of our Faithful, so I found out about it before our prince came home and before they questioned the *melamed* about the matter.

These are the words of
....

#150

**From Reb Avrohom Moyshe
To Reb Yankl Rivke's, Grocer**

Reb Yosl Fradel's ran away from here and we don't know where he ran off to. He left with me an IOU for you that I should send you for two hundred and twenty zlotys, so I'm sending it to you here enclosed.

As I see it, the wickedness grows worse and worse, because the *goye* and her father already spilled the beans. The *melamed* too, when he saw it looked bad for him, converted [to Christianity]* and told the whole story just like it happened. We'll never -- don't kid yourself! -- recover from this. Reb Noson Bakilinik was also forced to pull out of here, and the other people ran away too. Luckily, we had notice beforehand.

I'm also letting you know the court sent to the home of our *rebe,* THE SAINT and Holy Man OF BLESSED MEMORY, to take all his papers and belongings, but luckily, the second night after he passed away, our *rebe* came in a dream to the *tsadkones,* the *rebetsn,* she should live, and ordered her to hide all the papers and belongings and other treasures, and she did. The clothes of our *rebe,* The Hidden Light, she sold the very next day. Believe me, she sold the clothes for next to nothing, because what could she do at that time, when there was no way she could wait with the sale until many of our Faithful would gather? At some other time the clothes would've fetched a thousand times what they made now.[1]

---

[1] I know that the *misnagdim* will make a laughingstock of this -- how one could make so much money from old clothes. Therefore I'm demonstrating to them the potent power of the clothes of the *tsadikim* of our time, as is explained in the books by the *tsadikim.* They'll see that no fortune can compare to the clothes, for the shirt of the *tsadek* atones for bloodshed, the hat is a remedy to remove pride, the girdle to nullify [sinful] thoughts, the trousers atone for sexual immorality, the *tfiln* for arrogance. All of the above you will find in *Seyfer ha-Mides** 10:5;

And I don't got to tell and repeat all THE TROUBLES THAT HAVE OVERTAKEN US lately on account of the conspiracy of sinners,* that is, the infamous prince and Mordekhai Gold and the local rabbi and the judge Mikhal Kahane and their ilk. We're hiding out under cover. Even the Christians, when they see some Jew in the marketplace going with a tafetta girdle or his sidelocks in front of his ears, start laughing and ask, "Are you a *khosed?*" and make of us a complete laughingstock.* Many of our Faithful who have business with other people, especially with Christians, have left our faction under pressure, and only some people who just stay in the *kleyzl* still belong to the group.

Altogether now we don't got more than one *minyen,* because some ran away and some left the group. As I see it, even them few who stayed will also have to leave here or leave the group, since the members of the community don't even want to give them a handout, because in our community now, the title *'khosed'* is worse than 'atheist,' G-d save us! Unless G-d performs some prominent miracle, I don't know *what* will be. I want to leave here for the grave of the Besht and cry out there to him to have mercy on us.

These are the words of

....

The main thing I forgot. Burn this letter at once, for G-d's sake, because I'm very frightened of the villains. I risked my life by writing to you, but I saw it was urgent to let you know all this.

These are the words of the aforesigned.

13:26; 20:8; 41:23; 46:5. It cannot be said that the reference there is to the things of some Talmudist, because aside from the proofs we wrote in the Notice, we see that no one ever bought some article of clothing left from any Talmudist, but our group pays a lot of money for some article of clothing of a *tsadek.* If only every *misnaged* would buy for himself a hat or *tfiln* of some *tsadek,* they would see how through this the pride and arrogance would drop away from them.

#151*

From the Travelers to The Holy Land To Reb Meyer Yankev in Zaslav

Praise G-d WHO DID NOT FAIL IN HIS LOVINGKINDNESS to us and who brang us here to the city of Istanbul. On the 18th day of Sivon* we arrived in

Galats, 'cause every one of us, when he ran away from home, went first to the grave of the Besht, and the Besht ordered everybody to go to The Holy Land.[1]

THE L-RD PREPARED FOR US a vessel that was going from Galats to Istanbul.* We boarded the boat and started sailing on the Black Sea. During the first twenty-four hours there was a storm so strong the waves crashed over the boat and it was terrifying. Sixteen days later we arrived at Istanbul.

Now you know, of course, we didn't have much money for expenses, so our Faithful traveled quietly through the nearby towns to collect some amount so we would have at least enough for expenses from Galats to Istanbul. But we couldn't wait 'cause we were terrified of plots and libels and hatred from the conspiracy of sinners in the town of Zalin, so we were forced to leave with what little money we had from home.

Please, since you are -- with G-d's help -- in another province where there isn't this conspiracy of sinners, so make sure to collect the money our Faithful used to collect there. Make sure also to talk about this with the *tsadikim* in your province they should give the order to collect funds for us 'cause right now we don't got nothing to eat.

It was lucky we caught up with the Dishpoler in Galats and we went to him to be subject to him. Even though he didn't give us nothing, at least other people in Galats honored us for his sake and gave us money. Also, Reb Aharon Kaliner, who was the *Ertsisroel* fund collector in Pilshtin and the nearby villages, took with him some letters from our holy *rebe,* The Hidden and Concealed Light, THE SAINT and Holy Man OF BLESSED MEMORY, and some emissaries from the Land of Israel know him and got to know us too, and they also send us money sometimes or invite us to their table.

So for cryin' out loud, do all you can to collect for us money as much as you can. G-d willing, when we're privileged to come to The Holy Land, we'll also do all we can for your sake and for the sake of the people who keep faith with us.

Please send regards in our name to all our Faithful, especially to the few who stayed in our province, who are suffering now on account of

---

[1] **I heard this from the rabbi of our community. When Rabbi Nakhmen wanted to go to The Holy Land a second time, he went to the grave of the Besht with Reb Yoysef Kaminker. When he returned from the cemetery, he was beside himself with joy, and he said, "The Besht instructed me to go to The Holy Land." Reb Yoysef was very surprised and said, "Where did he speak with you?" Rabbi Nakhmen was surprised at him and said, "Did you not see him standing next to me and speaking with me...?"** *Shivkhey ha-Besht* 21:2 [Mintz, 152].

the conspiracy of sinners, their name and memory should be wiped out! Tell them they shouldn't worry nohow and they shouldn't be the least bit melancholy, G-d forbid!, 'cause soon all is sure to be well. When we arrive, G-d willing, in The Holy Land, everything will be okay, of course, 'cause we agreed amongst ourselves before anything else we'll go to the graves of the real *tsadikim* of our country who rest in The Holy Land and tell them the whole state of affairs -- the wickedness of the Kripen prince, and the wickedness of Mordekhai Gold, and the doings of the rabbi of the town with his judge Mikhal, their name and memory should be wiped out! We won't let them rest until they go to take vengeance against them persecutors, and soon, G-d willing, for sure you'll see wonders.* *Omeyn Selo* forever.

These are the words of your friends who look forward soon to redemption* through you and through all our Faithful, they should live, with their wives and their sons and daughters and all they got --

The holy Zaynvl Verkhievker
The holy Khayim Kaliner
The holy Noson Bakilinik
The holy Yekusiel Klinkvitser
The holy Avrohom Moyshe
The holy Aharon Kaliner, collector of *Ertsisroel* funds in Pilshtin
The holy Moyshe, son of the Preacher, in charge of lighting candles for Rabbi Meyer Balanes, of Pilshtin
The holy Peysekh, *arendar* of Slabudshik
The holy Yoysef Kupeler, who is called Fradel's
The holy Khayim, son of Zev Khaladivker, tavern-keeper of Pilshtin
And fifteen more men among us, and also Reb Leybele Khedve who was an attendant and Dovid who was a wagon driver by our *rebe*, The Hidden Light, THE SAINT and Holy Man OF BLESSED MEMORY

They all look forward to redemption and help from you and from all our Faithful.

We're also informing you the Dishpoler made a whole lot of money in Galats and other places, and he and his people don't need no money at all. Soon he'll send for his wife and his children to come to him to The Holy Land.

The main thing we forgot. When you send us the money, write us a list of all the people who gave money, with their wives and their children and their children's children, so we can pray for them in The Holy Land.

These are the words of all the aforesigned.

I forgot to write you something. I had a letter from home that Mordekhai-His-Name-Should-Be-Wiped-Out Gold left mine house for mine sister and mine children and took mine eldest son for his own, since he has no children. I know this sinner didn't do this out of compassion, but to raise mine son to be, G-d forbid!, an *apikoyres* like *he* is. So please, speak about this with mine sister, and tell her I don't agree to this unless this sinner sends mine wife -- who remains on route due to illness -- to me here in Istanbul at his own expense, so I won't be **half a man**. Then I'll be able to pray in The Holy Land that mine son won't learn from his evil deeds.

These are the words of Zaynvl (aforesigned).

EPILOGUE

As I have heard from some people who expressed their opinion that they very much wish to know the reason for the death of the *tsadek* of Zalin, and I was privileged to hear it, consequently I hereby inform the public of the reason, for there is no telling or imagining the important moral that emerges for us from this.

I will tell you the story as it happened. After the *tsadek* of Zalin passed away, I went to our Chief. I came to his room of meditative seclusion while invisible, and the *tsadek* of Zalin came to him while he [the Chief *Rebe*] was awake, on *Motse Shabes,* **wearing *Shabes* clothes, with an ordinary hat on his head.* He said in a loud voice, "A good week to our *rebe!*" and walked about as in life with a staff in his hand,** just as the Preacher Reb Yoysef came after the death of the Besht.[1]

The Chief *Rebe* began to discuss with the Zaliner many things and matters of which I cannot yet inform the whole public, for the generation is not yet worthy of it. But I *am* revealing what they said about the reason he passed away.

The *tsadek* of Zalin said the *bukh* that was published in the German language caused all this, because on account of this *bukh,* serious accusations were made on high against our whole faction and he -- that is, the Zaliner -- when he realized that on account of this *bukh* the case would become a big deal, got very excited and did not conceal his words but just said right out whatever he wanted because he was extremely agitated. On account of this the accusations grew.[2] On account of this *bukh* and the growing accusations, some people began writing against our faction, whereby the accusations grew worse. Since he had allied himself with the Dishpoler, the accusations grew even worse,[3] and the Talmudists there on high began to cry out against the group. They shouted that because of our faction the Toyre would be completely forgotten.

---

[1] *Shivkhey ha-Besht* 17:2 [Mintz, 125].

[2] "The *tsadek* who is praying must conceal his words so that the accuser will not understand so as to accuse, G-d forbid! Were it not for the accusations, the *tsadek* would be able to verbalize all the things he wishes to. But on account of the accusations, he has to conceal his words under his tongue and his lips." *No'am Elimelekh* 29:4.

[3] "The moment the *tsadikim* join together, then immediately the *Sitre Akhre** gets stronger there...and incites disagreements and disputes against the *tsadikim." No'am Elimelekh* 73:4.

As a result of this, a major controversy was created on high. A few of them said to pluck up our people by the root -- G-d save us! -- and a few said the opposite. Some of them started saying to bring the Zaliner on high so he could decide the case.[4] Many on high started to argue against this, saying on this account there was no need specifically to bring him on high, because he could decide this in the lower world as well, especially since several times on high they had already relied on him when he spoke in the lower world.[5] The reason several tsadikim on high didn't want them to take him from this world was that while he was in this world, those tsadikim make use of the portion in paradise that is his.[6] But others said, as long as he was in the lower world he was an interested party. The Talmudists in particular argued this and said on no account would they rely on him as long as he was in the lower world because he was a highly interested party. So it was impossible any other way but to take him on high.

They agreed to take him up from this world and he decided the case there after he passed away. But what he decided on high in this case, and what they decreed in Heaven about this, he didn't reveal even to the Chief *Rebe.* But he did say that soon, G-d willing, we would see in this world too what he decided about this, and what they decreed about this matter in Heaven, and we would know whether, G-d forbid!, the L-rd's PEOPLE HAD FALLEN WITH NONE TO HELP, until FROM ON HIGH HE WILL POUR OUT His MERCY upon him TO RESCUE him, or whether ISRAEL WOULD NO LONGER BE A WIDOWER and the word of the prophet would be fulfilled through us -- "NO MORE WILL ANYONE TEACH HIS NEIGHBOR OR HIS BROTHER, SAYING: 'KNOW THE L-RD,' FOR THEY WILL ALL KNOW ME, YOUNG AND OLD," IS THE WORD OF THE L-RD.... *Omeyn Selo* forever.

---

[4] "Sometimes the *tsadek* dies so that he can decide some case on high." *Mides* 52:76.

[5] "When there is a controversy on high in some matter, they rely on the *tsadek* who is in *this* world." *Ibid.*, 18:68.

[6] "As long as the *tsadek* is in this world, the other *tsadikim* who are in paradise make use of the portion in paradise that belongs to him." *Ibid.*, 52:72.

[LEXICON]

When I was in Hungary, I saw that some of the books of the *tsadikim* of our time they don't understand well, since there appear in them some words as they are used in our country, Russia, and by them they don't know of these words. Even in Galicia, which borders our country, there are many people who don't know those words as they are [used] by us.

Now, since many such words are also found in the letters I collected in this composition, and since my whole purpose is that the composition should be understood completely in all countries -- even to our kinfolk who live in Ashkenaz,* so they too would recognize the greatness and power of our faction -- I asked Reb Yisroel Reb Berish's, who was by the *tsadek* of Zalin, as YOU MAY SEE FOR YOURSELF within this composition,* to explain all of these words in language all our kinfolk understand. He did this for the benefit of the whole of our brethren, explaining those words that appear in this composition in the holy tongue or in the language spoken there in those countries.

I hereby thank him sincerely for his trouble, because still greater benefit will come from this to our kinfolk who live in those other countries, who will be able to understand these words when they see them in the books by the *tsadikim* of our time, as a result of which they will have a stronger desire to peruse those holy books. Let them DRAW AN ENLIGHTENING MORAL for themselves AND SET their EYES AND their HEART to understand and to become enlightened* about all the details of the matters WHICH WILL BE WITH them AND OF WHICH they SHALL READ ALL THE DAYS OF their LIVES. *Omeyn.* May this be G-d's will.

[There follows a list of one hundred twenty-six Yiddish and Slavic words or expressions that appear in the text, each accompanied by a Hebrew or Yiddish translation or explanation...]

[BIBLIOGRAPHY OF ḤASIDIC TEXTS]

Since the holy books by our *tsadikim* have been reprinted, with G-d's help, several times in succession, and the editions are not identical page for page, therefore we have listed here the place of publication and the year of printing of the holy books that are cited in this composition as they appeared to the author, so whoever wishes to peruse the passages taken from these books,

in their spot will find the lot without excessive essay
and undertake their study without undue delay,
in which favor we may savor to know and to relay,
DISSEMINATING KNOWLEDGE, EXPOUNDING OUR WAY,*
to rescue G-D'S ELECT* from THOSE WHO LEAD ASTRAY,*
TO UPLIFT AND TO HEAL THOSE WHO TO WILDERNESS AWAY,*
that G-d in love may CAUSE HIS LIGHT TO SHINE on us, [we pray].

These are the words of the proofreader, Eyliohu, grandson of the late prominent *khosed,* Our Teacher the *Rov,* Rabbi Yehude Leyb,* of blessed memory in life eternal, who is called The Grandfather *(Der Zeyde).*

BOOK TITLES	PLACE OF PUBLICATION	YEAR OF PUBLICATION
Or ha-Meyer	Poritsk	5575 [1814-15]
Or Peney Moyshe	Meziretch	5570 [1809-10]
Darkhey Tsedek	Lvov	5556 [1795-96]
Yesamakh Leyv	Zolkiew	5560 [1799-1800]
Keser Shem Tov (Part One)	Zolkiew	5554 [1793-94]
Keser Shem Tov (Part Two)	Zolkiew	5555 [1794-95]
Likutey Amorim	Lvov	5552 [1791-92]

Likutey Yekorim	Lemberg	5552 [1791-92]
Likutey MohoRa"N	Ostraha	5568 [1807-08]
Likutey MohoRa"N, Book 2	Mohiluv	5571 [1810-11]
Likutey MohoRa"N, Book 3*	(missing)	5575 [1814-15]
Mevaser Tsedek	Greater Dubno	5558 [1797-98]
Mides mi-MohoRa"N	(missing)	5571 [1810-11]
No'am Elimelekh	Lvov	5548 [1787-88]
Sipurey Mayses mi-MohoRa"N (two parts)	(missing)	5575 [1814-15]
Kitser Likutey MohoRa"N (two parts)	Mohiluv	5571 [1810-11]
Shivkhey ha-Besht	Barditchuv	5575 [1814]
Toldes Yankev Yoysef	Mezhebush*	5540 [1779-80]
Tanye of Rabbi [Shneur] Zalmen of Liozna	Slavita	5556 [1795-96]

Afterword: Was Perl Fair?

Though it is not within the scope of the present study to evaluate Perl's critique of Ḥasidism or of the activities and writings of some of the *tsadikim*,[1] it should be pointed out that it is unfair to raise this question with respect to Perl's work alone. Was Mendele fair? Were *any* of the Hebrew or Yiddish writers of the nineteenth century -- most of whom were propagandists for the Haskala -- fair? Were their ḥasidic counterparts fair? Moreover, the question of fairness pertains no less to scholars than to writers. Was Graetz fair? Was Dubnow fair? Was Scholem fair? Each had his predilections, preconceptions, prejudices. There is no justification for singling out the works of Perl on the issue of fairness.

The works of Rabbi Naḥman of Bratslav figure prominently in *Revealer of Secrets*, and Rabbi Shneur Zalman of Liozna (subsequently of Liady) is the model for one of Perl's chief protagonists, the Zaliner *Rebe*. But it should be noted that Perl never "exposes" a *rebe* himself. Rather, his scorn is reserved for their writings (in the case of Rabbi Naḥman) or their followers (in the case of the Zaliner *Rebe*). His chief criticism of the *rebes*, therefore, concerns their teachings and their toleration of their adoring henchmen.

It should also be pointed out that neither Rabbi Naḥman nor Rabbi Shneur Zalman were less learned or clever than was Perl, though the response they urged to the challenges of modernity was quite different from that urged by Haskala. Because they were dealing with people of simple faith as well as with scholars, they had to communicate on (at least) two levels -- one for the masses, the other for the cogniscenti. Perl faced the same challenge, which is why he wrote *On the Nature of the Ḥasidic Sect* in good German, but translated *Revealer of Secrets* into Yiddish.

Shneur Zalman was the founder of the *ḤaBa"D* school of Ḥasidism, which sought to effect a synthesis of mysticism and rationalism and which is the most intellectual of the various expressions of Ḥasidism. Zalman's major work, *Likkutei Amarim*, popularly known as the *Tanya*, expresses the thinking of an original mind. The school he founded is known in our day as the *Lubavitcher* movement, the largest and most influential of all of the branches of Ḥasidism, and the dynasty he established lasted for two centuries, coming to an end in 1994 with the death of Rabbi Menaḥem Mendl Schneerson, who left no heir (though there are other members of the Schneerson line alive).

Naḥman of Bratslav was a man of some genius, as is evident in his *Tales,* which are often viewed as having anticipated Kafka and the existentialists. Indeed, he told his Kafkaesque tales seventy-five years before Kafka was born. "It is very good to let a madman loose among the people," he said. "Everyone fools somebody, and that somebody is himself. He deceives himself and makes a fool of himself. The one who takes care not to deceive himself deceives the whole world."[2] Naḥman was familiar with Haskala and friendly with individual *maskilim.* He understood the implications of modernity for Judaism. His amanuensis wrote that "the *Rebe*...warned us to keep as far as we possibly could from...[philosophical] works and not so much as to glance at them. This particularly applied to the works written by the philosophers of our time."[3] As for the *maskilim* who used to visit with him in Uman and discuss their ideas, he suggested that "quite soon they will have used up all their stock. It won't be long before they won't have anything more to say."[4]

If we hazard the guess that he had in mind not science's ability to reveal the secrets of the universe but its inability to speak to the human heart, then the events of the past two centuries suggest that he was prescient -- as was Shneur Zalman, who correctly foresaw that "if Bonaparte is victorious, the Jewish people will prosper economically and politically, but they will separate themselves from, and their heart will draw far away from, their Father in Heaven."[5] He saw Napoleon, of course, as the symbol of emancipation.

Obviously, an accurate diagnosis is not the same as an effective prescription. Modernity brought on a split in the Jewish psyche. Ḥasidism denied it, Haskala embraced it. Neither prescription worked. Neither movement succeeded in bringing redemption. The patient continues to live with his illness as best he can. He has become used to it and often forgets that he is ill.

---

1. For a discussion of Perl's use of ḥasidic sources, see Rubinstein, *OnThe Nature,* 24-30.

2. Aryeh Kaplan, *Tzaddik: A Portrait of Rabbi Nachman* (Jerusalem: Breslov Research Institute, 1987), 102; cf. Aryeh Kaplan, *Rabbi Nachman's Wisdom* (Jerusalem: Breslov Research Institute, 1973), 51.

3. Kaplan, *Tzaddik,* 341f.

4. Kaplan, *Tzaddik,* 101.

5. Chayim Meir Heilman, *Beit Rebe* (Berditchev: Ḥayyim Yaakov Sheftil, 1902) Quoted in *Encyclopedia Judaica,* s.v. "Ḥasidism."

Excursus 1: Ḥasidic Masters

Following is a list of ḥasidic (with the notable exception of the first entry) masters mentioned by name, by title or by work in *Revealer of Secrets:*

The AR"I

Not a ḥasidic master, as he lived in the 16th century, two hundred years before the advent of Ḥasidism. Rabbi Isaac Luria was an outstanding kabbalist who created a new school of Jewish mysticism that bears his name -- Lurianic Kabbala. Some of its concepts were used in early Ḥasidism. His acronym, "The AR"I," also means "The Lion." *Shivḥei ha-Besht (The Praises of the Besht)* was modeled on *Shivḥei ha-AR"I (The Praises of the AR"I),* first published in Constantinople in 1766.

Israel ben Eliezer Balshemtov

1700-60. Regarded as the patron saint of Ḥasidism, though he never actually founded a movement or published anything. Also known as "**The Besht**," an acronym for the title "**B**aal **Sh**em **T**ov." A *balshem* was a wonder-worker or faith healer. The primary source of legendary material about his life and work is *Shivḥei ha-Besht (Praises of the Baal Shem Tov),* published for the first time in Kopys in December 1814. See *Introduction,* pp. *xxxviii-xli.*

Dov Baer of Meziretch

d. circa 1772. Known as "The *Maged* of Meziretch" or "The Great *Maged,*" he was a disciple of the **Balshemtov** and organizer of the ḥasidic movement. Author of *Maggid Devarav Le-Ya'akov.*

Yaakov Yosef of Polnai

d. circa 1782. Jacob Joseph HaCohen, a disciple of the **Balshemtov** and author of the first work of ḥasidic thought, *Toldot Yaakov Yosef* (1780), which elucidates, among other things, the doctrine of the centrality of the *tsadek.* He is known as "The *Toldes,*" after the title of this major work.

Yekhiel Mikhel of Zlotchuv

1721-1786. *Maged* of Zlotchuv and a disciple of the **Balshemtov**.

Elimelekh of Lizhensk

1717-1787. A disciple of **Dov Baer of Meziretch** and brother of **Zusha of Anipol**, founder of his own school of thought and father of Ḥasidism in Galicia. Author of *Noam Elimelekh*, which elaborates on the role of the *tsadek* as the "broker" between God and man.

Menakhem Nokhem of Tchernobil

1730-1787. A disciple of the **Balshemtov** and of **Dov Baer of Meziretch**. Author of *Me'or Eynayim* and *Yesamakh Leyv*.

Zusha of Anipol

d. 1800. A disciple of **Dov Baer of Meziretch** and brother of **Elimelekh of Lizhensk**.

Zev Wolf of Zhitomir

d. 1800. A disciple of **Dov Baer of Meziretch** and author of *Or ha-Meir*, an important source for the ideas of early Ḥasidism.

Moshe of Prshevorsk

d. 1805. Moses Sofer, a disciple of **Elimelekh of Lizhensk**.

Barukh of Mezhebush

1757-1810. Grandson of **The Balshemtov**. Moved for a period of time to Toltchin but subsequently returned to Mezhebush, where he inherited his grandfather's seat. Reported to have been a man of little learning, he inspired awe and fear in his *ḥasidim*. Remembered as living a life of excess and conducting himself in an arrogant way, especially toward *rebes* not of the Besht's family line. Had an adversarial relationship with Shneur Zalman of Liozna regarding the collection of funds for The Land of Israel. See **The Zaliner *Rebe*** and **The Dishpoler *Rebe*** in *Excursus 2: Deciphering the Names*.

Naḥman of Bratslav

1772-1811. Great-grandson of the **Balshemtov**. Author of many ḥasidic works, including *Likutey MohoRa"N*, *Seyfer ha-Mides* and *The Tales of Rabbi Nakhmen (Sipurey Mayses)*, which are quoted throughout *Revealer of Secrets*.

Aryeh Leyb of Shpola

1725-1812. Known as *Der Zeyde (The Grandfather), Der Shpoler Zeyde, Ha-Zakeyn (The Elder, The Old Man).* Had met the Besht personally. A fierce opponent of **Naḥman of Bratslav**.

Yaakov Yitsḥak of Lublin

1745-1815. Jacob Isaac, popularly known as The Seer of Lublin or The Lubliner. A disciple of **Dov Baer of Meziretch, Elimelekh of Lizhensk** and Levi Yitsḥak of Berditchev.

Joshua Heschel of Apt

d. 1825. "The Chief of the *rebes* who always stays in Mezhebush." Had a stake in the local publishing house, whose publications carry his Approbations. See **The Chief of All the *Rebes*** in *Excursus 2: Deciphering the Names.*

Nathan of Nemirov

d. 1845. Nathan Sternhartz, referred to in the text as Rabbi Noson, amanuensis of Rabbi **Naḥman of Bratslav** and author of several books of his own, including *Tsaddik,* a biography of his late master. His collected letters are published under the title, *Alim li-Terufa.*

Excursus 2: Deciphering the Names

In the *Prologue* to *Revealer of Secrets,* the editor indicates with mocking irony that he is reproducing verbatim the letters he has collected:

> I knew that because of their exceeding humility they would not agree to make public those things they do in secret. Therefore I have reproduced all the tales and letters in the very same language as I have them from the correspondents. Only in this respect have I made a change -- in that several names of people and towns I have not transcribed as they are in my letters, for I thought, "Perhaps it is not the wish of these *tsadikim* to make themselves and their deeds public"....So I disguised their name and the name of their town and wrote them in the secret language of *gimatrie* and such, and the one who is enlightened will understand.[1]

Implicit is an invitation to the "enlightened" reader to reveal what the narrator has disguised, which effort will parallel (cleverly enough) the effort on the part of the ḥasidic protagonists to find the *bukh* and to unmask its author. "The one who is enlightened will understand" the reasons for the disguise in the first instance, will crack the code, and from the new information gleaned thereby will be privy to a level of understanding reserved for the cogniscenti.

What *are* the reasons for the disguise? The ostensibly ḥasidic narrator provides two:

- I knew that *because of their* [the *tsadikim*'s] *exceeding humility* they would not agree to make known to the public those things they do in secret.[2]
- Perhaps it is not the wish of these *tsadikim* to make themselves and their deeds public, because much *publicity can...cause death,* as happened in the time of...Rabbi Nakhmen.[3]

The maskilic author elsewhere offers a third reason:

- The *gimatries* found in *Revealer of Secrets* I cannot make known to you. Even though we are enjoined to expose evil acts and evildoers so as to warn our kinfolk not to follow crooked ways and not to stray from the paths of Torah and faith, surely *it is forbidden to us to embarass or to shame our fellow publicly* [emphasis added].[4]

The author camouflages not only the names and locations of his characters, but his own name as well. He has his characters plant in the mind of the reader a plausible reason for this anonymity at the very outset of the plot when Reb Zelig announces his intentions concerning the author of "this here *bukh.*" He is eager for "the privilege of seeing this sinner and of getting the pleasure of revenge -- of hitting him, denouncing him, burning everything he owns and so forth."[5] As Rubinstein has demonstrated, however, the suggestion that the author chose to remain anonymous out of fear of reprisal by the *ḥasidim* themselves must be rejected in light of the fact that while *Megallé Temirin* appeared under the pseudonym of Ovadye ben Psakhye, there was never any question as to the author's real identity, even among his contemporaries.[6] Consequently, *the author's anonymity is simply a literary device* designed to increase the sense of mystification as though this really were an authentic ḥasidic text, *and a game of hide-and-seek* in which the author provides clues for the reader to decipher, a game which parallels the search for the *bukh* on the part of the *ḥasidim.*

In 1938, Simcha Katz reported having found in Perl's library in Tarnopol a key to the names which appear in disguise in *Revealer of Secrets.*[7] Apparently, Perl had distributed copies of this key to his immediate circle of fellow-*maskilim* for their own edification and amusement. Katz announced his intention to publish a decryption of the names based on the key but his untimely death prevented him from doing so. Chone Shmeruk also found a copy of the key, on the basis of which he deciphered several of the most important names in his 1957 article, "Authentic and Imaginative Elements in Joseph Perl's 'M'galeh T'mirin.'"[8] He also discussed the special significance of the names "Mordekhai" and "Gold" in his 1960 article, "The Name Mordecai-Marcus -- Literary Metamorphosis of a Social Ideal." To date, however, he has not published the key. More of the *gimatries* are deciphered by Werses and Shmeruk in their 1969 book, *Joseph Perl: Ḥasidic Tales and Letters;* and by Rubinstein in his 1974 article, "Etymology of the Names in Joseph Perl,"[9] and his 1977 publication of the German text of Perl's *On the Nature of the Ḥasidic Sect* with Hebrew commentary.

The names which have been deciphered to date are listed below in the order in which they appear in the text, with only their first appearance cited:

Revealer of Secrets *(Title Page)*

The biblical Joseph has the gift of prophecy, is elevated by Pharaoh to a high position, and is the savior of his people. Pharaoh names him צפנת פענח/*Tsaphenat Pa'anei'aḥ,*[10] which Targum Onkelos translates as, "דמטמרן גליין ליה, To Whom Secrets Are Revealed."[11] So the biblical Joseph is the original Revealer of Secrets, and his namesake, Joseph Perl, who sees himself as the prophet of the future and the savior of his people and is decorated by the monarchs of both

Russia and Austria is the contemporary Revealer of Secrets. צפנת פענח is also the title of an important ḥasidic holy book published in 5542/1782 by Yaakov Yosef, disciple of the Besht and author of the *Toldes.* Perl's allusion to this name, therefore, simultaneously establishes *his* claim to be the real Revealer of Secrets as over and against the ḥasidic author. It suggests a surreptitious battle of books, each of which claims to reveal the truth.

A second possible source of the title, *Megallé Temirin,* is Zohar I:32a, which reads:

> Hence the rabbinic exposition of the text, HE REVEALS DEEP THINGS *(MEGALLÉ 'AMUKOT)* OUT OF DARKNESS [Job 12:22], about which R. Yose says, "This cannot be the original darkness, since all the supernal crowns contained therein are still undisclosed, and we call them DEEP THINGS. The term 'reveals' *(megalleh)* can be applied to those supernal mysteries *(temirin)* only insofar as they are contained in that darkness which is in the category of 'Night'...."

In this context, *"megallé temirin"* means, "revealer of supernal mysteries." The gulf between the divine supernal mysteries to which the Zohar refers and the dirty little "secrets" which are "revealed" in *Megallé Temirin* is grotesque -- which fact would have made this mystical title perfect for Perl's parody.

Finally, the title resonates with Daniel 2:18f., 28f. and 47, where God is referred to as "the Revealer of secrets," and *Shivḥei ha-Besht* 1:1 [Mintz, 8], which alludes to the verses in Daniel.

Yehude son of Moshe of Turbusme *(Approbation)*

By *gimatrie,* Menakhem Mendl Lefin of Satinov.[12] Lefin, who spent the years 1808-1826 between Brody and Tarnopol,[13] was considered to be the leader of the Tarnopol circle of *maskilim* and may have been brought by Perl from Berlin for this very purpose. As Perl's mentor and friend, and as the *maskil* who first promulgated satire as the weapon of choice against Ḥasidism,[14] it is entirely fitting that Lefin's Approbation should appear at the beginning of Perl's work.

Ovadye ben Psakhye *(Acknowledgments)*

By *gimatrie,* Joseph Perl.[15]

Rubinstein finds an additional connotation in the name.[16] In Isaac Ber Levinson's *Megallé Sod,* which was published in 5591/1831 under the title *Divrei Tsaddikim* and which contains a dialogue concerning *Revealer of Secrets,* one Reb Hirsh Itsik says:

> I knew the *khosed* Ovadye ben Psakhye like I know you...When I was still traveling to the Lubliner[17]...I saw maybe a thousand times or more Reb Ovadye who served the Rabbi...and the Rabbi...said of him that Reb Ovadye could burn up the whole world with his breath, but the Rabbi ordered that his status as a *tsadek* not be made known until a certain time.

As to why Reb Ovadye had his holy book published in Vienna, Reb Hirsh Itsik explains that by *gimatrie*, "Vienna/ווין" is equivalent to "*khesed* (piety)/חסד,"[18] and *khesed* is the quality of a priest of God, which is why he was called Ovadye, that is to say, *Oved Ya*, Servant of the Lord.

Reb Hirsh Itsik's interlocutor, Reb Henikh Sofer, relates the fact that in their study hall there is a book "by an ancient author, which was published two thousand years ago and which is called *Sefer de-Razin/The Book of Secrets*, which mentions all the holy books that the *tsadikim* of our group have composed and will compose." The author of *Revealer of Secrets* is alluded to therein as follows:

> In latter days there will arise a wise man to whom are open all hidden gates, and because he is *khesed*, which is from the side of the priesthood,[19] he will be called *Ovadye* and he is *bar Psakhye* [He Who Can Unlock Things] of course because all the keys to the secrets will be passed down to him, that is, the book about Ḥasidism which is based on the secrets of the *ḥasidim*.[20]

Levinson makes the author of *Revealer of Secrets* a priest on the basis of the priest Ovadyahu in the days of King Ahab.[21]

According to Levinson, this Ovadye is wise -- obviously in esoteric matters -- and has the keys to all the secret things. Thus does Levinson provide a fictitious etymology for the name Ovadye ben Psakhye, rooting it in an imaginary past. It is difficult not to hear in Levinson's legendary hagiography a parody on the 13th-century author of the Zohar, Moses de Leon, who ascribed authorship of his work to the 2nd-century teacher Shimon bar Yoḥai, so as to retroject its provenance into antiquity.

Greater Tsidon *(Prologue)*

A city in Phoenicia condemned to destruction in Ez. 28:20-24. By *gimatrie*, the name is equivalent to Tarnopol.[22] Thus Perl's own city is identified by Ovadye as the hotbed of *apikorses*.

The Zaliner *Rebe* (Letter #1)

Rabbi Shneur Zalman (1745-1813), author of the *Tanya* and founder of the *ḤaBa"D* school of Ḥasidism, came to Liozna sometime between 1767 and 1773 and remained there, with occasional periods of travel, until moving to Liady in 1801. He served as *maged* in Liozna and established a seminary there in which he taught regularly.[23] In addition to his intellectual and spiritual pursuits, he was devoted to raising funds for the poor. He relates that when he traveled through the Jewish communities to collect money for suffering Jews and came to Podolia, Reb Borukh of Tultchin was angry with him for encroaching on his territory. "I asked him, 'Why are you angry at me?' and he replied, 'Why have you intruded on my turf?'"[24] "Zaliner" is a metathesis of "Liozner."[25] See below, **The Dishpoler *Rebe*.**

Mordekhai Gold (Letter #8)

"Psakhye [פתחיה] is Mordekhai. Why was he called 'Psakhye'? Because he would open [Heb.: פותח/*posei'aḥ*] with words and explain them and knew seventy languages."[26] In Haskala literature, the name Mordekhai is used to denote someone with the characteristics of the biblical Mordekhai, i.e., one who knows languages, is on good terms with the governmental authorities, and is a benefactor of his people. The use of the name "Psakhye" (= Mordekhai) and the identification of Ovadye as "ben Psakhye" alludes to Perl's own qualities as a *maskil*. He disguises himself as a faithful *khosed* (Ovadye) but is really a *maskil* (ben Psakhye).[27]

In the early nineteenth century in eastern Europe, the ḥasidic leaders opposed as assimilationist the drive to give Jews family names, while the *maskilim* welcomed this step toward integration. Jews were compelled to pay in order to receive a "nice" name rather than an ordinary one, and names derived from precious metals (e.g., Gold) or precious stones (e.g., Pearl, Perl) were the most expensive. Perl's choice of the family name "Gold" for his hero is thus highly significant, as Mordekhai is pure gold and wealthy to boot.

The name "Mordekhai Gold" is thus the incarnation of the social and educational ideal of the Haskala[28] -- the wealthy, educated merchant, conversant with secular culture and able to speak foreign languages, on good terms with the government, an intercessor for his people and a benefactor on their behalf. In Perl's eyes, no one fit this description better than Perl himself.

Yokltse (Letter #16)

See especially Letter #98. By *gimatrie,* Meyer (ben Aron-Leyb) of Premislan.[29] He was a popular *tsadek* who figured in many folktales. At the end of the Introduction to *On The Nature of the Ḥasidic Sect,* Perl notes (anonymously) that the work was completed during the fall festivals at the court of this *rebe.* Pursuant to Perl's attempt in 1825-6 to publish a new edition of Israel Loebl's 1798 antiḥasidic pamphlet, *Sefer ha-Vikkuaḥ,* R. Meyer of Premislan became the subject of police investigations in Galicia.[30] See below, **Kalashke**.

Kalashke (Letter #16)

By *gimatrie,* Premislan.[31] See above, **Yokltse**.

Akhziv (Letter #48)

A Canaanite city in the territory of Asher. By *gimatrie,* Lvov,[32] also known as Lemberg. Lemberg, Brody and Tarnopol, the three commercial cities in eastern Galicia along the Russian border, were the centers of Haskala in Galicia. In Hebrew, the name **Akhziv** means, "I will falsify, disappoint, disillusion," which perfectly suited Lvov with its fickle and perverse population.[33]

Meyer Yankev (Letter #55)

Meyer Yakov of Zaslav was the name of a real publisher involved in distributing ḥasidic books in Galicia in 1818, and the appearance here of an itinerant bookseller as a kind of Jewish picaresque is the first such appearance in Hebrew literature, which may well have been the inspiration for S. Y. Abramovits' pen name, "Mendele Moykher Sforim, Mendele the Bookseller," as well as for his protagonist, Alter Yaknehaz.[34] In a contemporary letter written by Reb Hirshele of Zhidotchev to Reb Joshua Heschel of Apt, Reb Meyer Yakov is mentioned in connection with the printing of a new edition of Vital's *Eyts Ḥayyim* and *Peri Eyts Ḥayyim.* Reb Hirshele writes: "Last week Meyer Yakov of Zaslav, who deals in book-publishing, came and told me...." In Letter #121, the connection between Reb Hirshele of Zhidotchev and Reb Meyer Yakov concerning the reprinting of Vital's book is mentioned explicitly: "I had a correspondence with the *rebe* of the holy community of Kalktsig [= Zhidotchev] and with other people there to supply them the holy books *Toldes Yankev Yoysef, Eyts Ḥayyim* and *Pri Eyts Ḥayyim."* Reb Meyer Yakov was arrested for smuggling ḥasidic books from

Russia into Galicia, and whatever correspondence he had with him at the time was confiscated by the authorities. In a letter of 1827, Perl alludes to the fact that back in 1818, he had translated that correspondence for the authorities![35] It is in this light that Ovadye's comment in footnote 1 to Letter #121 must be understood: "I was overjoyed when I saw from this letter that I had brought it about that they didn't find Reb Zelig's letters on Reb Meyer Yankev because I continually took them away from him when I was invisible, so even Reb Meyer Yankev didn't know where they were." See below, **Asher Dan** and **Kalktsig**.

Nakhal Ha-Motsa (Letter #55)

Mentioned in Josh. 18:26, Motsa was a town in the territory of Benjamin. The name **Nakhal Ha-Motsa** means "The Wadi of Motsa." By *gimatrie,* it is equivalent to Zbariz,[36] a neighboring town of Tarnopol and a ḥasidic stronghold.[37] In 1826 Perl denounced "a certain head of the very injurious ḥasidic sect," Hirsh Eichenstein of Zhidotchev, who had been accused in 1818 of conspiring with Yakov Meyer to smuggle banned ḥasidic books from Russia into Galicia, and successfully petitioned the district office in Tarnopol to prevent him from visiting Zbarazh and sabotaging the fund from which Perl's school in Tarnopol was supported.[38] See below, **Asher Dan** and **Kalktsig**.

The Chief of All the *Rebes* (Letter #56)

Joshua Heschel of Apt, who lived in Mezhebush at the time of the events under discussion and had a stake in the local publishing house, whose publications carried his Approbations.[39]

The Dishpoler *Rebe* (Letter #62)

By *gimatrie,* Dishpol is Mezhebush.[40] Rabbi Borukh (1757-1810), grandson of the Baal Shem Tov,[41] who inherited his grandfather's seat in Mezhebush, moved for a period of time to Tultchin, and subsequently returned to Mezhebush. He is reported to have been a man of little learning, but to have engaged in such ecstasy in prayer that he inspired awe and fear in his *ḥasidim.*[42] He is remembered as living a life of excess[43] and conducting himself in an arrogant way, particularly toward *rebes* who were not of the Besht's family line.[44] He is also known to have had an adversarial relationship with Shneur Zalman of Liozna, particularly regarding the collection of funds for The Land of Israel.[45] See above, **The Zaliner *Rebe*.**

This suggests that the character of the Dishpoler *rebe* is modeled after that of Rabbi Borukh, though the Dishpoler *rebe* himself is not to be equated with him, since the *rebe*'s secretary refers to Rabbi Borukh as having died some years earlier.[46]

Hirtsele, son of our holy *rebe* (Letter #94)

Only once did Perl openly identify one of his characters. In a private letter to Shmaryahu Horovitz near the end of 1837 (2 Kislev 5598), he mentions Rabbi Ḥaim Kozover, subsequently known as Rabbi Ḥaim Tshernovitser, whom he calls a real *tsadek*. He then goes on to say, "I also knew his son Hirtsele, whom I used as a prototype in *Revealer of Secrets*."[47]

Asher Dan (Letter #102)

By *gimatrie*, Hirshele, i.e., Hirsh of Zhidotchev.[48] See above, **Nakhal Ha-Motsa**. See also below, **Kalktsig**.

R. Nekhoray in Rektsits (Letter #105)

By *gimatrie*, R. Mordekhai of Kremenits.[49] The son of the famous *tsadek*, R. Yekhiel Mikhel, *maged* of Zlotchuv, he lived from 1746-1817 and was the teacher of R. Meir of Premislan. See below, **Rabbi Tan Yats Halevi**. See also *Notes*, note to *Lines 21f.: a letter that a local judge wrote to the prominent rebe...about a ritual slaughterer*

Rikmoh (Letter #105)

By *gimatrie*, Moshe, son of Yekhiel Mikhel of Tarnopol. See below, **Rabbi Tan Yats Halevi**.

Rabbi Tan Yats Halevi (Letter #105)

By *gimatrie*, R. Yekhiel Mikhel Halevi.[50] If so, he could be R. Yekhiel Mikhel ben R. Moshe, 1788-1855, grandson of R. Yekhiel Mikhel of Zlotchuv.[51] See above, **R. Nekhoray in Rektsits**.

Kalktsig (Letter #121)

By gimatrie, Zhidotchev.[52] See above, **Nakhal Ha-Motsa** and **Asher Dan**.

---

1. *Prologue*, lines 141-52.
2. *Prologue*, lines 141f..
3. *Prologue*, lines 147-50 and note thereto.

4. Letter, *Kerem Ḥemed* 3 (1838): 61. Cf. 2: 24, where Perl expresses the same rationale in *"Katit la-Ma'or."* The reference is to B.M. 58b: "Whoever shames his fellow in public is as if he had shed his blood."

5. Letter #1. Cf. what happens to Mendele Odele's as reported in Letters #45 and #49.

6. See Rubinstein, *On The Nature,* 19 and note 27 there. See also Perl's letter in *Ha-Shaḥar* I (1868): 9.

7. Simcha Katz, "Additions to the List of Tarnopol Publications", *Kiryat Sefer* 15 (1938): 515.

8. Chone Shmeruk. "Authentic and Imaginative Elements in Joseph Perl's 'M'galeh T'mirin,'" *Tsion* 21 (1957): 92-9.

9. Avraham Rubinstein, "Etymology of the Names in Joseph Perl," *Tarbiz* 43 (1974): 205-16.

10. Gen. 41:46.

11. See Rubinstein, "Etymology," 206.

12. See Rubinstein, "Etymology," 210 (משה מטורבוסמי [במוהר׳ר] יהודא = 744 = מנחם מענדל לעפין מסטינאב).

13. See Rubinstein, "Etymology," 211 and note thereon.

14. See *Introduction,* p. *xxiii.*

15. By a special form of *gimatrie* known as *mispar katan,* in which only the first digit of the numerical value of each letter is counted, the name עובדי׳ [בן] פתחי׳ totals 41, as does יוסף פערל. See Rubinstein, "Etymology," 207.

16. See Rubinstein, "Etymology," 207f..

17. I.e., Rabbi Jacob Joseph Horovits, The Seer of Lublin.

18. Both add up to 72.

19. Zohar 3:145b and 224b, based on Deut. 33:8.

20. Ms. of *Megalleh Sod,* 8f..

21. I Kings 18:3.

22. Shmeruk, "Imaginative Elements," 94 (צידון הרבה = טארנאפאל = 372).

23. Roman A. Foxbrunner, *ḤABAD: The Hasidism of R. Shneur Zalman of Lyady* (Tuscaloosa and London: University of Alabama Press, 1992), 47-50.

24. Chayim Meir Heilman, *Beit Rebe* (Berditchev: Ḥayyim Yaakov Sheftil, 1902), 86.

25: זאלינער = ליאזנער.

26. Shek. 5:1.

27. Rubinstein, "Etymology," 210f..

28. See Shmeruk, "The Name Mordecai-Marcus -- Literary Metamorphosis of a Social Ideal," *Tarbiz* 29 (1959-60): 76-98.

29. Shmeruk, "Imaginative Elements," 94 (יאקילצי = מאיר = 251).

30. See Rubinstein, *On The Nature,* 9-11 and 68, n. 26. See also Mahler, *The Jewish Enlightenment,* 85-9.

31. See Shmeruk, "Imaginative Elements," 94 (קאלאשקי = פרעמיסלאן according to the "key," though Shmeruk notes that the *gimatrie* is off by 1).

32. See Shmeruk, "Imaginative Elements," 94 (אכזיב = לבוב = 40).

33. Suggested by Shmeruk in "Mordecai-Marcus," 94.

34. See *Introduction,* p. *lxiii.*

35. See Shmeruk, "Imaginative Elements," 94f..

36. See Shmeruk, "Imaginative Elements," 94 (זבאריז = נחל המצה according to the "key," though Shmeruk notes that the *gimatrie* is off by 1).

37. Suggested by Shmeruk in "Mordecai-Marcus," 94.

38. See Mahler, *The Jewish Enlightenment,* 127f. and notes thereon.

39. See Shmeruk, "Imaginative Elements," 96.

40. See Shmeruk and Werses, *Tales and Letters,* 27, n. 22 (מעזבוש = דישפאל = 425) and 36.

41. See Letters #64, line 44 and #71, lines 4-6, where The Dishpoler *Rebe* is identified as the grandson of the Besht.

42. See Dubnow, *History of Hasidism,* 208f. and notes thereon. Cf. Letters # 34 and #60.

43. See A. B. Gotlober, "Memories from My Youth" in *Ha-Boker Or,* Warsaw, 5641, 312ff..

44. See Dubnow, *History of Hasidism,* 211. Cf. esp. Letter #130. Cf. also Letters #128, #131, #132, #133 and #134.

45. See, for example, Letters #70, #116, #126 and #128.

46. Letter #70, footnote 1.

47. See Rubinstein, "Etymology," 206, n. 3. See also Perl's letter in *Ha-Shaḥar* I (1868): 9.

48. See Shmeruk, "Imaginative Elements," 95 (אשר דן = הירשלי = 545). See also note to Letter #55, *Line 5: Meyer Yankev of Zaslav.*

49. See Shmeruk, "Imaginative Elements," 97 (קרעמניין = רעקציין = 560; מרדכי = נחורי = 274).

50. See Shmeruk, "Imaginative Elements," 97 (יחיאל מיכל = טן יין = 159).

51. Suggested by Mendel Piekaż in a private communication of 16 Tishri 5755 (21 September 1994).

52. See Shmeruk, "Imaginative Elements," 95 (זידאטשאב = קאלקצינ = 334) See also note to Letter #55, *Line 5: Meyer Yankev of Zaslav.*

Excursus 3: Perl's Yiddish *Prologue*

Jewish fiction writers of the nineteenth century were committed to the Haskala and its goals of enlightening and modernizing the Jewish masses and of revivifying the Hebrew language. But the very masses whom the Haskala sought to "elevate" were for the most part ignorant of Hebrew except for a few phrases of prayer. As Dan Miron observes,

> Even *Revealer of Secrets*...undoubtedly the best-known and the most brilliant Hebrew satire written in the course of the anti-hasidic campaign, had a very limited circulation....*Revealer of Secrets,* in which the language of the ignorant *hasidim* was exquisitely mimicked in crippled Hebrew, could be fully enjoyed only by those who were able to see its parodic point, i.e., by those who knew Hebrew well enough to feel the comic effect of its methodical disfiguring....[1]

Eventually it became clear that if the Haskala were ever to attain its goal, it would have to speak to the common people in the language they knew and trusted -- Yiddish. This realization led some writers to switch to Yiddish, while others published some of their works in parallel Hebrew and Yiddish versions.

Perl himself translated *Revealer of Secrets* into Yiddish. It was not until 1937, however, that Yisroel Vaynlez finally published the translation,[2] which had lain undiscovered in Perl's library in Tarnopol for a century. The following year, Simkha Katz discovered and published Perl's *Prologue* to the Yiddish version.[3]

It is now clear that despite his publicly professed opinion of Yiddish as a "coarse language"[4] -- a view characteristic of most of the Haskala writers -- Perl produced a fine Yiddish version with the intention, unfulfilled in his lifetime, of distributing his book among the masses who could not understand Hebrew. Perl achieves in correct and highly idiomatic Yiddish the satiric effect that requires corrupt Hebrew. After all, the *ḥasidim* of his day may not have written grammatically correct Hebrew, but Yiddish was their mother-tongue!

The Yiddish *Prologue,* however, is not a translation of its Hebrew counterpart. It is a completely new composition, reflecting Perl's understanding of the audience for whom it was intended. David Roskies suggests that

> Perl's main artistic achievement [in the Yiddish *Prologue*] is to replace the ornate bookish style of the Hebrew *Prologue* with a free-flowing, super-idiomatic *shmues.* Besides having an unerring sense of the differentiated audience, Perl throws in some interesting observations on the different read-

ing habits of the Yiddish and Hebrew audience. This, in turn, sheds new light on the difference between a *bukh,* a *mayse-bikhl* and a *seyfer.*[5]

It is not within the purview of the present study to compare the Hebrew and Yiddish texts of *Revealer of Secrets.* Zelig Kalmanovitch undertook the first literary and linguistic analysis of Perl's Yiddish version in his classic Yiddish article, published by Vaynlez together with Perl's Yiddish translation.[6] And Shmuel Werses has just published a penetrating study detailing the enormous differences in the flavor of the Yiddish version that followed from Perl's use of the language that bore a natural affinity to the reality he was describing and in which he himself was rooted.[7]

Werses writes that meticulous examination of the manuscripts in the Perl archive "proves conclusively that Perl was also a Yiddish writer, whether as translator of the works of others, as translator of his own works, or as author of an original creation -- the novel *Antigonos...* confirms the originality of his Yiddish writings, and establishes him as a unique and multi-talented Yiddish author despite his doctrinal opposition to Yiddish." Had his Yiddish version of *Revealer of Secrets* been published at the time it was composed, suggests Werses, "it is reasonable to suppose that it would have left its unique impression and influence on the development of Yiddish literature." As it is, he must be recognized as having preceded Mendele as the classic Jewish exemplar of a bilingual author who creates "two parallel and distinct artistic versions, each of which stands on its own merits."[8]

Following is an English translation of the full text of Perl's Yiddish *Prologue.* The reader is invited to compare it with the translation of Perl's Hebrew *Prologue* on pages 9-19. Since the ungrammatical Hebrew of ḥasidic holy books could not serve as a source of parody in a text intended for Yiddish readers, Perl omitted the footnotes, with their extensive quotations from ḥasidic works, from his Yiddish translation.[9] Bear in mind that the footnotes in the following translation are the translator's, not the author's.

Revealer of Secrets -- Yoysef Perl's Yiddish *Prologue*

As soon as the book *Revealer of Secrets* came out, I realized that many people were reading it. But once I was visiting a certain town and I noticed that the householder with whom I was staying was sitting with a neighbor and a villager was sitting off at some distance from them. The villager called out:

"I just don't know why you get so much pleasure from this book. I've never seen anybody so happy with a book as you are with this one. Could anyone ask for more than *Praises of the Besht* and *The Tales [of Rabbi Nakhmen]*, where you find whatever you want? But still, one doesn't revel in them as you do in the *Revealer of Secrets*."

"Is it my fault," the householder replied, "that you don't know any Hebrew[10] and don't know what the book contains?"

"What could be so wonderful in there? Could anything in the world be as wonderful as what's written in *Praises of the Besht* and in *The Tales?*" the villager called out.

"You see," says the householder, "this book was written after the *Praises of the Besht* and after *The Tales* were published, and it contains the best stories from the *Praises of the Besht*, and many others as well."

"Even so," says the villager, "how can you compare the stories from that book to those of the *Praises of the Besht?* Those, we know, are as true as the Holy Writ. The stories were written down by the ritual slaughterer of Linits, whose father-in-law, Reb Sender himself, may he rest in peace, was, I believe, ritual slaughterer and scribe to the Besht, and he himself knew lots of stories. But as for the book you're reading there -- G-d shouldn't punish me for these words -- I don't know if the stories are true. Suppose they're lies, G-d forbid!, especially since I heard there are subjects in that book from every corner of the world -- from Russia and from Galicia and even from The Land of Israel. So really, I ask you, how is it possible for one man, expert[11] though he be, to be able to know all this? Does he perhaps have wings?"

"You're right," says the householder, "but what you don't know is that the one who wrote this book was invisible, that is to say, when he wanted to, he could see the whole world but no one would see him. And whenever he wanted, he did something so that a cloud came and carried him wherever he wished."

"Please," the *arendar* exclaimed, "don't you have anyone else to make fun of besides me? What are you trying to tell me here? I don't believe such stuff!"

"Why don't you believe it? What's so hard for you here?" asks the householder. "If you're really familiar with the *Praises of the Besht,* you'll certainly remember that the Besht was once at his commissar's and there was a nobleman there who was the Besht's enemy and who always said that when he saw him he'd shoot him with a gun. Nevertheless, the Besht was standing near him twice and he [the nobleman] didn't see him.[12] And this you must have also read in *Praises of the Besht* -- how many times the Besht traversed the world in a short time! In a single night he once travelled a zillion miles -- every quarter of an hour they saw another city.[13] Anyhow, you see that anything is possible in this world."

"Fine, upon my word," says the *arendar,* "but what you're telling me here about the Besht, now that was something else. He had the writings of Adam Balshem, and with them he could do whatever he wanted."

"You see, this here already isn't true," says the householder.

"What are you saying isn't true?!" the *arendar* screamed.

"Just don't scream," the householder replies. "What you're saying -- 'Rabbi Adam was a *balshem'* -- isn't true."

"Who are you telling this isn't true?!" the villager screams again. "What I read with my own eyes, no one can deny!"

"I know," says the householder, "you read it in the Yiddish *Praises of the Besht.* Don't get so upset. You must know that the Yiddish *Praises of the Besht* is only a translation from the Hebrew."

"Indeed," says the *arendar,* "you're not telling me anything new. I read it right on the title page!"

"Well," says the householder, "you may believe me that in Hebrew it doesn't say anything that Rabbi Adam was a *balshem.* It was only the one who translated *Praises of the Besht* who added that on his own."

"What does that mean, 'added on his own'?" says the villager. How can he add something on his own? How does somebody who translates *add* something of his own?"

"Well, believe me," says the householder, "this wasn't all he did. He added lots of things out of his own head, and lots of things he didn't even include. What more proof do you need than this -- right at the beginning he didn't write that the Besht's mother was a midwife, yet in the Hebrew version it says so!"

"Well, you might think that this is a trifle. Let me tell you, this is a very important matter, because I heard from a great *tsadek* that the

Besht's mother was a reincarnation of the midwife Puah, who appears in the Torah! And if it were not so, G-d forbid!, the Besht's people nowadays wouldn't be who they are.[14] So now do you understand why it certainly wasn't right to leave out such things? And if it comes to that, I'll show you stories in the Yiddish that don't appear at all in the Hebrew, and many more -- maybe ninety -- things that are in Hebrew but not in Yiddish, and there are some here that he didn't write at all as they are in Hebrew."

"Please," says the villager, "let's not talk about this. Better you should tell me what you started to tell about the Besht's power to make it so he could see everything while nobody could see him, or to fly in one night a zillion miles away. Is anything really possible in this world?"

"You see," says the householder, "you yourself read that the Besht could do this through Rabbi Adam's manuscripts. Well, you should know that the author of the *Revealer of Secrets* received one of these manuscripts."

"What's that supposed to mean?" says the *arendar*. "How is it possible? The Besht locked them up in a stone and also posted a watchman near them."

"Indeed," says the householder, "exactly so! The Besht locked them up in a stone, but why then did he also have to place a watchman? Who would know how to take those manuscripts out of a stone that opened and closed by a magical incantation? But the Besht knew that there are some things in the manuscripts that someone else must show the world. *That*'s why he placed the watchman -- not so that he should guard them, but so that he should give them to the one who was supposed to have them."

"Oh, woe is me!" says the *arendar*. "Now I understand for the first time what it says in *Praises of the Besht* -- that 'the manuscripts were revealed to the world five times, namely, to Father Abraham, to Joshua bin Nun, to Rabbi Adam' (I won't say any more, 'Rabbi Adam Balshem') 'and to the Besht. And the fifth one we don't know.' *Now* it seems that the fifth one was the author of the *Revealer of Secrets*."

"You see," says the householder, "that here, too, the Yiddish *Praises of the Besht* is written different from the Hebrew. In Hebrew, it says that 'the manuscripts were revealed to the Besht the fifth time. The Reprover of Polnoye said: They were by Father Abraham, may he rest in peace, by Joshua bin Nun, and the others I don't know.'"

"G-d shouldn't punish me for these words," says the villager, "but what does it mean? I don't understand. Then the Hebrew version is also -- G-d forbid! -- I dare not even utter it [-- mistaken]. First he says they were by Rabbi Adam and by Rabbi Adam's son and by the Besht and then by Father Abraham, may he rest in peace, and by Joshua bin Nun. There's all five for you!"

"Rabbi Adam's son," says the householder, "doesn't count. All the while they were lying in the stone, the son wasn't fit for them."

"Nevertheless," says the villager, "something still isn't right, but I don't want to raise problems. What good would it do? So be so good as to tell me how the author of *Revealer of Secrets* got them from there."

"About that there's lots to tell," says the householder. "He describes it in the *Prologue.* It's really amazing."

"What good is it?" says the villager. "It's not available in Yiddish, and Hebrew -- because of our many sins -- I don't understand. But I'll tell you the truth, from what you just told me, I already lost my desire to read such things even in Yiddish. It's no joke at all that a person could do such things, to write something different than it says. What the big idea?! In such a book there are things that are no joking matter -- and along comes somebody and makes of it I don't know what!"

"Of course, you're right," says the householder. "Who can know what's contained in such books? The one who published the Hebrew version of *Praises of the Besht* even says that people shouldn't think that he wrote the book simply as stories for entertainment. There are great things there. And with the *Revealer of Secrets* it was the same. Just now someone published a little booklet called *Divrey Tsadikim.*[15] We learn from it that in the *Revealer of Secrets* are secrets that will make your hair stand on end."

"This," says the *arendar,* "I don't believe. I was once in Dobri at a grocer's. He started to read this booklet and someone ran up and grabbed it and tore it up. Well, had it been something worthy, he certainly wouldn't have dared to tear it up."

"You were there?" calls out the neighbor. "I was also in there at the time. I'll prove it to you. The one who tore it up is called the Russian broker."

"Yes," says the *arendar.* "That's right. There were so many people in there at the time that they couldn't recognize each other."

"So, what do you make of that Russian broker?" says the neighbor. "Don't you remember how no sooner did he come in than he said to the grocer, 'You know, Khaya, today we'll be Jews'?"

"And she said to him, 'What does that mean? What then are we now?'

"And he replied, 'Do you understand? Today we'll really be Jews, Jews, real Jews! Now do you understand?'

"But she just said, 'No, I don't understand.'

"'Do you understand?' he said. 'Today we'll have a drink.' And when he said that, they made him tea -- not tea with arak, but a couple of big glasses of arak with a little warm water!"

"Yes, indeed," says the *arendar,* "I remember very well. Really, as I live and breathe, really."

"Surely you must remember," says the neighbor, "that when the Russian broker had just arrived, he was already pretty tipsy. And eventually he said he wants to have a drink, and he got stinking drunk like a common peasant. Well, from such a coarse fellow, from such a drunk, you want to prove that since he tore up a book, it stands to reason that it's bad?"

"Then of course you're right," says the *arendar.* "What do *I* know? I'm just a simple man. I swear, we common folk, when we hear somebody extolling a person or a book, we're used to praising it to high heaven, and when we hear shameful things, we run away from it. We common folk are, unfortunately, like blind sheep."

"That's right," says the neighbor. "A simple man should listen to what others say. But still, he shouldn't hang on their every word. If he sees a learned, pious Jew, he should turn to listen to him, but if he sees a drunkard doing something, he shouldn't be concerned with him. Because you saw the Russian broker dare to tear up a book, you already thought to yourself, 'Obviously, that's how it has to be.' And it's plain as day he tore it up because he's a common drunkard, an insolent lout. Even the greatest man, if he doesn't keep himself from drink, one mustn't rely on him. One who decides matters of rabbinic law, if he's drunk, doesn't render verdicts. You should see what it says in *Medresh Rabbe* in *Bemidbar,*[16] and in *Medresh Tankhume, Parshes Shemini*[17] -- how one should keep himself from drunkenness and everything drunkenness leads to. In brief, it says there explicitly that drunkenness leads one to fornication, to bloodshed, to stealing and to all the transgressions mentioned in the Torah. So, do you want to pay attention to such folk?"

"What do *I* know?" says the *arendar.* "G-d shouldn't punish me for these words -- a simple man might as well not even be born. He doesn't even know what he's supposed to do in this world. I know what you're saying seems to make perfect sense. You're absolutely right! And especially since you're telling me this from such books, it must be true. Listen, just a few years ago I was in a certain town, and I don't want to say that there was a great *tsadek* there, practically the greatest one. I went there to see him. I gave him -- don't repeat this to anyone, as I live and breathe -- what I could, maybe even more than I could. I saw how he lived, G-d shouldn't punish me for these words! Right after prayer, they brought him vodka. From then until it was time to eat, he drank a quart and a half, and at mealtime, a lot of very expensive wine. He was carried from the table to his -- but why should I go on talking off the top of my head? Better we should talk about something else. Please, tell me, you said the author of the *Revealer of Secrets* received some of the manuscripts that the Besht had. Is this really true?"

"I don't understand," says the householder. "I tell you that the whole story is printed in the *Prologue,* and it says that a very pious Jew wrote the book. And it's even repeated in the *Approbation,* written by a great kabbalist from Turbusma. And after all that you're still asking me if it's true!"

"Why are you upset with me?" says the villager. "I'm just a simple man. Do I know what's going on? I can't read Hebrew at all, I can't even repeat [the name of] the city you just now mentioned from the *Approbation."*

"The name of the city," says the householder, "is Turbusma."

"Turbusma," says the villager. "I never heard of such a city. Please, where is this city located?"

"Apparently," says the householder, "it's in The Land of Israel because the name is Aramaic. Where outside The Land of Israel is there a city with an Aramaic name?"

"Aramaic?" says the villager. "So it appears that the one who gave the *Approbation* is a Jew from The Land of Israel! Well then, there certainly can't be any doubt that the book *Revealer of Secrets* must really be something amazing. But what good is it if it's not in Yiddish, and in the holy tongue I don't have anyone who'll explain it to me? I asked my *melamed* to read it to me. At first he said to me, 'You don't have the book.' And once I was on my way home from town and I told him that someone promised [to lend] me the *Revealer of Secrets* to read, and he gave me excuses. So when I saw he doesn't want to read it to me, I thought to myself, 'Obviously, there must be something bad in it.'"

As soon as the villager said this, the householder asked him, "What's your *melamed*'s name and what does he look like?"

The villager told him his name and described him completely, and added, "He's not a fool or a loser. He speaks Polish well and is a bit of a scoffer, but lately he's been walking around without a head."

The householder took the *Revealer of Secrets,* began reading one page of it, called his neighbor over and showed him everything inside, and the two of them started to whisper. When the villager saw this, he started begging them to tell him what they're whispering about.

"I see," he said, "that you're saying something about my *melamed,* so don't be upset with me that I want to know why."

At first, they didn't want to tell him, but he kept begging them until they told him they would tell him, but he must shake hands with them that it would remain secret. The villager shook hands with them and they told him that the *melamed* is in *Revealer of Secrets*. There was a whole to-do with him. He had once become an apostate, and subsequently they heard that he has since quietly reconverted to Judaism. That's why he doesn't want to read the *Revealer of Secrets* and goes around without a head.[18]

"If it's really so," says the villager, "then I see that the *Revealer of Secrets* is no trifle. If it even knew what's going on with my *melamed*, it's really no joke. Now why doesn't somebody translate it into Yiddish? Why shouldn't we common folk have the privilege of being able to read such a book? Upon my word, when a Sabbath or a holiday comes, or the wintry nights, we can almost go crazy.[19] I know that if someone were to translate this into Yiddish, as I live and breathe, he would have acquired for himself the world-to-come, and for his trouble he'd also earn a pretty penny. Let's see, the Hebrew version, I hear, costs one ruble -- or *there*,[20] one and a half silver Rhenish gulden. Let's say the Yiddish will cost even just half that, one could still earn good money."

"Please," says the neighbor, "you think one buys Yiddish books just like that? If the author doesn't travel around from town to town and go around with his books from door to door like some pauper and doesn't let himself be scorned by some rich young boors, he can't sell any books. In the old days things were different. *Then* Jews bought books because they wanted to learn. Now they buy books just out of of conceit, so people should know they have a bookshelf! And once they already have the bookshelf -- which they don't look at even once a year -- what's the point of buying more?"

"Listen here," says the villager, "that's only with Hebrew books. But Yiddish chapbooks, upon my word, we common folk buy as many as we can. Hebrew books are bought by people who don't understand them, but we unfortunates read all the Yiddish chapbooks and have ourselves a real pleasure with them. I know that I -- as sure as you see me -- and -- as I live and breathe -- also many more people like me, would gladly pay even a whole Rhenish coin for a *Revealer of Secrets.* From what I hear of it just from you, it must be a great pleasure to read."

"See, don't be upset with me," says the householder. "The fact is that common folk buy chapbooks just because they love to read stories, but the rest of the people don't like to read stories. They think they're above it."

Until now, I was sitting off at a distance and I didn't mix in, but now I couldn't restrain myself any longer. I said to them:

"Do you also think that the one who wrote *Revealer of Secrets* just wanted to write stories to entertain the public?[21] It seems to me that when the author copied the letters, more than once there were tears in his eyes, and it was with a bitter heart he copied them because he saw our gloomy condition -- that one can't address people nowadays in a serious vein as one could in the past. Because of our many sins, we're deaf to serious talk and our eyes are closed. I compare us to a sick child. When you have to give him medicine, you need to mix it in sugar or in preserves for him because otherwise he won't take the medicine. He doesn't understand that he must have the medicine, he doesn't know that he's sick. That's how it is with us. The author of the *Revealer of Secrets* knows his brothers. He didn't intend just to write stories, he intended something different. He sees we're critically ill and we won't take any medicine, so he mixed the medicine with sugar for us. But what good is it? The public, I see, laps up the sugar, and the medicine they don't touch!"

"Dear friend," the two townfolk say to me, "how do you know all this?"

"If one reads the *Revealer of Secrets* intelligently, one knows what I just said," I replied to them. "And furthermore, I must tell you that I know the author very well, as well as I know myself."

As soon as I had said this, the two people came up to me and shook my hand. They were so overjoyed they didn't know what to do.

"Praised be G-d," they said, "that He sent us such a man as you! Both of us understood this on our own, but nowadays who dares to talk this way? For the villager has no one to look out for him. Indeed, if you're really such a close friend of Reb Ovadye, then tell me why he hasn't published anything since the *Revealer of Secrets?* Doesn't he himself say in *Revealer of Secrets* that he'll publish more things? -- and now, many years later, there's not another thing from him."

"I've seen many more good books by him," I told them. "Two are coming out soon. He couldn't publish anything until now for several reasons that I can't reveal."

"What good are new books to me?" says the *arendar*. "Better he should put out the *Revealer of Secrets* in Yiddish. As I live and breathe, people will sooner buy Yiddish books than Hebrew books. But it should be an honest translation, not like I just heard from you about the Yiddish *Praises of the Besht.*"

"If you wish, I will translate the *Revealer of Secrets* honestly and faithfully, but who will publish it?" I answered the *arendar*.

"You want to translate it?!" the *arendar* shouted. "You know what, my landlord has a paper mill. I'll get paper from him -- he'll give it to me on credit 'til the books are sold. I'll also chip in some money, and I have a couple of neighbors who'll also lend money."

"I don't need paper or money," I told him. "I also don't have time to spend on printing or selling. I'll translate it for you and I'll give you the handwritten *Revealer of Secrets* -- a full, faithful Yiddish translation -- and you take care of the printing and send it around to sell. I don't even want anything from you for my trouble."

"Fine," says the *arendar* and the two townfolk, "but you also have to translate the *Prologue* of the *Revealer of Secrets* for us,[22] and in addition, you must also write another separate Yiddish prologue."

I promised them this too. I translated it accurately, along with the Hebrew *Prologue,* and as for the Yiddish *Prologue,* I thought to myself, why do I need to write another prologue? This here whole conversation among the householder, the neighbor, the villager and me -- let *it* be the prologue. In a prologue, one must tell why one wrote the book and what the book's purpose is. This here conversation that just took place includes it all. But I must also say this, that a very few things in all -- maybe two or three from the book itself and something from the Hebrew *Prologue* -- aren't translated because in Yiddish they can't be expressed. In the Hebrew version there are also many footnotes, which appear beneath [the text]. These too aren't in the Yiddish version because they can't be translated into Yiddish. Such things appear in those [Hebrew] books that, were they in Yiddish, people would stuff their ears so as not to hear them, while the Hebrew-reading public is already used to hearing them, because people say them and no one can make sense of them anyway. For example, lots of Jews study Zohar and don't know what it says there, or they recite Targum,[23] *yoytsres* and *slikhes*[24] and have no idea what they mean. And what's more, if the public knows they'll see a footnote here from the *Praises of the Besht* or from *The Tales* and won't find this footnote in the Yiddish version of those books, they shouldn't be at all surprised because they read here that the Yiddish translation of those books isn't accurate and the footnotes from the Hebrew version are left out.[25]

I hope that honest common folk will thank me for translating the *Revealer of Secrets* for them, and if others will be angry, I couldn't care less. G-d, praised be He, knows my intention is honest. In their merit,[26] may G-d, praised be He, help me to translate more useful books for the benefit of my people. Amen. May this be His will.

1. Dan Miron, *A Traveler Disguised* (New York: Schocken, 1973), 4f..

2. In Vaynlez, *The Yiddish Writings of Joseph Perl,* 1-217.

3. Simkha Katz, "New Materials from the Perl Archive: Joseph Perl's Prologue to His *Revealer of Secrets* in Yiddish," *YIVO-Bleter* XIII (1938): 566-75. The manuscript of Perl's Yiddish *Prologue* is lost. It is doubtful whether Katz brought it to Jerusalem with other manuscripts from the Perl Archive in Tarnopol. More likely, he delivered it to YIVO in Vilna in conjunction with its publication, and it was destroyed, together with other writings of Perl, during the Holocaust.

4. Expressed in a sermon Perl delivered in the new synagogue in Tarnopol in 1838. Quoted in Kalmanovitch, "Linguistic Analysis," LXXIX-LXXX.

5. In a private communication of July 6, 1995. *Shmues* is the folksy Yiddish of a chat or informal conversation. A *bukh* is a book on a secular subject; a *mayse-bikhl* is a story booklet or chapbook; a *seyfer* is a holy book. See also Roskies *A Bridge of Longing,* 58-60.

6. "Joseph Perl's Yiddish Writings -- A Literary and Linguistic Analysis," in Vaynlez, *The Yiddish Writings of Joseph Perl,* LXXI-CVII.

7. Shmuel Werses, "From One Language to Another: Nuances of the Yiddish Version of Joseph Perl's *Revealer of Secrets,*" *Ḥuleyot* 3 (1996): 59-108.

8. Werses 1996: 61, 83-4.

9. On the footnotes, see *Introduction,* pp. *xxxv, xl, xli, lviii, lix, lxiii* and especially *xliv-xlvi.* In the Yiddish translation, Perl kept the footnote citations (i.e., the numbers) but omitted the footnotes themselves. See also below, note 25.

10. Lit., "the holy tongue," i.e., the Hebrew of holy books.

11. The Yiddish phrase -- זאל אים אידום זיין -- is problematic. First, the word אידום does not appear in any extant reference work. I suspect that it is a conflation of א ידום, similar to Perl's construction, איאם for א ים, and that ידום is the printer's corruption of ידען, *yadn,* "an expert, a know-it-all." In a handwritten manuscript, the letters ען would be run together and easily mistaken for ום. Also, the word אים, "him/to him" does not fit the context syntactically or thematically. The translation, "expert though he be," is an educated guess which fits the context of the sentence. In a private communication of December 22, 1995, Shmuel Werses concurs with my suggestion to read אידום as א ידען, "an expert," despite the problematic אים.

12. *SB* 27:1 [Mintz, 193]. Cf. *Revealer of Secrets,* Letter #77 and footnote 6 there.

13. *SB* 29:4, 34:3 [Mintz, 213, 245].

14. Pharaoh commanded the Hebrew midwives, Puah and Shifra, to kill any baby boys born to the Israelites. But the midwives were God-fearing and disobeyed the command, for which God rewarded them by establishing households, i.e., family lines, for them. See Ex. 1:15-22. If the Besht's mother were a reincarnation of Puah, then she too helped to save her people. But more importantly, it makes the Besht a "descendant" of Puah and places him in the company of Moses, whom Puah presumably helped to deliver. Cf. Hebrew *Prologue,* footnote 1 and note to *Footnote 1: Introduction to...Shivkhey ha-Besht...first printing.* The implication is that "the Besht's people" know that their leader is a reincarnation of Moses.

15. A fictional work by Isaac Ber Levinsohn, consisting of a conversation and exchange of letters between two *ḥasidim* about *Revealer of Secrets.* It was first published in Vienna in 1830.

16. The section in Midrash Rabba that discusses Num. 1:1-4:20. See specifically chap. 10.

17. The section in Midrash Tanḥuma that discusses Lev. 9:1-11:47.

18. See Letters #149 and #150, and note to Letter #150, *Lines 8f.: the melamed... converted to Christianity.* The fact that the Yiddish *Prologue* specifically mentions that the *melamed* became an apostate and subsequently reconverted to Judaism makes it even more likely that the real-life model for the character was Rabbi Shneur Zalman's third son, Moshe. See note to Letter #150, *Line 9: converted [to Christianity].*

19. Roskies reports that "chapbooks sold for two to five kopecks, and itinerant booksellers lent them out for the duration of the Sabbath for...a mere penny." Roskies, *A Bridge of Longing,* 58.

20. In Austrian Galicia.

21. Cf. the householder's statement on p. 268, "The one who published the Hebrew version of *Praises of the Besht* even says that people shouldn't think that he wrote the book simply as stories for entertainment." The parallel language here is intended to reinforce the identification of *RS* as a holy book that is every bit the equal of *Praises of the Besht.*

22. Perl's Yiddish translation of the Hebrew *Prologue* was inadvertently left out when YIVO published the Yiddish version of *Revealer of Secrets* in 1937. It is included in manuscript form as an appendix to Werses new study. See Werses 1996: 94-108.

23. The Targum is the Aramaic translation of the Pentateuch and certain other parts of the Bible.

24. *Yotserot* and *seliḥot* are liturgical poems. The former are recited after the *Yotser Or* prayer in the festival morning service, the latter on fast days, in times of trouble and during The Ten Days of Penitence.

25. The Yiddish versions of *Praises of the Besht, The Tales of Rabbi Nakhmen* and other works are often significantly different from their Hebrew originals. Consequently, if the narrator in the Yiddish *Prologue* were to translate the Hebrew footnotes from the Hebrew *Revealer of Secrets* into Yiddish, readers would be confused when they did not find these passages in the Yiddish versions of the works quoted. And since there is no point in including the Hebrew footnotes in a translation intended for Yiddish readers, he will omit the footnotes entirely, except for their numbers in the text. See also above, note 9.

26. I.e., in the merit of the common folk for whom the translation is intended.

Glossary

Entries appear in boldface. Hebrew/Yiddish entries are given in their Yiddishized Ashkenazic pronunciation, as they would have been pronounced by the masses of Jews in Eastern Europe, and/or in Sephardic pronunciation if it is used in the *Introduction, Excursuses* or *Notes,* e.g., **Havdo´le** (Ashkenazic), **Havdala´** (Sephardic).

apikoy´res (pl., **apikor´sim**). A heretic, an unbeliever, an infidel.
apikor´ses. Heresy, apostasy.
arendar´ (pl., **arendars´**). One who leases a business or property on a Polish lord's estate. Often, a tenant farmer.
arendar´ke. Wife of an **arendar**.
aren´de (pl., **aren´des**). The business or property leased to an **arendar**.

bal´shem (pl., **baley shei´mes**). Lit., "master of the Name." A wonder-worker.
besmed´resh. Study hall for the study of Jewish holy books.
Besht. Israel Baal Shem Tov, the "founder" of Ḥasidism.
bukh (pl., **bikh´er**). A secular book, as opposed to a **seyfer**.

drosh, drush. The homiletical exposition of Scripture.
dvey´kes. A key ḥasidic concept – "clinging to God" or "communion."

Ertsisro´el. The Land of Israel.

ga´be (pl., **gabo´im**). In this context, the personal secretary of a **rebe**.
Go´´on/Ga'on´. Lit., "Excellency, Exalted One." In ancient times, the title of the head of any of the Babylonian talmudic academies, and signifying genius in respect to Talmud learning. Used derivatively to signify any brilliant mind.
Gemo´re/Gemara´. The rabbinic discussions of the **Mishne** from the 3rd through the 5th centuries, printed together with the **Mishne** to form the **Talmud**.
gimat´rie. A technique of mystical speculation involving the calculation of the numerical value of Hebrew words and the search for connections with other words or phrases of equal value.
godl (pl., **gdoy´lim**). A worthy, a great man.
goy (f., **go´ye**; pl., **go´yim**). A Gentile.
griv´ne. A Russian coin worth ten (Austrian) kreuzer.
gvir (f., **gvi´re**; pl., **gvi´rim**). A rich man.

Ḥasidism. A Jewish revivalist movement which began in the second half of the eighteenth century in southern Poland.

Hasko´le/Haskala´. The Jewish Enlightenment. The 19th century movement which saw western culture as the key to the modernization of Eastern European Jewry.

Havdo´le/Havdala´. A ceremony marking the conclusion of the Sabbath on Saturday night. The braided candle used in this ceremony is also known as a **havdole** (pl., **havdoles**).

ḥey´der. The traditional Jewish elementary school.

heshay´nes. A bunch of willow twigs beaten against the reading stand of the synagogue in accompaniment with a particular Sukkot prayer.

ḥev´ra kadi´sha. Jewish burial society.

hislay´ves. A key ḥasidic concept -- rapture. Literally, "burning enthusiasm" with which one is supposed to pray.

kabo´le/kabbala´. The Jewish mystical tradition.

kavo´ne. A key ḥasidic concept. Ḥasidism dispensed with the **kavvanot** and stressed instead the importance of **kavone**, which word it uses in the singular form only and which comes to mean the generalized intention or concentration with which one prays.

kavvana´ (pl., **kavvanot´**). In its original meaning in kabbalistic tradition, a mystical meditative preamble to a particular prayer, intended to get the worshiper to recite the prayer with the focus or intention necessary for it to have the desired effect of **tikkun** (restoration, repair, correction) in the supernal worlds which constitute the Godhead. Kabbalistic prayerbooks are filled with such **kavvanot**.

kho´sed (pl., **khsi´dim**)/**ḥasid** (pl., **ḥasidim**). A follower of a **rebe**.

khsi´des. Ḥasidism, piety.

ki´desh/kiddush´. The prayer of sanctification of the Sabbath or festival or holyday, usually using wine. The main version is recited on the eve of the day, a shorter version following the morning service.

kloyz (diminutive: **kleyzl**). A ḥasidic house of prayer.

ko´desh (pl., **kdoy´shim**). A holy man.

May´se Merko´ve/Ma'aseh´ Merkava´. That branch of Jewish mysticism dealing with metaphysics. It takes its name from the description of the Divine chariot-throne in Ezekiel 1, which became the focus of such speculation.

ma´ged. A preacher.

mas´kil. A devotee of **Haskole**. An enlightener, an intellectual.

ma´tse (pl., **ma´tses**). Unleavened bread eaten during Passover, in accordance with Ex. 12:15.

may´se-bikhl. A book of folktales, a storybook.

Megi´le. Lit., a scroll. Can refer to any one of the five short books of the Hagiographa (Esther, Song of Songs, Ruth, Lamentations, Ecclesiastes), but most often, as in this context, refers to The Book of Esther.

mazl´ tov. Congratulations.

mela´med. A teacher of young children.

meshu´ge. Crazy, mad, daft.

mezu´ze (pl., **mezu´zes**)/**mezuza´**. Lit., "doorpost." Based on Deut. 6:9 and 11:20, it consists of a small roll of parchment containing the texts of Deut. 6:4-9 and 11:13-21, enclosed in a case of wood, metal or ceramic and fastened to the upper part of the doorpost. It is the distinctive symbol of a Jewish home or institution.

med´resh (pl., **midro´shim**)/**midrash**. Ancient rabbinic expositions of Scripture.

mekhu´tn. The father of one's current or future son-in-law or daughter-in-law.

mi´de (pl., **mi´des**). Depending on the context, an attribute, a quality, a virtue, a trait, a characteristic, a measure.

mik´ve. A ritual bath. Attended by Jewish women following their menstrual period and by ḥasidic men daily.

min´khe. The afternoon worship service. Traditionally, it may be recited any time between 12:30 p.m. and sunset, but in the 19th century it was postponed to very near sunset so that it could be followed by *mayrev,* the evening service. On the Sabbath, the **shaleshudes** is eaten between **minkhe** and *mayrev.*

min´yen. A quorum of ten adult males traditionally required for public worship.

Mish´ne/Mishna´. The Oral Torah as compiled by Judah HaNasi in 210 C.E. Each individual paragraph in the **Mishna** is called a **mishna**.

misna´ged (pl., **misnag´dim**)/**mitnagged** (pl., **mitnaggedim**). Lit. "opponent, adversary." *Ḥasidim* used this appelation to refer to Jews who were opposed to Ḥasidism, and also to refer to *ḥasidim* of a rival **rebe**.

mits´ve/mitsva´. A commandment, one of the 613 traditionally found in the Torah. In Yiddish, by extension, "a good deed."

Moy´she Rabey´ne. Traditional title for Moses, lit., "Moses our Rabbi," "Moses our Master" or "Moses our Teacher."

Mo´tse Sha´bes. Saturday night following the conclusion of the Sabbath.

nign. (pl., **nigu´nim**)Lit., *melody* or *tune.* A wordless melody sung by *ḥasidim* and regarded as the highest form of prayer. Mystical in nature, it is intended to bring the worshiper into ecstatic communion with God. Typically, each **rebe** teaches **nigunim** which become characteristic of his court.

no´gid (pl., negidim). A community dignitary.

O´meyn Se´lo. **Omeyn** is an affirmation at the conclusion of a prayer, "So be it." **Selo**, whose meaning in The Book of Psalms is open to question, comes to mean "forever" in medieval Hebrew texts. **Omeyn Selo** suggests a most emphatic affirmation -- "May it be so forever!"

pshot/pshat. The plain, straightforward or literal interpretation of Scripture.

pid´yen (pl., **pidyoy´nes**). Lit., "redemption." Abbreviated form of **pidyen nefesh**, "soul-redemption." The monetary gift brought or sent to a **rebe** with the request that he intercede in the supernal realms for someone who is ill or in danger or has some special need.

prince. Chief or leader. Honorary title used of a *tsadek.*

pru´te. A small coin.

push´ke. An alms-box.

Rab´bi. Lit., "My Teacher, My Master." Title used beginning in the year 68 C.E. for Jewish spiritual leaders who were ordained as teachers of Torah.

Rabbon´. An honorific title, somewhat more exalted than **Rabbi**, used by *ḥasidim* only with reference to the Baal Shem Tov.

Rov. An ordained rabbi. The word means "teacher" or "master."

Reb. The title preceding the name of every married Jewish man. Akin to "Mister."

re´be. A ḥasidic master, a charismatic spiritual guide and mentor for a group of *ḥasidim*. May be but is not necessarily an ordained rabbi. Familiar term for a **tsadek**.

re´betsn. Wife of a **rabbi** or **rebe**.

Reshkhoy´desh/Rosh Ḥo´desh. The first day of each lunar month, hence, the new moon, sanctified with special prayers. The eve of **Rosh Ḥo´desh** became particularly important among the Jewish mystics and, later, the *ḥasidim*.

sage. In rabbinic Judaism, refers to a **Rabbi**. In Ḥasidism, refers to a **rebe** or **tsadek**.

scholar. A scholar in talmudic learning. In rabbinic Judaism, refers to a **Rabbi**. In Ḥasidism, refers to a **rebe** or **tsadek**. **Sage** and **Scholar** are used interchangeably.

sey´fer (pl., **sforim**). A sacred book, as opposed to a **bukh**.

Sey´fer Toy´reh. A scroll of the Torah (Pentateuch), kept in The Holy Ark in a synagogue and read thrice weekly and on special days.

Sha´bes (pl., **Shabo´sim**). The Sabbath, beginning at sundown on Friday and concluding at nightfall on Saturday. Traditionally a day of rest, prayer and Torah study. Also called **Shabes Koydesh**, "Holy Sabbath," literally, "Sabbath of Holiness."

shaleshu´des/se'uda´ shelishit´. The traditional third meal of Sabbath, eaten late Saturday afternoon. Among **khsidim**, the **shaleshudes** became the most sacred time of Sabbath, when the **rebe** would say his **toyre**.

Shkhi´ne/Shekhina´. In **kabbala**, the female element in the Godhead, corresponding to the tenth *sefira*, Malkhut ("Sovereignty"), through which God's sovereignty over His creatures is established. It is the divine element "closest" to man.

shlima´zl, shlime´zalnik. One who always has bad luck, a "loser."

shmu´es. A chat or conversation.

shoy´khet/shoḥet´. A Jewish ritual slaughterer, trained in the ritual requirements and professional technique of slaughtering animals for human consumption, using a specially honed knife to slit the animal's throat.

Shul´khn O´rekh/Shulḥan´ Arukh´. Literally, "The Set Table." Sixteenth century code of Jewish law compiled by Joseph Karo and still normative for Orthodox Jews.

sod. The mystical or esoteric interpretation of Scripture.

ta´les. A prayer shawl worn by married Jewish males, generally during morning worship. The fringes at its four corners are in fulfillment of the command in Num. 15:38f.: "...Instruct them to make for themselves fringes on the corners of their garments throughout the ages.... Look at it and recall all the commandments of the Lord and observe them...."

ta´les-kotn. "Short **tales**." A garment worn under the shirt by pious Jews. The fringes at its four corners emerge over the trousers and are generally tucked into the trouser pockets. See **tales**.

Tal´mud. The Oral Torah, as compiled at the end of the fifth - beginning of the sixth centuries. It consists of **Mishna** and **Gemara**, and is the main source and primary focus of study of rabbinic Judaism.

tfi´le. Prayer. Also, specifically, the second major section of the worship service, traditionally recited in silence and during which the worshipers sway forward and backward.

tfiln. Two small boxes containing parchment on which is written the passages Ex. 13:1-10, 11-16, Deut. 6:4-9 and 11:13-20, which speak of the obligation to love and serve God. Attached to the boxes are leather straps used to fasten one to the forehead and the other to the left arm. The **tfiln** are worn during the daily morning service by religiously observant Jewish males above the age of thirteen. They are not worn on Sabbaths and festivals.

tikn/tikkun´. The mending, repair or restoration of the supernal unity which, according to the Lurianic myth, was shattered during the Creation, giving rise to the existence of evil. All Jews are responsible for bringing about this **tikkun**, but ín Ḥasidism it is the **tsadek** who is uniquely qualified to effect a **tikn**.

Toy´re. God's word as expressed in the Bible, Talmud and later rabbinic literature.

toy´re. The doctrine or teaching of a particular **Rabbi** or **rebe**.

treyf (pl., **trey´fes**). Unkosher food forbidden by Jewish dietary laws, because of the ritual impurity of the animal, the improper slaughtering or preparation of the meat, or the mixing of meat and milk products. By extension, **treyf** comes to mean illegitimate, shady, or nefarious.

tsade´kes, tsadko´nes. Honorary title for the wife of a **tsadek**.

tsa´dek (pl., **tsadi´kim**)/**tsaddik** (pl., **tsaddikim**). In Ḥasidism, a charismatic spiritual leader, a saint. See **rebe**. Ḥasidism knows two kinds of **tsadikim** -- the *nistar* or hidden saint, and the *mefursam* or publicly revealed saint.

tshu´ve. Repentance.

tsi´tsis. The four fringes at the corners of the prayer shawl, intended as a reminder of God's commandments.

yeshi´ve/yeshiva´. An academy of higher Talmud learning.

yey´tser. The inclination or propensity to do evil.

Yo´mim Nero´im. Days of Awe, i.e., Rosh HaShana (The New Year) and Yom Kippur (The Day of Atonement).

yon´tef. A Jewish holiday.

zmi´re (pl., **zmi´res**). Sabbath table songs, sung after meals and at the close of the Sabbath.

Notes

Notes to *TITLE PAGE*

Lines 2f.: Revealer of Secrets

See *Excursus 2: Deciphering the Names.*

Line 4: It is just what its name says

I Sam. 25:25. To avoid repetition, the source of the phrase is identified only here in its first appearance in the text.

Line 6: and hidden from all human sight

Job 28:21. To avoid repetition, the source of the phrase is identified only here in its first appearance in the text.

Line 12: the Jews of Poland

I.e., the *ḥasidim*.

Line 14: the tsadikim of our time

The founders and leaders of Ḥasidism, in contradistinction to the *tsaddikim* of talmudic Judaism. In the Talmud, the term *tsaddik* denotes a righteous person who always tries to follow the laws of the Torah, while a *ḥasid* is a person of great piety who voluntarily goes beyond the letter of the law. In Ḥasidism, these terms undergo a change in meaning as well as in position relative to one another. *Tsadek* comes to mean a saint, a charismatic spiritual leader of a circle of followers, while a *khosed* is a follower of a *tsadek.*

Line 19: May it please the wise

Calqued on Prov. 9:17 and 24:25. There is *double entendre* in Perl's use of "*ḥakham,* the wise." To the *ḥasidim,* the *ḥakham* is the *tsadek,* as is clear in footnote 1 to the *Important Notice,* pp. 7f.. To everyone else, the *ḥakham* is either the talmudic sage or scholar, or the contemporary man of science. Ostensibly written "so that our kinfolk who are not amongst the Jews of Poland will understand the holy books composed by the *tsadikim* of our time who reside in the land of Poland," the "concealed" message is that those who are really "wise" are those who oppose Ḥasidism and who "will understand" that the real purpose of this book is not to praise but to damn.

The use of *double entendre* is a staple of satire, but it takes on a new dimension in *Revealer of Secrets.* Appropriating symbolism derived from the Jewish mystical tradition, Ḥasidism speaks of *nigla* and *nistar* -- the revealed and concealed meanings of things; of *pshat* and *sod* -- the plain and esoteric interpretations of a biblical text; of *mefursam* and *nistar* -- the *tsadek* who has revealed himself publicly and the one whose identity remains secret. In a very real sense, then, it may be said that Ḥasidism has its own system of *double entendre* in theory as well as in practice. Consequently, Perl's very use of the literary technique of *double entendre* -- apart from its specific content in any particular instance -- itself becomes a satire of ḥasidic forms of thought and language.

In a private communication of December 18, 1996, Abraham Aaroni points out that the Hebrew וינעם לחכם, *Va-yin'am le-ḥakham,* "May it please the wise," can also be read *Va-yin'am le-ḥikam,* "May it be pleasing to their palate/taste," i.e., may it be to the liking of those who oppose Ḥasidism. This adds yet another level of meaning to the satire.

Line 21: Vienna

Megallé Temirin was published in Vienna in 1819 and reprinted three times in Lvov (Lemberg) -- in 1864, 1879 and 1881, the last time together with Isaac Ber Levinsohn's *Divrei Tsaddikim.*

Line 22: Printed by ANTON STRAUSS, royal imperial licensed printer

This line is printed in German in the text. Why would a ḥasidic holy book be printed by a Christian printing house in Vienna, a city barred to most Jews? This is the only obvious giveaway to the hoax; the "explanation" was provided in Levinsohn's *Divrei Tsaddikim,* written around 1821 and published by Perl in 1830. See Roskies, *A Bridge of Longing* (Cambridge: Harvard University Press, 1995), 60 and n. 12 thereto.

Notes to *APPROBATION*

Line 1: The Approbation

It was generally the custom for authors of sacred Jewish books to preface their works with one or more endorsements from respected rabbinic authorities of the day in order to lend credence to and rally support for the book, as well as to guard against plagiarism and to serve as a kind of copyright protection for a specified period of time.

The inclusion of a fictitious *Approbation* here -- set in the original in the Rashi script in which such endorsements normally appear -- serves several purposes. It lends an air of verisimilitude to the text; it parodies both the custom of appealing to rabbinic authority and the literary content of such *Approbations* -- typically formulaic, both in the florid encomium to the writer of the *Approbation* and in its pastiche of scriptural and other quotations marshaled in the service of the objective; it adumbrates its satirical theme in its absurd word play, lines 25-37.

The rhyme scheme in the first four lines of the translation is suggested by that of the Hebrew.

Line 2: brimful

Lit., *full to overflowing.* Tam. 5:4.

Line 3: Filled with ancient wine, a vessel new [and fine]

Avot 4: 20: "Rabbi [Judah the Prince] said: 'Do not look at the vessel but at what is in it; there may be a new vessel that is full of old wine and an old one in which there is not even new wine.'" The implication here is that the writer of the *Approbation* is among "the *tsadikim* of our time," i.e., a new vessel, yet full of old wine, i.e., the correct understanding of Torah.

The allusion to this *mishna* from Avot is an allusion to R. Naḥman as well. See *Acknowledgments,* lines 34-9; see also *Excursus 1: Ḥasidic Masters.* R. Nathan reports that "I once heard the *Rebe* say: 'I am a new vessel full of old wine.'" Aryeh Kaplan, *Tzaddik: A Portrait of Rabbi Nachman* (Jerusalem: Breslov Research Institute, 1987), 280.

However, "a new vessel full of old wine" can also signify a *maskil,* an enlightener, so we have here a *double* (at the very least) *entendre.*

Line 4: khosed

Double entendre. The word can be read as Hebrew *ḥasid,* meaning "pious," or as Yiddish *khosed,* identifying someone as an adherent of Ḥasidism.

Line 5: The Lamp exceeding bright...resides the light

Botsina de-Nehora, San. 14a. Lit., "The Lamp of Light," an honorary title. Also the title of a book (Pietrikov, 1889) by Barukh of Mezhebush, grandson of the Besht. But "the Lamp exceeding bright, with him resides the light" can also refer to a *maskil,* so again the words can be understood in mutually antithetical ways.

Line 8: Rabbi Moyshe of Turbusme

See *Excursus 2: Deciphering the Names.*

Line 11: to disseminate in Jacob

Cf. Jer. 10:16, 51:19.

Line 12: scatter over the face of the whole earth
Gen. 11:9.

Lines 12f.: All dwellers on earth and its inhabitants
Is. 18:3.

Lines 13f.: will recognize and know
The *Aleinu* prayer, which concludes every Jewish worship service, incorporates the first part of the above verse into a new phrase, "Let all dwellers on earth recognize and know...."

Lines 14f.: that the name of the L-rd is proclaimed...will fear
Deut. 28:10.

Line 15: one who is unclean or far away
Num. 9:10.

Line 16: seen the deliverance of the L-rd
Ex. 14:13, II Chr. 20:17; cf. Is. 52:10, Ps. 98:3.

Lines 17f.: fulfill the wishes of those who fear Him
Ps. 145:19.

Line 18: who tremble at His words
Cf. Is. 66:5.

Lines 18f.: will resolve not to defile himself with the food of the king
Dan. 1:8. See below, note to *Lines 19f.: the kings of the rabbis.*

Lines 19f: the kings of the rabbis
Though not attested in rabbinic literature, the term is quoted later as though it were a rabbinic statement. In a private communication, Marc Saperstein suggests that it is a conflation of two phrases, playing on the similarity of the words "*melakhim,* kings" and "*mal'akhim,* angels" -- "How do you know that rabbis are called kings? (Git. 62a) מנא לך דרבנן אקרו מלכים?," and "Who are the ministering angels? -- Rabbis. (Ned. 20b) מאן מלאכי השרת? -- רבנן."

The author of *Toledot Yaakov Yosef* complains about rabbis and communal leaders who persecute the *tsadikim.* "Who are the kings of the rabbis?" he asks (*Toledot,* "Naso"). They are the rabbis who purchase their office from Polish noblemen. It is they to whom the author of the *Approbation* alludes as "unclean or far away," who have "not yet seen the salvation of the L-rd." By implication, the *ḥasidim* are those upon whom "the Name of the L-rd is called ...those who revere Him and who tremble at His words." "The food of the king," therefore, may refer either to the perquisites enjoyed by "the kings of the rabbis" or to the incorrect -- indeed, heretical -- exposition of Scripture by rabbis and Talmudists who do not embrace ḥasidic doctrines. See below, notes to *Line 21: predatory preachers who prey upon,* and to *Line 22: through drosh.* See also Shimon Dubnow, "The Maggid of Miedzyrzecz," in *Essential Papers on Hasidism,* ed. G. D. Hundert (New York: NYU Press, 1991), 73.

Lines 20f.: who are bent on mischief
Cf. Ex. 10:10.

Line 21: predatory preachers who prey upon
The Hebrew -- דורשים דורסים האוכלים (*doreshim doresim ha-okhelim*) -- begs to be explained, as it cannot be reproduced in English. *Doreshim* are expounders or preachers. *Doresim* can signify (a) those who tread recklessly; (b) beasts or

birds of prey that tear the flesh of their victims; and (c) slaughtering an animal by cutting its throat with one swift, deep stroke of the knife instead of several back-and-forth strokes. Furthermore, *doreshim* are expounders of a particular type, here identified with *mitnaggedim*. See below, note to *Line 22: through drosh*. The coincidental fact that the two Hebrew words rhyme as well as differing in but a single letter makes possible the delicious word play, the point of which is to equate the two, i.e., those who expound Scripture through *drosh (doreshim)* are the very ones who tread recklessly *(doresim)* on its meaning, or tear it up like predators, or kill it in one fell swoop. The rhyming continues with yet another synonym, *"ha-okhelim,* who destroy/devour/prey upon." The translation, "predatory preachers who prey upon" is faithful to the meaning of the Hebrew and captures through alliteration something of the impact of the Hebrew rhyme scheme. And the phrase, "who prey upon," follows from the earlier phrase, "kings of the rabbis," with its implication that the rabbis make a handsome living from their perverse preaching and exposition of Scripture. The translation also contains an aural word play -- "who prey/pray upon."

R. Naḥman of Bratslav, whose works are frequently quoted or alluded to throughout *RS,* speaks of "wild beasts of prey *(doresim),"* whom he equates with "natural scientists [i.e., *maskilim*] who demonstrate through their erroneous science that everything happens naturally, as if there were no Divine will, God forbid!, and even the awesome signs that G-d, praised be He, performed for us, they subsume within natural categories. These scholars are in the category of wild beasts, for they prey upon *(doresim)* and tear apart/away many of our kinfolk." *Likkutei MohaRa"N,* Book 2, 4:6.

Consequently, "predatory preachers who prey upon" may refer either to *mitnaggedim* or *maskilim,* and probably refers to both.

Line 22: through drosh

Jewish exegetical tradition knows four methods of scriptural exegesis or exposition, signified by the acronym "**p**a**r**d**e**s" (פרדס, which means "an orchard"): **p**eshat *(pshot),* **r**emez, **d**erash *(drosh)* and **s**od (פשט רמז דרש סוד). **P**eshat pertains to the plain or literal meaning of the text. **R**emez refers to its allegorical or symbolic interpretation. **D**erash, "to draw out, expatiate upon," describes the homiletical style of exposition and is the core of classical rabbinic midrash. **S**od signifies the mystical mode of interpretation, and is referred to by kabbalists as "the way of truth." The author of the *Approbation* here states that those who interpret Scripture via *drosh,* i.e., *mitnaggedim* and their rabbis, commit sacrilege and actually strengthen the demonic forces. He goes on to say that only the other three modes of scriptural exegesis -- not coincidentally, those employed by *ḥasidim* -- are legitimate.

Line 24: the Kabbalists

The term *yode'ei ḥen* (יודעי חן) is calqued on *yode'im ḥen* (יודעים חן) in Eccl. 9:11. It means literally, "those who know/experience grace." The second word, ***ḥen*** (חן), came to be interpreted as an acronym for **ḥ**okhma **n**istara (חכמה נסתרה, esoteric knowledge) and *yode'ei ḥen* -- now, "those who have esoteric knowledge" -- became a technical term for kabbalists. In the present context, of course, the kabbalists are "the *tsadikim* of our time," i.e., the ḥasidic *rebes*, Cf. below, note to *Lines 56f.: pour out...a favorable spirit.*

Line 25: Such must not be done

Gen. 34:7.

Lines 25f.: the essence of Toyre study is through pshot, remez or sod

See above, note to *Line 22: through drosh.*

Line 27: SeyferYetsire

Sefer Yetsira (The Book of Formation) is the oldest and most esoteric of all kabbalistic texts. The first *mishna* in Chapter I states that "He created His universe with three *sepharim* -- with *sephar,* with *sepher* and with *sippur."* There is no agreement among scholars as to how to translate the names of the three *sepharim,* which in modern terms might be called "time, space and spirit." The *sepharim* are the roots of the concept of the ten *Sephirot,* the Divine emanations through which God's creative power unfolds. The author of the *Approbation* is here reading the *sepharim* as acronyms -- *s-p-r* -- for the three modes of scriptural exegesis he wishes to validate. See above, note to *Line 22: through drosh.*

Lines 29f.: Velorosh ein kol, The poor man had nothing

II Sam. 12:3.

Line 31: this is a Jewish demon

See below, note to *Line 34: A [Talmud] sage is a Jewish demon.*

Line 32: Who has complaints?

Prov. 23:29.

Lines 34f.: A [Talmud] sage is a Jewish demon, as is explained in the book

See Letter #65 and footnote 2 thereto. In its discussion of demons, the Zohar states that there are Jewish demons and non-Jewish demons, and defines the difference between them. It states further that "one type (of demon) are like ministering angels, and another like human beings, and a third like animals. There are among them scholars of the Written and Oral Torah." See Zohar III:253a, 277a. Tishby observes that "the author's main purpose in classifying demons in this way is to denigrate certain specific types of persons among his contemporaries, which he does in other ways too." Isaiah Tishby, *The Wisdom of the Zohar* (Oxford: Oxford University Press, 1989), 2:529-32. Cf. Samuel H. Dresner, *The Zaddik* (New York: Schocken, 1974), 107 on *Toledot* 179c and 58c. The author of the *Approbation* draws on well-established images in Jewish mystical tradition in order to categorize his opponents, i.e., Talmudists.

Lines 36f.: Descend, for your people have acted basely

Ex. 32:7.

Lines 38f.: to gird himself with strength

Ps. 93:1.

Line 39: hasten in the vanguard

Num.32:17.

Line 40: a war of mitsve, an obligatory war

Sot. 44b.

Lines 40f.: for it is a law unto Israel

Ps. 81:5.

Lines 41f.: are encamped at the command of the L-rd
Ex. 17:1, Num. 9:18, 20, 23.

Lines 42f.: the demon Samoel and his troupe
Lit., *the Sa"M and his troupe*. In kabbalistic thought, Samael is The Prince of Evil, the leader of the demonic realm, the Jewish name for Satan. Isaac Luria introduced the practice of not pronouncing the name of Samael, following which it became customary to refer to Samael by the euphemism, "the Sa"M" (הס"ם). See Hayyim Vital, *Sha'ar ha-Kavvanot, Kitvei Rabbeinu ha-AR"I* (Jerusalem: Yeshivat Kol Yehuda Press), 1:339a (in *Derush ha-Laila 1*).

Lines 43f.: ground the manna between millstones or pounded it in a mortar
Num. 11:8.

Lines 44f.: because they didn't know what it was
The fictitious author of the *Approbation* suggests that *mitnaggedim*, unaware of the real (i.e., esoteric) meaning of Scripture, in effect grind its words between millstones or pound them in a mortar through their erroneous interpretation, thereby destroying them. The savvy reader is supposed to understand that *these* words are really a diatribe *against* esoteric (i.e., ḥasidic) exegesis.

Line 46: he has my unflagging support
Lit., "my hand shall be constantly with him." Ps. 89:22.

Line 47: approach the sacred altar
Num. 8:19.

Line 48: compound its like
Ex.30:33. A warning not to reprint or plagiarize the author's text.

Lines 49f.: the blessings of Heaven above
Gen. 49:25.

Line 50: boundless blessings
Calqued on Rashi to Gen. 49:26.

Lines 50f.: ascending and descending
Gen. 28:12.

Lines 51f.: from the Sanctuary on high to the Sanctuary below
Calqued on Gen. Rab. 69:7.

Line 52: to couple the tent
Ex. 36:18, where the verse reads, "to couple the tent together so that it might become one whole." The tent is the Tent of Meeting, where God enables Moses to encounter Him. As used here, the crucial idea is that of unification, in this case of the heavenly and earthly Sanctuaries.

Lines 52f.: shall be one and its name one
Zech. 14:9. The verse anticipates the day when "the Lord shall be one and His Name one," i.e., when all will worship the one God. Subsequently, it acquired messianic overtones. Its use here fittingly concludes the idea discussed in the preceding two notes but also seems to be ironic, i.e., "when the Tabernacle shall be one and its name one" seems to anticipate the messianic day when there will be but one kind of house of worship, presumably a ḥasidic *kloyz*.

Lines 53f.: the highest cistern and the conduits that bring abundance
"Cistern" *(bereikha)* is a common kabbalistic symbol for the tenth *sephira*,

called *Malkhut* or *Shekhina*. The *tsadek* is the conduit through which the heavenly abundance comes to the people and through which they rise upward toward the Divine.

Line 55: no harm will befall him

Ps. 91:10.

Lines 56f.: will pour out His spirit, a favorable spirit, on all flesh

A conflation of Joel 3:1 and Zech. 12:10. *Ru'aḥ ḥen* (רוח חן), here translated as "a favorable spirit," may also be understood as "the spirit of Kabbala." See above, note to *Line 24: the Kabbalists.*

Line 57: herald

Is. 52:7. "The herald" announces the coming of the messiah.

Lines 58f.: for the purpose of dating the week

The week is identified by the name of its assigned Torah reading. The verse, Num. 11:29, is from the weekly lection *Beha'alotekha,* which is read in the synagogue calendar around June.

Line 59: and year

There follows the first of several *gematriot,* or arithmetic word puzzles, a favorite device of ḥasidic authors. The purpose of this *gematria* is to date the *Approbation*. Its composer presents a biblical verse with certain letters enlarged, indicating that only these enlarged letters are to be included in the reckoning:

ויאמר לו משה המקנא אתה לי ומי יתן כל־עם ה׳ נביאים כי־יתן ה׳ את־רוחו עליהם:

Solving the puzzle requires knowing that each of the twenty-two letters of the Hebrew alphabet has a numerical value, as follows:

א	1	כ	20	ק	100
ב	2	ל	30	ר	200
ג	3	מ	40	ש	300
ד	4	נ	50	ת	400
ה	5	ס	60		
ו	6	ע	70		
ז	7	פ	80		
ח	8	צ	90		
ט	9				
י	10				

Adding the numerical value of the enlarged letters, the arithmetic works out as follows: 6+30+40+5+1+30+6+10+20+70+5+50+20+10+5+1+200+70=579.

The verse is followed by the term, "by the abbreviated count," which means that the thousands digit has been omitted and is to be understood. Since the readers of the book knew the millenium in which they lived, they knew that 579 (by the abbreviated count) meant 5579 (by the full count). To convert from the Gregorian to the Hebrew calendar, subtract 3760. The Hebrew year 5579 thus corresponds to the Gregorian year 1819.

Lines 63ff.: But Moses said to him...His spirit upon them

Numbers 11:29. The composer of the *Approbation* could presumably have chosen any one of a number of biblical verses that would tot up to the desired sum, so the fact that he chose this particular verse is significant. In Num. 11, Joshua complains to Moses about the ecstatic prophesying in the camp of two young men, Eldad and Medad -- a mode of behavior generally associated with pagan mantics and regarded with abhorrence by the biblical authors. Moses, however, here approves the questionable behavior, as verse 29 indicates. What better verse for a *ḥasid* to use to express his approbation of a book intended to defend Ḥasidism, in which religious ecstasy plays such an important role! Furthermore, as Dinur points out, Ḥasidism's proposed solution to the problem of social disintegration in the Jewish communities was that instead of rabbis and lay community leaders appointed by Polish authorities, leadership ought to be bestowed by God via the mantle of prophetic -- not rabbinic -- authority, hence, *Would that all the Lord's people were prophets!* See Benzion Dinur, "The Origins of Hasidism and Its Social and Messianic Foundations," in *Essential Papers on Hasidism*, ed. Gershon Hundert (New York: NYU Press, 1991), 151f..

The same verse is quoted in *Toledot Yaakov Yosef*, the first ḥasidic text. See, for example, *Parashat Vayakhel* (67:2, bottom) in the Jerusalem 5726/1966 photo-offset of the original Korets 5540/1780 edition.

Line 66: 1819

See above, note to *Line 59: and year.*

Line 68: Be strong

Deut. 31:7, 23; Josh. 1:6 et. al.

Notes to *ACKNOWLEDGMENTS*

Line 1: [ACKNOWLEDGMENTS]

[Brackets] indicate that the word/phrase is not explicit in the original.

In both the preceding *Approbation* and here in the *Acknowledgments,* Perl parodies the penchant of ḥasidic texts for making extensive use of *notarikon,* a system of acronymic abbreviation in which a formulaic phrase is represented by a single "word" made up of the first letter of each of the words in the phrase. Taken to its extreme as it is here, it results in a string of abbreviations and a kind of private language familiar only to its initiates. To get a sense of what the page looks like in Hebrew, it should be noted that the English translation of the *Acknowledgments* requires almost five hundred words to render what is expressed in Hebrew by fewer than half that number.

Line 8: it is incumbent upon us

The *Aleinu* prayer, which concludes every Jewish worship service, begins with the words, "It is incumbent upon us to praise the Lord of all...." The allusion to *Aleinu* suggests that God has been replaced by the Balshemtov as the object of praise.

Line 11: Israel Balshemtov

Also known as the Besht. *Excursus 1: Ḥasidic Masters* identifies and locates each of the *tsadikim* named or alluded to in *RS.* More detailed information will be found in several of the sources included in the *Select Bibliography,* beginning on p. 373.

Lines 16f.: dwelt in his shade

Cf. Ps. 91:1, where the faithful dwell in God's shade, i.e., under His protection. The use of the phrase here casts the Besht in the role of God. "In his shade" suggests also, "in his shadow," i.e., in a subsidiary role.

Line 20: the priest

In the Pentateuchal cult, every Israelite was either a priest, a Levite or an ordinary Israelite. Traditional Jews to this day continue to identify themselves as being descended patrilineally from one of these three castes.

Lines 22f.: that which is revealed, and in that which is concealed

"That which is concealed" refers to the esoteric aspects of Scripture, i.e., the allegorical/symbolic *(remez)* and mystical *(sod)* interpretations of Scripture, in contrast to "that which is revealed," i.e., the straightforward, plain or literal *(peshat)* meaning. See above, note to *Approbation, Line 24: through drosh.*

Lines 27f.: remembered for eternal life

To say of the deceased that he is remembered for eternal life (lit., "life in the world-to-come") is to affirm his worthiness. The phrase is formulaic and characteristic of traditional Jewish texts.

Line 30: prominent

In Hebrew, *mefursam.* Ḥasidic lore knows two types of *tsadikim* -- the *nistar* or hidden saint, and the *mefursam* or public figure. To be a *mefursam* is to accept the mantle of leadership and therefore involves greater dangers and requires greater preparation. See Arthur Green, *Tormented Master,* (University, Alabama: University of Alabama Press, 1979), 41f.

Lines 35f.: The Hidden and Secret Light

A title used of R. Naḥman. Cf. *Prologue,* line 165; Letter #22, line 43; and Letter #151, line 30.

Lines 37f.: the saint of blessed memory

Prov. 10:7. To avoid repetition, the source of the phrase is identified only here in its first appearance in the text.

Lines 38f.: the great-grandson of the Besht

See above, note to *Line 11: Israel Balshemtov.* Perl refers to R. Naḥman as "*nekhed ha-Besht,* the grandson of the Besht." He was, in fact, the son of Feige, daughter of Odel, daughter of the Besht, i.e., the *great*-grandson of the Besht.

Lines 40f.: The Lamp of Israel, The Right-hand Pillar, The Strong Hammer

Ber. 28b, addressed to Rabban Yoḥanan ben Zakkai. Cf. I Kings 7:21. Used by the Besht in a letter to Yaakov Yosef, *SB* 8:4. See Dresner, *The Zaddik,* 51, for a good translation of the letter. Also, see Letter #105; and see below, note to Letter #105, *Line 3: Rabbi Neḥorai in Rektsits.*

Line 42: The Prodigy of the Generation

Ḥull. 103b.

Lines 42f.: The Holy Diadem

Ex. 29:6, 29:30; Lev. 8:9.

Lines 43f.: The Pride of our Strength

Cf. Lev. 26:19; Ez. 24:21, 30:18, 33:28.

Line 44: Light of our Eyes

Cf. Prov. 15:30.

Line 55: a holy one speaking

Dan. 8:13.

Line 56: fear of G-d

In *kabbala,* fear of God corresponds to the *sephira* of *Gevura,* love of God to *Ḥesed.* To approach God through the performance of *mitsvot* in love and fear is to help harmonize *Ḥesed* and *Gevura* in *Tif'eret,* the male principle, so that it can can be united with *Malkhut,* the female principle. See Zohar I:11b-12a and Isaiah Tishby, *The Wisdom of the Zohar,* III:1064ff..

The twin concepts of love of God and fear of God take on an especially important role in R. Shneur Zalman's ḤaBa"D Ḥasidism, as articulated in *Tanya.* See, for example, Israel Zinberg, *A History of Jewish Literature,* vol. IX, *Hasidism and Enlightenment* (New York: KTAV, 1977), 118-21 and the selections from *Tanya* cited there.

Line 57: Ovadye ben Pesaḥye

See *Excursus 2: Deciphering the Names.*

Line 60: Job 21:5

The citation appears in Hebrew in the body of the text because it has been counted in the computation.

Line 61: 579 (by the abbreviated count) = 1819

פנו־אלי והשמו. איוב כ״א, ה. The computation works out as follows: (80+50+6)+(1+30+10)+(6+5+300+40+6)+(1+10+6+2)+(20+1)+(5) = 579 (by the abbreviated count) = 5579 (by the full count) - 3760 = 1819.

Notes to *IMPORTANT NOTICE*

Line 1: IMPORTANT NOTICE

See below, note to Letter #15, *Line 100: there's even a Notice about this.*

Line 10: "Talmudists"

The Hebrew term *lomedim* is used by *ḥasidim* to refer to the leaders of the *mitnaggedim,* who consider themselves Talmudists. Since it means "learners," it is in this context a term of scorn, hence, the quotation marks: "Talmudists," i.e., "They *think* they are Talmudists, but they are mere beginners."

Line 11: light has ...dawned

Is. 9:1. To avoid repetition, the source of the phrase is identified only here in its first appearance in the text.

Line 14: syphilitics

Ket. 77b and Tosefta Ket. 7:11. The Hebrew *ba'alei ra'atan* (בעלי ראתן) may mean "syphilitics" or "those having a skin disease." See *Siḥot HaRa"N,* #106, where *ra'atan* is called "a brain disease" and where Rashi's comment on Ket. 77b to the effect that "they have a worm in their brains" is taken to mean that the mind of a scholar without faith "is filled with filth and *apikorses.*"

New evidence suggests that syphilis did afflict the Old World before Columbus. In medieval Europe the symptoms and transmission of leprosy were inaccurately described and many leprosy cases may actually have been syphilis. Even the biblical term for "leprosy" may have referred in actuality to syphilis. *The New York Times,* Nov. 17, 1992, B5f..

Whichever it means, it is clearly a term of denigration. The use of indelicate terminology to describe the opposition was not infrequently part of the polemics between *ḥasidim* and *mitnaggedim.* Linguistic flourishes with equivalent emotional weight and shock value would not be difficult to find in contemporary English usage, and are perhaps best left to the reader's imagination.

Lines 19ff.: a haughtiness that...has been taken from them for some time now

Double entendre. On the one hand, the "real" *tsadikim* have revealed the arrogance and pretentiousness of the Talmudists. But the sophisticated reader is also to understand that the ḥasidic rebes have outdone the talmudic rabbis in these very "qualities."

Lines 23f.: attire themselves in a tales that is not theirs

A *tales* is a prayer-shawl. The phrase is used in late medieval Jewish literature for plagiarism. In this context it means that the "talmudists" misappropriate the honorific epithets that properly belong to "the *tsadikim* of our time."

Footnote 1: truth my mouth utters

Prov. 8:7.

Footnote 1: the way of truth

The mystical interpretation of Scripture. See above, note to *Approbation, Line 22: through drosh.*

Footnote 1: feels a craving

Num. 11:4.

Footnote 1: I am fully prepared

The *ḥasidim* were bitterly criticized for their custom of reciting before the performance of every *mitsva* the formula, "I am fully prepared for the sake of the unification of The Holy One Blessed be He and His *Shekhina*..."

Footnote 1: Rabbi Elozor said in the name of...your builders
Ber. 64a, Yev. 122b

Footnote 1: All your children...peace of your children
Is. 54:13.

Footnote 1: There is a single pillar from heaven to earth and Tsadek is its name
Sefer ha-Bahir, Part 1, #102. Cf. Ḥag. 12b.

Footnote 1: There is a single pillar...Abundance, named 'Word'
See Scholem's discussion thereof, *On the Kabbalah,* 105.

Footnote 1: This is the Toyre
Deut. 4:44.

Footnote 1: This is the Word
Ex. 16:16, 32; 35:4 *et al.*

Footnote 1: grope...like blind men
Cf. Is. 59:10.

Footnote 1: the name that is really fitting for them
The text of *Kitsur Likkutei MohaRa"N,* Book 2, par. 174, reads as follows:

> There are sages who are learned even in the holy Toyre but they have no faith. These sages are called 'syphilitics' *(ba'alei ra'atan),* and one must keep far from them and their vicinity in all the possible ways which our sages of blessed memory warned [us] to keep far from actual syphilitics. For what comes out of their mouth [i.e., the breath of actual syphilitics = the teachings of Talmud sages] is very harmful to an honest man, who can fall into carnal desire, G-d forbid!, on account of what comes out of their mouth, because these aforementioned sages are for the most part very great fornicators.

See also *Siḥot HaRa"N,* #106.

Notes to *PROLOGUE*

Lines 2ff.: Praised be...to our gaze through

The first letters of the first thirteen words of the *Prologue* spell out the Hebrew name of The Balshemtov, YISRAEL BEN ELIEZER, as follows:

ישתבח שם רבינו אין לנו בין נביאים איש לו ידמה עשיותיו זמן רב...

In an attempt to convey this stylistic device while remaining faithful to the meaning of the text, I have rendered the name in English by enlarging selected letters in the opening lines. The translation is quite faithful to the original, though in order to supply the letters "ZE" for the name ELIEZER, I have taken the liberty of introducing the words "to our gaze" where the Hebrew simply says "to us."

Line 10: secure position

Num. 24:21.

Line 12: Spiritual Guide

Lit., "Teacher of Righteousness." Hebrew, *Moreh Tsedek,* commonly used in acronymic form, *Ma"TS.* Title of the spiritual leader of a local ḥasidic community, appointed by and responsible to the *rebe.* In contrast to the traditional rabbi, he is neither preacher, judge, counselor nor scholar, but concerns himself with issues of domestic ritual and piety. See Minkin, *The Romance of Hassidism* (New York: Thomas Yoseloff, 1955) 316 and n. 1 thereto, 383.

Line 14: an infinitesimal part

Lit., *a thousandth part of thousands of thousands.* Cf. *Nishmat* in *Pesukei De-Zimra* of the daily morning liturgy, where we acknowledge that no matter how we might try, we would still be unable to thank God sufficiently for "one part of the thousands of thousands" of benefactions that He has performed for our ancestors and for us. Here, in ironic contrast, the narrator praises Yaakov Yosef for having privileged us by revealing in his books "a part of the thousand thousands of thousands" of the teachings of the Besht who -- implicit in the analogy as well as in certain ḥasidic teachings -- has functionally replaced God. Cf. below, note to *Lines 21f.: Were all the oceans ink....*

Lines 14f.: Toldes Yankev Yoysef...

Compiled by one of the Balshemtov's favorite disciples, R. Jacob Joseph Ha-Kohen of Polonnoye (Polnai), *Toledot Yaakov Yosef* was the first work of ḥasidic literature. Published simultaneously in Korets and Mezeritch in 1780, it is a primary source for the teachings, previously transmitted orally, of the Besht.

Lines 21f.: Were all the oceans ink and...all the grasses paper

Cf. Shab. 11a, "Were all the oceans ink and all the reeds quills and all the grasses paper" it would not be sufficient for us to declare God's praise. Here, ironically, the same conditions would not be sufficient simply to list the *names* of all the holy books produced by the Besht and those who followed him. Hyperbole aside, considering the fact that the story is set barely half a century after the death of the Besht, it is clear that the literary output of the early ḥasidic leaders was prodigious. The narrator finds this highly praiseworthy and borrows the language of the prayer to describe it, supplanting God with the *tsadikim,* as was commonly done in ḥasidic literature, e.g., the description of R. Naḥman's Sabbath table in *Siḥot HaRan,* #169. Cf. above, note to *Line 14: an infinitesimal part.* The author ridicules the phenomenon by having his narrator glorify it.

Lines 26f.: all those books...must already have been known in the days of the Besht

This is the ḥasidic equivalent of and counterclaim to the rabbinic claim of Oral Torah, according to which all holy books composed in the generations since Sinai were already revealed to Moses at Sinai and passed down through the centuries by word of mouth. It is the Oral Torah that underwrites rabbinic authority. This alternative Oral Toyre, by contrast, underwrites the authority of the ḥasidic teachers and casts the Besht in the role of Moses. See also below, note to *Footnote 1: Introduction to...Shivkhey ha-Besht...first printing.*

Line 27: the toyre...

Throughout the book the word is used with different meanings, distinguished in the translation by the use of upper and lower case letters. "Torah/Toroh/Toyre" refers to Scripture and its classical exposition in Talmud and Midrash, while *"torah/toroh/toyre"* may refer either to the specific teachings and doctrines of the Besht and his various successors (as in this instance) or to the learning that anyone has acquired from his teacher(s).

Line 30: the generations were not yet worthy of them

Calqued on Sot. 48b.

Line 47: our faction

The Hebrew word is כת, usually translated as "sect." It seems unlikely that a *ḥasid* would refer to his own circle as a sect since the word carries a negative tone. Consequently, when the word is used by a *ḥasid* with reference to his own circle, I have chosen to translate it as "faction," "circle," "group" or, in one instance, "bunch." When, however, it is used by a *mitnagged* or a non-Jew to refer to the *ḥasidim* as in Letters #17, #76, #106 and #117, it is translated as "sect."

The Hebrew title of Perl's German manuscript, *Über das Wesen der Sekte Chassidim,* is על מהות כת החסידים/*Al Mahut Kat ha-Ḥasidim* (see below, note to *Prologue, Lines 36f.: the large lettering on the title page...isn't German – but maybe Latin.)* It parallels Perl's use of the Hebrew word כת/*kat* to mean "class." He categorizes Jewish society into four classes, i.e., (1) the masses of simple folk who follow traditional ways unthinkingly and passively as they struggle to make a living; (2) the few enlightened people *(maskilim),* who want Jews to enter modern society by learning languages and sciences without discarding the pure faith of their ancestors; (3) the fanatical adversaries of the second class, namely, the *ḥasidim,* and (4) the conservative Orthodox rabbis. See Shmeruk and Werses, *Tales and Letters,* 39f. and notes 10-14 thereto.

Line 47: sacred fellowship

The term used of various pietist groups, especially after the beginning of Lurianic kabbala and the rise of Jewish mysticism.

Line 49: are further laid bare...

"Said R. Simeon: 'Alas for the man who regards the Torah as a book of mere tales and everyday matters! If that were so, we, even we could compose a torah dealing with everyday affairs, and of even greater excellence....The Torah, however, contains in all its words supernal truths and sublime mysteries....The stories of the Torah are thus only her outer garments, and whoever looks upon that garment as being the Torah itself, woe to that man...!'" Zohar V:152a.

Lines • ?f.: we will be privileged to study the Toroh without any attire whatsoever

The ambiguity and resulting *double entendre* are deliberate.

Line 51: I was dumbfounded

Lit., "I stood trembling and amazed." Calqued on Dan. 10:11.

Line 53: when shall I make provision for my own household

Gen. 30:30. Quoted also in Yehuda Halevi's *piyyut,* "Lord, all my yearning is before You" *(Adonai negdekha kol ta'avati),* which is part of the liturgy of The Day of Atonement and was certainly familiar to Perl.

Lines 53f.: the end is...approaching

Ezek. 7:2 and 7:6. The "end" here refers to the coming of the messiah. Cf. Letter #1, lines 28f., "in these times -- when the generation is very near to the coming of the *meshiekh.*"

Line 55: it will be too little too late

Ḥull. 58b. Lit., *later on whoever adds takes away.*

Lines 57f.: I have performed all kinds of service...close in every way possible

The *ḥasid* regards it as a duty and a privilege to perform "all kinds of service" for the *tsadek,* and hopes that the *tsadek* will "draw him close in every way possible." Whether the author intends any sexual innuendo is at least open to discussion, as the accusation of homosexual behavior among the *ḥasidim* had been made as early as 1772 in Vilna. See Mordecai Wilensky, *Ḥasidim and Mitnaggedim,* I:41, 43 and 65. At the end of the eighteenth century, R. David of Makow states that "they all gather at night and sleep together in a loft, and who knows what disgusting things are done there." Wilensky, 2:174.

Line 60: I didn't disburse my fortune to them

In a parable about a king and his two sons, R. Naḥman distinguishes himself from other *tsadikim* in that, unlike the others, he does not disburse the king's treasury. The king is God, the foolish son represents the other *tsadikim,* the wise son is Naḥman, and the treasures refer to miracle-working. See *Siḥot HaRan,* #130, *Ḥayyei MohaRa"N* 32b, #20 and Yehuda Liebes, *Studies in Jewish Myth and Messianism* (Albany: SUNY Press, 1993), 124.

Ovadye paraphrases R. Naḥman here, though the king's fortune in the parable has now become "my fortune" in Ovadye's statement. The net effect is to do R. Naḥman one better, i.e., "I am superior to all the *tsadikim* including Naḥman: Not only have I not performed *God's* miracles -- I have not even performed my *own* miracles!"

Cf. also Kaplan, *Portrait,* 64, where Nathan uses "the hidden treasures of the king" to refer to the hidden meanings of the *Rebe*'s journeys and suffering. If this is the literary model, then Ovadye is aping R. Naḥman, i.e., just as Naḥman said that his followers could never understand or appreciate the hidden meanings of his journeys and sufferings, so too Ovadye's readers will never be able to understand or appreciate the meanings hidden in his text (though, of course, they will -- because Perl wants them to!) or even the hidden meaning of the author's "journeys" to the civil authorities in his relentless battle against Ḥasidism or his "sufferings" at the hands of his ḥasidic adversaries, who ultimately broke out in unrestrained dancing on his grave.

Lines 66f.: I lost my way...to search for the way

SB 26:3 (Mintz, 188).

Line 69ff.: very high mountains...like a cut off region

SB 3:2 (Mintz, 22).

Lines 70f.: a cut off region

Lev. 16:22, quoted in *SB* 3:2 (Mintz, 22).

Line 71: the rigor of the journey

Rashi on Eruv. 65a.

Line 71: a rock...

Cf. the parallel with Jacob at Beth El, Gen. 28:11.

Lines 75f.: the manuscripts of Rabbi Odom

See *SB* 1:4 (Mintz, 13).

Lines 91f.: I could be invisible

Ḥag. 5b, cf. Ber. 10a of God. Cf. also *SB* 27:1 (Mintz, 193), where it is the Besht who can make himself invisible at will.

Lines 94f.: a cloud would...carry me wherever I wish

Cf. *SB* 29:4, 34:3 (Mintz, 213, 245), where the Besht covers distances in an instant.

Line 124: Revealer of Secrets

Perhaps an allusion to *SB* 1:1 (Mintz, 8). See also *Excursus 2: Deciphering the Names.*

Line 125: hidden from every human eye

Job 28:21.

Lines 131f.: a lie is only with the mouth, not in a manuscript

The citation from Naḥman seems to suggest that it is permissible to lie in print, as long as one does not lie in speech. If this is what the narrator understands, then the author is satirizing all ḥasidic books or, at the very least, those of R. Naḥman.

Lines 136ff.: which falsehood would accomplish good...would be harmful

The author here satirizes the patronizing manner of the *tsadikim,* who arrogate to themselves the right to lie to their followers, since "they know which falsehood will accomplish good in our behalf and which will be harmful," and also the self-deprecating attitude of their *ḥasidim,* who are perfectly willing to permit to the *tsadikim* that which they deny to themselves.

Lines 143f.: in the very same language as I have them from the correspondents

Language is a critical aspect of this novel and central to its satire. The grotesque Hebrew of the letters authored by Perl's ḥasidic characters is well attested in ḥasidic writings of the period. See, for example, *Alim li-Terufa,* the collected letters of R. Nathan, R. Naḥman's secretary. Conversely, the elevated style of those letters authored by *mitnaggedim* (the Rabbi and the Judge Mikhal Kahane, see Letters #62, 66, 68, 69, 76, 77, 78, 83, 84, 113 and

117) is perfectly consistent with the contemporary belletristic Hebrew of Talmudists. The claim of Perl's narrator to have reproduced the letters "in the very same language...as I have them from the correspondents" is, from a linguistic perspective, entirely trustworthy. See "The Language of *Revealer of Secrets*" in *Introduction*, pp. lii-lv. See also below, note to *Line 219: verbatim.*

Cf. also in The Author's Preface to *Shivḥei ha-Besht:* "I was careful to write down all the awesome things that I heard from truthful people....I neither added nor omitted anything. Every word is true, and I did not change a word." Mintz, 4f.

Lines 148ff.: publicity can...cause death...in the time of...Rabbi Nakhmen

The reference here is to the death from tuberculosis in the summer of 1806 of R. Naḥman's young son, Shlomo Ephraim. R. Naḥman attributed the boy's death to "the accusers," led by R. Aryeh Leyb, the Grandfather of Shpola. "I knew when I handed the book [*Sefer ha-Nisraf,* "The Burned Book"] over to those two that *they* (the accusers) would brace themselves for an attack on this little baby." Kaplan, *Portrait,* 82.

Lines 150f.: I disguised their name...in the secret language of gimatrie and such

See *Excursus 2: Deciphering the Names.*

Lines 151ff.: and the one who is enlightened will understand

Cf. Dan. 12:10 and 11:33.

Lines 155f. they can't write properly...like common ignoramuses

See below, note to Letter #51, *Footnote 1: the scoffers say that the tsadikim can't write.*

Line 174: language we call "pure"

The ideal of the Haskalah was "pure Hebrew," which meant biblical Hebrew, with its own unique grammar, syntax and vocabulary.

Line 177: they totally forgot grammar

In *Siḥot HaRa"N*, #235, R. Naḥman is quoted as saying, "Real devotion consists mainly of simplicity and sincerity. Pray a lot, study Toyre a lot, do a lot of good deeds. Don't worry yourself with unnecessary restrictions -- just follow the way of our ancestors....*This is why people no longer study grammar.* People have abandoned it because this type of precision is not really necessary. This is true of all areas. You should not be overly precise in seeking out restrictions [italics added]."

The study of grammar became one of the preoccupations of the Haskala in its desire to recreate the Hebrew language as a vehicle suited to a modern literature. And the disregard of grammar reflected in ḥasidic texts became the object of ridicule on the part of the *maskilim.* Nowhere is this ridicule more powerfully apparent than in *RS,* in which Perl puts in the mouth of his ḥasidic characters a Hebrew so grammatically grotesque as to be hardly Hebrew at all. Insofar as the study of Hebrew grammar became symbolic of Haskala, it came to be the object of scorn on the part of the *ḥasidim.* See, for example, the conclusion of Letter #60, where the *rebe*'s horrible dream that requires exorcism is that someone had laid a book of grammar on top of a ḥasidic text!

Line 179: experts

See below, note to Letter #54, *Line 28: experts in the sciences.* Ovadye claims that reading his composition without any scientific preconceptions or pseudo-sophistication can even lead to healing people who are ill.

Lines 184f.: the publisher of...Slavita

Slavita was the place of publication of the *Tanya*. See *Bibliography of Ḥasidic Texts*. The remark is a jibe at R. Shneur Zalman, author of the *Tanya*, who is the model for the Zaliner *Rebe* in the novel. See *Excursus 2: Deciphering the Names*.

Lines 187f.: in language we call "beautiful"

The Haskala considered "beautiful" language to be grammatically correct biblical Hebrew, while the language that ḥasidic authors typically wrote was, for the most part, a highly ungrammatical mix of Yiddish and rabbinic Hebrew with a sprinkling of Slavic words.

Line 190: Greater Tsidon

See *Excursus 2: Deciphering the Names*.

Line 197: I have provided footnotes

The footnotes and their relationship to the body of the text constitute one of the distinctive features of the novel. See *Introduction*. See also Shmuel Werses, "Joseph Perl's Methods of Satire" in *Story and Source*, esp. 21-34.

Line 203: tsadikim of the highest standing

Lit., *who stand at the pinnacle of the universe*. From the *Yotser* prayer in the Morning Service, where it is used of the angels who sing God's praises. *Yotser* is the source of several other phrases in the novel. Cf. below, notes to *Prologue (Line 235: the L-rd will overturn clear language)*; Letter #1 *(Line 38: all of them alike answer and speak respectfully)*; Letter #76 *(Lines 24f.: to recount his praises, to sanctify him and to adore him)* and Letter #126 *(Lines 4f.: happily rejoice to do the will of their Creator)*. In each case, the referent of the prayer has been shifted and its meaning inverted. "Clear language" has a positive ring in *Yotser*; here it is a term of opprobrium. It is the *tsadikim*, not the angels, who now "stand at the pinnacle of the universe." It is the erstwhile opponents who "answer and speak with reverence" to the *ḥasidim*, not the angels who behave thus toward God. And ultimately, instead of the angels "recounting His (i.e., God's) praises, sanctifying and adoring Him," we now have the *ḥasidim* recounting his (i.e., the *rebe*'s) praises, sanctifying and adoring *him*.

Perl's choice and absurd recasting of these phrases from *Yotser* is not accidental. The full name of the prayer is *Yotser Or*, Creator of Light. It is the first of the benedictions preceding the recitation of the *Shema* in the Morning Service, and it is woven in its entirety around the symbol of light. Since light was also a symbol of the Haskala, or Jewish Enlightenment, it makes perfect sense that Perl should portray his ḥasidic characters as those who overturn the meaning of light, who represent the antithesis of clarity, understanding, reason, light, enlightenment.

Lines 215f.: those who speakwantonly

Ps. 31:19.

Line 216: to bow like a bulrush the head

Is. 58:5.

Line 217: as clear as the noonday sun

Isaiah Horowitz, *Shenei Luḥot ha-Berit, Vavei Ha-Amudim,* chap. 7.

Line 218: to blame me

Calqued on Ramban to Ex. 32.

Line 219: verbatim

See also above, note to *Lines 143f.: in the very same language as I have them from the correspondents.* In addition to the verbatim quotations from ḥasidic sources cited in Ovadye's footnotes and the extensive phrases and even whole passages drawn from *SB* without attribution, the syntax (or lack thereof), the ungrammatical nature of the writing and many of the words and phrases used throughout the book are drawn directly from ḥasidic texts of the period. For an analysis of much of the phraseology, see Kalmanovitch's essay, "Joseph Perl's Yiddish Writings: A Literary and Linguistic Analysis" in Vainlez' *The Yiddish Writings of Joseph Perl.* Ovadye's claim to "have brought the quotations from the books by the *tsadikim* of our time...in their actual language" is, despite the grotesque language, no exaggeration.

Line 219: those of little faith

Sot. 48b, Ber. 24b *et al.,* used here to refer to the *mitnaggedim* and the *maskil* who appear in the novel.

Lines 219f.: the disputants

In this context, the disputants include "those of little faith" as well as the followers of other *rebes.*

Lines 224f.: the language of falsehood

Ps. 109:2, Prov. 6:17, 12:19, 21:6 and 26:28.

Lines 231f.: the current generation is not yet worthy

Sot. 48b; Rashbam on B.B. 134a.

Line 235: the L-rd will overturn clear language

Calqued on Zeph. 3:9, but where the original means, *I will make the peoples pure of speech,* this phrase turns the meaning upside-down.

In the *Yotser* prayer of the morning service, the angels are described as "sanctifying their Creator...in clear language." *Sefer Ta'amei ha-Mitsvot* indicates that "clear language" (*safa berura,* שפה ברורה) is equivalent by *gematria* to "the holy tongue" (*leshon ha-kodesh,* לשון הקדש), i.e., Hebrew. Cf. above, note to *Line 203: tsadikim of the highest standing.*

Lines 235f. so that all will call upon the Name of the L-rd

Zeph. 3:9.

Lines 236f.: credulous children of credulous parents

Shab. 97a. The use of this quotation is an allusion to R. Naḥman as well. R. Nathan states that "as for us, however, we have no need of proofs...for we are 'believers, the sons of believers,' the seed of Abraham, Isaac and Jacob, and we believe in God and His holy Torah unquestioningly and with perfect faith...." Kaplan, *Portrait,* 352.

Lines 238f.: a heart to know and ears to hear

Deut. 29:3.

Line 239: stopped up his ears

Cf. Is. 33:15.

Line 240: made his heart insensitive

Cf. Is. 6:10.

Line 242: Today is Tuesday, the 17th of Kislev, a lucky day

The Hebrew היום יום ג׳ טוב כסליו is intentionally ambiguous. It can be read, "Today is Tuesday, the 17th (reading טוב for its numerical value of 9+6+2=17) of Kislev," or "Today is a lucky Tuesday (referring to the Jewish superstition that Tuesday is a lucky day because in the story of creation in Genesis 1, Tuesday is the only day concerning which the phrase, 'God saw that it was good' appears twice) in Kislev." I suspect that the ambiguity is intended to convey both meanings, which I have reproduced in the translation.

Line 242: in the year...

The computation works out as follows: (50+60+3+6)+(1+8+6+200)+(10+2+300+6)+(2+300+400)+(5+2+9+8+10+40) +(2+80+60+30)+(5+1+40+200+10+40)+(30+40+60+20+5)+(1+400+40+1+30 +5+10+50+6)+(5+8+200+300+10+40)+(300+40+70+6)+(6+5+70+6+200+10 +40)+(5+2+10+9+6)+(30+200+1+6+400)+(10+300+70+10+5)+(100+1+80+1 0+9+70+30)+(40+2)+(80+ 60+6+100)+(10+7) = 5579 (by the full count). 5579-3760 = 1819

Line 254: thirstily drinks in their words

Avot 1:4.

Footnote 1: verily the word of G-d was

Ezek. 1:3.

Footnote 1: nor will there ever be any like him on earth

Calqued on Job 19:25.

Footnote 1: Introduction to...Shivkhey ha-Besht...first printing

Printer's Preface to *SB* (Mintz, 2 and n. 7 thereto). Dinur writes that "In this line...the following message is communicated: that the BeSHT was bestowed with the prophetic spirit in exile, so that through him the Divine Presence would watch over the Jewish people even when they are in exile; that he was a perfect Zaddik who had the privilege of cleaving to God to such an extent that all his 'decrees' were fulfilled; he was unique, no contemporary having the same relationship with God, for he incorporated within him aspects of both Moses and Elijah." Benzion Dinur, "The Messianic-Prophetic Role of the Baal Shem Tov," in *Essential Papers on Messianic Movements and Personalities in Jewish History*, ed. Marc Saperstein (New York: NYU Press, 1992), 383.

Footnote 1: Likutey MohoRa"N, Book 2, 16:1-2

The statement is in 5:15. It reads in part as follows: "We must...renounce the intellect...discard all cleverness and serve the L-rd in simplicity without any cleverness. Not only foolish 'wisdom' of ordinary people, but even perfect wisdom of one who really has a great intellect. He must even behave and do things that seem crazy for the sake of worshiping the L-rd....We must roll ourselves in mud and mire for the sake of the worship of the L-rd and His commandments....When his love for the L-rd...is so very strong that he renounces all his wisdom and throws himself into mud and mire for the sake of His worship...and His pleasure, then...he is privileged to understand...the problem of why the righteous suffer and the wicked prosper...which is the problem of theodicy...which even Moses did not understand while...alive."

Footnote 2: Israel son of Eliezer

See "Proper Names" in *Introduction,* p. lvii.

Footnote 3: What a disgrace!

Midr. Tehillim 42. Lit., "Woe to the ears that hear this!"

Footnote 3: fool enough to believe

Prov. 14:15.

Footnote 5: Generation to generation will praise Your deeds

Ps. 145:4.

Footnote 5: Gemoro, 'Before the sun of Eli set...'

Yoma 38b.

Footnote 5: the AR"I

R. Isaac Luria was the center of a circle of mystics in Safed in the 16th century and founder of Lurianic *Kabbala,* whose doctrines greatly influenced Ḥasidism.

Footnote 5: Gemoro, 'The tsadikim are greater in death than in life'

Ḥull. 7b.

Footnote 6: pshot

The straightforward or plain meaning of a text, hence, unclothed, stripped bare.

Footnote 6: His Shkhine

In rabbinic thought, the *Shekhina* is simply the female *manifestation* of the Deity. But in kabbala, the *Shekhina* acquires a life of its own. It is understood as the female *part* of the Deity, and the purpose of Jewish existence is to help unify The Holy One Blessed be He with His *Shekhina.*

Footnote 6: From my own flesh I behold G-d

Cf. Job 19:26.

Footnote 6: Yesamaḥ Leyv 4:3

Cf. Zohar Vayikra, end of fol. 51; *Toledot, Parashat Shelaḥ,* Mezhebuzh 5577 edition, fol. 11b.

Footnote 7: the Adversary

I.e., the Accuser, the Satan.

Footnote 7: very near to the end

I.e., the coming of the messiah.

Footnote 11: In proportion to the number of persons

Ex. 12:4.

Footnote 17: meditate therein day and night

Calqued on Ps. 1:2.

Footnote 17: Say to Wisdom: You are my sister

Prov. 7:4.

Footnote 17: 'tsomid posil' (a lid fastened down)

Num. 19:15. The author of *Likkutei Yekarim* is relating the the words "פתיל, fastened down" and "תפילין, *tfiln,*" since they share the three letters פ-ת-ל, albeit not in the same order.

Footnote 17: 'One third in Talmud,'...as it says in the Gemoro

B.M. 33a.

Footnote 17: near to minkhe

The afternoon service.

Footnote 17: minkhe...is a high rung

Cf. *SB* 32:4 (Mintz, 232): "...in the *minkhe* prayer, which is when the soul ascends to the highest palaces...."

Footnote 17: And if he occupies himself 'with Toroh alone'

A.Z. 17b.

Footnote 17: he is 'like one who has no God'

A.Z. 17b.

Notes to *LETTERS*

Notes to Letter #1

Lines 5f.: sweeter than honey or the honeycomb

Ps. 19:11. *SB* 18:4 (Mintz, 135).

Line 10: a human being

Dan. 7:13.

Line 12: his pipe

The *ḥasidim* were very fond of tobacco, a fondness that prompted polemics on the part of the *mitnaggedim*. "The main reason...is... because of the need to elevate the holy sparks...Tobacco was unknown in Luria's day because the time had not yet come for the very subtle sparks in tobacco to be released by smoking. But now that almost all the coarser sparks had received their restoration, tobacco was sent by God so that the Ḥasidic masters should elevate these 'new' and subtle sparks!...This is the 'sweet savor unto the Lord' mentioned in Scripture in connection with the sacrificial system. Also found in Ḥasidic sources is the idea that smoking corresponds to the incense in Temple times, having the same effect of elevating the holy sparks." Louis Jacobs, *Hasidic Prayer* (London: Routledge & Kegan Paul, 1972), 121.

Line 14: our Faithful

Anshei shelomeinu, "people of our persuasion." Probably calqued on Ps. 37:37 and 41:10, the term is used specifically by *ḥasidim* to refer to members of their own circle.

Lines 15f.: it wasn't our rebe's wish to be accompanied to the outhouse

Cf. *SB* 36:1 (Mintz, 257).

Line 21: It shook me up

Lit., "trembling seized me." Calqued on Is. 33:14 and Ps. 48:7. To avoid repetition, the source of the phrase is identified only here in its first appearance in the text.

Line 22: treyf travesty

Literally, *treyfe posl,* "unclean flawed [book]." Cf. below, note to *Line 68: trashy books.* "The Jewish alphabet was the attribute of Jewishness; Gentiles used... Latin, the language of the priests....The aversion for the language of the clerics was transferred to their script. In the Middle Ages a *seyfer posl* (flawed book) was any book in non-Jewish characters. The aversion went so far that up to the Emancipation hardly a Jew knew the non-Jewish alphabet." Max Weinreich, *History of the Yiddish Language* (Chicago and London: University of Chicago Press, 1980),185, 278. The literary creations of the Haskalah were called by pious Jews *treyf-poslen.*

Line 24: bukh

Yiddish has two words for "book." *Seyfer* (pl. *sforim*) is derived from Hebrew and refers to a holy book, i.e., a book of Torah, while a secular book is referred to in Yiddish as a *bukh* (pl. *bikher*). To preserve the distinction, *"seyfer/sforim"* is translated as "book/s," while *"bukh/bikher"* is transliterated.

Line 31: no secret is hidden from them

The word used here for "secret/hidden thing" -- *tamir* -- is the same as that used in the title of *Revealer of Secrets* -- *Megallé Temirin.* The "secret" is thus introduced linguistically as well as literarily in Letter #1. Cf. above, note to *Title Page, Line 3: Revealer of Secrets.*

Line 32: praise is silence

Ps. 65:2. Maimonides interprets this verse to mean that silence can be a form of praise of God, i.e., *silence is praise.* Here the meaning is reversed, i..e., *praise is silence* -- any praise is inadequate to express the greatness of the *tsadek.*

Lines 32ff.: The times...are past when there were still those...who opposed us

Zeitlin pointed out that those Jews who did not accept the ideas of the Besht "were called by the *ḥasidim* the epithet, *'mitnagdim*/opponents,' as if...they were opposed not only to the sect that followed the path pointed out by the Besht but...to Judaism itself." See "Sadducees and Pharisees," *Ḥorev,* 5696. Historians still use the terms *ḥasidim* and *mitnaggedim,* though it is common knowledge that there never existed any breakaway group known as *mitnaggedim* and that at the beginning of the ḥasidic movement the so-called *mitnaggedim* accounted for the overwhelming majority of Jews. See Aharon Wertheim, *Laws and Customs in Ḥasidism* (Jerusalem: Mossad Ha-Rav Kook., 1960), 234. Various groups of *ḥasidim* referred to their ḥasidic competitors as *misnagdim* as well.

The observation that "the times...are past when there were still people...opposed to us" sets the story in the beginning of the 19th century, after the battles between the *ḥasidim* and their adversaries had subsided and the erstwhile foes had joined forces against the Haskalah. Furthermore, since reference is made throughout *RS* to *Shivḥei ha-Besht,* published in December 1814, this date is the *terminus a quo* for the events in *RS.*

Line 34f.: the whole people, small and great...male and female slave

A conflation of II Kings 25:26, Jer. 42:1. Jer. 51:22 and Gen. 32:6.

Line 38 : all of them alike answer and speak respectfully

Lit., *with reverence.* From the *Yotser* prayer of the morning service. Cf. above, note to *Prologue, Line 203: tsadikim of the highest standing.*

Line 46: vodka

Yayin saraf, lit., astringent wine. See note to Letter #122, *Line 17: vodka.*

Lines 47f. : push away melancholy with both hands

Cf. San. 107b, where the verb is *daḥaf* rather than *daḥa.* Cf. also the 1781 Vilna proclamation of excommunication against the *ḥasidim,* urging people "to push them away with both hands." M. Wilensky, *Ḥasidim and Mitnaggedim* (Jerusalem: Bialik Institute, 1970), 2:151.

Lines 64f.: to buy the bukh and burn it up and wipe it out

Zinberg notes with reference to Israel Loebl's *Sefer ha-Vikkuaḥ,* published in 1798, that "because the Hasidim very diligently bought out this edition and promptly burned the copies they collected, *Sefer ha-Vikkuaḥ* is now extremely rare." Zinberg, *Hasidism and Enlightenment,* 181, n. 25. Cf. below, note to Letter #109, *Lines 42f.: the books...some Talmudists...wrote against our faction.*

Line 68: trashy books

Literally *sifrei posl,* "flawed books." See above, note to *Line 22: treyf travesty.*

Lines 69f.: our rebe will look at his picture and will punish him by looking

The belief that the *tsadek*'s gaze has extraordinary powers that are effective even from a distance is echoed in the notion that wine at which a *tsadek* has peered has curative qualities (Letter #88 and footnote 1 thereto) and in Reb Zelig's demise, inadvertently brought about by the *rebe*'s gaze (Letter #123).

Line 71: A word to the wise...

Midr. Mishlei 22.

Line 75: the Lubliner's people

R. Yakov Yitsḥak, the "Seer" of Lublin, one of the great masters of Ḥasidism's classical period. See *Excursus 1: Ḥasidic Masters.*

Notes to Letter #2

Line 4: otherworldly

Lit., *a reflection of the world-to-come.* B.B. 16a, 17a *et al.,* with reference to Shabbat. "The world-to-come" is an expression for reward in the hereafter.

Line 26: the German schools

In its attempt to "Germanize" the Jewish population, the Austrian government created a system of German schools for Jewish children in Galicia. These were closed in 1806 when Francis I became apprehensive that education might have a revolutionary influence on Galician Jewry. In a memorandum to the provincial presidency at the end of 1819, the year of publication of *RS,* Perl argued that separate German schools for Jewish children should be reestablished along the lines of his own school in Tarnopol, but the government rejected the proposal. See Raphael Mahler, *Hasidism and the Jewish Enlightenment* (Philadelphia: JPS, 1985), 70, 76-80. Accordingly, Reb Zaynvl's son-in-law from Galicia must have studied in "the German schools" prior to 1806. Cf. below, note to Letter #4, *Line 74: that he studied by royal edict in school.*

Lines 36f.: the large lettering on the title page...isn't German – but maybe Latin

The title page that Reb Zaynvl's son-in-law saw was that of *Über das Wesen der Sekte Chassidim,* Perl's non-fiction *bukh,* which had not been published but which, for purposes of the novel, Perl treated as though it *had* been. The language of *Über das Wesen der Sekte Chassidim* is German. The manuscript is written in Gothic letters, except for non-Germanic words, such as the names of persons, places and books, which are almost invariably written in Latin letters. The son-in-law obviously could not read the Gothic letters or else he would have known that the language was German. See also above, *Introduction,* pp. xxvii-xxviii, and below, note to *Footnote 2: The letter [for] Ḥ that he saw was from the word "Chassidim."*

Footnote 2: The letter [for] Ḥ that he saw was from the word "Chassidim"

He knew enough of the Latin alphabet to recognize that the letter combination "Ch" in the word *Chassidim* (which, as a non-Germanic word, is written in Latin letters in the manuscript) has the sound of the Hebrew/ Yiddish letter ḥet/ḥes (ח), which is in fact the first letter of the word *"ḥasidim"* in Hebrew and Yiddish. But since he also knew that German words don't begin with the guttural "Ch," and that German-speaking Jews pronounce an initial "Ch" as though it were simply "H," he concluded that this language could not be German, though since the letters "Ch" were of the Latin alphabet, it might be Latin. The irony, of course, is that the word at which he was looking -- *"Chassidim"* -- should have been a dead giveaway that this was indeed the *bukh* for which he was searching, but he obviously did not know *enough* of the Latin alphabet to sound out the entire word *"Chassidim,"* and to understand that it was simply a transliteration of Hebrew/Yiddish "חסידים, *ḥasidim."*

Notes to Letter #3

Line 13: a mockery and laughingstock

Eruv. 68b. To avoid repetition, the source of the phrase is identified only here in its first appearance in the text.

Lines 15f.: why the Jews sway during the Tfile prayer

The *Tefilla* or "Prayer" is part of the three daily Jewish worship services. In contrast to the rest of the service, which is recited aloud, the *Tefilla* is recited silently, as if being whispered so that only God may hear. Pious Jews, earnestly engaged in this private audience, sway to and fro as they recite the *Tefilla.*

Line 19: the justice of gentiles is husks

The husks represent the material realm of evil, which hold captive sparks of Divine light. See below, note to *Lines 21f.: to extract the holy sparks.* Cf. above, note to Letter #1, *Line 12: his pipe.*

Line 20: gentile justice

I.e., the non-Jewish courts of law. See footnote 2 to this Letter.

Line 20: holy justice from among the husks

See below, note to *Footnote 2: to put the fear of You in their heart.*

Lines 21f.: to extract the holy sparks

See above, note to *Line 19: the justice of gentiles is husks.* Each time a Jew fulfills a *mitsva* with the proper intent, he performs an act of rectification *(tikkun)*, extracting a holy spark from the husk that holds it captive and restoring it to its Divine source. Cf. above, note to Letter #1, *Line 12: his pipe.*

Lines 24f.: to high heaven

Deut. 4:11.

Line 29: I'm urging him

The use of the third person while speaking directly to someone is a form of respect, still in vogue in parts of the *yeshiva* world. Occasionally I translate it in the second person. Cf. below, note to Letter #63, *Line 4: his lovely letter.*

Footnote 2: to put the fear of You in their heart

Lev. 26:36. Cf. above, note to *Line 20: holy justice from among the husks.* For a discussion of the affinities of this teaching of R. Naḥman's with Sabbateanism, see Liebes, *Jewish Myth and Messianism,* 140-2.

Notes to Letter #4

Lines 20f.: in case our rebe...wills

A play on an expression of Jewish piety, *"im yirtse ha-Shem,* God willing." Here God has been replaced by "our *rebe,* he should live."

Line 37: he didn't send for her for several days

Calqued on Esth. 4:11, this phrase introduces the biblical Book of Esther, itself a parody, as a paradigm for present events. Zaynvl's letter casts the Polish prince in the role of the non-Jewish king, Ahasuerus; Freyda, the noble whore, in the role of Esther, savior of her people; and his own pathetic self in the role of Mordekhai, the hero. As events unfold, however, there will be an actual Mordekhai, a *maskil,* who turns out to be pure Gold, a real hero. And in an ironic twist, the *ḥasidim* will be cast in the role of the villain, Haman.

Lines 38ff.: Queen Esther wasn't called to the king...but...she went on her own

See Esther 4:11-5:2.

Line 67: what Rabbi Wolf of Zutomir wrote in his book

Or ha-Meir, published in 5575 (1815-16) in Poritsk.

Line 70: I began to tremble

Lit. "trembling seized me." Calqued on Is. 33:14 and Ps. 48:7. To avoid repetition, the source of the phrase is identified only here in its first appearance in the text.

Line 74: that he studied by royal edict in school

See above, note to Letter #2, *Line 26: the German schools.*

Line 75: the language of wickedness

Any language other than Hebrew or Yiddish could be the vehicle for secular knowledge and would be regarded, consequently, as the language of wickedness. In practice, the language of wickedness was German, since it was the language of western culture, of science, of Enlightenment and of Austrian Galicia, where the *bukh* was published.

Line 77: he'll be a great vessel

I.e., for Torah. The irony here is that it is precisely his ignorance of anything other than Torah that will qualify him to be a great vessel for Torah.

Lines 78f.: relief and deliverance will arise for us from somewhere else

Esther 4:14.

Footnote 1: A happy heart makes a lovely face

Prov. 15:12.

Footnote 5: Your love is more wonderful to me than women's love

II Sam. 1:26.

Footnote 7: Reuben went and lay with Bilhoh his father's concubine

Gen. 35:22.

Notes to Letter #5

Lines 23f.: a sealed letter...from the lieutenant governor

I.e., a forged letter, made to appear *as if* it were from the lieutenant governor.

Line 31: Shabes Koydesh

The holy Sabbath, beginning at sunset on Friday and concluding at nightfall on Saturday. Observant Jews spend *Shabbat Kodesh* in prayer, study and rest.

Line 32: shaleshudes

The third of the traditional three Sabbath meals, eaten at twilight on Saturday before concluding the Sabbath with the *Havdala* ceremony. This ritual meal had been important since rabbinic times, but the *ḥasidim* turned it into a communal meal (for men only), when the faithful would gather, eat a small meal, chant songs and *niggunim* and hear the *rebe's toyre.*

Line 35: speaks and does

The *rebe* is likened to God, who words and deeds are miraculous.

Footnote 4: Place it on an ensign

Num. 21:8. A word play: Hebrew *nes* means both "miracle" and "ensign."

Notes to Letter #6

Line 9: a bit of a clown

The jester performed a quasi-official function as entertainer and master-of-ceremonies at Jewish weddings and other functions. Presumably, being "a bit of a clown" would enable the *melamed* to carry off the ruse.

Lines 22f.: a thorough investigation

San. 4a

Notes to Letter #7

Lines 10f.: dwelt in the house of the L-rd

Ps. 23:6.

Lines 17f.: and on my watch I shall remain

Hab. 2:1.

Lines 19f.: take leave of my father-in-law's house according to the law...

Jewish law enjoins a man to "be fruitful and multiply," which is understood to mean that he father at least two children. If he is unable to procreate with his wife within a period of ten years, the law permits him to divorce her and to try to fulfill the commandment with a new wife. See Yev. 64 and Ket. 77b.

Lines 21f.: from whom the lack stems, whether from me or from my spouse

In pre-modern times, childlessness was seen as the woman's fault. The recognition that infertility could stem from either partner clearly reflects an awareness of science and marks Moshe Fishls as a modern man for his time.

Line 33: the way of truth

The phrase ordinarily refers to the mystical interpretation of Torah. Moshe Fishl's is torn between what his wife and her friends say and what seems rational to him. His plea is really to be told which *is* the way of truth, superstition or science? Cf. above, note to *Approbation, Line 22: through drosh* and below, note to Letter #78, *Line 50: the way of truth.*

Line 36: we await

Ps. 69:4. Lit., "Our eyes wait."

Notes to Letter #8

Line 5: a great miracle

Nes gadol – an analogy with the miracle of Ḥanukka. To avoid repetition, the source of the phrase is identified only here in its first appearance in the text.

Lines 11f.: he fell on my neck and kissed me

Gen. 33:4.

Line 18: if you'll need more receipts

I.e., forged receipts.

Line 22: Mordekhai Gold

See *Excursus 2: Deciphering the Names.*

Line 26: the forbidden books

Secular books.

Line 26: speaks evil

Deut. 13:6, Jer. 29:32.

Lines 26f.: of the L-rd and His meshiakh

Ps. 2:2, cf. I Sam. 12:3.

Line 33: features

B.M. 2:7.

Lines 35f.: he has long hair on his head

In the western (i.e., German) style. The *ḥasidim,* in contrast, keep the hair of the head trimmed very short, only the sidelocks being left untrimmed. R. Naḥman said, "The mere fact that they [today's religious leaders] are careful not to grow their hair long except for their sideburns ensures that they do not follow the current fashions in hairstyles for men. This automatically distances them from...the gentiles...freethinkers and philosophers." Kaplan, *Portrait,* 354.

Line 37: his speech is measured

I.e., he speaks in a dignified manner, in contrast to the *ḥasidim,* who speak rapid-fire. Reb Zelig sees this as a shortcoming of Mordekhai the *maskil.*

Lines 37f.: he knows arithmetic

Another flaw, as far as Reb Zelig is concerned. Arithmetic is part of western science and Enlightenment, condemned by *ḥasidim.*

Lines 39f.: he can't stand a stain on his clothes

R. Zelig sees Mordekhai's clean clothes as proof that he is crazy. Perl, of course, is expressing elliptically his contempt for "the unwashed masses" who make up the ḥasidic minions. We see reflected here both the cultural and socio-economic gaps between *maskilim* and *ḥasidim.*

R. Naḥman advised his *ḥasidim* of the importance of wearing clean clothes (See, for example, Kaplan, *Portrait,* 103, 355), which advice represents both a departure from the common practice and an acknowledgment of that practice.

Lines 40f.: when he sees a poor goy he gives him charity

Giving charity *(tsedaka)* is a *mitsva* incumbent on every Jew. But implicit in this "telltale feature" is the fact that the *ḥasid* practices charity only toward other *ḥasidim* or, at most, toward fellow-Jews, whereas the *maskil* (enlightened, modern, western-style Jew) gives charity without regard to the religion of the recipient. The difference is crucial. The frame of reference of the former is limited to his own kind; non-Jews are the enemy. The latter sees himself as part of the larger human family and feels an ethical obligation to all the poor.

Line 41: he doesn't drink vodka or smoke a pipe

In contrast to *ḥasidim,* who make abundant use of alcohol and tobacco.

By the end of the 18th century, some forty per cent of the revenues of royal properties in Poland came from the manufacture and sale of grain-based intoxicants, the supply of which was largely controlled by Jewish *arendars.* Cf. below, note to Letter #31, *Line 7: our prince made a franchise.*

Ḥasidim established in their prayer-houses the custom of toasting "to a good life and to peace" on occasions such as the anniversary of a death of a loved one, the arrival of an important visitor, the successful completion of a journey, the engagement of a child, the purchase of a new home or object, the illness of a family member, or the prospect of a reversal in business. The money for the purchase of liquor and delicacies was called a *tikn,* short for *tikkun nefesh,* a repair or restoration of whatever blemish or lack existed in the soul of the individual on whose behalf the *tikn* was given. This custom made the consumption of alcohol into a primarily communal and quasi-religious practice. See Wertheim, *Laws and Customs,* 221-4.

See also above, note to Letter #1, *Line 12: his pipe.*

Lines 41f.: throughout our province there's no one, thank G-d, like him...nowadays

I.e., the Haskala has not yet come to Poland.

Notes to Letter #9

Line 14: hurry, quick, get going

The Hebrew achieves a comic effect through the use of three rhyming verbs, עושה! גושה! חושה! In a linguistic nod to Perl, Mendele uses the very same phrase in *Susati.* See *Kol Kitvei Mendele Mokher-Sforim* (Tel Aviv: Dvir, 5723), 324.

Line 28: the Ertsisroel funds

Funds collected by *ḥasidim* through the use of alms boxes and distributed to their colonies in Hebron and Tiberias in the Land of Israel.

Line 28: Rabbi Meyer Balanes funds

R. Meir was a prominent second-century talmudic teacher. The title "Baal ha-Nes/The Miracle-Worker" was added to his name at the end of the eighteenth century by Aaron of Apt, author of *Keter Shem Tov. Ḥasidim* collected funds to maintain the oil lamps on the grave of R. Meir Baal ha-Nes in the Land of Israel. These funds were the subject of a denunciation by Perl in a Hebrew brochure entitled *Katit la-Ma'or,* published in 1836. See *Introduction,* p. xxxii.

Reb Zelig's instructions to "take whatever money you need for this from the *Ertsisroel* funds or the Rabbi Meyer Balanes funds" reflects the historical charge that the *rebes* vied with one another for control of these funds and that they used them for their own purposes. The theme is continued in Letters #22, 41, 42, 70, 80, 108, 116, 128, 130, 133 and 151. See above, note to Letter #9, *Line 28: the Ertsisroel Funds,* and below, note to Letter #128, *Footnote 1: Keser Shem Tov, Part 2, 23:2.*

Lines 29f.: there's no greater mitsve...the members of our fellowship

Cf. San. 4:5, "Whoever saves one life is regarded by Scripture as having saved an entire world." The statement exists in two versions. The one quoted here has "one *Jewish* life," implying that the *ḥasidim* consider only *Jewish* life sacred, and the lives of their own members *most* sacred. Though the saving of a human life is a very great *mitsva* in Judaism, it is not true that "there is no greater *mitsve* than to save...lives," as Jewish law requires one to sacrifice one's life rather than commit murder, idolatry or sexual immorality.

Line 35: we sanctified the new moon

In the Jewish calendar, each month begins with the new moon. Pious Jews recite a special prayer called *Birkat ha-Levana,* The Blessing of the New Moon, three days after the new moon is first sighted or at the first Saturday night before the seventh day of the month. Cf. San. 42a.

Line 39: put fat on...our bones

Prov. 15:30.

Notes to Letter #10

Line 15: czerwone zlotys

Eighteen zlotys equal one czerwone zloty. Cf. *SB* 20:2 (Mintz, 146) and Murray Jay Rosman, "Miedzyboz and Rabbi Israel Baal Shem Tov," in *Essential Papers on Hasidism,* 210. "Czerwone" is Polish for "red." Though the word "zloty" means "gold," an ordinary zloty was made of silver, a czerwone zloty of gold -- hence, "red." Cf. Letter #124: *I took a ducat in my hand...but...I understood that one czerwone zloty is a small sum...,* hence, one czerwone zloty equals one ducat *(rendl).* Ducats, incidentally, were always gold.

Footnote 1: The L-rd loves the gates...more than all the dwellings of Jacob

Ps. 87:2.

Footnote 1: Therefore 'their toroh' is called 'their profession'

Shab. 11a.

Notes to Letter #11

Line 9: judgments pending against him

"Judgments" *(dinim)* are the spiritual consequences of sin. The power of the prayers of the *tsadek* to temper or "sweeten" judgments decreed on high became a prominent feature in early Ḥasidism. The idea is developed at great length in *No'am Elimelekh.* See also Jacobs, *Hasidic Prayer,* 126-39.

Line 18: the forbidden books

In this context, any book opposed to the teachings of Ḥasidism.

Footnote 1: in our land...a Reshkhoydesh prayer booklet...they all pray the Sephardic rite

In Galicia they follow the Ashkenazic rite, whereas the *ḥasidim* in Poland use the Lurianic prayer book, which is based on the Sephardic rite.

Notes to Letter #13

Line 4: Now this man Moyshe I don't know what's become of him

Ex. 32:1.

Lines 5f.:: like a dead man, unremembered in my heart

Ps. 31:13.

Lines 6f.: you have made me...happy

Ps. 92:5.

Line 11: innumerable

I Sam 29:2, II Sam. 18:4. Lit., "by the hundreds and thousands."

Line 14: belongs to his soul-root

SB 2:2 (Mintz, 15f.). "As a result of Adam's disobedience, there was a second cosmic fall....Adam's soul became fragmented, each of his descendants having a mere spark of Adam's mighty soul. Thus the Lurianic school thinks of two kinds of sparks. The first are those that fell when the vessels were shattered. The second are the sparks of Adam's soul....Every soul has to assist in its own *tiqqun,* that is, in the perfection of that particular spark of Adam's soul....The souls of his descendants were present in Adam's soul in families or groups, each with its own soul-root. Since Adam's sin, when the souls were scattered, Adam's descendants each receive their souls in this pattern of roots....A soul not yet perfected while in one body has to return to another body in order to perform the *tiqqun* it requires....The return...may be in the form of an animal or a bird...[or] another human being....Ḥasidic legend tells of certain masters having the souls of saints who lived long ago and with whom they share the same soul-root....This is the reason...for the many tales of disciples going from master to master without finding spiritual rest until they discover a master with the same soul-root as themselves." Louis Jacobs, "The Uplifting of Sparks in Later Jewish Mysticism," in *Jewish Spirituality from the Sixteenth Century Revival to the Present* (New York: Crossroad, 1987), 107, 121f..

Lines 23f.: has not been performed or reported

In Ex. 24:7, the Israelites tell Moses that all that God has spoken "we will faithfully do (lit., do and hear/obey)," in Hebrew, "נעשה ונשמע." Playing on this phrase, Perl has Gedalye say, "לא נעשה ולא נשמע," which in this context means, "has not been performed or reported/heard," but which the knowledgeable reader immediately recognizes as the negation of Israel's promise, i.e., "was not done and not obeyed/we will neither do nor obey."

Lines 26f.: like the skin of a garlic clove

I.e., insubstantial. *SB* 22:4 (Mintz, 162f.). The original use of the expression is in Bekh. 58a, where Ben Azzai says, "All the sages of Israel are to me as the skin of a garlic clove, apart from this bald one." R. Naḥman goes a step further: "I can now say, 'All the sages of Israel are to me as the skin of a garlic [clove],' except that in my case there is no 'apart from.'" Kaplan, *Portrait*, 280.

Line 32: what can I do for you

II Kings 2:9, 4:2; Ez. 35:15; Hos. 6:4. *SB* 17:4 (Mintz, 128).

Line 36: a form for written petitions

The *ḥasid* would list on a note *(kvitl)* his needs and those of his family, together with their names and their mothers' names, according to a set formula. The *kvitl* would then be delivered to the *rebe*, along with money for a *pidyen*.

Lines 58f.: you will see wonders

Rashi on San. 111a.

Footnote 1: the tale of the king and the only son and the beggars

Probably the best-known of R. Naḥman's tales, commonly known as the tale of "The Seven Beggars."

Notes to Letter #14

Line 14: and never left his side

Lit., "his hand never let go of his hand." Calqued on Ket. 2:9.

Notes to Letter #15

Line 42 : faithful servant

I.e., *trustee, right-hand man*. Num. 12:7, of Moses. It comes to be a technical term, referring to a specific position within the household, workplace or other organization. To avoid repetition, the source of the phrase is identified only here in its first appearance in the text.

Lines 57ff.: He took a pipe to smoke the tobacco...put it to his pipe

SB 34:3 (Mintz, 245f.).

Line 60: gratefully

Lit., *with great thanks*. Zech. 4:7. To avoid repetition, the source of the phrase is identified only here in its first appearance in the text.

Lines 79f.: took out the infamous bukh and...says, The book is Shivkhey ha-Besht

Published in December 1814, *Shivḥei ha-Besht (The Praises of The Balshemtov)* is a collection of tales and legends about the life and wonders of the Balshemtov, who died in 1760. While he never founded a movement, he is generally regarded as "the patron saint" of the movement that came to be known as Ḥasidism. The figure of the Besht and the book, *Shivḥei ha-Besht* -- when they are not explicitly referred to or quoted in *RS* -- provide backdrop for the book as well as objects of Perl's satire. See *Introduction*, pp. xxxviii-xlii.

Line 80: you must have it in Judeo-German

The Polish lord refers to the spoken language of the Jews not by its Jewish name, "Yiddish," but by its non-Jewish name, "Judeo-German."

Lines 100f.: there's even a Notice about this, as all the Jewish authors have

Such disclaimers appear regularly in Jewish books of the period. E.g., the following appears on the obverse of the title page of *Toledot Yaakov Yosef*:

> IMPORTANT NOTICE
>
> These things too will be self-evident to the discerning -- that the nations in whose lands we dwell are not like the nations who lived in the time of the mishnaic sages of blessed memory, for those were idolators and held fast to all the abominations. They did not know the L-rd nor did they recognize His holy word. But the nations of our time revere the L-rd and honor His Toroh. They practice justice in their lands and kindness toward the Jews who take refuge beneath their wings. G-d forbid that we should speak or write anything disparaging about them! Everywhere the books mention *goy* (non-Jew) or *nokhri* (foreigner) or *umos ho'olom* (Gentile nations) and such, the reference is to idolators, those who lived in the period of the sages of the Mishna.

Cf. above, note to *Important Notice, Line 1: IMPORTANT NOTICE.*

Line 107: Pray for the well-being of the government

Avot 3:2.

Line 126: vodka

See above, note to Letter #8, *Line 41: he doesn't drink vodka....*

Line 129: cut him down to size

Lit., "bring him down to the dust." Is. 25:12.

Lines 130f.: the celestial prince of any nation

Refers to the talmudic belief that each nation is represented on high by an angel, its celestial prince.

Line 141: holding a holy object

Shev. 38b.

Line 158: seen a little something

SB 16:4 (Mintz, 121 and n. 1 thereto, where he calls this a euphemism for carnal intimacy, "a paintbrush in a tube," as in Makkot 7a and B.M. 91a). Cf. San. 68a.

Lines 171f.: I'll lease him the mill for three more years

Under the *arenda* system, three years was the most common length of time for a lease. See, for example, Baron and Kahan, 127, 135.

Lines 233f.: send...a gift of a wagon with all kinds of flour and fowl

SB 17:4 (Mintz, 129).

Line 248: from here to there

San. 5a, where "here" refers to Babylonia and "there" to the Land of Israel.

Footnote 1: all in all

Eccl. 9:2.

Notes to Letter #16

Lines 4f.: wagon with all kinds of flour and...fowl

SB 17:4 (Mintz, 129).

Lines 19f.: Yo'el, wife of Khever the Kenite

Judges 4:17ff.. The prophetess Deborah summoned Barak to mass an army against Jabin's army, commanded by Sisera. Barak lead a successful counter-attack at Mount Tabor, from which Sisera fled on foot to the tent of Yael, with whose husband's family Jabin had had an old friendship. Yael offered Sisera hospitality and protection in her tent, and when he lay fast asleep, she killed him by driving a tent pin through his temple with a mallet.

Lines 21f.: Why must you ask about what's not permitted to you?

Ecclesiasticus 3:21. Cf. Hag. 13a and Ber. Rab. 8:2. Cf. also below, note to Letter #116, *Footnote 1: Into what is too wondrous for you don't inquire.*

Line 47: from Wallakhia

Now part of Rumania, Wallakhia was until 1861 an independent principality between the Danube River and the Transylvanian Alps.

Line 50: You can bet...he's merely Yokltse

The name is a pun based on the Yiddish word, "*yok*, a simpleton." The line can be read, "It must be obvious that he's merely a simpleton." Also, see *Excursus 2: Deciphering the Names.*

Lines 92f.: our chief opponent Elijah...who excommunicated the whole group

Elijah *(Eyliohu)*, the Gaon of Vilna, the most revered rabbinic authority of his day, led the first wave of opposition to Ḥasidism at the end of the 18th century, proclaiming a ban against the entire sect in 1772 and again in 1781.

Lines 95f.: the wicked Seyfer ha-Vikuakh

Literally, *The Book of Controversy* -- an anti-ḥasidic tract written by R. Israel Loebl, *Maggid* in various Lithuanian and White Russian communities. Published in Warsaw in 1798, it was bought up by the *ḥasidim* and burned. Perl tried without success to have it reprinted, but his efforts did lead to a three-year investigation of Ḥasidism by the Austrian government. See Mahler, *The Jewish Enlightenment*, 85ff.. Also, cf. above, note to Letter #1, *Lines 64f.: to buy the bukh and burn it up and wipe it out.*

Lines 97f.: the holy book Shivkhey ha-Besht was published...first...in Kopust...in Lithuania

I.e., Ḥasidism has so vanquished its opponents that even *Shivḥei ha-Besht*, the quintessential literary symbol of the movement, was published in Lithuania, the home of talmudic scholarship and former hotbed of opposition to Ḥasidism.

Line 100: the tsadikim and their disciples and their disciples' disciples

Calqued on the distinctive phrase of the *Kaddish de-Rabbanan*, "For our rabbis and their disciples and their disciples' disciples...," which gives this version of the *Kaddish* its unique name. But in Reb Zelig's use of the phrase here, *"our rabbis"* have been supplanted by "the *tsadikim.*"

Line 101: be so brazen

Ps. 110:7.

Footnote 3: My prayer is against their evil deeds

Ps. 141:5.

Footnote 3: angry every day

Ps. 7:12.

Footnote 3: G-d's mercy is all day

Ps. 52:3.

Footnote 3: 'when there is judgment below there is no judgment on high'
Tanh. Mishpatim 5 et *al.*

Footnote 4: bad-mouths them with abuse and vilification
A conflation of Job 16:10 and Ez. 5:15.

Footnote 4: She will be cut off cut off
I.e., *utterly cut off.* Num. 15:31.

Footnote 4: the final conclusion of the Gemoro
The source is Rashi to Lev. 22:3, which in turn is based on Sifra 4:10.

Notes to Letter #17

Lines 7f.: wagon with the assorted flour and fowl
SB 17:4 (Mintz, 129).

Line 13: I got no business with mysteries
Calqued on Ḥag. 13a. Cf. notes to Letter #60, *Line 50: we have no business in mysteries* and to Letter #78, *Lines 4f.: you have no interest in esoteric matters.*

Lines 16f.: a unification of The Holy One, blessed be He, and His Shkhine
"Unifications" *(yiḥudim)* are meditations on combinations of letters of the name of God, or on configurations of God's name with unusual vocalizations, designed to bring about an act of unification between The Holy One and His *Shekhina,* thereby restoring the primordial unity of the Godhead.

Line 19: caused a menstrual flow to the Shkhine
See below, note to *Footnote 1: the wicked cause a separation...a menstrual flow.*

Line 20: Their gold [shall be] as something unclean
Ez. 7:19.

Line 23: to follow the king
Eccl. 2:12. In this context, "Who am I to criticize or second-guess you or our *rebe?*" Cf. Introduction to *Sippurei Ma'asiyot,* where it alludes to the "scholars" *(lomedim)* and where the King is clearly R. Naḥman. Aryeh Kaplan, *Rabbi Nachman's Stories* (Jerusalem: Breslov Research Institute, 1987), 4.

Footnote 1: the wicked cause a separation...a menstrual flow
See Piekaż' discussion of this teaching in conjunction with the opposition of the Grandfather of Shpola. *Ḥasidut Breslav,* 68.

Footnote 1: men of blood
Ps. 55:24.

Footnote 1: The turbid blood is...made into milk by a nursing mother
Bekh. 6b, Nid. 9a.

Footnote 1: He declared to you His covenant
Deut. 4:13. See Zohar, *Vayishlaḥ,* 176b.

Footnote 1: 'Shaddai' because it fires (shadei)
Rashi on Gen. 49:25.

Footnote 1: and the fear of the L-rd is his treasure
Is. 33:6.

Notes to Letter #19

Line 12: And the gold of the land is good

Gen. 2:12.

Line 19: the renowned story of the pearls

The Hebrew word for "pearls" is "מרגליות/*margaliot,"* but the Yiddish word is "פערלס/perls." The otherwise anonymous author reveals his identity to the careful reader with a phrase that can now easily be read, "the renowned story of Perl's." In the Yiddish version, the author changed the plural to the singular, "דער מעשה פון דיא פערל, the story of the pearl/Perl," making the hint even more obvious. Such a playfulness would be consistent with the theme of the novel: The *ḥasidim* search for the *bukh* and try to identify its author, while the reader of the novel tries to discover *its* author. Such a device would also fit well with the theme of revealment and concealment that runs through both the plot and the kabbalistic concepts alluded to in the text and footnotes. Cf. below, note to Letter #80, *Line 33: who deals in pearls,* and note to Letter #103, *Lines 45ff.: a hundred...zlotys' worth of pearls...to give the tsadekes pearls.*

Further support for this interpretation may be adduced from Shmeruk's observation that in the manuscript of the Yiddish version of Perl's story, "The Tale of the Loss of the Prince," Perl first copied the word *margalit* (pearl) from his earlier Hebrew version of the story, and subsequently "corrected" it to something else entirely so as to hide his identity. *Tales and Letters,* 12.

Lines 22f.: The living, the living shall thank You

Cf. Is. 38:19, which is part of a poem by King Hezekiah of Judah upon recovering from a life-threatening illness he had suffered. There are strong parallels with all of Is. 38:1-20. The verse is quoted in Zohar I:207b.

Line 26: twice eighteen zlotys

The numerical value of the letters of the Hebrew word *ḥai* (חי, life, living) totals 18 in *gematria* (ח=8, י=10), so the number 18 represents the Hebrew word for "life, living." The *rebe* said, "The living, the living...," hence the need for twice eighteen zlotys to correspond to the words of the *rebe*'s *pidyen.*

Line 31: the kavone of the smoke of the incense that stops the plague

See Num. 17:11-13. The *kavvana* accompanies the liturgical unit entitled "The Compounding of The Incense *(Pittum ha-Ketoret)."* See Vital, Part I, 87ff. Hirsh of Zhidotchev called the *tsadek* the "healer of the sick among his people Israel." His remedy for cholera was to "recite all of Psalms every week, pledge to charity after completing each of the five books of the Psalms...and examine the *mezuzes* to insure that they are ritually fit." Mahler, *The Jewish Enlightenment,* 15f. and n. 50 thereto. On Hirsh of Zhidotchev, see in *Excursus 2: Deciphering the Names,* "Asher Dan," "Kalktsig" and "Nakhal Hamotsa."

Line 37: in a coma

Pes. 50a, Ta'an. 25a. *SB,* Writer's Preface, col. I (Mintz, 4). Cf. *SB* 36:3 (Mintz, 260).

Line 49: bread of silver (nahamo dikhesifin)

Beggar's bread, charity. Cf. Dresner's discussion of *kosef* (*The Zaddik,* 193) in connection with *Tsafenat Pa'anei'aḥ* 54c.

Line 59: honor and glory
Ex. 28:2.

Notes to Letter #20

Lines 5ff.: seen a boy...with the empty wagon
SB 28:4 (Mintz, 205).

Lines 14f.: a parasang from his village
A Russian *mal,* equivalent to 10 versts or 6.629 miles. See Aryeh Kaplan, *Rabbi Nachman's Wisdom* (Jerusalem: Breslov Research Institute, 1973), 314, n. 578.

Lines 17ff.: if it was possible for him to get...from the pond a big fish
SB 33:1 (Mintz, 235f.).

Line 31: from the arendar they sent him food and drink at the manor
Presumably, the Jewish steward would require kosher food; hence, his meals were sent to his apartment by the Jewish *arendar.*

Line 61: there was no 'eruv there
The *'eruv,* or Sabbath limit, is an area physically encircled by wire or twine and defined as one's "home." Since it is forbidden to travel more than a specific distance from home or to carry any object outside home on the Sabbath, the *'eruv* enlarges the definition of "home" for these purposes. In practice, the *'eruv* made it possible for Jews to carry the Sabbath stew *(tcholent)* from the baker's oven to their home at mealtime. In Letter #20, R. Zelig mentions the absence of an *'eruv* in conjunction with his carrying the piece of glass -- and provides a rationalization so that the absence of the *'eruv* is no deterrent.

Lines 78f.: I'm moving with tremendous dveykes in the upper worlds
A scathing take-off on the ḥasidic goal of "*bittul ha-yesh,* the annihilation of the self," in which the self is left behind as the soul soars aloft through contemplative prayer. The contrast between sublime and ridiculous is devastating.

Notes to Letter #21

Line 51: by himself
Reb Zelig's observation that the *misnaged* actually carried the merchandise to the cellar by himself may reflect both surprise that a Jew *could* be strong enough to do physical labor and contempt that a Jew *would* do physical labor. His remark expresses his contempt for such labor and implies his belief that physical labor is for gentile servants -- labor that only a *misnaged* would do!

Notes to Letter #22

Lines 24ff.: One...collects funds...the other is...a grandson of Reb Yoyne Kaminker
See Letter #151, lines 61f.. See also below, note to Letter #125, *Line 17: as our rebe wrote it.* Reb Yonoh Kaminker is mentioned in *SB* 12:1, Mintz, 89.

Notes to Letter #23

Line 24: whom no mystery baffles
Cf. Dan. 4:6.

Line 24: said gimatrie
Cf. *SB* 29:1 (Mintz, 207).

Line 25: And he found written that Mordekhai had told
Esther 6:2, cf. 3:4.

Lines 25f.: Higgid (הגיד) plus 2 adds up to goyo (גויה)
הגיד = 5+3+10+4=22; גויה = 3+6+10+5=24; 22+2=24.

Line 28: also meat with milk
The biblical laws of *kashrut* forbid eating certain parts of the animal (See below, note to *Line 29: the sinew.*) The rabbinic laws, based on Ex. 34:26, proscribe in addition the eating of meat with milk. Reb Zelig's point here is that Mordekhai has undoubtedly violated *all* the laws of *kashrut.*

Line 29: the sinew
Gen. 32:33 -- "That is why the children of Israel...do not eat the thigh sinew...since Jacob's hip socket was wrenched at the thigh sinew."

Lines 31f.: in its mother's milk
Ex. 34:26.

Lines 34f.: the covenant of the tongue and the covenant of the flesh
Sefer Yetsira 1:2, 1:3 and 6:7. The tongue (via speech) and the penis are both organs of creation and must be covenanted to the service of God. The covenant of circumcision *(mila)* is given to Abraham and later restated to Moses: WHEN A WOMAN AT CHILDBIRTH BEARS A MALE...ON THE EIGHTH DAY THE FLESH OF HIS FORESKIN SHALL BE CIRCUMCISED (Lev. 12:3). The covenant of the tongue is from II Sam. 23:2, THE SPIRIT OF THE LORD HAS SPOKEN THROUGH ME; HIS WORD *(MILA)* IS ON MY TONGUE. Playing on the two meanings of *mila* ("circumcision" and "word"), the verse can be read, "His circumcision is on my tongue." See Aryeh Kaplan, *Sefer Yetzirah* (York Beach, Maine, 1990), 35-7.

"There is a particular relationship in Naḥman's writings between the purity of speech and sexual purity, based upon an older Kabbalistic association between the sexual (*berit ha-ma'or* [the covenant of the flesh], i.e., circumcision) and verbal (*berit ha-lashon* [the covenant of the tongue], i.e., the acceptance of Torah at Sinai) covenants between God and Israel." Green, *Tormented Master,* 179f., n. 60. Cf. also *SB* 9:2 (Mintz, 68).

Lines 38f.: There was a Jewish man...son of Kish, a Benjaminite
Esther 2:5.

Lines 41f.: Why is your clothing so red?
Is. 63:2.

Line 46 : Though your sins be like crimson
Is. 1:18.

Lines 46f.: the sin of the capitol (ha-biro)
In context, Isaiah is addressing Jerusalem.

Line 51: vayeshama Sho'ul, Saul gathered
Yoma 22b on I Sam. 15:4.

Line 53: A stone in a pitcher goes 'Rattle, rattle (kish, kish)'
B.M. 85b.
Line 55: and He readied
Jonah 2:1.
Line 56: May his lips be kissed
Prov. 24:26. I.e., *Bravo! He said something wonderful!* An expression of appreciation common in ḥasidic literature.
Footnote 1: The choicest of the first fruits of your soil
Ex. 23:19.
Footnote 1: Bring to the house of the L-rd your G-d
Ex. 23:19.
Footnote 1: Do not cook a kid with its mother's milk
Ex. 23:19.

Notes to Letter #24

Line 9: the Megile
The biblical Book of Esther, referred to in the *rebe*'s *gimatrie* in Letter #23.

Notes to Letter #25

Line 11: He just rested his head...
Cf. *SB* 7:2 (Mintz, 52).
Footnote 1: the Shkhine was ablaze around them
At Elisha ben Avuya's *berit mila,* R. Eliezer and R. Joshua were engaging in the esoteric study of Torah "and the words were as happy as when they were given from Sinai, and the fire was ablaze around them." Eccl. Rab. 7:8, par. 1.
Footnote 1: He was very upset
Cf. Jonah 4:9.

Notes to Letter #26

Lines 7f.: He was riding on the back of an animal
B.M. 1:3.
Lines 17f.: Whoever studies Toroh...having borne him
San. 19b, where it says 'teaches.'
Line 19: His Exalted Eminence
Maharal of Prague, *Netivot Olam,* part 2, p. 84.
Line 26: Let me not become contemptible
Gen. 38:23.
Line 29: the laws of the Shulkhen Orukh
The codification of Jewish law compiled by Joseph Karo in the 16th century. It remains the authoritative guide for observant Jews to this day.

Line 30: Vatikin

"The pious men of old" who would rise early to synchronize their morning prayers with sunrise. "Abaye says: In regard to the *Shema,* [the *halakha* is] as practiced by the *vatikin.* For R. Yoḥanan said: 'The *vatikin* used to finish it [the recital of the *Shema*] by sunrise...and say the *Tefilla* in the daytime.'" (Ber. 9b) "The practice of synchronizing the morning prayers with the sunrise received a strong impetus from the kabbalists during the 17th and 18th centuries, and the number of early risers increased." Abraham E. Millgram, *Jewish Worship* (Philadelphia: JPS, 1971), 504. Vital states that "those who pray in the manner of the *vatikin* and recite the *Shema* at sunrise must be complete *ḥasidim* whose *kavvana* and thought are efficacious... and not every man is fit for this at the present time." Vital, *Sha'ar ha-Kavvanot, Kitvei Rabbeinu ha-AR"I,* I:127b. Moshe Fishls follows the traditional custom of reciting the morning service *(shḥarit)* early, whereas the *ḥasidim* were more casual about the time for worship.

Line 33: Duties of the Heart

A widely read and beloved work by R. Baḥya ibn Pakuda of eleventh-century Spain, it was the first systematic presentation of the ethics of Judaism.

Lines 37f.: we shouldn't imitate Aharon the priest with the fire-pan of incense

In ḥasidic tradition, smoking tobacco is akin to the ancient priestly offering of incense. Some holy sparks must be raised by being smelled. Wertheim, *Laws and Customs,* 224. Cf. note to Letter #1, *Line 12: his pipe.*

Lines 39f.: If the ancients were human beings, we are like asses...

Shab. 112b.

Line 42: I started shuddering

Calqued on Job 21:6.

Notes to Letter #27

Line 4: I'm sending you some good news

Cf. Grace After Meals, where it says, referring to Eliyohu, herald of the messiah, "He will bring us good news...."

Line 10: to make for her a remedy

The use of amulets, "cures" and folk remedies for illness and for current needs such as help in making a living or raising children was common among *ḥasidim* until recent times. Cf. below, notes to Letter #57, *Lines 61f.: a common wonder-worker* and to Letter #98, *Line 76: the remedies this rebe has.*

Line 11: hemorrhoids

SB 10:3 (Mintz, 77).

Footnote 1: Healing he will heal

I.e., *he will heal completely.* Ex. 21:19.

Notes to Letter #30

Line 33: anguish, healing, loss of time and indignity

B.K. 8:1.

Notes to Letter #31

Line 7: our prince made a franchise

The franchise *(propinacja)* was "a specialized form of the *arenda,* the manufacturing, wholesaling, and retailing of grain-based intoxicants. In Poland, from the middle of the 17th century to the end of the 18th century, there was a dramatic increase in the manufacture and sale of alcohol....By 1789 the proportion of revenues from the sale of alcohol reached 40.1 percent [of the overall income of royal properties]....The increased revenue from alcohol does indicate greater success in institutionalizing the monopoly on its manufacture and distribution within the economy of feudal estates, as well as the increased quantities of grain that the gentry deployed particularly for this purpose....The supply became increasingly managed by Jewish *arendars* and their sublessees on behalf of the Polish noble landlords." Hillel Levine, *Economic Origins of Antisemitism* (New Haven and London: Yale University Press, 1991), 140ff..

Line 11: treyf trash

See above, note to Letter #1, *Line 22: treyf travesty.*

Notes to Letter #34

Lines 5f.: You have perceived well

Jer. 1:12.

Line 7: his father's filth

His father's semen or genetic legacy.

Line 8: his teacher's toyre

The "false" teaching of his teacher, who was obviously not a *khosed.*

Line 22: what a great celebration there was last night

The setting of this celebration is either *Simḥat Torah* or *Simḥat Beit ha-Sho'eiva.*

Lines 23f.: Open for me the gates of righteousness. I will enter into them...

Ps. 118:19. The word for "righteousness" is *tsedek.* The next verse reads, "This is the gateway to the Lord; *Tsaddikim* shall enter it." The *rebe* and his *ḥasidim* understand the verses to mean, "Open for me the gates of the *tsadek.* This is the gateway to the Lord; the *tsadikim* (i.e., the *rebes)* shall enter it."

Line 25: It came to pass at midnight

Ex. 12:29. In its biblical context and in later Hebrew usage this phrase is invariably linked with Passover and specifically with Seder night, but in Yiddish it came to be used idiomatically and does not necessarily refer to Passover.

Lines 27f.: Blessed be the Omnipresent who has drawn me near to His service...

Num. Rab. 4:6 is the source of the expression, "who has drawn me near to His service." The earliest liturgical context in which this phrase is echoed is *Kedushat ha-Yom* of the festival *Tefilla:* "You, our Sovereign, have drawn us near to Your service." But it is the Karaite prayerbook that contains the formula, "Blessed are You...who has drawn us near to Your service..." in conjunction with the reading of Scripture. It is this formulation that is echoed by the *rebe* here in Letter #34, and that also appears in the Reconstructionist prayer book. See *Karaite Siddur,* vol. 2 (Vilna, 1890), 182. See also *Sabbath Prayer Book* (New York: Jewish Reconstructionist Foundation, 1965), 160. I am grateful to Sid Leiman for the identification of the source of this blessing. Leiman further suggests that it probably came to the *ḥasidim* via one of the texts they studied, e.g., *Yesod ve-Shoresh ha-Avoda, Reishit Ḥokhma* or *Shenei Luḥot ha-Berit.*

The opening formulation, "Blessed be the Omnipresent," distinguishes this prayer from a formal *berakha* (which must begin with the words, "Blessed are You, Lord our God..."). In a private communication, Yehoshua Eichenstein indicates that this is one of a number of informal and spontaneous prayers common in ḥasidic usage. It is used to say, in effect, "Thank You, God, for removing the veil from my eyes and permitting me to see another aspect of Your truth, thereby drawing me closer to Your service."

Lines 25f.: his face aflame like torches

SB 34:2 (Mintz, 243).

Line 51: because no one from the arende saw it

The *arendar* is supposed to deal only in goods produced on the lord's estate.

Footnote 1: Rabbi Koppel

Probably refers to R. Yakov Koppel Lifshitz, whose prayerbook, *Siddur Kol Yaakov,* appeared in Slavuta in 1804 and was highly esteemed by the *ḥasidim.*

Notes to Letter #35

Lines 21f.: don't tempt the devil

Literally, *don't open [your] mouth to Satan* by uttering ominous prophecies, lest he hear you and carry them out. Cf. Letters #53, 67, 87, 101, 106 and 145.

Lines 29f.: Should they really be condemned for such a trivial act

Cf. *SB* 26:2 (Mintz, 188).

Notes to Letter #38

Lines 4f.: The Lord caused...to happen my way

Gen. 27:20.

Notes to Letter #40

Line 23: like a slave before his master

Shab. 10a in manuscript versions.

Line 30: goy

I.e., Christian.

Line 30: Ishmaelite

I.e., Moslem or Turk.

Notes to Letter #43

Line 27: to find out what he really thinks
Men. 4a.

Line 48: there's nothing more to say
A formula used to signify the end of a talmudic discussion. Its use at the end of Reb Gershon's cunning letter is an ironic commentary on the letter itself.

Notes to Letter #44

Lines 20f.: the goye should act like she's dumb so no one will recognize she's a goye
Language distinguishes not only *ḥasidim* from *mitnaggedim* and *maskilim;* it also distinguishes Jews from non-Jews.

Line 24: a Canaanite slave
A servant from the Slavic lands. See Max Weinreich, 80.

Line 25: to go to Lvov to the doctor
Lvov (Lemberg), in Austrian Galicia, was a center of commerce and Haskala. It is sophisticated enough to have a doctor (as opposed to a healer).

Line 25: our holy rebe looked
The *rebe* "looked" in the supernal realms to see what was pending for her.

Notes to Letter #45

Line 24: this week was Legboymer
The *Omer* (lit., barley sheaf) is the seven-week period from the second day of Passover until the first day of Shavuot, the period of the barley harvest in ancient Israel. It came to be associated with various tragic events in Jewish history and legend, and joyous celebrations were forbidden during this time, except on the thirty-third day of the *Omer*, La"g Ba'Omer, a day of rejoicing.

Lines 24f.: it was always his custom to go on Legboymer...to shoot a bow
When the Romans forbade the teaching of Torah, R. Shimon bar Yoḥai hid in the woods where his students came to study with him. They would carry bows and arrows and pretend to be hunting. The custom of La"g Ba'Omer outings and shooting toy bows and arrows traces back to this legend and is observed to this day by *ḥasidim* in Israel, who make a pilgrimage to the tomb of Shimon bar Yoḥai, the pseudepigraphic author of the Zohar.

Lines 24f.: a Jewish custom is toyre
Beit Yosef on *Tur, Yoreh De'ah* 39, citing Rashba.

Line 45: Whoever didn't saw this celebration never saw celebration
Suk. 5:1.

Line 60: very deep– who can discover it?
Eccl. 7:24.

Line 104: as an everlasting memorial
Ps. 112:6.

Lines 112f.: be strong and courageous

Deut. 31:7, 23 *et al.* To avoid repetition, the source of the phrase is identified only here in its first appearance in the text.

Notes to Letter #46

Lines 20f.: expert in Shimesh Tilim

Shimmush Tehillim (The Use of Psalms), a medieval manual for the magical uses of individual psalms or verses thereof provides formulae against illness, attack by highwaymen, wild animals and evil spirits, imprisonment and involuntary baptism. Cf. Joshua Trachtenberg, *Jewish Magic and Superstition* (New York: Behrman House, 1939), 109ff..

Line 42: look to the L-rd

Ps. 27:14, 37:34.

Notes to Letter #48

Line 25: Akhziv

See *Excursus 2: Deciphering the Names.*

Notes to Letter #49

Line 29: for ransoming captives

In Ḥasidism, "freeing captives" meant providing a lump sum to someone who was otherwise in danger of bankruptcy. See Benzion Dinur, "The Origins of Hasidism and Its Social and Messianic Foundations" in *Essential Papers on Hasidism,* 156.

Notes to Letter #50

Line 27: he'll...extend himself every which way

From Yiddish, lit., "he'll lay himself out lengthwise and breadthwise." Its use here may allude to a statement attributed by R. Nathan to R. Naḥman: "[R. Naḥman] revealed the Ten Psalms of the *Tikkun ha-Klali* and said that whoever will come to his grave and give a penny to charity and recite these ten psalms, no matter how great his sins, 'I will do everything in my power, spanning the length and breadth of the creation, to help this person.'" Kaplan, *Portrait,* 70.

Footnote 1: 310 immersions

The letters of the Hebrew number 310 (ש"י) also spell the word *shai,* "a gift."

Notes to Letter #51

Line 11: have been a stranger in a strange land

Ex. 2:22, 18:3.

Lines 11f.: it was the Omnipresent who sent you thither

Cf. Gen. 45:5, Ex. 3:14 *et al.*

Line 36: I have nothing more to say

Calqued on Job 32:5.

Footnote 1: the scoffers say that the tsadikim are unable to write

The charge that some of the *tsadikim* were unable to write appears frequently in the 19th century. Tishby cites this passage and another from the *Prologue* to *RS* among several such examples. See Isaiah Tishby, "Tsvi Herman Shapira as a Writer of the Haskala," in *Studies in Kabbalah and Its Branches,* 2:554, n. 65. Cf. *Prologue,* lines 153ff.: "The scoffers of the generation make a dreadful mockery of our Faithful and say they can't write properly in the holy tongue and always write full of errors and mistakes like common ignoramuses."

Notes to Letter #54

Lines 28f.: experts in the sciences

"Like many...Christian sects during the Middle Ages and the Reformation, Ḥasidism attacked science not only because it was hostile to...religion but also because it was closely allied to the new socioeconomic order of capitalism, which was undermining the old relationships of production and the medieval ways of life connected with them.... Science was regarded by Ḥasidism to be such a great threat to faith that even medicine was rejected by some of the *rebes.*" Mahler, *The Jewish Enlightenment,* 15.

Notes to Letter #55

Line 5: Meyer Yankev of Zaslav

Meyer Yakov of Zaslav was the name of a real publisher involved in distributing ḥasidic books in Galicia in 1818. In a letter written by R. Hirshele of Zhidotchev to R. Joshua Heschel of Apt, he is mentioned in connection with the printing of a new edition of Vital's *Eits Ḥayyim* and *Peri Eits Ḥayyim,* i.e., "Last week Meyer Yakov of Zaslav, who deals in book-publishing, came and told me...." In Letter #121, the connection between R. Hirshele and Reb Meyer Yakov concerning the reprinting of Vital's book is mentioned explicitly: "I had a correspondence with the *rebe* of the holy community of Kalktsig [=Zhidotchev] and with other people there to supply them the holy books *Toldes Yankev Yoysef, Eyts Khayim* and *Pri Eyts Khayim.*" In Letter #102, the name of this *rebe* is Asher Dan (=Hirshele). See Chone Shmeruk, "Authentic and Imaginative Elements in Joseph Perl's M'galeh T'mirin" *Tsion* 21 (1956): 95. See also *Excursus 2: Deciphering the Names.*

Line 5: a draft card

This would indicate that the bearer is not fleeing military service -- a frequent reason for crossing the border.

Lines 6f.: Nakhal Hamotsa, which is near the district seat

See *Excursus 2: Deciphering the Names.* The district seat is Greater Tsidon, i.e., Tarnopol. Nakhal Hamotsa is its neighboring village of Zbariz.

Lines 14f.: he carried packets of contraband

"Abraham Ber Gottlober tells...of knowing 'such persons who call themselves *ḥasidim*' who come over the border to Galicia to the son of *Rebe* Israel of Ruzhin and whose visits are 'merely coverups' for smuggling contraband on their way back home." Mahler, *The Jewish Enlightenment,* 12 and n. 34 thereto.

Notes to Letter #56

Lines 28f.: printed in Mezhebush where the Chief of all the rebes always stays

The Besht moved to Mezhebush between 1740-45, remained there until his death in 1760, and was buried there. Mezhebush subsequently became the unofficial "capitol" of the ḥasidic movement. For the identity of "the superior of all the *rebes,*" see *Excursus 2: Deciphering the Names.*

Footnote 1: the holy tongue

I.e., Hebrew.

Notes to Letter #57

Lines 25f.: the tsadek of Hanipoli...of Tcharna Ostra...of Prshevorsk

The historical persons were Zusha of Hanipoli, Ze'ev Wolf of Tcharna Ostra and Moshe of Prshevorsk. See *Excursus 2: Deciphering the Names.* Also, regarding the last, see footnote 1 to Letter #63, p. 115.

Lines 27f.: pray before the Ark

Literally, "before the lectern." Traditionally, the prayer leader presents the congregation's prayer before the Divine Throne. Hence, he and the lectern face the Ark. To translate the phrase as "before the lectern" would be confusing to the reader in whose experience the lectern faces the congregation.

Lines 32f.: The Elder (Der Zeyde, The Grandfather)

R. Aryeh Yehuda Leyb, known as *Der Shpoler Zeyde,* The Grandfather of Shpol. Cf. below, note to *Bibliography of Ḥasidic Texts, Lines 15ff.: the late prominent khosed....Yehude Leyb...who is known as The Grandfather (Der Zeyde).*

Line 37: fit as a fiddle

Ps. 73:4. Lit., "healthy and strong." To avoid repetition, the source of the phrase is identified only here in its first appearance in the text.

Lines 61f.: a common wonder-worker (balshem)

Solomon Maimon notes that a "*balshem* is one who occupies himself with the practical Kabbalah, that is, with the conjuration of spirits and the writing of amulets, in which the names of God and of many sorts of spirits are employed." See "On A Secret Society," in *Essential Papers on Hasidism,* 23.

Line 99: The Rov, Our Teacher, Rabbi Yehude Leyb

The rabbi of whom this story is told is identified in the text as *MohaRY"L,* the same acronym used in the *Bibliography of Ḥasidic Texts* at the end of the book to refer to R. Aryeh Yehuda Leyb, The Grandfather of Shpol. See below, note to *Bibliography of Ḥasidic Texts, Lines 15ff.: the late prominent khosed...Yehude Leyb...known as The Grandfather (Der Zeyde).* But it is unlikely that it refers here to The Grandfather of Shpol. Though Aryeh Leyb was old enough to have met the Besht, there is no reason to believe that he was antagonistic towards him. Also, R. Aryeh Leyb is referred to earlier in this letter, where he is identified as "The Elder (*Der Zeyde,* The Grandfather)," and it seems highly unlikely that Perl would refer to him again by a completely different title in the same letter. Who, then, is this *MohaRY"L?*

In Letters #16 and #109, we read of *Sefer ha-Vikkuaḥ,* a diatribe against Ḥasidism published in 1798 by Israel (Yisrael) Loebl, *Maggid* of Slutsk. See above, note to Letter #16, *Lines 95f.: the wicked Seyfer ha-Vikuakh,* and below, note to Letter #109, *Lines 42ff.: the books...like Seyfer ha-Vikuakh.* See also in *Introduction,* pp. xxiv, xxvi. Dubnow reports that the author's name does not appear on the title page of the first edition of *Sefer ha-Vikkuaḥ,* but that it does appear in the *Approbation,* where the rabbis of Vilna state: "In witness whereof we have signed below, so that this great man...Yisroel son of MohaRY"L (Leybl) may succeed...in publishing his *Sefer ha-Vikkuaḥ (Book of Controversy).*" See Dubnow, 420. Yisrael Leyb's father was Yehuda Leyb (see Dubnow, 279), the acronym for which is Moha**RY"L** (= our teacher the *Rov,* **R**abbi **Y**ehuda **L**eyb). Since the son, Yisrael Loebl, was active at the end of the eighteenth century, his father could have been a contemporary of the Besht. And since the son was a fiery *mitnagged,* Perl may have cast the father in the role of antagonist of the Besht half a century earlier.

Alternatively, *MohaRY"L* here may be **R**. Aryeh **Y**ehuda **L**eyb, scribe of Brody and editor of *Zemir Aritsim ve-Ḥarevot Tsurim,* published in 1772. See below, note to Letter #109, *Lines 42ff.: the books...some Talmudists and rabbis wrote against our faction, like...Zemir Aritsim.* The scribe of Brody was probably not a young man when he did his work of editing in 1772 at the behest of the Gaon of Vilna. Since the Besht died in 1760, the time frame fits.

Footnote 4: the back part of the Divine countenance...called Father

For a discussion of the *partsufim* (configurations of *sephirot* or Divine countenances), see Jacobs, esp. 104f.. The back part of a *partsuf* is its judgmental aspect, so the judgment (or guilt felt) for sin is reflected in the pulse. In a private communication, Pinchas Giller suggests that the source of the statement in *SB* 35:3 (Mintz, 253f.) was probably R. Shalom Buzaglo's commentary, *Kissei Melekh,* to *Tikkunei ha-Zohar* 106a-107b. See also Hayyim Vital, *Sha'ar Ruaḥ ha-Kodesh,* 14a-15a.

Notes to Letter #58

Line 39: left...in despair

Shab. 127b.

Notes to Letter #59

Line 10: small brains

Hebrew *moḥin ha-ketanim* (small brains) may be a play on the mystical concept, *moḥin dekatnut*, that imperfect spiritual state in which the soul is only partially immersed in the Divine glory because it is still actively involved in worldly existence. See Hayyim Vital, *Eits Ḥayyim, Sha'ar* 6.

Notes to Letter #60

Line 5: the Musef Kdushe

Part of the Additional Service immediately following the Morning Service.

Line 8: to ameliorate the dream

See Trachtenberg, *Jewish Magic*, 244-8 and 311, n. 30. The ritual for "ameliorating a dream" was practiced through the Middle Ages. See Ber. 55b.

Line 14: get all excited

Lit., "burst into flame." Calqued on Song 8:6.

Line 16: as it's written in the prayerbook

See, for example, Zeligman Baer, *Seder Avodat Yisrael* (Frankfurt-on-Main: Schocken, 1937), 578f..

Lines 23f.: nothing would be too wondrous...

Jer. 32:17.

Lines 24f.: I remained stupefied too – at his not telling me beforehand

The *rebe* doesn't make a move without first informing his personal secretary.

Line 33: tsapikhis with honey

Ex. 16:31. The word appears only once in the Bible. Whatever it means, the phrase "*tsapikhis* with honey" came to mean "something ambrosial."

Line 33: and I remained alone

Is. 49:21, Dan. 10:8. To avoid repetition, the source of the phrase is identified only here in its first appearance in the text.

Line 38: the glory of our strength

Lev. 26:19, Ez. 24:21.

Line 39: How long will you refuse to obey

Ex. 16:28.

Lines 41ff.: not just one has arisen against us...but rather in every single generation

"Vehi she'ameda" in narrative section of Passover Haggada.

Line 46: Poskim and Tosfes

Posekim are medieval codifiers of Jewish law. *Tosafot* are critical and explanatory glosses to the Babylonian Talmud, composed in France and Germany in the 12th-14th centuries.

Line 50: we have no business in mysteries

Calqued on Ḥag. 13a. Cf. note to *Letter #17, Line 13: I got no business in mysteries* and note to *Letter #78, Lines 4f.: you have no interest in esoteric matters.*

Line 64: Is the present generation better?

Yev. 39b.

Lines 64ff,: the saying of the Medresh...outside the Land

Tanḥuma Bo, #5, for example, states that the *Shekhina* does not reside outside the Land of Israel. I am unable to locate a source expressly stating that the *Shekhina* did not rest on *Moses* because he was outside the Land.

Lines 70f.: as you can see in...folio 36, column 4

Mintz, 261.

Line 81: ordered that he enter a carcass

SB 36:4 (Mintz, 261).

Lines 81ff.: he saw that the printers of the holy community of Barditchev...left this out

The last story in the Kopust edition of *SB*, omitted in the Berditchev edition.

Line 96: took some grammar book and laid it on those holy books

By Jewish custom, a holy book should lie on top of a *bukh*, not vice versa.

Line 97: Come see

A Hebrew version of an Aramaic phrase, *"ta shema,* come [and] hear!," used in the Talmud to introduce a prooftext or raise a difficulty. Its use here suggests that the *rebe*'s dream is the proof of everything alleged in the letter.

Notes to Letter #62

Line 6: novel interpretations

The rabbis "discover" *ḥiddushim,* novel interpretations of a text.

Line 6: does great things beyond number

Job 9:10.

Line 7: signs and wonders

Deut. 4:34 *et al.*

Line 21: secluded in his meditation room

This and further references (Cf. Letters #78, 80, 88, 123 and *Epilogue*) to the *rebe*'s room of meditative seclusion reflect the emphasis of R. Naḥman, whose works are frequently quoted in Ovadye's footnotes. "The most essential religious practice of Bratslav, and that which Naḥman constantly taught was to be placed above all else in his disciples' hierarchy of values, was this act of *hitbodedut,* lone daily conversation with God." Green, *Tormented Master,* 145.

Lines 22f.: Even I don't have permission...if he don't call for me

See Esther 4:10f.. The parallel with Esther and Ahasuerus is hardly accidental.

Line 54: above and beyond

From a version of the *Kaddish* prayer used during The Days of Awe, which states that God's praise is "above and beyond all blessings and praises" that we can utter. Here the phrase is used to describe the words of the *rebe*. Cf. below, note to Letter #80, *Line 14: above and beyond.*

Line 58: When the jester interrupts the discourse of the bridegroom

"Between meals the groom begins his discourse. At this point the *badkhn* (jester) interrupts and begins a mock discourse...he calls out: 'Wedding gifts!'... The *badkhn* announces the names of the donors and the kind of gift, until the ceremony is over." A. B. Gotlober, quoted by E. Lifschutz, "Merrymakers and

Jesters Among Jews", YIVO Annual of Jewish Social Science, 7 (1952): 43-83, esp. 64 and 46f. See also *Siḥot HaRa"N*, #86.

Line 59: the fragments of the Tablets [*broken by Moses*]

I.e., useless. The expression comes to mean "ignorance." See below, note to *Footnote 2: Moses became wealthy....*

Line 61: badekns

The veiling of the bride prior to the wedding ceremony.

Lines 61f.: the wheels...(the letters of "hops")

The word-play involves the similarity between *ha-ophanim* (האופנים, the wheels) in Ez. 1:12 and Yiddish *hopn*. In his translation of *Siḥot HaRa"N*, #86, Kaplan states that "an *ophan* is an angel. Baked goods are *Ophin*. The similar spelling indicates a similarity in essence. The spirit of the groom. Wherever the groom goes, baked goods are lifted up." He further notes that in kabbalistic imagery, "spirit *(ruaḥ)* is the counterpart of *Ze'ir Anpin*, the groom. The *Ophanim* are angels of *Asiyah*, the lowest supernal world, which also corresponds to the feminine element. Throwing baked goods thus unites male and female." Kaplan, *Wisdom*, 198. In Yiddish, *hopn* (האפען) are hops, and it is the custom to this day among some *ḥasidim* to throw a mixture of rice and hops at the wedding. Kaplan's explanation of the mystical symbolism in the custom works perfectly well if we translate *hopn* as hops rather than "baked goods."

Lines 61f.: The wheels went wherever the spirit impelled them to go

A conflation of Ez. 1:12 and 10:16. See *Siḥot HaRa"N*, #86.

Line 63: a bridegroom is like spirit (ruaḥ)

There is a play here on the word *ruaḥ*. In Hebrew it means "wind" or "spirit" but in Yiddish, it means "ghost" or "devil."

Lines 64f.: I shall go down with you to Egypt and I shall bring you up

Gen. 46:4. *Siḥot HaRa"N*, #86.

Lines 69f.: it won't be absent from...posterity forever.

A conflation of Deut. 31:21 and Is. 59:21.

Line 74: Mendl Barer

I.e., Mendl of Bar. Perhaps modeled on Menaḥem Mendl of Bar.

Lines 74f.: the fake rebe of Dishpol

See *Excursus 2: Deciphering the Names.*

Footnote 2: Moses became wealthy...from a sapphire quarry

Ned. 38a, Ex. Rab. 46:2 *et al.* This footnote explains the *rebe*'s *toyre* to mean that the bridegroom's homiletical discourse is akin to the fashioning of the second set of Tablets by Moses. Since Moses became wealthy from the fragments of precious stone that fell when he hewed out those Tablets, it is appropriate that the bridegroom should similarly become wealthy when his discourse is interrupted, i.e., fragmented, by the wedding jester. But since "the fragments of the Tablets" are useless and a symbol of ignorance, the parody here is that the bridegroom is an ignoramus and is rewarded for his ignorance. See above, note to *Line 58: When the jester interrupts.*

Footnote 5: These three reasons...also in Likutey MohoRa"N, Book 3, folio 13

In a private conversation, Arthur Green confirms that there was never a Book 3 of *Likkutei MohaRa"N*. The reference, however, is not fictitious. These three reasons are mentioned in #86 of *Siḥot HaRa"N,* published for the first time (though only through #116) as an appendix to the 5575/6 Ostrog edition of *Sippurei Ma'asiyot,* where it is imprecisely identified as *Likkutei MohaRa"N.* It would appear that Perl had before him this edition of *Sippurei Ma'asiyot* with its appendix identified as *Likkutei MohaRa"N,* which Perl, who had before him also Books 1 and 2 of *Likkutei MohaRa"N* (in their original 5568 and 5571 editions, respectively), called Book 3. See Shmeruk and Werses, *Tales and Letters,* 15f., n. 2. See also Rubinstein, 77, n. 34, where he adds that the first mention of *Likkutei MohaRa"N, Book 3* appears in Lepin's pamphlet, *Alon Moreh,* 19.

Footnote 5: The whole world is sustained for the sake of my son Khanine

Ber. 17b. The text recounts the praise of the first-century *ḥasid* and wonder-worker, R. Ḥanina ben Dosa, known for his asceticism. But yhe Besht's interpretation of the passage (reported in *Ben Porat Yosef* 80b; ed. Warsaw 1883) highlights Ḥanina's *charisma.* This passage and its new interpretation became paradigmatic in Ḥasidism, underscoring "the claim...to be the successors of Ḥanina, the *ẓaddikim* who will sustain the world in this time." Arthur Green, "Typologies of Leadership and the Hasidic Ẓaddiq," in *Jewish Spirituality,* ed. Arthur Green (New York: Crossroad, 1987), 131f. and 155, nn. 15, 16 and 17.

Notes to Letter #63

Line 4: His lovely letter

Cf. above, note to Letter #3, *Line 29: I'm urging him.*

Line 4: sparkled before me

Cf. Ex. 25:37.

Lines 4f.: I rejoiced as over any treasure

Ps. 119:14.

Line 6: of His good health

See above, note to *Line 4: his lovely letter.* "His good health" refers to the recipient of the letter, i.e., Zelig Letitchiver.

Line 6: May G-d grant this and more

Cf. Ps. 120:3, Ruth 1:17 *et al.*

Lines 6f.: to hear of your well-being

"Your" is in the plural, i.e., formal, impersonal and respectful, form.

Line 9: May His Eminence

I.e., Zelig Letitchiver.

Line 13: a piece suitable for presentation

Ḥull. 100a.

Lines 27f.: they have given...an opportunity to distinguish himself

Ḥull. 7a.

Lines 31ff.: a remembrance for Him from me His friend who sends Him

See above, note to *Line 4: His lovely letter.*

Line 33: who sends Him regards always

SB 9:1 (Mintz, 65). To avoid repetition, the source of the phrase is identified only here in its first appearance in the text.

Lines 48f.: the matter has proceeded from the L-rd

Gen. 24:50. To avoid repetition, the source of the phrase is identified only here in its first appearance in the text.

Notes to Letter #64

Lines 21f.: the judge Mikhal

SB 26:3 (Mintz, 188).

Lines 29ff.: laid his head on the table and...lifted his head

Cf. *SB* 7:2 (Mintz, 52).

Lines 31ff.: Eyliohu...has a new and very lofty soul and I see a bright light upon him

The name Eyliohu (Elijah) is a symbol of the struggle between Ḥasidism and its opponents. Four persons bear the name. First is Elijah, Gaon of Vilna, the quintessential *mitnagged,* cited first in Letter #16 by Reb Zelig as "our major adversary." Second is the contractor's only son, mentioned for the first time here in Letter #64. He is courted by the *ḥasidim* because of his father's wealth and power in the community, and he is also a symbol of the younger generation, pulled in opposite directions by his teacher Mikhal Kahane -- himself a student of The Gaon -- and Ḥayyim Gavriel, the Dishpoler *rebe*'s man.

Third is Elijah the prophet, whose story appears in I Kings and who becomes in later Jewish legend the herald of the messiah. Both sides here claim him as their own (See, for example, Letter #77). To the *mitnaggedim,* he is the essence of traditional Jewish religiosity. To the *ḥasidim,* he is the prototypical *ḥasid,* cloaked in the mantle of prophecy. It is *his* soul to which the Dishpoler *rebe* refers when he says that "Eyliohu [the contractor's son]...has a new and very lofty soul...." According to Jewish legend, when Elijah comes he will resolve all disputed questions. If so, will he appear as a *ḥasid* or as a *mitnagged?* Finally, in the *Bibliography of Ḥasidic Texts,* Perl has given the name to "the proofreader, Eyliohu, grandson of the late prominent *khosed*...Rabbi Aryeh Leyb...who is called The Grandfather *(Der Zeyde).*" See below, notes to *Bibliography of Ḥasidic Texts, Line 15ff.: the late prominent khosed...R. Yehude Leyb...who is called The Grandfather (Der Zeyde).*

Line 56: the Prince of the Toyre

"The angel who can grant perfect knowledge of all fields of the Law, both in its exoteric and its esoteric aspects." Gershom Scholem, *Jewish Gnosticism, Merkabah Mysticism and Talmudic Tradition,* 12f.. See discussion there.

Notes to Letter #65

Footnote 2: Who has contentions? Who has trouble?

Prov. 23:29.

Notes to Letter #66

Lines 9f.: whoever didn't see...never in his life saw beauty

Calqued on Suk. 5:1 (re. *Beit ha-Sho'eiva*). Cf. Letter #45: *Whoever hasn't seen this celebration has never seen celebration.*

Notes to Letter #67

Line 4: I rejoiced like one who finds great spoil

Ps. 119:162.

Line 42: sang Lekho Dodi

The name of a well-known hymn welcoming the Sabbath, written by Solomon Alkabets in 1529 and used by Isaac Luria and his disciples. It has inspired countless melodies.

Lines 44f.: a small besom for the bathhouse

A small broom made of birch branches with the leaves still attached and used to flog the body to stimulate the circulation so as to sweat out the impurities.

Notes to Letter #68

Line 5: not lifted a finger

Lit., "hidden your hand in your pocket." Prov. 19:24.

Lines 5f.: Do you not know – have you not heard

Is. 40:28. To avoid repetition, the source of the phrase is identified only here in its first appearance in the text.

Lines 14f.: What right have you to tell of My laws?

Ps. 50:16. The verse alludes also to Ḥag. 15b and San. 106b. The first is a legend about R. Elisha ben Abuya, the quintessential heretic. When he asks a child to tell him the biblical verse corresponding to the boy's name, he replies, "What right have you to tell of My laws?" -- taken to be a condemnation of Elisha's heresy. The second is a reference to Doeg the Edomite, King Saul's courtier,who in I Sam. 22 kills the priests of the Lord for supporting David. The Rabbi's allusion to these contexts equates the *ḥasidim* with Elisha ben Abuya and with Doeg the Edomite, i.e., they too are heretics and villains.

Line 15: There is nothing new under the sun

Eccl. 1:9.

Line 16: swayed his heart

I Kings 11:4.

Line 18: which way to turn

II Sam. 14:19.

Line 20: at my righteous right hand

I.e., be my defender, Is. 41:10.

Line 22: sway his...heart

See above, note to *Line 16: swayed his heart.*

Line 28: are considered as chaff

Calqued on Job 41:21.

Line 38: judge me kindly

Avot 1:6, lit., "Judge everyone meritoriously," i.e., Give everyone the benefit of the doubt. Cf. below, note to Letter #76, *Lines 7f.: judged me generously.*

Line 41: whose value no fortune could equal

Cf. Job 28:17, 19.

Line 45: who can hide

Jer. 23:24.

Line 47: ruler's sceptre

Is. 14:5.

Lines 48f.: with a willing heart and soul

Ramban on Gen. 27. To avoid repetition, the source of the phrase is identified only here in its first appearance in the text.

Notes to Letter #69

Lines 29f.: that have brought...to this point

II Sam. 7:18 and I Chr. 17:16.

Line 16: within his power

Calqued on Gen. 31:29.

Notes to Letter #70

Lines 7f.: digging a well by the home of our rebe

R. Issachar Ber of Radoszyce, the "Holy Grandfather," used drinking water from the well in his yard for curing all kinds of ailments. Mahler, *The Jewish Enlightenment,* 265 and n. 140 thereto.

Line 41: "transaction permits"

A rabbinic institution designed to overcome the biblical prohibition against accepting interest, the transaction permit *(heter isko)* allows a lender to accept interest by regarding him as a partner of the borrower. That which the lender-partner now receives is not interest but a share of the profits.

Line 49: how can I bring myself

II Sam. 2:22.

Footnote 1: an ensign for the peoples

Cf. Is. 11:12 and 62:10. The reference here is probably to the "Holy Grandfather" of Radoszyce. See Mahler, *The Jewish Enlightenment,* 265.

Footnote 1: still water

In contrast to fresh ("living") water from rivers.

Footnote 1: stop up the mouths of those who speak heresy

Gen 26:15 reports that the Philistines stopped up the wells dug in the days of Abraham. Here it is the miracles performed with the magical water from the well that "stop up" the mouths of the skeptics. There is also an echo here of "those who speak wantonly" (Ps. 31:19), as it is used in the *Prologue*, "to strike dumb those who speak wantonly." See *Prologue*, p. 18, lines 215f..

Notes to Letter #71

Line 8: treasures of kings

Eccl. 2:8.

Line 43: ***E****sh* ***D****at* ***L****amo*

"Lightning flashing at them." Deut. 33:2.

Line 45: the youngest of the fellows

Ḥull. 12b.

Notes to Letter #72

Lines 4f.: I got your letter and saw one piece of evidence...where it says

SB 8:4 (Mintz, 65).

Line 8: children, life and sustenance

M.K. 28a ("Rava said: Life, children and sustenance depend not on merit but on *mazzal*.") "*Mazzal* is...destiny, luck, fate, and there are obvious astrological implications. R. Elimelech's interpretation is to take *mazzal* as referring to the 'upper worlds' which can only be influenced by the prayers of the Zaddik." Jacobs, *Hasidic Prayer*, 177, n. 10. The phrase became a conventional formula describing the benefits the *tsadek* provides for his *ḥasidim*.

Lines 13f.: like he found a great treasure

Ps. 119:162.

Line 18: the Merciful One desires the heart

Rashi's paraphrase of the text in San. 106b. Also in the Introduction to *Duties of the Heart* and in the Zohar (Ter. 162b and Tetsei 281b).

Line 39: shmire wheat

Grain protected against dampness since reaping to guard against the possibility of fermentation, which would render it unusable for Passover *matsa*. See below, note to Letter #142, *Line 9: when you bought by me the shmure*.

Footnote 1: The shopkeeper is absolved and the householder is liable

Alludes to the talmudic case of a householder who has instructed a shopkeeper to furnish the householder's workers with goods in the amount of wages he owes them. Subsequently, the shopkeeper claims that he has supplied the goods, but the workers deny having received them. The rabbis rule that both the shopkeeper and the workers must take an oath affirming their claim, following which the householder must pay both parties, i.e., *the householder is liable* (B.M. 3a, Sheb. 7:5 and 47b). *Noam Elimelekh's* application of the text casts the *tsadek* in the role of householder and God in the role of shopkeeper.

Notes to Letter #75

Lines 6ff.: he walked back and forth...in his customary manner

SB 4:2 (Mintz, 30).

Lines 7f.: Azamer Bi-Shvokhin

Composed by Isaac Luria, this hymn was an indispensable part of the Shabbat eve ritual for the kabbalists. It describes the joining in sacred marriage of the King and the Shekhina/Sabbath-Bride. For a full translation and discussion, see Scholem, *On The Kabbalah and Its Symbolism,* 139-45.

"Anyone who never heard the way he [R. Naḥman] sang *Azamer bi-Shevachin* on Friday night...never heard anything good in his life!" Kaplan, *Portrait,* 416f.

The episode in *SB* (see above, note to *Lines 6ff.: he walked...in his accustomed manner*) occurs in the morning and has the Besht singing *Asader li-Se'udata,* Luria's hymn for Shabbat morning. Perl used the episode from *SB* but switched the time to evening because he needed the line from the evening hymn, "At the wine in the cup" (see below, notes to *Lines 10f. didn't take his eyes off the vessel* and to *Line 11: "At the wine in the cup"*) to use in connection with the stolen goblet.

Line 8: the Great Kidesh

Maimonides suggests that as it is not biblical but rabbinic, its name is a euphemism in much the same sense as a blind person is called "greatly illumined." See Baer, 252. The Great *Kiddush* is normally recited at the Shabbat *midday* meal, Pes. 106a, but it is the custom among many *ḥasidim* also to recite it Friday night following the singing of *Azamer bi-Shevaḥin.*

Lines 10f.: didn't take his eyes off the vessel

It is the custom to look at the Shabbat candles while reciting the preliminary passage of the *Kiddush* (Gen. 1:31b-2:3) and at the wine goblet beginning with the actual blessing over the wine. Baer, 197. But here the *rebe* did not take his eyes off the vessel because he did not want it stolen by one of his *ḥasidim!*

Line 11: "At the wine in the cup"

From the hymn, *Azamer bi-Shevaḥin.* See above, note to *Lines 7f.: Azamer Bi-Shvokhin.*

Lines 13f.: the kaiser took...to conceal in his breastpocket

SB 2:1 (Mintz, 15).

Notes to Letter #76

Line 4: Your pleasant words

Lit., *his pleasant words.* See above, note to Letter #63, *Line 4: his lovely letter.*

Line 4: sparkled before me

Cf. Ex. 25:37.

Lines 6f.: you have revived me

Lit., "revived my soul." Calqued on Gen. 19:19.

Lines 7f.: judged me generously...judge you generously
Avot 1:6. Cf. above, note to Letter #68, *Line 38: judge me kindly.*

Lines 13f.: on the tablet of...heart
Jer. 17:1.

Line 19: great and small alike
Deut. 1:17, I Chron. 25:8, 26:13.

Line 19: listen to your voice
Song 8:13.

Lines 19f.: the L-rd has given...a learned tongue
Is. 50:4.

Line 22: not so I
Job 9:35.

Line 22: I, who dwell among a people of unclean lips
Is. 6:5.

Lines 22f.: a people that does not know the way of the L-rd
Deut. 28:33 or Ruth 2:11 and Jer. 5:4.

Lines 24f.: to recount his praises, to sanctify him and to adore him
Calqued on *Yotser* prayer in Morning Service, where it describes the angels who "praise...and adore and sanctify" God's Name. Cf. above, note to *Prologue, Line 203: tsadikim of the highest standing.*

Line 28f.: reaches the very sky
Ezra 9:6.

Line 38: spread an evil rumor about
Deut. 22:19.

Line 41: small and great
Gen. 19:11, I Sam. 5:9 *et al.*

Line 42: it is easy in ...view
II Kings 3:18.

Line 45: do not be surprised
Eccl. 5:7.

Lines 45ff.: if they had lashed...
Ket. 33b on Dan. 3.

Line 50: believe me
Lit., *may he believe me.* See above, note to Letter #3, *Line 29: I'm urging him.*

Lines 51f.: so as to remove there my filthy garments
Cf. Zech. 3:4. The filthy garments are the sins of the past.

Line 53: sin with my tongue
Ps. 39:2.

Lines 54f.: the Toroh of the L-rd was our delight
Ps. 1:2.

Lines 62f.: Whoever saves one Jew...
San. 4:5.

Footnote 1: and wait but a moment
Is. 26:20.

Footnote 7: The first fruit of your soil...in its mother's milk
Ex. 23:19.
Footnote 7: To know Your ways on earth
Ps. 67:3.
Footnote 7: Odom knew
Gen. 4:1.
Footnote 7: Know the G-d of your father and serve Him
I Chr. 28:9.
Footnote 7: Odom knew
Gen. 4:1.
Footnote 7: When a man seduces a virgin
Ex. 22:15.
Footnote 7: For if he had a claim as to her virginity
Ket. 1:1.
Footnote 7: In order to raise up His covenant
Deut. 8:18.
Footnote 7: I am alive because of you
Gen. 12:13.
Footnote 7: As the excrement burns
I Kings 14:10.
Footnote 7: the Divine essence could enter excrement too
In which case, the verse means, "I am alive in your excrement."
Footnote 7: Put your hand under my thigh
Gen. 24:3.
Footnote 7: my thigh, which is called 'yesod'
Zohar, II:61a and Tikkunei Zohar, *Introduction,* 17:1.
Footnote 7: Make for it four golden rings
Ex. 25:26.
Footnote 7: tranquillity for themselves
Lit., "respite for their souls." Calqued on Jer. 6:16.
Footnote 7: And on the company of youths together
Jer. 6:11.
Footnote 7: See, their ear is uncircumcised...became a reproach to them
Jer. 6:10.

Notes to Letter #77

Line 22: I was aghast
Lit., "fear and trembling seized me." Calqued on Ex. 15:14, Is. 33:14, Ps. 48:7.
Lines 24f.: believes...with perfect faith
Each of Maimonides' Thirteen Articles of Faith begins with the words, "I believe with perfect faith...." Since Ḥasidism is the antithesis of Maimonidean rationalism, there is irony in using these words to describe this young *ḥasid.*
Line 26: more splendidly
Gen. 49:3.

Line 27: Elijah bent over and put his face between his knees
I Kings 18:42.

Lines 29f.: Elijah stretched himself out over...the boy's life to him
I Kings 17:21.

Lines 33f.: The pitcher of meal...and the jar of oil would not be diminished
I Kings 17:14.

Lines 38ff.: very zealous...be known to...the people that the L-rd is G-d in Israel
I Kings 19:10 and 18:36f.

Lines 44f.: and he went to the wilderness and wanted to die
I Kings 19:4.

Line 52: an angel...a cake baked in ashes and a jar of water
I Kings 19:5f. Cf. *SB* 3:2 (Mintz, 22).

Lines 58f.: to eat twice of the foods the angel had brought...on the strength of the meal
Cf. I Kings 19:6-8.

Lines 64f.: The dogs will lick up Aḥav's blood, and they will devour Izevel
I Kings 21:19, 23.

Lines 68f.: The bed which Aḥaziohu is lying on he would not rise from
II Kings 1:4,6,16.

Line 72: Elijah struck the water with his mantle and it parted right and left
II Kings 2:14, but note that it was Elisha who struck the water with the mantle of Elijah. Eyliohu the contractor's son is confused.

Line 80: Does he know the ritual slaughterer of Linits
The author of the manuscript of *SB* was the son-in-law of R. Alexander, the ritual slaughterer of Linits, who had been the Balshemtov's scribe for eight years and was the source of fifteen of the tales in the manuscript. See Mintz, xv, 108, 185.

Line 85: Rabbi Elijah
See above, note to Letter #16, *Lines 92f.: our chief opponent Elijah...who excommunicated the whole group*

Line 99: spoke disparagingly
See above, note to Letter #8, *Line 26: speaks evil.*

Line 101: he was out of his mind
Lit., "a spirit of confusion had been poured into him." Cf. Is. 19:14.

Lines 107f.: the forced converts
The term *anusim* generally refers to Marranos, Jews who were forced to convert to Christianity or face expulsion from Spain and Portugal. It is used here ironically to refer to Jews who have been "forcibly converted" to Ḥasidism in order to maintain their livelihood.

Lines 111f.: the permit concerning the rabbinate
The *consenz* was one of a number of special taxes on Jews in the Kingdom of Poland. A permit fee was imposed on those engaged, e.g., in tenancy, innkeeping or the sale of liquor in the villages. See Mahler, *The Jewish Enlightenment,* 177ff.. The fact that the community had to obtain a permit for the rabbi reflects the degree to which the government manipulated religious life.

Notes to Letter #78

Lines 4f.: you have no interest in esoteric matters

Ḥag. 13a. Cf. above, notes to *Letter #17, Line 13: I got no business with mysteries* and *Letter #60, Line 50: we have no business in mysteries.*

Line 10: Make the heart of this people fat....

Is. 6:10.

Lines 14ff.: Therefore let everyone...Toyre that emanates from the story...

SB, Author's Preface, col. 2 (Mintz, 5).

Line 16: with insight

Be-ein ha-seikhel, lit., "with the mind's eye." The term is found in the poetry of Y. Alnaqua and Moses ibn Ezra and, subsequently, in the Maharal of Prague.

Line 23: I grieve for you

II Sam. 1:26.

Line 32: published in Kopust

Cf. Letter #16, lines 97f., and see above, note to Letter #16, *Lines 97f.: the holy book Shivkhey ha-Besht was published for the first time in Kopust...in Lithuania.*

Lines 33ff.: in these words: "The word of the L-rd was in the power...on earth."

Printer's (not, as per the rabbi of Kolne in this letter, Author's) Preface to *SB* (Mintz, 2 and n. 7 thereto, 306f.). Cf. Job 19:25 and Footnote 1 to *Prologue.*

Line 39: this will be utterly baffling in your coarse sight

Cf., "It is baffling to me," Rashi, Responsa, #355.

Lines 40ff.: the Ramban...was incredulous that the khsides...of our father Avrohom

In fact, Ramban observes that the piety of R. Pinḥas ben Ya'ir was *not* greater than that of Abraham. See Ramban on Gen. 24:32. In this context, חסידות *(ḥasidut/khsides)* conveys two meanings, i.e., "piety," as intended by Ramban, and "Ḥasidism," as intended by the rabbi of Kolne. To preserve both, the Hebrew/Yiddish is transliterated rather than translated.

Lines 40f.: He unloaded the camels

Gen. 24:32.

Line 47: the way of truth

Ramban uses the phrase in his Torah commentary to allude to the mystical interpretation. See above, note to *Approbation, Line 22: through drosh.*

Line 52: the paths of righteousness

Prov. 2:13.

Line 53: we grope about like blind men

Is. 59:10.

Lines 53f.: save you and your soul from hell

Calqued on Jer. 20:13 and Ps. 33:19. I see three ways of explaining the sudden *volte face* of the Rabbi of Kolne toward his friend, and the response of the judge in Letter #83. The first is that the Rabbi of Kolne has caved in to the realities of survival and has indeed cast his lot with the Zaliner and his *ḥasidim* so as to have their support in acquiring the rabbinic post. If so, then the entire novel must be read as a satire not only of *ḥasidim* but of *mitnaggedim* as well. And, in fact, the *mitnaggedim* did even-tually join forces with the *ḥasidim* in order to oppose the Haskala, which threatened both of them.

The second possibility is that both the Rabbi and the judge, aware of the highly tenuous nature of the situation and of the presence everywhere of spies who open letters, are "covering themselves" in case their letters fall into the wrong hands. They would have to keep up this pretense until the Rabbi receives the official permit for the rabbinic post.

Or we may read the letter tongue-in-cheek. The Rabbi teases his friend, writing *as if* he has become a *khosed* and the judge responds in kind. See below, note to Letter #83, *Line 13: I shall be your student.* There is a hint of this in Letter #68, when the Rabbi writes, "I am sending you...some reasons for Jewish customs, which the secretary of that *rebe* sent me in the name of his master. In his opinion this was a gift whose value no fortune could equal [i.e., a worthless gift] and I know that you will find it as favorable as do I [i.e., as unfavorable as do I]." The hidden message (the mystical interpretation?) in the *double entendre* is the very opposite of the plain one. Letters #113, #117, #118, #136 and #151 leave no doubt that the Rabbi's feelings and actions remain strongly opposed to Ḥasidism.

Footnote 1: The eyes of the L-rd belong to the tsadikim
Ps. 34:16.

Footnote 1: All your children shall be taught of the L-rd
Is. 54:13.

Footnote 1: opening Your hand
Ps. 145:16.

Footnote 5: Rabbi Pinḥos ben Yo'ir's ass...between tithed and untithed
Shek. 18b. Also in *Ein Yaakov* and in *Ma'aseh Book*, #55, p. 97.

Footnote 5: He pursued as far as Dan
Gen. 14:14.

Footnote 5: deployed against them by night
Gen. 14:15.

Footnote 5: He separated 'H' from 'LaYLoH' and...with this he pursued them
The sound of the letter *H* is the sound of breathing, the source of life. By removing this letter from the word *"LaYLoH"* (night) through contemplative prayer, Abraham was able to able to remove the vitality of the five kings, to prevent them from acting in concert and to bring them to judgment. In effect, he was able to leave them in the dark *(LaYiL)*. See Schatz-Uffenheimer, 137.

Notes to Letter #80

Line 13: secret
Temirim, the same word used in the title of Perl's book. It is such secrets as these that Ovadye wishes to reveal.

Line 14: above and beyond
Part of a version of the *Kaddish* prayer used during The Days of Awe. Cf. above, note to Letter #62, *Line 54: above and beyond.*

Line 33: who deals in pearls

See above, note to Letter #19, *Line 19: the renowned story of the pearls.* The Yiddish translation here reads, געהן נאך דער פערל האנדלרין, *geyen nokh der perl handlern,* "to go after the pearl (Perl?) dealer." See also below, note to Letter #103, *Lines 45ff.: a hundred...zlotys' worth of pearls...to give the tsadekes pearls.*

Notes to Letter #81

Lines 14f.: them who cry out and aren't answered

B.M. 75b.

Notes to Letter #83

Line 11: repute

Is. 56:5. In Hebrew, *yad vashem.*

Line 13: I shall be your student...

Cf. above, note to Letter #78, *Lines 56f.: save you and your soul from hell.*

Notes to Letter #84

Line 8: a lie don't fly

Lit., "a lie has no feet." Rashi on Prov. 12:19, based on Shab. 104a.

Lines 10f.: nothing remains unfulfilled of all he has spoken

II Kings 10:10.

Lines 11f.: the efforts...were in vain

Calqued on Is. 49:4, 65:23 and Job 39:16.

Lines 37f.: Zimri son of Salu, chieftain of a Simeonite patriarchal house

Num. 25:14.

Lines 38f.: If this contemptible character encounters you, drag him...

Suk. 52b and Kidd. 30b.

Line 41: prickling briers

Ez. 28:24.

Line 43: nesi beis av

A play on נשיא, *nesi.* In Num. 25:14 it is a noun -- "*chieftain* (i.e., one who is raised up) of a...patriarchal house." Here it is read as a verb -- "שא (incorrectly written as נושא in Zelig's letter), *carry* it (i.e., raise it up) to the father's house."

Lines 48f.: According to the Toyre that they will teach you...

Deut. 17:11.

Lines 55ff.: And to the sons of Kehas he did not give any...carry by shoulder

Num. 7:9.

Footnote 1: who opens the eyes of the blind

One of the daily Morning Benedictions.

Footnote 1: You bring life to them all

Neh. 9:6.

Notes to Letter #85

Lines 11ff.: came out to greet him...words of toyre
SB 4:2 (Mintz, 31), where the rabbi is the Besht.

Notes to Letter #86

Lines 12f.: a miser who would die for less than a perute's worth
Er. 62a, Yev. 47b.

Notes to Letter #88

Lines 15f.: note with the names...for profuse bleeding and that she shouldn't abort
See above, note to Letter #13, *Line 36: a form for written petitions.* The request or need expressed in such notes might concern "profuse bleeding" or "that she shouldn't abort," as it does here, or it might be about some other illness, a need for a livelihood, a desire for children, a search for a suitable bridegroom or anything else for which the individual sought intercession.

Footnote 1: wine that reddens
Prov. 23:31.

Footnote 1: The wine enters – that which is hidden, exits.
Eruv. 65a. The efficacy of the treatment is based on arithmetic. "יין (***yayin***)" means "wine" and "סוד (**sod**)" means "secret/that which is hidden." The sum of the numerical values of the letters of each word is 70 (See above, note to *Approbation, Line 59: and year*). Hence, the words are "equivalent" and may be exchanged for one another -- "the *wine* enters -- *that which is hidden*, exits."

Notes to Letter #90

Line 6: a source
Gittin 65a.

Line 40: sustain me
Gen. 19:19.

Notes to Letter #94

Line 14: Hirtsele, son of our holy rebe
See *Excursus 2: Deciphering the Names.*

Footnote 1: The wine enters; that which is hidden, exits
See above, note to Letter #88, *Footnote 1: the wine enters – that which is hidden, exits.*

Notes to Letter #95

Line 28: I done their family...a very big favor

Shlomo Umner is a relative of Freida Reb Isaac's. See Letter #89.

Notes to Letter #96

Lines 40f.: some devotional practices

Manuals of devotion, which made their appearance even before the rise of Ḥasidism, were a popular means of introducing kabbalistic ideas and mystical customs to a wide population. The major work on this genre is Ze'ev Gris' *Conduct Literature*, Jerusalem: Bialik Institute, 1989.

Line 66: Nakhal Hamotsa

See *Excursus 2: Deciphering the Names.*

Lines 66f.: the local rabbi whose name is Shlemiel ben Lemekh

"Shlemiel" means "bungler" or "clod." "Lemekh" means "good-for-nothing." The local rabbi's name is something like "Good-for-Nothing Clod."

Lines 70f.: involved in all the affairs of the community

Perhaps an allusion to the teaching of R. Yaakov Yosef that "one should not habituate oneself to constant diligence in Torah study, but should also become involved with other human beings." See *Toledot* on *Vayetsei.* This was one of many statements to which the *mitnaggedim* pointed in order to show that persistent Torah study had been devalued in Ḥasidism.

Lines 73ff.: Tsidon...Hamotsa...Akhziv

Three biblical towns Perl uses to disguise three towns in Galicia. See *Excursus 2: Deciphering the Names.*

Notes to Letter #98

Line 17: Yokltse of Kalashke

See above, note to Letter #16, *Line 50: you can bet...he's merely Yokltse.*

Line 18: Animal dealers...kept oxen...

"Merchants would ask R. Isaac of Warka to write a deed of partnership for them, and a trader in oxen from Hungary was even privileged to get from the *rebe* a list of all the market days on which it was worth his while to do business." Mahler, *The Jewish Enlightenment*, 274 and notes 197 and 198 thereto.

Line 19: some German merchant from Olmits

He may be only culturally or linguistically German. Olmits is in central Moravia, 62 km. northeast of Brno, in the Austro-Hungarian Empire but south of Germany proper. The "German" merchant was probably a *maskil*, as the *maskilim* were regularly referred to by Yiddish-speaking Jews as *Daytshn*, "Germans," because of their adoption of western language, culture and style. See also below, note to *Lexicon, Lines 9f.: even to our kinfolk...in Ashkenaz.*

Lines 30f.: I am a partner in this transaction (that is, an inside partner)

The *rebe* announces his intention to be a real partner (as opposed to a silent partner) with the two animal dealers, so as to reassure them that all will be well if they follow his advice, for which they have paid a handsome thirty czerwone zlotys. Jewish law stipulates that in a limited partnership in which one partner furnishes all the capital and no services while the other partner provides services but no capital, in the absence of an express agreement to the contrary, any profits are to be divided one-third to the "capitalist" and two-thirds to the provider of "services," and any losses are to be shared equally between them, though the *Shulḥan Arukh* states that the partner who provides services is liable for only one-third of any losses. Since the *rebe* has furnished none of the assets, only "services," he will be entitled to two-thirds of any profit. If his advice proves disastrous, as it ultimately does, it is doubtful that his *ḥasidim* would know of his legal liability or try to collect from him.

Line 76: the remedies this rebe has

Folk remedies for illness, childlessness and other needs were in use among *rebes* until recent times. E.g., the "pharmacy" of the "Holy Grandfather," Issachar Ber of Radoszyce, contained "remains of jars, the residue of oil from Ḥanukka lamps, the leftover wine from the *Kiddush* and *Havdala* and of the *afikoman* of the...Seder and of the four species of the *lulav*...and the drippings from the Havdala candles, the wax from the candles for Yom Kippur, and other such residues of objects used in performing a mitsva." Mahler, *The Jewish Enlightenment,* 265; Wertheim, *Laws and Customs,* 236; cf. above, note to Letter #27, *Line 10: to make for her a remedy.*

Line 102: broke pots

The breaking of clay vessels confirmed the signing of the engagement contract.

Notes to Letter #100

Lines 13ff.: ten copies of the holy book...to...the border...to Galicia

"When the government outlawed the publication of Ḥasidic...works, the *ḥasidim* established secret presses and printed false dates and places of publication. In spite of the decree of 1800 that forbade the importation of Hebrew and Yiddish books from abroad, the Jews smuggled books from Russia." Mahler, *The Jewish Enlightenment,* 21.

Notes to Letter #101

Line 22: slapped him around

Lit., "gave him some gifts of the hand."

Lines 61f.: privileges with regards to their houses

Everything on the estate belongs to the landlord. Privileges regarding the houses, therefore, might involve some sort of equity.

Notes to Letter #102

Line 69: this coming Teyves

A Hebrew month, corresponding to December-January.

Notes to Letter #103

Lines 45ff.: a hundred...zlotys' worth of pearls...to give the tsadekes pearls

See notes to Letter #19, *Line 19: the...story of the pearls* and Letter #80, *Line 33: who deals in pearls.* This is the third and fourth mention of pearls (Perl's?).

Line 55: the land was stilled

Judges 5:31.

Notes to Letter #104

Lines 21f.: a letter that a local judge wrote to the prominent rebe...about a ritual slaughterer

See below, Letter #105. Ettinger and Shmeruk indicate that "there is no doubt that this letter is authentic and the fictitious names that appear in the letter itself may be deciphered through *gimatrie*. R. Nekhoray of Rektsits is R. Mordekhai of Kremenits, the judge Rikmoh son of Tan Yats of Greater Tsidon is the judge Moshe son of Yekhiel Mikhel of Tarnopol." The letter attests to the great influence of R. Mordekhai even across the border in Galicia. See S. Ettinger and C. Shmeruk, *The Community Ledger of Kremenits,* 34. See also *Excursus 2: Deciphering the Names.*

Lines 36f.: the image of G-d

Gen. 1:27. The rabbinic interpretation of this verse is that *all* human beings are created in the image of God. R. Naḥman states that "the faces of those who study this work [Maimonides' *Guide for the Perplexed,* a philosophical work] change for the worse, because they are bound to lose 'the image of God' which gives holiness to the face." Kaplan, *Portrait,* 344f.

Lines 37f.: The fear of you...shall be upon every creature on earth

Gen. 9:2.

Lines 84f.: like the monkey who performs acts that he sees a man do

R. Naḥman calls the *tsadikim* who oppose him "lying hypocrites ...who imitate the real *tsadek* like monkeys." *Likkutei MohaRa"N,* Book 2, #15.

Lines 93ff.: the instrument that arrests the thunder...How does the instrument work?

This circumlocution expresses more than the fact that early 19th-century Hebrew did not have a word for "lightning rod." A lightning rod arrests lightning, not thunder, yet Meyer Yankev says, "the thunder or the lightning" and affirms his uncertainty by adding that he no longer remembers. That he does not understand becomes clear when he explains that "thunder strikes a place where there's a husk" and "iron is capable of driving away the husks." The discussion reflects the superstition, ignorance and contempt for science on the part of the Jewish masses and of Meyer Yankev, the ḥasidic envoy.

The discussion alludes to a statement of R. Naḥman, related by R. Nathan:

"The *Rebe* once spoke about scientific advances and progress in secular knowledge. 'Anyone who discovers something new never comes to a good end.... There is the famous case of the man who discovered a way of avoiding the dangers of lightning. In the end he died in a storm....'" The editor informs us that "a Russian inventor, Georg Wilhelm Richmann, was a pioneer in experiments with lightning in the early 18th century. While setting up an experiment, a storm struck and he was killed." Kaplan, *Portrait*, 93.

Lines 103f.: iron is capable of driving away the husks

"The power of iron to drive off...evil spirits and supernatural beings...is almost universal....Throughout Europe iron is one of the most potent charms against witchcraft." S.v. "Iron" in Funk & Wagnalls *Standard Dictionary of Folklore, Mythology, and Legend*, ed. Maria Leach, Harper & Row, San Francisco, 1972. "Foods placed under a bed for safekeeping during the night are...contaminated by evil spirits...Even a covering of iron...is no security against nocturnal invasion...[A] Kabbalistic explanation was that the consonants of the Hebrew word for iron, ***barzel***, are the initials of Jacob's wives, **B**ilhah, **R**achel, **Z**ilpah, and **L**eah...[who] protect the water against the spirits." Trachtenberg, *Jewish Magic*, 46, 160, 258 and 313, n. 14.

Line 128: where his mikve still is

In ḥasidic teaching, immersion in the *mikve* is an important form of worship in its own right and not only as preparation and purification for worship. "They said of the Besht 'that he merited all the illuminations and rungs that he had by virtue of the *mikva'ot* and immersions that he always had, and regular *mikva'ot* are better than fasting....'" Wertheim, *Laws and Customs*, 66.

Line 138: one of the icicles

The Yiddish translation reads, "one of the icicles hanging..."

Lines 143f.: a lady Tomorl, wife of Reb Berki of Warsaw

On "the wealthy lady Temerl of Warsaw," see Mahler, *The Jewish Enlightenment*, 272 and n. 180 thereto.

Lines 147f.: Don't it say explicitly in the Zohar, "Tomor is male and female"?

"The palm tree *(tamar)* is male and female, for one is not effective without the other." Zohar II:37b (not in the Soncino English translation), where the reference is not to the biblical Tamar, but to *tamar*, the palm tree, used symbolically, as in the proof text Song 3:6. The speaker quoted by Meyer Yankev knew the quote from the Zohar but thought it referred to the Tamar of Genesis, and therefore (mis)used it as an explanation.

Notes to Letter #105

Line 3: Rabbi Nekhoray in Rektsits

See above, note to Letter #104, *Lines 21f.: a letter that a local judge wrote...about a ritual slaughterer.* See also *Excursus 2: Deciphering the Names.*

Lines 9f.: The Delight...The Joy...The Glory of our Generation

The first two honorific titles are calqued on Ez. 24:21 and 25.

Line 11: The Holy Seed
Is. 6:13.

Line 11: through whom Israel is glorified and on whom she relies
Calqued on Judg. 7:2 and Is. 50:10. In the biblical texts, Israel relies on God; here, God has been replaced by the *tsadek*, R. Nekhoray.

Line 12: The Lamp of Israel, The Right-hand Pillar, The Strong Hammer
See above, note to *Acknowledgments, Lines 40f.: The Lamp...The Strong Hammer.*

Lines 16f.: another ritual slaughterer for our community here
See Chone Shmeruk, "The Social Significance of the Ḥasidic Sheḥita," *Tsion* 20 (1955-56): 47-72.

Line 21: presented his knife to him for inspection
Ḥull. 18a and Rashi thereon. "Levinsohn related that whenever the *rebe* arrived in a town, he would summon the *shoḥet* to present his knife for inspection. If the latter did not appear, his *sheḥita* would be declared invalid." Mahler, *The Jewish Enlightenment,* 25.

Line 22: skilled in his work
Prov. 22:29.

Lines 22f.: both in slaughtering as well as in examining
The ritual slaughterer must be skilled in the ritually correct way of slaughtering the animal and adept at examining its lungs for defects. Improper slaughtering renders the animal unkosher, as does a defect on the lungs.

Line 26: whose authority is diminished
Ket. 79a, Kidd. 20b *et al.*

Lines 28f.: his prior presumption of ownership
Heb., *ḥazaka.* Jewish law recognizes three kinds of *ḥazaka*, i.e., physical occupation or possession, right or privilege based on possession or occupancy, and presumption of fact.

Lines 34f.: a sage is superior to a prophet
B.B. 12a. R. Mendl of Kock, a rationalist of the *ḥasidim* of Przysucha in Poland, interpreted this talmudic aphorism to mean that intelligence *is* prophecy. Mahler, *The Jewish Enlightenment,* 283 and n. 266 thereto.

Line 38: to forgo the honor due him
Kidd. 32a.

Line 42: a doormat trampled
Eruv. 98a. Cf. *Ketonet Passim* 4a, where Yaakov Yosef says that the leader should *not* become as something to be trampled upon (Dresner, 163).

Line 48: Rabbi Tan Yats Halevi
See *Excursus 2: Deciphering the Names.*

Notes to Letter #106

Lines 40f.: in the most secret places
Beitsa 9a, Ber. 10a *et al.*

Lines 67f.: Then I was pleased mine son-in-law couldn't read German...better if he could've
Cf. Letters #2, #4 and #101. An important change in Reb Zaynvl's thinking.

Even *he* now sees that there could be an advantage in the study of foreign languages (a prominent aspect of the program of Haskala) -- if only to serve as a defense *against* the forces of Enlightenment.

Notes to Letter #107

Lines 14f.: light has...shone on them

Is. 9:1.

Line 21: the rung of faith in khakhomim

The centrality of faith in the *tsadek (emunas khakhomim)* who elevates one's prayers on high as well as providing the channel whereby blessings flow from on high, is already present in the teachings of the Balshemtov and is one of the core teachings of virtually all varieties of Ḥasidism.

Line 41: out in the open

Lev. 14:7, Num. 19:16, Jer. 9:21, Ez. 16:5 *et al.*

Footnote 1: Fatten the heart

Is.6:10.

Notes to Letter #108

Lines 16f.: in...Rektsits the misnagdim took a fat man and made him a "rebe" as a joke

"The reference here is to R. Mordekhai [of Kremenits], since *RS* was written and also submitted to the Austrian censor before 5577 [1817, the year of R. Mordekhai's death]." Ettinger and Shmeruk, *The Community Ledger of Kremenitz,* 34-5 and n. 135 there. See also above, note to Letter #104, *Lines 21f.: a letter that a local judge wrote...about a ritual slaughterer,* and note to Letter #105, *Line 3: Rabbi Nekhoray in Rektsits.*

Lines 26f.: the mockery

Eruv. 68b.

Lines 32f.: I stirred up

Ez. 31:16 and Hag. 2:7.

Notes to Letter #109

Line 14: their books

I.e., non-Jewish books in the vernacular. He reads secular books such as travelogues and atlases but not scholarly Jewish books that may corrode his faith.

Lines 27f.: On the Nature of the Ḥasidic Sect

At last we have the name of the *bukh, Über das Wesen der Sekte Chassidim*, which turns out to be none other than the non-fiction anti-ḥasidic polemic that Joseph Perl first tried to publish in 1816 but was regarded by the Austrian censors as too incendiary! Unable to publish his non-fiction *bukh,* Perl made it the focus of the plot in *RS* as though it *had* been published. The *bukh* was finally published by the Israel Academy of Sciences and Humanities in 1977 in its original German in a critical edition with a Hebrew Introduction and Annotations by Avraham Rubinstein. Its Hebrew title is על מהות כת החסידים. See *Introduction,* pp. xxvii-xxix.

Lines 42ff.: the books...some Talmudists and rabbis wrote against our faction...and such

Sefer ha-Vikkuaḥ, by Israel Loebl, *Maggid* of Slutsk, was published in Warsaw in 1798. Almost the entire first edition was bought up by the *ḥasidim* and burned. *Zemir Aritsim ve-Ḥarevot Tsurim,* edited by R. Aryeh Yehuda Leyb, scribe of Brody, and published in 1772, includes the first bans and most of the objections against the new sect. *Kivrot ha-Ta'ava,* also by Israel Loebl, was published in Warsaw in 1797 and is no longer extant. The three remaining works are mentioned together in Loebl's German treatise. See Wilensky, *Ḥasidim and Mitnaggedim,* 2:253, 330. *Noda bi-Yehuda,* by R. Yeḥezkel Landau, chief rabbi of Prague, was published in 5536/1776; *Zikhron Yosef,* by R. Yosef Shteynhart of Pirta, in Anspach in 5533/1773; *Merkevet Mishna,* by R. Shlomo of Ḥelm, chief rabbi of Lvov, in 5511/1751 in Frankfurt-an-der-Oder. These are the main anti-ḥasidic polemics of the *mitnaggedim.*

Footnote 2: I know that the fools...the "experts" in greater Tsidon

Piekaź found that in later editions of *Sippurei Ma'asiyot,* the word "chronicles" was corrected to "land maps." This correction could have been prompted by Perl's comment here. See *Tales and Letters,* 162.

Notes to Letter #111

Line 10: under the rug on the table

In Eastern Europe, rugs are still put on tables when the tables are not in use.

Notes to Letter #113

Lines 14f.: at the hour of eleven...the members of our community have left me

Cf. Dresner, 189, that the Besht would speak with those who needed his counsel until the eleventh hour.

Line 18: who has not withdrawn His kindness

Ruth 2:20.

Line 19: I am inundated with concerns

A conflation of "*ḥavilei teradot,* bunches of concerns" (calqued on "*ḥavilei zeradim,* bunches of green shoots (Shab. 18b)") and "*hikifuni,* encompassed me (Ps. 22:17)."

Line 19f.: that do not permit me to catch my breath

Calqued on Lev. 25:28.

Line 21: safe

I Kings 5:18. Lit., "without mishap."

Line 23: who has led me on this path

Gen. 24:27.

Lines 25f.: people in it who stand in the breach and erect a bulwark against
Ez. 22:30.

Notes to Letter #114

Lines 7ff.: They presented their words...postponed on any account.
SB 13:1 (Mintz, 95f.).
Line 12: Sign [it] as you see fit regarding our gevir
Cf. Esth. 8:8.
Line 14: Shvues
The summer harvest festival, which comes in late May or early June.
Lines 19f.: even those who always went for Rosheshone...here by our holy rebe
Ta'amei ha-Minhagim, part 4, p. 44 cites R. Naḥman's view that one must go to real *tsadikim* for Rosh Hashana,. i.e., make a pilgrimage to the *rebe*.
Lines 30f.: the rejoicing was greater than...the House of Water-drawing
Suk. 5:1. Cf. Letter #45: *Whoever hasn't seen this...has never seen celebration.*
Lines 37f.: The sons of G-d saw...whomever they chose
Gen. 6:2.
Footnote 1: When your eyes behold a king in his splendor
Is. 33:17.
Footnote 1: your eyes will see a distant land
Is. 33:17.

Notes to Letter #115

Line 16: Sukes
The autumn harvest festival, the ritual objects of which include *etrogim* (*esroygim*, citrons), *lulavim* (*lulovim*, branches of date palms) and *hoshanot* (*heshaynes*, willow branches).
Line 17: Peysekh
The spring harvest festival. The primary rite of Passover *(Pesaḥ)* is the ritual meal or *Seder*, during which various symbolic foods are eaten. These include *matsa* (unleavened bread), *maror* (bitter herbs), *karpas* (green vegetable such as parsley) and *ḥaroset* (a mixture of chopped apples, wine, raisins and cinnamon).
Line 18: Rosheshone
The Jewish New Year, announced by the sounding of a *shofar* (ram's horn).
Line 19: Shminatseres and Simkhes-Toyre
The concluding days of *Sukkot*, when the annual cycle of Torah reading is also concluded and begun anew. The event is marked by parading around the synagogue carrying the Torah scrolls.
Line 20: streamers
See Alexander Harkavy, *Yiddish English-Hebrew Dictionary* and O. M. Lipschitz, *New Yiddish-Russian Dictionary*, both of which indicate that one meaning of the word *ratsye* (ראַציע) is "a flying paper snake (a kind of toy)." Hence,

"streamers" which children waved aloft while parading around the synagogue with the Torah on *Simḥat Torah.*

Lines 20f.: even for Purim

A minor festival in early spring, based on The Book of Esther. When the story is read aloud, *gragers* (noisemakers) are used to drown out the name of the villain, Haman. *Homen-clappers* or hammers portray Haman's head and have a hinged piece which, when the device is swung back and forth, has the effect of hammering the villain's head. *Homentashn* are triangular pastries, traditionally filled with poppy seeds, which may represent Haman's pockets, his ears or his three-cornered hat. The hanging of Haman and his sons is described in Esth. 7:9f. and 9:7-10. *Even* for Purim because, as a minor festival, Purim is not ushered in with the lighting of candles. The fact that this man has an elaborate candelabrum *even* for Purim testifies to both his wealth and his foolishness.

Line 35: honor and glory

Ex. 28:2.

Footnote 1: as related in Letter #67

Page 123, lines 70-4 and footnote 9 there. Ovadye suggests that Zalmon Brezner could not have been exaggerating since he is the grandson of Eliezer Brezner, who reported seeing the lintel of a passageway raise itself so that the Besht's wagon could enter the passageway. Q.E.D.!

Notes to Letter #116

Lines 4f.: a letter came to our holy rebe...from The Holy Land

I.e., from the ḥasidic communes in Palestine. See above, notes to Letter #9, *Line 28: the Ertsisroel funds* and *Line 28: the Rabbi Meyer Balanes funds.*

Lines 5f.: they accepted him there as President over them

Honored members of the community were appointed to collect funds for their brethren in Palestine and given the title, 'President of Eretz Israel.' Jacob Barnai, *The Jews in Palestine in the Eighteenth Century,* 65.

Lines 14f.: the kolel fund-collectors

Ashkenazi settlers in Palestine from the same country or district received financial support from their country of origin. The term *kolel* may originally have referred to the organization in the country in which the funds were collected; later it came to be applied to the recipients of the funds. *Encyclopedia Judaica,* s.v. "Ḥalukkah" and "Kolel." See also Barnai, 53-73.

Lines 15f.: send them to The Holy Land through...Istanbul

See below, note to Letter #128, *Lines 30f.: institute this...people come to the fairs.*

Line 24: lionthalers

In Yiddish, *leben thaler.* The Dutch leeuwendaalder, or lion-dollar, circulated extensively in the Ottoman Empire at the time. Six thousand lionthalers was a huge sum, reflecting the greed of the local pashas and the foolishness of the *ḥasidim* who would pay such a sum for the privilege of cutting down a reed. I am grateful to Alan Stahl of The American Numismatic Society for the identification of *"leben thaler."*

Lines 29f.: our holy rebe is his spark

"Katnuso" means "the smallest," "the last," "the least," "the uncomprehending one" or "the worthless one." It has a mystical meaning as well, i.e., *katnus* (smallness) is the imperfect spiritual state of the soul when it cannot achieve *gadlus* (greatness). The "real *tsadek*" in footnote 1 to this Letter explains that he was named "Katnuso" because he was the last of *khsidim* and his spark is placed in a different *tsadek* in each subsequent generation, most recently in the Zaliner. But the name also conveys the satirical implication that the Zaliner is a man of diminutive physical and spiritual stature.

Lines 32f.: have a lot to rectify with this stem

See above, note to Letter #1, *Line 12: pipe.*

Line 35: Whoever didn't see this never in his life saw beauty...

Calqued on Suk. 5:1. Cf. Letter #45: *Whoever hasn't...has never seen celebration.*

Footnote 1: Since Rabbi Yose Katnuso died, khsidim ceased to exist

Sot. 9:15.

Footnote 1: because he was the last

See above, note to Letter #116, *Lines 28f.: our holy rebe is his spark..*

Footnote 1: The words from a khokhem's mouth are lovely

Eccl. 10:12.

Footnote 1: in the Gemoro there

Sot. 49b.

Footnote 1: Into what is too wondrous for you don't inquire

Hag. 13a, quoted at end of Ramban's Introduction to his commentary on Genesis. (Cf. Ecclesiasticus 3:21 and Ber. Rab. 8:2. Cf. also above, note to Letter #16, *Lines 21f.: Why must you ask about what's not permitted to you?*)

Notes to Letter #117

Line 15: and you will set your mind at ease

Lit., "and you will find rest for your soul." Jer. 6:16.

Notes to Letter #118

Line 4: Please do not be angry

Gen 44:18.

Line 10: sinners

Lit., "men of wickedness." Job 34:8.

Line 15: break off the...yoke...from you

Calqued on Gen. 27:40.

Line 17: I...dwell among them

Is. 6:5.

Line 17: poured out their wrath

Jer. 10:25, Ps. 79:6, Lam. 2:4.

Lines 18f.: even if a man hides in secret places

Jer. 23:24.

Line 27: who cleaves closer than a brother

Cf. Prov. 27:10. Employed by the Besht in a letter to Yaakov Yosef, *SB* 8:4. See Dresner, 51, for a good translation of the letter.

Notes to Letter #120

Lines 25f.: under solemn oath

Lit., "under oath and curse." Neh. 10:30.

Line 33: gnash their teeth

Cf. Ps. 35:16, 37:12, 112:10 *et al.*

Lines 34f.: the rabbi...is busy writing a responsum

A legal opinion in response to a question of Jewish law. Perl is poking fun at the *mitnaggedim,* whose rabbis labor at producing learned legal opinions more than at involving themselves in the lives of ordinary people.

Notes to Letter #121

Line 4: Up to now the L-rd has helped us

I Sam. 7:12.

Lines 16f.: no one's allowed to make a minyen...without...permission from the district

The Jewry Ordinance of 1776 prohibited private *minyanim* except for those where the Torah was not read. It was repealed, but in 1789 a tax for the benefit of the German-Jewish schools was levied on *minyanim* where the Torah was read. Jews tried to evade this tax by claiming that in these *minyanim* they prayed without a Torah scroll. Letter #121 prefigures an event in 1823: "The district chief of Jaslo...dispatched a police commissioner and a military detachment to Dukla. They raided the Hasidic congregation...arrested all the worshippers, and all the religious books and Torah scrolls...were transported in carts to Jaslo." See Mahler, *The Jewish Enlightenment,* 81-3.

Line 24: under guard

Lit., *with an escort.* By the Edict of Toleration of 1789, "a Jew who was apprehended...for not having a special permit to reside in the village would...be returned under guard to his place of birth." Mahler, *The Jewish Enlightenment,* 3.

Notes to Letter #122

Line 17: vodka

Lit., *aqua vitae.* From the 16th century onwards, *aqua vitae* refers to very strong vodka made out of wine and used medicinally. It is sometimes called *yayin saraf,* astringent wine. See above, note to Letter #1, *Line 46: vodka.*

Notes to Letter #123

Lines 18ff.: The pictures they put on this page...for Rosheshone

Nathan Neta Horowitz mentions "the famous engraving of the *rebe*'s secretary greeting a visitor, which Perl ordered in Berlin," possibly to adorn his German treatise which was not published in his lifetime. See Rubinstein, 18.

Line 25: his Reb Noson

R. Naḥman's personal secretary was Noson ben Naphtali Herz of Nemirov (Nathan Sternharz). The Zaliner *Rebe* has *his* Reb Noson -- Noson Bakilinik.

Line 46: he ordered Reb Noson to throw the bukh into the fire

It was not unusual for *ḥasidim* or *mitnaggedim* to burn each other's books, but this particular incident seems to be inspired in part by the accounts of *Sefer ha-Nisraf, The Burned Book* of R. Naḥman, which took place in the spring of 1808. He himself gave the order to burn this most esoteric of his writings up to that time because he blamed his sufferings on its existence. Two copies of the book were extant -- the original, presumably written by the author himself, and a copy made by his personal secretary, Rabbi Nathan. The order to burn the book was given to Reb Shimon, who carried it out: "He told him [Reb Shimon] about a book that he had in his house, which had brought about the deaths of his wife and his children. He had also risked his own life for this book, and now he did not know what to do. He saw that he would have to die there...but if the book were burned he would live." The story is reported by R. Nathan in *Ḥayyei MohaRa"N,* Part 1. See Chaim Kramer, *Through Fire and Water,* 148-50. See also Green, *Tormented Master,* 241f. and Joseph G. Weiss, *Studies in Breslov Ḥasidism* (Jeru-salem: Bialik Institute, 1974), 215-43.

Even though it is a *bukh* and not a book that is burned here, it was nonetheless responsible for the death of Reb Zelig, and its burning effects a *tikn* and serves to purify and to elevate him -- hence the parallel with *The Burned Book.*

Lines 48f.: He poured out his wrath on trees and stones...and likewise on paper

I.e., he may as well have railed against the wind. The quotation is from Lam. Rab. 4:14. *Likewise on paper* alludes to the *bukh* with its photograph.

Notes to Letter #124

Line 14: lock, stock and barrel

Eccl. 9:2. Literally, *everything without exception*

Lines 14ff.: I took a ducat in my hand...one czerwone zloty is a small sum

Therefore, one ducat equals one czerwone zloty equals eighteen zlotys. Cf. above, note to Letter #10, *Line 15: czerwone zlotys.*

Notes to Letter #125

Line 17: as our rebe wrote it

As "President of Eretz Israel" (see Letter #116 and note thereon to *Lines 5f.:*

they accepted him there as "President" over them), the Zaliner *rebe* would have had the task of appointing collectors of the contributions for The Land of Israel. The bearer of Letter #126, the man whom the *goye* claims fornicated with her in the woods and from whom she stole the letter as evidence (see Letter #33), was none other than "the great, wonderful and distinguished rabbinic sage, the G-d-fearing elder...Rabbi Aharon Kaliner...a man who...has turned away from all the affairs of this world and all of whose labors have only been to be busy with *mitsves* to the extent of his ability," appointed by the Zaliner to be the collector in the Pilshtin area and therefore carrying his credential with him. In Letter #22, Zaynvl reports that two men spent the night in the woods, one who collects funds in Pilshtin for *Ertsisroel* (Aharon Kaliner) and the other a grandson of Reb Yoyne Kaminker, in charge of of lighting candles for the soul of Rabbi Meyer Balanes. In Letter #151, Zaynvl informs us that the name of the latter is Moyshe, son of the preacher.

Shneur Zalman, leader of the *ḥasidim* in White Russia, was imprisoned in St. Petersburg in 1798 after being denounced by the *mitnaggedim* of Vilna for sending money to Turkey. See Wilensky, *Ḥasidim and Mitnaggedim,* 1:213f..

Lines 19f.: money and blood are the same

Meg. 14b, but with a different meaning. Lit., *damim has two meanings (money, blood).* Zaynvl complains that having to pay for the vodka he has received is like giving blood!

Lines 44f.: in desperate straits

Deut. 28:53, 55, 57; Jer. 19:9.

Notes to Letter #126

Lines 2f.: Copy of the letter...the goye stole from the man from Pilshtin in the woods

See Letter #33. See also note to Letter #125, *Line 17: as our rebe wrote it.*

Lines 4f.: happily rejoice to do the will of their Creator

From the blessing of the New Moon. Cf. above, note to *Prologue, Line 203: tsadikim of the highest standing.*

Line 6: Men of Truth

Ex. 18:21.

Line 6: Pursuers of Righteousness

Is. 51:1.

Lines 6f.: deeds are recorded in the book

Avot 2:1.

Line 9: all the blessings

Lit., "all the seals of the blessings" or "all who seal the blessings," after Ber. 9:5. On the mystical function of the seal of a blessing, see R. Shneur Zalman's *Torah Or,* 6:3. Perl's Yiddish translation has simply, "all the blessings."

Lines 14f.: one whom I love well

Song 1:7, 3:2-4.

Line 21: I hereby give an order

Dan. 3:29, 4:3; Ezra 4:19, 6:8, 6:11, 7:13 and cf. 7:21.

Notes to Letter #128

Lines 30f.: institute this in your community where...people come to the fairs

The money donated in Eastern Europe for the Jewish settlements in the Land of Israel was collected twice a year at the fairs in Lublin and Jaroslav, transferred to "the President of Eretz Israel" and subsequently to Palestine via The Istanbul Committee of Officials for Palestine in Istanbul or other centers. See Barnai, *The Jews in Palestine*, esp. 70f..

Line 36: we can make the air of Ertsisroel anywhere

"Just as all the nations exist only by virtue of the Jewish people, so the earth endures thanks only to the Land of Israel." "Ertsisroel is the essence of the world and all vitality stems from it (Mendl of Rymanow, *Menaḥem Tsiyyon*, 46f.)." See Mahler, *The Jewish Enlightenment*, 17 and 342, n. 60. Also see below, note to *Footnote 2: By means of hand-clapping.*

Footnote 1: Keser Shem Tov, part 2, folio 23, col. 2

The passage, Par. 388, reads: "In the name of the Besht...if a man comes into danger and needs a miracle, then he should give eighteen large coins for candles for the synagogue and...say aloud: 'I pledge those eighteen large coins for candles for the soul of Rabeyne Meyer Balanes. G-d of Meyer, answer me!...And thus may it be Your will, L-rd our G-d and G-d of our fathers, just as You heard the prayer of Your servant Meyer and performed miracles and wonders for him, so may You do for me and for all Israel Your people who are in need of hidden and revealed miracles. Amen. So may it be Your will.'"

Footnote 2: By means of hand-clapping...

Cf. Editor's note in Kaplan, *Portrait*, 29: "I heard that the *Rebe* said: 'We conquered Breslov with hand-clapping and dancing.' (...As soon as the *Rebe* entered Breslov he immediately started talking about clapping one's hands while praying and how this is the way to drive away the air of the lands of the exile and draw in the air of the Land of Israel....)." Cf. also *Likkutei MoHaRa"N* I:44. See also above, note to *Line 36: we can make the air of Ertsisroel anywhere*

Notes to Letter #130

Lines 39f.: according to civil law it's forbidden to take money out of the country

In Poland, the policy of "containing the borders" included the prohibition on the export of money, as the aristocracy believed that exporting currency impoverished the country. See Levine, *Antisemitism*, 100f..

Lines 41f.: to keep an oil light burning continually

Cf. Ex. 27:20, Lev. 24:2 and note to Letter #9, *Line 28: the...Meyer Balanes funds.*

Notes to Letter #131

Line 26: of the royal seed

II Kings 25:25, Jer. 41:1, Ez. 17:13 and Dan. 1:3.

Notes to Letter #133

Line 4: I almost peed in my pants

Lit., "my hands and feet started trembling under me."

Lines 20f.: how can the husk bear that the holiness should be uplifted and strengthened

In Lurianic kabbala, the husk represents the evil that imprisons the holy spark of Divine light and prevents it from being uplifted and reunited with its Divine source. The letter writer uses "the husk" to characterize "the fake *rebe*" of Dishpol. "The holiness," of course, refers to his own *rebe*, the Zaliner.

Line 34: the tsadikim decreed with the X

"The X" is a euphemism for the penalty of excommunication, *ḥerem*. "All the *tsadikim* decreed on penalty of excommunication not to set up a box...." The Hebrew too uses a euphemism, גזרו בחית, *gazeru be-ḥet* instead of גזרו בחרם, *gazeru be-ḥerem*, i.e., it uses only the letter *ḥet* of the word *ḥerem* to represent the entire word. The Yiddish translation too reads, *Alle tsadikim hobn goyzer geven mit der ḥes*. For this euphemism in Yiddish, see Yudel Mark's *"Die Shprakh Fun Der Komedye 'Die Genarte Velt',"* *Yiddishe Shprakh* 3, no.3:74, n. 26. I am grateful to Mordkhe Schaechter for the meaning of the Yiddish phrase, and to Marc Saperstein for the translation, "with the X," which conveys the feeling and meaning, as "X" is the first sound in "excommunication."

Line 39: alive and kicking

Lit., "lives and endures (חי וקים)." Calqued on Ber. 32a.

Notes to Letter #134

Line 21: decreed with the X

See above, note to Letter #133, *Line 34: the tsadikim decreed with the X.*

Notes to Letter #136

Line 26: and they all united

Lit., *made one group*. From the prayer, *Uvekhein tein paḥdekha* in the *Tefilla* of the Rosh Hashana liturgy. The phrase reads, "Let all Your creations revere You...and let them all become united to do Your will with a whole heart." The letter writer takes a phrase familiar to all his contemporaries in its liturgical context and uses it to refer now not to uniting to do God's will but rather uniting "against that liar [the Zaliner]," thereby introducing a note of absurdity.

Notes to Letter #137

Line 9: under guard

See above, note to Letter #121, *Line:24: under guard.*

Notes to Letter #139

Lines 11f.: this follower...must've come...just for the sake of the wine goblet

This would square with the fact that "the *Rebe* [R. Naḥman] once told someone he should make a special effort to use a beautiful and valuable goblet for *kiddush,* this being a *segulah* [remedy] for wealth." Kaplan, *Portrait,* 441.

Lines 13f.: troublemakers

Eccl. Rab. 3:12.

Footnote 1: Mides 55:114

The correct citation is 55:154.

Footnote 4: It is permissible...so that people should not go astray after it

Ber. 59a.

Notes to Letter #140

Footnote 2: nor a spade to dig with

Avot 4:7.

Notes to Letter #141

Footnote 2: Do not make of them a crown...nor a spade to dig with

Avot 4:7.

Footnote 2: Karno, who was a judge...used to live by drawing water

Ket. 105a.

Footnote 2: Each person shall give a ransom

Ex. 30:12.

Footnote 2: intercourse with itself

In Lurianic *kabbala, Arikh Anpin* is the only *partsuf* (configuration of *sephirot*) of *Adam Kadmon* which has no female counterpart. It participated in the process of creation by copulating with itself. Scholem, *Kabbalah,* 167. Cf. *Eits Ḥayyim, Sha'ar* 28, Chap. 2. The idea as used in the passage from *Noam Elimelekh* is that the *tsedaka* from below and the blessings from above are both channeled through the *tsadek,* who becomes the conduit for "intercourse back and forth." Ovadye quotes the passage to underscore the importance of not coming to the *tsadek* empty-handed.

Footnote 3: an impairment in his brain marrow

Lit., *in his brain drops.* Scholem quotes *Sefer Bahir* (Sect. 104) to the effect that "'the spinal marrow extends from the brain of man to the phallus, and that is where the semen originates....' The idea that the semen has its origin in the brain was widespread in the Middle Ages and taken from Galenus." *Origins of the Kabbalah,* 154. "R. Naḥman's view is based on an ancient medical outlook often cited in kabbalistic books claiming that the seminal drop has its source in the brain and, while descending, it spreads throughout the limbs. R. Naḥman hence concluded that the sexual sin, related to semen, is linked to the intellectual sin, whose source is also in the brain....This point is discussed at length in *Likkutei MohaRa"N* I:29." See Liebes, *Studies in Jewish Myth and Jewish Messianism,* 194, n. 53. So when one pays attention to the quarrels between *tsadikim,* it is a sign that one is intellectually and sexually sinful, i.e., impaired.

Notes to Letter #142

Line 9: when you bought by me the shmure

I.e., the special wheat for Passover. See above, note to Letter #72, *Line 39: shmire wheat.*

Line 38: by their laws

I.e., by civil law, not Jewish law. Cf. note to Letter #3, *Line 20: gentile justice.*

Line 43: wicked people

Job 34:8.

Notes to Letter #143

Lines 38f.: against the L-rd and against His meshiekh

I Sam. 12:3. In its biblical context, *mashiaḥ* means "anointed one," and the priest-prophet Samuel speaks these words referring to King Saul. But *meshiekh* ultimately came to mean "messiah," and so the use of this verse to refer to the *rebe* illustrates three of the roles that the *tsadek* fills, i.e., priest, prophet and messiah. Cf. Green, *Typologies,* 127-56.

Footnote 1: A person must go back and search for what he has lost

Cf. B.M. 2:11.

Footnote 1: overturned the living words of G-d

Eruv. 13b.

Footnote 1: He who has studied...is worse than all of them

Pes. 49b. The statement concludes a discussion of the vices of the unlearned who despise Torah and its teachers. "He who has studied and then abandoned [Torah, hates the students of Torah] more than all of them," i.e., he is the worst adversary. Ovadye applies this talmudic statement to the rabbi of Koven -- ironic in light of the fact that it is precisely the talmudists *(lomdim)* for whom the *ḥasidim* have the greatest contempt. He implies that the Torah referred to is *khsidishe Toyre,* so the quotation describes Perl himself, who "studied and then abandoned [Torah]," i.e., who was a *khosed* for a couple of years and then abandoned the movement and became its adversary.

Notes to Letter #144

Lines 24f.: a lie don't fly

See above, note to Letter #84, *Line 8: a lie don't fly.*

Lines 27f.: we knew beforehand it would be so

Reb Noson goes on to tell that "we sent one of our people to spend *Shabes* at the Dishpoler's" as a cover for his mission. In Letter #143, Reb Dovid Tsere's acknowledges that "apparently there was someone from our holy *rebe*'s household who revealed to them how they had hidden the vessel." In Letter #139, Yankl Pulnaer quotes the Dishpoler to the effect that "the reconciliation won't help the Zaliner...because it's already too late," and adds that "we don't know what he meant by this." But Ovadye notes that "they really didn't know the meaning but *I* know...several times I saw that he [the Dishpoler] received a letter from some adherent of the Zaliner who was always at the Zaliner's but really was secretly an adherent of the Dishpoler. The Dishpoler's spy was in the Zaliner's home but this was so secret that even the Dishpoler's secretary didn't know it. This spy always informed the Dishpoler by letter how the affairs of the Zaliner stood...." The idea that the *rebes* have spy networks was articulated by the lord of Kripen in his remark to Freida in Letter #106, "Even to *my* servants they must be giving money to inform them what I do. Everyone in my town...is a spy for them."

Notes to Letter #146

Line 6: they have a holiday for several days

Yiddish *khoge,* either Christmas or Easter, probably the former.

Notes to Letter #147

Line 4: Woe is us! Fallen is the crown of our head!

Lam. 5:16.

Lines 5f.: I'll write...a little about his passing away

SB 35:4 (Mintz, 257).

Lines 9f.: went to the cellar herself...wanted

SB 11:1 (Mintz, 81).

Lines 24f.: Afterwards he...went to the outhouse

SB 36:1 (Mintz, 257).

Line 30: like a bluish flame

SB 36:2 (Mintz, 257).

Footnote 2: the world is left as though defiled

In Jewish law, only those who come into proximity with a corpse are impure for a time. If "the world is...defiled," then the whole world mourns the *tsadek.*

Notes to Letter #149

Lines 5ff.: was bragging...praising it to the skies and...asked him

SB 33:3 (Mintz, 239).

Notes to Letter #150

Line 9: converted [to Christianity]

The historical allusion here is probably to Shneur Zalman's third son, Moshe, who converted to Christianity, though he returned to Judaism toward the end of his life. Heilman has a veiled reference to it (See *Beit Rebe,* 113f.):

> What happened with him afterwards...was a great sorrow to our rabbi and to our Faithful. By great effort they rescued him...and from then on his whereabouts were unknown. They sent...his family to The Holy Land....In recent years..he would wander from town to town...looking for a handout...and would spend the night in the *besmedresh.* He would put a stone under his head and bind his feet with rope. No one knew who he was or what he had done, except for a few people who knew that he was our rabbi's son and who said that he looked very much like our rabbi. He was usually in the vicinity of Kiev, Zhitomir...Tcherkas... or Tchernobil....When they saw that his time had come, they called the *khevre kdishe,* and before his death they asked him his name and his father's name so they would know what to inscribe on his gravestone. He answered, "Write 'Moshe' on the gravestone, and also...that you don't know his father's name." They asked him where the members of his family were so they could notify them. And he replied, "They will know on their own." And he died....

See also *The Universal Jewish Encyclopedia,* s.v. "Shneor Zalman Ben Baruch of Ladi." See also *Excursus 3: Perl's Yiddish Prologue,* p. 270 and n. 16 there. Embarrassed by this apostasy, the *ḥasidim* tried to keep it secret so as to protect the reputation of their *rebe,* but it was made to order for Perl.

Line 18: conspiracy of sinners

Rashi on Yev. 61a.

Lines 23f.: the troubles that have overtaken us

Cf. Deut. 31:17 and Ps. 116:3.

Footnote 1: All of the above you will find in Seyfer ha-Mides

The source of all the statements about the efficacy of clothing is Zev. 88b, where the claims are made with reference to the garments of the priest. Its use here reflects the fact that one of the roles in which the *tsadek* functions is that of priest. Cf. Green, *Typologies,* 127-56. See also above, note to Letter #143, *Lines 38f.: against the L-rd and against His meshiekh.*

Notes to Letter #151

Line 1: #151

Why are there 151 letters in *RS?* The speculation is unavoidable that Perl's choice of this number was not coincidental, because: (1) *gimatrie* is used in the novel (e.g., Letter #23 and #104, footnote 3); (2) the novel contains extensive references to the prophet Elijah (in Letters #43, #78 and especially #77); (3) Perl's own life was filled with his persecution *of* and *by ḥasidim.*

The Hebrew number that appears in the heading to Letter #151 is קנא,

which is also a word-root meaning "zealous, jealous, fanatical, obsessed, impassioned." I suspect that it alludes here to I Kings 19:10 (as do Eyliohu's diatribes reported in Letter #77). Elijah has fled to the wilderness away from the wrath of the wicked and idolatrous Queen Jezebel. God asks him, "Why are you here, Elijah?" He responds, "I have acted zealously for the Lord...for the Israelites have forsaken Your covenant, torn down Your altars, and put Your prophets to the sword. I alone am left, and they are out to take my life." The opening phrase -- "I have acted zealously" -- is קַנֹּא קִנֵּאתִי, a repetition of the letter combination that represents the number 151.

Since Letter #151 has the defeated and frightened *ḥasidim* fleeing to The Holy Land via Istanbul ("the wilderness"?) away from the wrath of the authorities, it is possible that Elijah here symbolizes the cowering *ḥasidim*. But such an interpretation casts them as martyrs and heroes and would be inconsistent with the rest of the work.

More likely Elijah symbolizes the author himself -- zealous for the Lord, outraged by the wholesale apostasy of the masses who have taken up with the idolatrous ways of Ḥasidism and rejected God's real prophets (Talmudists? *maskilim?*), leaving Perl to fight the good fight at great personal risk. This interpretation would suit Perl's purpose perfectly, i.e., the number of the novel's parting missive has him proclaiming, "I have acted zealously for the Lord."

Line 4: who did not fail in His lovingkindness

Ruth 2:20.

Line 5: the 18th day of Sivon

Cohen argues that this entire account is a parody of R. Naḥman's journey to The Land of Israel in 1798-99 ("Ḥasidism and The Land of Israel"). R. Naḥman set out on 18 Iyar (May 4, 1798) and finally arrived in Haifa on September 10, the eve of Rosh Hashana, after an extended stay in Istanbul, including the month of Sivan. Cf. below, note to *Lines 9f. : a vessel...from Galats to Istanbul.*

Line 9: The L-rd prepared for us

Cf. Gen. 27:20.

Lines 9f.: a vessel that was going from Galats to Istanbul

Literary models for this episode are a ḥasidic legend that tells of the Besht's attempted journey to The Holy Land and an account of R. Naḥman's actual journey there in 1798-99. In the first instance, on the way to Istanbul a great storm arose and almost sank the boat. The Besht reached Istanbul, then decided to return home. In the second account, R. Naḥman actually reached Haifa following a fierce storm at sea. See Dubnow, "The Beginnings: The Baal Shem Tov and the Center in Podolia," in *Essential Papers on Hasidism,* 39, 77.

On the significance of this account as a parody of R. Naḥman's journey, and also as an accurate reflection of the role of The Land of Israel in ḥasidic teaching and in Perl's own thought, see Tova Cohen's "Ḥasidism and The Land of Israel" and Joseph Dan's *The Ḥasidic Novella,* 145ff..

On R. Naḥman's journey, see also Green, *Tormented Master,* 63-93.

Perl leaves his fugitives in Istanbul -- possibly an allusion to the Sabbatian heresy of which the *ḥasidim* were frequently accused by their adversaries.

Lines 50f.: you'll see wonders
Rashi on San. 111a.
Lines 52f.: look forward...to redemption
Shab. 31a.
Line 91: half a man
Cf. footnote 1 to Letter #77.

Notes to *EPILOGUE*

Lines 10ff.: wearing Shabes clothes...in his hand
SB 17:2 (Mintz, 125).
Lines 10f.: an ordinary hat on his head
A western-style hat rather than a yarmulke or ḥasidic *strayml* (wide-brimmed hat edged with fur) or *spodik* (high fur hat).
Lines 50f.: the L-rd's people had fallen with none to help
Cf. Lam. 1:7.
Line 51: from on high He will pour out
Cf. Is. 32:15.
Line 52: mercy...to rescue
Ps. 109:21.
Lines 52f.: Israel would no longer be a widower
Jer. 51:5.
Lines 54f.: No more will anyone teach his neighbor...
Jer. 31:34.
Footnote 3: Sitre Akhre
Literally, "The Other Side," i.e., the realm of the demonic.

Notes to *LEXICON*

Lines 9f.: even to our kinfolk who live in Ashkenaz
In this context, Jews who live in the Germanic lands rather than in Poland or Russia. "Our kinfolk who live in Ashkenaz" would understand both Hebrew and Yiddish, but might not know several of the Slavic words or expressions that have become part of Eastern Yiddish. These Jews would include, of course, Perl's intended readership.
See also above, note to Letter #98, *Line 19: some German merchant from Olmits.*
Line 11f.: Reb Yisroel Reb Berish's...as you may see for yourself within this composition
Letter #123. Reb Yisroel can read German. *As you may see for yourself* -- lit., "in your view, in the sight of your eyes" -- is calqued on Is. 11:3 and Eccl. 6:9.

Lines 21f.: draw an enlightening moral
Prov. 1:3.

Line 22: and set...eyes and...heart
Perhaps a conflation of Is. 41:20 and Num. 15:39.

Lines 22f.: to understand and to become enlightened
"Ahava Rabba" in daily morning liturgy.

Lines 24f.: which will be with them...all the days of their lives
Deut. 17:19.

Notes to *BIBLIOGRAPHY OF ḤASIDIC TEXTS*

Line 11: disseminating knowledge, expounding our way
Cf. Is. 28:9. The first phrase, *yoreh de'ah* (Teaching Knowledge) was used by Jacob ben Asher (1270-1343) to designate the second section of his code of Jewish law, *Arba'a Turim*. The section deals with things forbidden and permitted.

Line 12: G-d's elect
II Sam. 21:6. Here implying the *tsadikim.*

Line 12: those who lead astray
Cf. Ps. 52:4 and 101:7. Here implying the *mitnaggedim* and *maskilim.*

Line 13: to uplift and to heal
Cf. Jer. 30:13 and 46:11.

Line 13: those who to wilderness away
Job 30:3. I suspect the reference is also to Elijah, who went to the wilderness and wanted to die, I Kings 19:4. If my supposition is correct in the note above to Letter #151, *Line 1: #151,* then "those who to wilderness away" are all those Jews who have been cowed by the power of the ḥasidic movement.

Line 14: cause His light to shine
Cf. Job 37:15.

Lines 15ff.: the late prominent khosed...Yehude Leyb...known as The Grandfather (Der Zeyde).
R. Aryeh Yehuda Leyb, who died in 1812. Cf. above, note to Letter #57, *Lines 32f.: The Elder (Der Zeyde, The Grandfather).* Making the grandson of this beloved *tsadek* the proofreader of the passages from the ḥasidic texts is Perl's parting touch of irony.

Line 30: Likutey MohoRa"N, Book 3
See above, note to Letter #62, *Footnote 5: These three reasons...also in Likutey MohoRa"N, Book 3, folio 13.*

Line 39: Mezhibush
There was no publishing house in Mezhibush until 5575. The 5540 edition of *Toldes Yankev Yoysef* was published not in Mezhibush but in Korets. The first Mezhibush edition of the *Toldes* was in 5576, and it is this edition that Perl had before him and is alluding to in his list. See Rubinstein, 76, n. 30.

Select Bibliography

On Ḥasidism, Kabbala and Related Topics

Ben-Amos, Dan and Mintz, Jerome R., trans. 1970. *In Praise of The Baal Shem Tov [Shivḥei ha-Besht],* by Dov Ber ben Samuel. Bloomington and London: Indiana University Press.

Ben-Yaakov, Y. I. 1880. *Bibliography* [Hebrew]. Vilna: Rom.

Carlbach, Eyliahu C., ed. 5750 [1989]. *The Complete Praises of the Balshemtov* [Hebrew]. Jerusalem: Naftali Memorial Institute

Cohen, Tova. "Ḥasidism and The Land of Israel" [Hebrew]. *Tarbiz* 48 (1979): 332-40.

Dan, Joseph. 1966. *The Ḥasidic Novella* [Hebrew]. Jerusalem: Bialik Institute.

______. 1975. *The Ḥasidic Story* [Hebrew]. Jerusalem: Keter.

______. 1983. *The Teachings of Hasidism.* New York: Behrman House.

Dov Ber ben Samuel. 1814. *Shivḥei ha-Besht (The Praises of the Besht)* [Hebrew]. Kopys, Lithuania: Israel Yafeh.

Dresner, Samuel H. 1974. *The Zaddik.* New York: Schocken.

Dubnow, S. M. 1930. *The History of Hasidism* [Hebrew]. Tel Aviv: Dvir.

Ettinger, S. and Shmeruk, Ch.. 5714 [1954]. "Toward a History of the Jewish Community of Kremenits," in A. S. Stein, ed., *The Community Ledger of Kremenits* [Hebrew]. Tel Aviv.

Fine, Lawrence, ed. and trans. 1984. *Safed Spirituality.* New York: Paulist Press.

Foxbrunner, Roman A. 1992. *ḤABAD: The Hasidism of R. Shneur Zalman of Lyady.* Tuscaloosa and London: University of Alabama Press.

Gaster, Moses, trans. 1934. *Ma'aseh Book.* Philadephia: Jewish Publication Society.

Green, Arthur. 1979. *Tormented Master: A Life of Rabbi Nahman of Bratslav.* Tuscaloosa, Alabama: University of Alabama Press.

______. 1987. "Typologies of Leadership and the Hasidic Ẓaddiq," in Arthur Green, ed., *Jewish Spirituality from the Sixteenth Century Revival to the Present,* 127-56. New York: Crossroad.

Greenbaum, Avraham, trans. 1983. *Advice (Likutey Etzot).* Jerusalem: Breslov Research Institute.

Gries, Zeev. 1989. *Sifrut ha-Hanhagot (Conduct Literature)* [Hebrew]. Jerusalem: Bialik Institute.

Heilman, Chayim Meir. 1902. *Beit Rebe* [Hebrew]. Berditchev: Ḥayyim Yaakov Sheftil.

Heilman, Samuel. 1992. *Defenders of the Faith.* New York: Schocken.

Horodetsky, S. 1927. *Ḥasidism and Ḥasidim* [Hebrew], 4 vols. Tel Aviv: Dvir.

Hundert, Gershon David, ed. 1991. *Essential Papers on Hasidism.* New York: New York University Press.

Jacobs, Louis. 1972. *Hasidic Prayer.* London: Routledge & Kegan Paul.

______. 1976. *Hasidic Thought.* New York: Behrman House.

______. 1987. "The Uplifting of Sparks in Later Jewish Mysticism," in Arthur Green, ed., *Jewish Spirituality from the Sixteenth Century Revival to the Present,* 99-126. New York: Crossroad.

Kaplan, Aryeh, trans. 1973. *Rabbi Nachman's Wisdom (Shevachay HaRan, Sichos HaRan).* Jerusalem: Breslov Research Institute.

______, trans. 1979. *The Bahir.* York Beach, Maine.

______, trans. 1983. *Rabbi Nachman's Stories.* Jerusalem: Breslov Research Institute.

______. 1985. *Until The Mashiach.* Jerusalem: Breslov Research Institute.

______, trans. 1987. *Tzaddik: A Portrait of Rabbi Nachman (Chayey Moharan, Shevachey Moharan, Sichot Moharan).* Jerusalem: Breslov Research Institute.

______, trans. 1990. *Sefer Yetzirah.* York Beach, Maine.

Kenig, Tsvi. 1969. *Nevei Tsaddikim* [Hebrew]. Benei Berak.

Kramer, Chaim. 1993. *Through Fire and Water: The Life of Reb Noson of Breslov.* Jerusalem: Breslov Research Institute.

Langer, Jiri. 1961. *Nine Gates.* London: James Clarke & Co.

Liebes, Yehuda. "Sabbath Meal Songs Instituted by The Holy AR"I" [Hebrew]. *Molad* 4 (1972): 23:540-55.

______. 1993. *Studies in Jewish Myth and Messianism.* Translated by Batya Stein. Albany: SUNY Press.

______. 1993. *Studies in the Zohar.* Translated by Arnold Schwartz, Stephanie Nakache and Penina Peli. Albany: SUNY Press.

Minkin, Jacob S. 1955. *The Romance of Hassidism.* 2d ed. [New York:] Thomas Yoseloff.

Mykoff, Moshe, trans. 1986. *The Aleph-Bet Book [Sefer Ha-Middot].* Jerusalem: Breslov Research Institute.

Piekaź, Mendel. 1972. *Ḥasidut Breslav* [Hebrew]. Jerusalem: Bialik Institute.

Rubinstein, Avraham, ed. 1991. *The Praises of The Ba'al Shem Tov,* by Dov Ber ben Samuel [Hebrew]. Jerusalem: Rubin Mass.

Saperstein, Marc, ed. 1992. *Essential Papers on Messianic Movements and Personalities in Jewish History.* New York: New York University Press.

Schatz-Uffenheimer, Rivka, ed. 1990. *Maggid Devarav le-Ya'akov of The Maggid Dov Baer of Mezhirech* [Hebrew]. Jerusalem: Magnes Press, Hebrew University.

Scholem, Gershom. 1928. *These are The Names* [Hebrew]. Jerusalem: Azriel.

______. 1965. *Jewish Gnosticism, Merkabah Mysticism and Talmudic Tradition.* New York: Jewish Theological Seminary of America.

______. 1965. *On The Kabbalah and Its Symbolism.* New York: Schocken.

______. 1971. *The Messianic Idea in Judaism.* New York: Schocken.

______. 1974. *Kabbalah.* New York: Quadrangle/The New York Times Book Company.

______. 1974. *Major Trends in Jewish Mysticism.* New York: Schocken.

______. 1987. *Origins of the Kabbalah.* Princeton: Jewish Publication Society.

Shmeruk, Chone. "The Social Significance of the Hassidic Shekhita" [Hebrew]. *Tsion* 20 (5715/1955): 47-72.

Spector, Sheila A.. 1984. *Jewish Mysticism: An Annotated Bibliography on the Kabbalah in English.* New York & London: Garland.

Sternharz, Nathan [Nathan ben Naphtali Herz]. 1968. *Alim li-Terufa* [Hebrew]. 4th ed. Jerusalem: Breslov Research Institute.

Tishby, Isaiah. 1989. *The Wisdom of the Zohar.* Translated by David Goldstein, 3 vols. Oxford: Oxford University Press (for the Littman Library).

______. 1993. *Studies in Kabbalah and Its Branches* [Hebrew], 2 vols. Jerusalem: Magnes Press, Hebrew University.

Trachtenberg, Joshua. 1939. *Jewish Magic and Superstition.* New York: Behrman House.

Vital, Hayyim ben Joseph. 5748 [1988]. *"Sha'ar ha-Kavvanot"* [Hebrew], 2 vols. In *Kitvei Rabbeinu ha-AR"I.* Jerusalem: Yeshivat Kol Yehuda Press.

______. 5748 [1988]. *"Sha'ar Ruaḥ ha-Kodesh"* [Hebrew]. In *Kitvei Rabbeinu ha-AR"I.* Jerusalem: Yeshivat Kol Yehuda Press.

Weiss, Joseph G. 1974. *Studies in Breslov Ḥasidism* [Hebrew]. Jerusalem: Bialik Institute.

______. 1985. *Studies in Eastern European Jewish Mysticism.* Oxford: Oxford University Press.

Wertheim, Aharon. 1960. *Laws and Customs in Ḥasidism* [Hebrew]. Jerusalem: Mossad Ha-Rav Kook.

______. 1992. *Law and Custom in Hasidism*. Translated by Shmuel Himelstein. Hoboken, New Jersey: KTAV.

Wilensky, M. 1970. *Ḥasidim and Mitnaggedim* [Hebrew]. 2 vols. Jerusalem: Bialik Institute.

Zeitlin, Hillel. 1965. *In The Orchard of Ḥasidism and Kabbalah* [Hebrew]. Tel Aviv: Yavneh.

On Haskala, Joseph Perl and *Revealer of Secrets*

Alter, Robert. 1994. *Hebrew & Modernity.* Bloomington and Indianapolis: Indiana University Press.

Davidson, Israel. 1907. *Parody in Jewish Literature.* New York: Columbia University Press.

Dubnow, S.M. 1931. "The First Struggle of the Enlightenment Against Ḥasidism" [Yiddish]. *YIVO-Bleter* 1: 4-8. Vilna: YIVO.

Friedlander, Yehuda. 1984. *Hebrew Satire in Europe in the Eighteenth and Nineteenth Centuries* [Hebrew], 3 vols. Ramat-Gan: Bar-Ilan University.

Gordon, Nathan. 1904. "Joseph Perl's Megalleh Temirin," in *Hebrew Union College Annual,* 235-42. Cincinnati: Hebrew Union College.

Halkin, Shimon. 1984. *Trends and Forms in Modern Hebrew Literature* [Hebrew]. Jerusalem: Bialik Institute.

Kalmanovitch, Zelig. 1937. "Joseph Perl's Yiddish Writings: A Literary and Linguistic Analysis" [Yiddish], in Israel Vaynlez, *The Yiddish Writings of Joseph Perl.* LXXI-CVII. Vilna: YIVO.

Katz, Simkha. 1938. "New Materials from the Perl Archive: Joseph Perl's Introduction to His *Revealer of Secrets* in Yiddish" [Yiddish]. *YIVO-Bleter* XIII: 557-61, 566-75. Vilna: YIVO.

______. "Additions to the List of Tarnopol Publications" [Hebrew]. *Kiryat Sefer* 15 (1938/5698-9): 515.

______. "Letters of *Maskilim* In Dispraise *of Ḥasidim"* [Hebrew]. *Moznayim* 10, nos. 2-3 (5700/1940): 266-76.

Klausner, Joseph. 1932. *A History of Modern Hebrew Literature.* London: M. L. Cailingold.

______. 1937. *History of Modern Hebrew Literature* [Hebrew]. Vol. 2. Jerusalem: Hebrew University.

Kurzweil, Barukh. 5730 [1969]. *In The Struggle Over Jewish Values* [Hebrew]. Jerusalem and Tel Aviv: Schocken.

Landau, Judah Leo. 1938. *Short Lectures on Modern Hebrew Literature.* London: E. Goldston.

Mahler, Raphael. 5745 [1985]. *Hasidism and The Jewish Enlightenment.* Translated from Yiddish by Eugene Orenstein, from Hebrew by Aaron Klein and Jenny Machlowitz Klein. Philadelphia: Jewish Publication Society.

Miron, Dan. 1973. *A Traveler Disguised.* New York: Schocken.

Patterson, David. 1988. *A Phoenix in Fetters.* Savage, Maryland: Rowman & Littlefield.

______. 1958. *Hebrew Literature: The Art of the Translator.* London: Jewish Book Council.

______. 1964. *Abraham Mapu: The Creator of the Modern Hebrew Novel.* London: Horovitz Publishing.

______. 1964. *The Hebrew Novel in Czarist Russia.* Edinburgh: University Press.

Pelli, Moshe. 1979. *The Age of Haskalah.* Leiden: E. J. Brill.

Perl, Joseph [Ovadye ben Psakhye, pseud.]. 1819. *Megallé Temirin (Revealer of Secrets)* [Hebrew]. Vienna: Anton Strauss.

______ [Ovadye, pseud.] to The Editor, letter (followed by three letters that appeared in *Katit La-Ma'or*) [Hebrew], 1836. *Kerem Ḥemed* 2:16-39.

______ [Ovadye, pseud.] to The Editor, letter [Hebrew], 1838. *Kerem Ḥemed* 3:53-61.

[Perl, Joseph]. 1838. *Boḥen Tsaddik (The Test of the Righteous)* [Hebrew]. Prague: M. J. Landau.

Perl, Joseph [Ovadye, pseud.] to The Editor, letter, 2 Kislev 5598 [1868] [Hebrew]. *Ha-Shaḥar* 1:6-10, 17-21.

Perl, Joseph [Ovadye ben Psakhye, pseud.]. 1937. *Megallé Temirin (Revealer of Secrets)* [Yiddish] in Israel Vaynlez, *The Yiddish Writings of Joseph Perl,* 1-217. Vilna:YIVO.

Rabinovich, Isaiah. 1968. *Major Trends in Modern Hebrew Fiction.* Chicago and London: University of Chicago Press.

Rapoport, Solomon J. [Pil'i, pseud.]. Review of *Megallé Temirin (Revealer of Secrets)* [Hebrew]. *Bikkurei ha-Ittim* 12 (1831):175-181.

______. "On The Book *The Test of the Righteous,* Newly Reprinted in Prague" [Hebrew]. *Kerem Ḥemed* 4 (1839):45-57.

Roskies, David. 1995. *A Bridge of Longing.* Cambridge, Mass.:Harvard University Press.

Rubinstein, Avraham. "The Manuscript of 'On The Nature of the Ḥasidic Sect'" [Hebrew]. Parts 1 and 2. *Kiryat Sefer* 38 (5713/1953): 263-72, 415-24 and 39 (5714/1954): 117-36.

______. "Etymology of the Names in Joseph Perl" [Hebrew]. *Tarbiz* 43 (1974): 205-16.

______. "The Enlightenment and Ḥasidism -- The Work of Joseph Perl" [Hebrew]. *Bar Ilan Annual,* 5734 [1974].

______. 1977. *Joseph Perl: On The Nature of the Ḥasidic Sect* [German, Hebrew commentary]. Jerusalem: Israel Academy of Sciences and Humanities.

Shmeruk, Chone. "Authentic and Imaginative Elements in Joseph Perl's 'M'galeh T'mirin'" [Hebrew]. *Tsion* 21 (5716/1956): 92-9.

______. "The Name Mordecai-Marcus -- Literary Metamorphosis of a Social Ideal" [Hebrew]. *Tarbiz* 29 (1959-60): 76-98.

Shmeruk, Chone and Werses, Shmuel. 1969. *Joseph Perl: Ḥasidic Tales and Letters* [Hebrew]. Jerusalem: Israel Academy of Sciences and Humanities.

Silberschlag, Eisig. 1973. *From Renaissance to Renaissance: Hebrew Literature from 1492-1970.* New York: KTAV.

Slouschz, Nahum. 1909. *The Renascence of Hebrew Literature.* Philadelphia: Jewish Publication Society.

Tamar, David. "'The Ḥasidic Sect' in the Eyes of Joseph Perl" [Hebrew]. *Ha-Arets,* 18 November 1977.

Vaynlez, Israel. 1937. "Joseph Perl: His Life and Work" [Yiddish], in Israel Vaynlez, *The Yiddish Writings of Joseph Perl.* LXXI-CVII. Vilna: YIVO.

Werses, Shmuel. "An Unknown Satirical Work by Joseph Perl" [Hebrew]. *Ha-Sifrut* 1, no. 1 (1968): 206-227.

______. 1971. "Joseph Perl's Methods of Satire" [Hebrew] in *Story and Source,* 9-45. Ramat Gan: Massada.

______. 5750 [1990]. *Trends and Forms in Haskalah Literature* [Hebrew]. Jerusalem: Magnes Press, Hebrew University.

______. "From One Language to Another: Nuances of the Yiddish Version of Joseph Perl's *Revealer of Secrets*" [Hebrew]. *Ḥuleyot* 3 (Spring 1996): 59-108.

Zinberg, Israel. 1977. *A History of Jewish Literature.* Translated by Bernard Martin. Vol. IX, *Hasidism and Enlightenment,* and vol. X, *The Science of Judaism and Galician Haskalah.* New York: KTAV.

General Reference

Baer, Zeligman (ed.). 5697 [1937]. *The Order of Jewish Worship* [Hebrew]. Rev. ed. Frankfurt-on-Main: Schocken.

Barnai, Jacob. 1992. *The Jews in Palestine in the Eighteenth Century.* Tuscaloosa: University of Alabama Press.

Barnavi, Eli (ed.). 1992. *A Historical Atlas of The Jewish People.* New York: Alfred A. Knopf.

Baron, Salo W. and Kahan, Arcadius. 1975. *Economic History of the Jews.* New York: Schocken.

Brichto, Herbert C. 1992. *Toward A Grammar of Biblical Poetics.* New York and Oxford: Oxford University Press.

Dubnow, S. M. 1916. *History of the Jews in Russia and Poland.* 3 vols. Philadelphia: Jewish Publication Society.

Horowitz, George. 1963. *The Spirit of Jewish Law.* New York: Central Book.

Levine, Hillel. 1991. *Economic Origins of Antisemitism.* New Haven and London: Yale University Press.

Lieber, Sherman. 1992. *Mystics and Missionaries: The Jews in Palestine 1799-1840.* Salt Lake City: University of Utah Press.

Lipschitz, O. M. 1876. *New Yiddish-Russian Dictionary.* Zhitomir.

Millgram, Abraham E. 1971. *Jewish Worship.* Philadelphia: Jewish Publication Society.

Mokotoff, Gary and Sack, Sallyann Amdur. 1991. *Where Once We Walked.* Teaneck, New Jersey: Avotaynu.

Rosten, Leo. 1976. *O Kaplan! My Kaplan!* New York, Evanston, San Francisco, London: Harper & Row.

Sachar, Howard M. 1958. *The Course of Modern Jewish History.* Cleveland and New York: World Publishing.

Weinreich, Max. 1980. *History of the Yiddish Language.* Chicago and London: University of Chicago Press.

About the Book and Author

The dawning of the nineteenth century found the Jews of Eastern Europe torn between the forces of progress and reaction as they took their first tentative steps toward the modern world. In a war of words and of books, Haskala—the Jewish Enlightenment—did battle with the religious revival movement known as Hasidism. Perl, an ardent advocate of Enlightenment, unleashed the opening salvo with the publication in 1819 of *Revealer of Secrets.* The novel tried to pass itself off as a hasidic holy book when it was, in fact, a broadside against Hasidism—a parody of its teachings and of the language of its holy books. The outraged *hasidim* responded by buying up and burning as many copies as they could.

Dov Taylor's careful translation and commentary make this classic of Hebrew literature available and accessible to the contemporary English-speaking reader while preserving the integrity and bite of Perl's original. With Hasidism presently enjoying a remarkable rebirth, the issues in *Revealer of Secrets* are all the more relevant to those seeking to balance reason and faith. As the first Hebrew novel, the work will also be of great interest to students of modern Hebrew literature and modern Jewish history.

Dov Taylor is rabbi at Congregation Solel in Highland Park, Illinois. He completed this translation as a Visiting Scholar at The Oxford Centre for Hebrew and Jewish Studies.